All You Can Eat!

All Occasion

entertaining

More than 600 delicious recipes for parties and celebrations anytime of the year!

Margaret Kaeter & Nicole Alper

JG
PRESS

Published by World Publications Group, Inc.
140 Laurel Street, East Bridgewater, MA. 02333
www.wrldpub.com

ISBN 10: 1-57215-721-6
ISBN 13: 978-1-57215-721-7

Printed and bound in the United States of America.

10 9 8 7 6 5 4 3 2

Many of the designations used by manufacturers and sellers to distinguish their
products are claimed as trademarks. Where those designations appear in this
book and Adams Media was aware of a trademark claim, the designations have
been printed in initial capital letters.

This publication is designed to provide accurate and authoritative information
with regard to the subject matter covered. It is sold with the understanding that
the publisher is not engaged in rendering legal, accounting, or other professional advice. If legal advice or other expert assistance is required, the services
of a competent professional person should be sought.
—From a Declaration of Principles jointly adopted by a Committee of the
American Bar Association and a Committee of Publishers and Associations

Previously published as the *Everything® Holiday Cookbook*
and the *Everything® Easy Gourmet Cookbook.*

Contents

INTRODUCTION V

INTRODUCTION TO HOLIDAY ENTERTAINING 1

CHAPTER 1 **Thanksgiving** 9

CHAPTER 2 **Christmas Meals** 27

CHAPTER 3 **Christmas Treats** 39

CHAPTER 4 **New Year's** 55

CHAPTER 5 **Valentine's Day** 71

CHAPTER 6 **Easter** 91

CHAPTER 7 **Passover Foods** 107

CHAPTER 8 **Cinco de Mayo** 119

CHAPTER 9 **Mother's Day and Father's Day** 133

CHAPTER 10 **Memorial Day** 151

CHAPTER 11 **Summer Picnics** 163

CHAPTER 12 **Fourth of July** 175

CHAPTER 13 **Labor Day** 189

CHAPTER 14 **Fall Favorites** 199

CHAPTER 15 **Kids' Celebrations** 211

CHAPTER 16 **Jewish Holidays** 221

CHAPTER 17 **Fancy Foods for a Diabetic Diet** 235

CHAPTER 18 **Low-Carb Celebrations** 243

CHAPTER 19 **Low-Fat Celebrations** 255

CHAPTER 20 **World Favorites** 267

INTRODUCTION TO GOURMET ENTERTAINING 277

CHAPTER 21 **Going Gourmet** 278

CHAPTER 22 **Vive La France** 287

CHAPTER 23 **Belgium: More Than Just Chocolate** 303

CHAPTER 24 **Germany: Have Your Own Octoberfest** 319

CHAPTER 25 **Greece: Gourmet Island Hopping** 335

CHAPTER 26 **Italy: Eating the Sun** 347

CHAPTER 27 **Spain: Dining after 10 p.m.** 361

CHAPTER 28 **Scandinavia: Straight from the Sea** 377

CHAPTER 29 **Great Britain: It's Not Just Fish and Chips** 397

CHAPTER 30 **Central and South America: Carnivalé in Your Own Home** 407

CHAPTER 31 **India: Spicing Up Your Life** 413

CHAPTER 32 **Thailand: Land of Lemongrass, Coconut, and Curry** 429

CHAPTER 33 **China: New Food for the New Year** 449

CHAPTER 34 **Japan: Japanese Without the Chopsticks** 471

CHAPTER 35 **The Middle East: At the Root of It All** 481

CHAPTER 36 **Africa: A Food Safari** 499

CHAPTER 37 **USA: The Melting Pot** 511

CHAPTER 38 **Oh Canada: Taste of the Provinces** 527

CHAPTER 39 **Mexico: Food for Any Fiesta** 539

CHAPTER 40 **Bermuda and the Caribbean: Island Eats** 553

APPENDIX A **U.S. to Metric Units Conversion** 566

APPENDIX B **Gourmet Cooking Glossary** 567

INDEX 570

Introduction

Everyone loves entertaining. Whether it's a family gathering together for a holiday feast, friends packing into the living room to watch the big game or a sophisticated dinner party, we all enjoy gathering together with those we care about.

While the most important part of entertaining is enjoying time with your guests, you would be hared pressed to find a celebration without food. Food and drink are an integral part of entertaining, and often a celebration centers around them. So, in keeping with that spirit, the All You Can Eat series present Entertaining.

The first part of our volume focuses on recipes and ideas centered on holiday celebrations. From the big holidays like Thanksgiving to others, such as Mother's Day, that are not typically recognized by large parties, we've got you covered.

The second part puts a different spin on helping you get your party together. You may think that it's difficult to create a gourmet style meal. Our recipes and planning advice will show you just how easy it can be. Organized by countries and regions around the world, our gourmet section will help you prepare parties with worldwide flavor. Your guests will no doubt be thrilled just to enjoy your party, but an impressive meal can only enhance everyone's enjoyment.

Introduction to Holiday Entertaining

▶ TO CELEBRATE IS TO EAT; TO EAT IS TO CELEBRATE. It may not be the most profound statement in the world, but it does sum up the way life should be. Every celebration imaginable, from a wedding to a job well done, includes a morsel of food or, at least, a glass of wine. And, on the other side of the equation, we really should celebrate every bite we eat.

It is a sign that we are vital human beings enjoying the most fundamental aspect of life. We eat, thus we celebrate. We celebrate, thus we eat.

As you peruse this book, you will find that statement imbedded in the very essence of all the recipes. Some are simple. Some are old favorites. Some are exotic and complicated. But all of them are worthy of celebrations and celebrating.

However, before you embark on this celebratory journey, it's important to keep a few things in mind. Follow good cooking practices and you will have the best celebration possible.

Before You Plan the Meal

Before you even page through the book, think about what you want to achieve with your celebration. Keep these things in mind:

• **Will children be present?** You don't want a lengthy meal with foods that are difficult to eat if there will be young children at the party. Unless you know the children are adventurous, you also likely want to stay away from new foods with exotic spices.

- **How many will be attending?** If you don't have an exact number, you want to stay away from meals with individual servings. There's nothing worse than having one steak too few or an entire lobster too many. If you don't know the exact number, make items that are flexible. Or, make too many if you know the leftover dishes can be frozen.

- **Does anyone have food allergies or other special needs?** Keep these in mind as you plan your menu. There are plenty of wonderful dishes for people on low-salt, low-carb, and low-fat diets.

Planning the Meal

As you look at the recipes, determine which ones will work best for your celebration. Keep these things in mind:

- **What will the weather be like?** If you live in a northern climate, don't plan a meal that must be served outdoors in the spring or fall. You never know if you will have super-cold weather. Likewise, you might not want to be outdoors at 110° during a Southern summer.

- **How much experience do you have as a cook?** Realistically, do you know what you're in for? Most of the recipes in this book are easy, but a few require precise cooking methods. Are you confident enough in your cooking abilities to know you can handle them?

- **Do you have the utensils?** Read each of the recipes thoroughly and determine if you have the right pots and pans as well as miscellaneous utensils. Remember that you will be making all of the recipes at the same time; so, if something is being chilled in a bowl, that bowl won't be usable for another recipe.

- **How much time do you have?** Again, read the recipes and determine how long it will take you to make the meal. If the event is on a Thursday night and you have an evening class on Wednesdays, you need to plan accordingly.

- **How big is your kitchen?** Be realistic, again. If you live in a small apartment, you likely don't have room to make meals that require a lot of dishes. Go with something simpler such as a pasta dish, salad, and easy dessert.

- **Are the ingredients available?** A few of the recipes in this book call for some exotic ingredients. Most are available in big-city grocery stores, but if you live in a small town, they might be impossible to find. If you have time, you could plan a trip to a larger town or you could get the spices via mail order, but you'll need to plan for it.

- **Do you have the money?** There is nothing worse than planning a celebration that depletes your bank account. It becomes less of a celebration and more of a burden for you. Don't overextend your budget. Instead, make a wonderful-tasting meal, perhaps accented with extra attention to presentation; add fresh garnishes to a plate of simple chops, for example.

Making the Meal

Keep the elements of good cooking in mind as you start to make your meal. These things are most important:

- **Try a new dish beforehand.** If you're at all concerned about something turning out right, make it for yourself a few days ahead of time. That way you can tweak the ingredients or your technique when it really counts.

- **Cut corners where you can.** Did we really say that? Yes, there is no harm in using a good-quality store-bought French bread if you don't have the time, space, or pans to make the real thing. Buy precleaned veggies or even precut salad greens. This will give you more time to attend to the important aspects of the meal.

- **Follow directions.** You may have cooked many complicated meals before, but if you haven't cooked these dishes, follow the directions carefully. Timing and temperature are especially important when cooking, because various spices and ingredients react differently at different temperatures and over different amounts of time.

- **Plan ahead.** Know which items you will make first, which can be made a day ahead, and which must be served fresh. Plan your cooking schedule just as you would the other aspects of a big celebration.

Pay Attention to Details

Good cooking is in the details. Follow these guidelines to make sure your meal turns out perfect:

- **Measure correctly.** Some ingredients aren't important, such as spices. The amounts can be altered according to taste. However, the main ingredients, such as flour, liquids, and sugars, should be measured exactly. There is no room for spillage or "good enough," especially in a celebration. You don't want a gooey cake or a runny stew.

- **Preheat.** If the recipe says to preheat, allow at least 15 minutes to get the oven up to the correct temperature. This is important; otherwise, the food will start cooking at the lower temperature, which could completely alter the chemistry of the baking.

- **Know what slicing means**. Become familiar with the various terms for cutting something:

  Zesting: Making small grated pieces from the thin, colored part of a citrus fruit's peel
  Bias slice: To cut at a 45° angle
  Chop: To cut into small irregular pieces
  Core: To remove the center of a fruit or vegetable
  Crush: To smash seasonings to release their flavor

Cube: To cut food into squares about ½-inch on each side

Cut up: To cut into small irregular pieces

Diagonal slice: To cut at a 45° angle

Dice: To cut into fairly uniform pieces about ¼-inch square

Grate: To rub food against a sharp-edged tool called a grater, making small or fine particles

Julienne: To cut into thin strips about 2 inches long

Mince: To chop into very small bits

Score: To cut through the surface about ¼-inch deep

Section: To cut the pulp of a peeled citrus fruit away from the membranes, separating its segments

Shred: To cut in narrow, thin strips

Slice: To cut into flat pieces that are usually thin and even

Snip: To cut herbs or other food into small pieces using scissors

Tear: To break into pieces using your hands

- **Know how to mix it.** Become familiar with the various terms for mixing ingredients:

  Beat: To stir briskly with a spoon, whisk, egg beater, or electric mixer

  Blend: To mix two or more ingredients until they make a uniform mixture

  Cream: To beat a fat until it is light and fluffy, often in combination with other ingredients

  Cut in: To combine a solid fat with dry ingredients until the fat is in very small pieces, about the size of small peas, by using a pastry blender or a fork

  Fold: To combine ingredients gently, using a spatula or spoon to lift ingredients from the bottom of the bowl and "fold" them over the top

  Knead: To work dough by continuous folding over and pressing down until it is smooth and elastic (Dough can also be kneaded with an electric mixer attachment called a dough hook.)

  Stir: To mix ingredients at a moderate pace to combine

Toss: To mix ingredients by gently lifting them from the bottom of the bowl and allowing them to tumble, usually using two forks or other utensils

Whip: To beat rapidly with a wire whisk, hand beater, or electric mixer (Whipping increases volume because it adds air to the ingredients.)

- **Know how to prepare it.** Become familiar with the various terms for preparing the meal:

Baste: To spoon or pour broth, sauce, or other liquid over food while cooking to prevent dryness or add flavor

Blacken: To cook Cajun-seasoned foods over a very high heat

Bread: To coat foods before cooking in bread or cracker crumbs

Caramelize: To coat the top of a food with sugar and then broil quickly until the sugar is melted; or, to melt sugar in a saucepan over a low heat until it turns into a golden syrup

Deglaze: To add liquid to a skillet in which meat has been cooked, stirring to loosen meat bits and make a broth (The broth can be used to make a sauce.)

Dot: To place pieces of butter randomly on top of a food

Drizzle: To pour a liquid topping in thin, irregular lines over a food

Dust: To sprinkle a dry ingredient lightly and fairly evenly over a food

Glaze: To spread a thin coating such as jelly on food, making it appear glossy

Grease: To coat the surface of a pan with shortening, oil, or cooking spray to prevent foods from sticking while they bake; to "grease and flour" is to dust the plan lightly with flour after applying the shortening

Marinate: To let food stand in a special liquid to flavor it or tenderize it (The liquid is called a marinade.)

Purée: To process ingredients into a thick liquid, usually by using a blender or food processor

Reduce: To boil a liquid until some of it evaporates, thus concentrating the flavor

Roux, to make: To combine melted butter, flour, and seasonings over heat to use as a thickening base for sauces

Sift: To process dry ingredients through a kitchen sifter (Sifting adds air to dry ingredients that have been compressed in storage and also removes any lumps.)

Skim: To remove fat or foam that has accumulated on the surface of a liquid, usually using a spoon

- **Know how to cook it.** Become familiar with the various terms for cooking the meal:

Bake: To cook food with the indirect dry heat of an oven (Covering food while baking it preserves moistness. Leaving food uncovered results in a drier or crisp surface.)

Barbecue: To cook with barbecue sauce or spices, or to cook slowly on a grill or spit, usually outdoors

Blanch: To cook fruits, vegetables, or nuts very briefly in boiling water or steam, usually to preserve the color or nutritional value or remove the skin; also called *Parboil.*

Boil: To cook a liquid at a temperature at which bubbles rise and break on the surface ("Bring to a boil" means to heat just until bubbling begins. In a full, or rolling, boil, the bubbles are larger and form quickly and continuously.)

Braise: To cook food slowly in a tightly covered pan in a small amount of liquid (Usually, food is first browned in a small amount of fat. Braising tenderizes food and can be done on either the stovetop or in the oven.)

Broil: To cook food under a direct source of intense heat or flame, producing a browned or crisp exterior and a less well-done interior

Deep-fry: To cook food in hot, liquefied fat, usually 350° to 375°, deep enough to cover and surround the food completely

Fry: To cook in hot fat or oil, producing a crisp exterior

Grill: To cook foods directly above a source of intense heat flame (Foods can be pan-grilled on a stovetop by using a specially designed pan with raised grill ridges.)

Oven-fry: To cook food, usually breaded, in a hot oven with a small amount of fat, usually dotted or drizzled on top of the food

Pan-fry: To fry with little or no added fat, using only the fat that accumulates during cooking

Parboil: See *Blanch*

Poach: To cook in a simmering, not boiling, liquid

Roast: To cook meat or poultry in the indirect heat of the oven, uncovered (Roasted foods are not cooked in added liquid but are often basted with liquids for flavor and moistness.)

Sauté: To cook in a small amount of fat over high heat

Scald: To heat a liquid to just below the boiling point, when small bubbles begin to appear around the edges of the pan (When milk is scalded, a film will form on the surface.)

Sear: To brown on all sides over high heat to preserve juiciness

Simmer: To keep a liquid just below the boiling point (A few bubbles will rise and break on the surface.)

Steam: To cook food above, not in, boiling or simmering water

Stew: To cook food, covered, very slowly in liquid

Stir-fry: To cook small pieces of food in a hot wok or skillet, using a small amount of fat and a constant stirring motion.

Chapter 1

THANKSGIVING

ROASTED GARLIC MASHED POTATOES	10
ROAST TURKEY WITH FRUIT STUFFING	11
TURKEY AND CRANBERRY ON BUTTERNUT SQUASH	12
FRUIT-STEWED TURKEY	13
WARM SWEET POTATO AND APPLE SALAD	14
OVEN-ROASTED ASPARAGUS	15
SWEET POTATO–GINGER SOUP	16
CRANBERRY SHERBET	17
CRANBERRY SCONES	18
CRANBERRY NUT BREAD	19
CRANBERRY-PECAN BARS	20
PUMPKIN PIE	21
PECAN PIE	22
SPICED CRANBERRY GLOGG	22
APPLE BLOSSOM	23
CRANBERRY CREAM COCKTAIL	23
CRANBERRY GIN SOUR	24
MAYFLOWER COCKTAIL	24
TURKEY SHOOTER	25
BRANDY COCOA	25

ROASTED GARLIC MASHED POTATOES

Serves 4

These potatoes are excellent without gravy. For even more flavor, sprinkle with crumbled blue cheese or grated Parmesan.

4 garlic cloves
$\frac{1}{4}$ teaspoon olive oil
$\frac{3}{4}$ pound potatoes
$\frac{1}{2}$ teaspoon salt
1 small head cauliflower
1 small yellow onion

$\frac{1}{4}$ cup buttermilk
$\frac{1}{8}$ cup nonfat cottage cheese
2 teaspoons butter
$\frac{1}{4}$ teaspoon freshly ground
    black pepper

1. Preheat oven to 350°. Brush the garlic cloves with the olive oil and place in a shallow baking pan. Bake for 1 hour or until the cloves are soft. Remove the skin and cut the cloves into fourths.
2. Peel the potatoes and cut them into quarters. Place in a large pot and cover with water. Add the salt and boil for 10 to 20 minutes or until the potatoes are tender. Drain.
3. Break the cauliflower into small pieces and place in a large pot. Cover with water and boil for about 10 minutes or until the cauliflower is tender. Drain.
4. Remove the skin from the onion and chop into $\frac{1}{4}$-inch pieces.
5. Combine all the ingredients and whip until fluffy. If the mixture is too thin, add the buttermilk gradually until the whipped mixture reaches the desired consistency.

Defatting Meat
To remove most of the fat from ground beef or bacon, cook it in the microwave, then lay it on several paper towels to drain. Lay a paper towel on top of the meat and pat it lightly before adding it to the dish you are making.

ROAST TURKEY WITH FRUIT STUFFING

1 (10- to 15-pound) turkey
1 small white onion
¾ pound prunes
6 dried apricots
2 large Granny Smith apples
5 tablespoons margarine

2 quarts cubed toast
1 cup apple juice
2 teaspoons dried sage
1 teaspoon dried basil
2¼ teaspoons salt
¼ teaspoon pepper

> **Serves 8**
>
> Serve as the center-piece for a traditional Thanksgiving turkey dinner. It is excellent with Roasted Garlic Mashed Potatoes (page 10).

1. Preheat oven to 375°.
2. Peel the onion and chop it into ¼-inch pieces. Slice the prunes into ½-inch pieces. Chop the apricots into ¼-inch pieces. Peel the apples and cut into 1-inch chunks.
3. In a medium-sized frying pan over medium heat, melt the margarine; sauté the onions until golden brown.
4. In a mixing bowl, toss the toast chunks with the onions, prunes, apples, apricots, apple juice, and seasonings.
5. Spoon the stuffing into the turkey. Fasten with poultry pins if necessary.
6. Place the turkey in a pan and roast in the oven for 25 minutes per pound. Scoop out the fat from the pan as it gathers. Check regularly the last 30 minutes of cooking. The juices should run clear when the bird is done. Do not overcook.

Low-Fat Sautéing
For a fat-free alternative, add flavored vinegars when sautéing meats and vegetables. They will add a light flavor to the dish and tend to blend well with almost any recipe.

TURKEY AND CRANBERRY ON BUTTERNUT SQUASH

Serves 6

This makes a complete meal by itself or can be used as the main dish in a larger meal, served with Oven-Roasted Asparagus (page 15) and Roasted Garlic Mashed Potatoes (page 10).

1 butternut squash
1 teaspoon salt
½ teaspoon nutmeg
12 ounces fresh-roasted turkey
6 ounces precooked cranberries

2 tablespoons extra-virgin olive oil
3 tablespoons orange juice
1 teaspoon fresh-cracked black pepper

1. Preheat oven to 250°.
2. Peel the butternut squash and cut in half lengthwise. Remove and rinse the seeds, and place the seeds on a baking sheet. Toast for 5 to 10 minutes, until golden. Sprinkle lightly with salt when done.
3. Thinly slice the butternut squash lengthwise. Brush another baking sheet with oil and lay out the squash slices. Sprinkle with nutmeg. Roast the squash for 20 to 30 minutes or until the squash is tender when pierced with a fork. Let cool, then place the cooled squash on serving plates.
4. Thinly slice the turkey. Arrange the turkey slices on top of the squash and sprinkle cranberries over the turkey. Drizzle with the olive oil and orange juice. Sprinkle the squash seeds on top. Season with salt and pepper.

Cooking Fresh Cranberries

While many people shy away from fresh cranberries, they are very easy to cook. Simply steam them and sprinkle lightly with sugar until they are slightly soft.

FRUIT-STEWED TURKEY

4 cups precooked turkey meat
1 small red onion
1 cup pineapple chunks,
   drained
6 pitted prunes
¼ cup dried apricots

1 tablespoon olive oil
½ cup fresh raspberries
1 teaspoon salt
1 teaspoon ground white
   pepper

> **Serves 4**
>
> Serve over white rice
> or fettucine noodles
> for a day-after-
> Thanksgiving treat.

1. Cut the turkey into 1-inch chunks. Remove the skin from the onion and cut the onion into quarters. Cut the pineapple into 1-inch chunks, if necessary. Cut the prunes and apricots in half.
2. In a large frying pan, preheat the olive oil to medium temperature. Add the turkey chunks and fry until lightly browned on all sides.
3. Drain off the oil and add the onion, pineapple, apricots, prunes, raspberries, salt, and pepper to the pan. Turn heat to low and cook for 1 hour, stirring periodically.

Mushrooms for Meat

To turn any meat dish into an instant vegetarian entrée, substitute morel mushrooms for the meat. Be sure to substitute by volume, not weight, because even these heavier mushrooms weigh less than meat.

WARM SWEET POTATO AND APPLE SALAD

Serves 12

This is the perfect complement to a traditional holiday turkey.

2½ pounds sweet potatoes
2 medium-sized Granny Smith
    apples
1 (20-ounce) can pineapple
    chunks

¾ cup mayonnaise
¾ cup plain yogurt
1½ tablespoons curry powder
½ teaspoon salt
½ cup golden raisins

1. Cook the sweet potatoes in boiling water. Drain and let cool. Peel the potatoes and cut into ¾-inch pieces. Peel the apples and cut into ½-inch pieces. Drain the pineapple.
2. In a large saucepan, whisk together the mayonnaise, yogurt, curry powder, and salt over low heat until well blended.
3. Stir in the potatoes, apples, pineapples, and raisins. Toss gently to mix and coat evenly.
4. Cover and continue to cook over low heat for 7 to 10 minutes, until the potatoes are heated through.

Seasonal Best

Because there are so many types of apples available year-round, you should always inquire about which ones are in season. This will ensure that you are using the tastiest ones in the bunch. Also, try combining different kinds for added flavor and variety.

OVEN-ROASTED ASPARAGUS

1 pound fresh asparagus
2 garlic cloves
1 teaspoon fresh parsley
2 tablespoons water
2 tablespoons dry white wine

2 teaspoons lemon juice
1 teaspoon olive oil
1/4 teaspoon salt
1/8 teaspoon freshly ground
   black pepper

Serves 4

This is the perfect simple-yet-elegant accompaniment to any holiday meal.

1. Preheat oven to 400°.
2. Break off the tough ends of the asparagus spears. With a vegetable peeler, peel the bottom half of the asparagus stalks. Peel the garlic and cut into slivers. Roughly chop the parsley.
3. Scatter the garlic and parsley in a 13" × 9" baking dish. Arrange the asparagus spears in a single layer.
4. In a small bowl, combine the water, wine, lemon juice, oil, salt, and pepper; pour over the asparagus.
5. Bake for 10 minutes. Turn the asparagus over and bake for 10 more minutes, or until the asparagus stalks are tender but slightly crisp and the liquid is almost gone.

Asparagus Knowledge

Although it is a popular belief, thick asparagus is not always woody and tough. In fact, it can have much more natural juiciness, sweetness, and silky texture than the pencil-thin variety. Check the cut bottoms of asparagus for freshness, making sure they are plump, moist, and recently cut.

SWEET POTATO–GINGER SOUP

Serves 6

Serve as a first course
to a large holiday meal.

1½ pounds butternut squash
4 large sweet potatoes
1 large russet potato
1 tablespoon olive oil
1 small yellow onion

2 tablespoons fresh minced
   ginger
8 cups chicken broth
½ cup plain yogurt

1. Peel, seed, and dice the squash. Peel and dice the sweet potatoes.
   Peel and dice the potato. Peel and chop the onion.
2. In a soup pot, heat the oil on medium for 30 seconds. Add the onion
   and sauté until translucent, about 5 minutes.
3. Add the ginger and cook for about 1 minute. Add the squash, sweet
   potatoes, russet potato, and broth. Bring to a boil, reduce heat to low,
   and cover; cook until the vegetables are tender, about 30 minutes.
4. Remove from heat and allow to cool slightly. Working in 1-cup
   batches, purée in a food processor or blender until smooth.
5. Pour into a clean pot, stir in the yogurt, and reheat gently. Ladle into
   bowls and serve.

The Squash Bowl

*Use squash as a soup bowl. Many small squash make excellent
complements to soups and stews. Cut them in half, remove the
seeds, and prebake in the microwave or oven. Ladle your soup
or stew into the squash for a festive look.*

CRANBERRY SHERBET

1½ teaspoons unflavored gelatin
2 cups cranberry juice
½ cup granulated sugar
⅛ teaspoon salt

2 tablespoons nonfat dry milk
  powder
½ cup corn syrup
3 tablespoons lemon juice

1. In a small saucepan, sprinkle the gelatin over ½ cup of the juice. Let stand for a few minutes to allow the gelatin to soften.
2. Place over low heat and stir until dissolved. Stir in the sugar and salt until dissolved.
3. Pour the remaining 1½ cups juice into a bowl. Sprinkle the milk powder over the top and beat with a fork to dissolve. Add the gelatin mixture to the milk-juice mixture, then add all the remaining ingredients. Stir until well mixed.
4. Pour into a metal ice cube train or loaf pan and freeze until almost firm. Beat until fluffy. Refreeze until firm, then serve.

Use Good Pans

Thin, flimsy stainless steel pans don't conduct heat well, resulting in hot spots where foods burn and cold spots where they don't cook at all. Better pans have a thick core of highly conductive aluminum or even copper bonded to their bottoms.

CRANBERRY SCONES

1 cup dairy sour cream
1½ teaspoons fresh-grated orange peel
2 cups sifted all-purpose flour
½ cup granulated sugar
2 teaspoons baking powder
½ teaspoon salt
¼ cup butter, softened
1 large egg, at room temperature
¼ cup dried cranberries

1. Preheat oven to 375°.
2. In a small bowl, combine the sour cream and grated orange peel. Set aside.
3. In a large bowl, mix together the flour, sugar, baking powder, and salt.
4. Using a pastry blender or 2 knives, cut the butter into the flour mixture until coarse crumbs form.
5. Break the egg into a small dish and beat well with a fork. Add the egg to the flour mixture and beat together until blended. Add the sour cream and orange peel mixture and beat just until blended.
6. Prepare a smooth surface by sprinkling it lightly with flour. Turn the dough out of the bowl. Using floured hands, knead the dough for about 30 seconds, or until smooth. Taking only ½ the dough at a time, roll it out with a floured rolling pin until it is about ½-inch thick. Using a 3-inch round cookie cutter or the mouth of an empty can or drinking glass, cut out rounds of dough.
7. Place the rounds 1 inch apart on a greased or nonstick cookie sheet. Before putting them in the oven, push 5 dried cranberries into the top of each scone. Bake until the tops are just barely browned, 12 to 18 minutes. Let cool on wire racks.

CRANBERRY NUT BREAD

½ cup butter, softened
1 cup granulated sugar
1 large egg
1 cup fresh orange juice
3 cups all-purpose flour

2 teaspoons baking powder
1 teaspoon fresh orange zest
1 cup fresh cranberries
1 cup chopped pecans

Makes 8 to 10 servings

For a special morning treat, use this bread to make French toast. Simply beat together an egg and ½ cup milk, then coat bread slices in the mixture and fry in a skillet on medium heat until lightly browned.

1. Preheat oven to 350°. Coat a 9" × 5" × 3" loaf pan with cooking spray or a light coating of cooking oil.
2. Mix together the flour and baking powder. Cream together the butter and sugar until light and fluffy. Add the egg, and beat for 2 minutes. Gradually stir in the juice, flour, baking powder, and orange zest; mix until just blended. Stir in the cranberries and pecans.
3. Pour the batter into the prepared baking pan. Bake for 50 to 60 minutes or until a toothpick inserted in the center comes out clean.
4. Let the bread stand in the baking pan for 8 to 10 minutes. Invert onto a wire cooling rack.

Hold the Yolk

Egg yolks contain all of the fat and cholesterol in an egg. Use egg whites instead of whole eggs when making pasta, cakes, and other dishes. Usually 2 egg whites can be substituted for 1 whole egg.

CRANBERRY-PECAN BARS

1 cup unsalted butter, chilled
1½ cups roasted pecans
2 cups all-purpose flour
¾ packed cup brown sugar

1 (10-ounce) jar seedless raspberry preserves
¾ cup dried cranberries
⅓ cup flaked, dried coconut.

1. Preheat oven to 350°. Grease a 9" × 13" × 2" pan. Cut butter into bits.
2. In a food processor, coarsely chop ½ cup of the pecans and place in a bowl. Add the remaining 1 cup pecans to the processor along with the flour, brown sugar, and butter. Process until the dough clumps together, occasionally scraping down the sides of the processor bowl with a rubber spatula.
3. Remove the dough from the processor and measure out 1 cup. Add the reserved pecans to the 1 cup of dough and set aside. Pat the remaining dough onto the bottom of the prepared pan.
4. In a bowl, mix together the preserves and cranberries, then spread over the dough in the pan. Mix the coconut with the reserved nut mixture, pressing some together to form clumps. Sprinkle over the preserves layer in the pan.
5. Bake for 40 minutes or until the top browns. Let cool on a rack, then cut into 2-inch bars.

Sweet Vanilla Sauce
Mix ¼ cup nonfat buttermilk, 2 teaspoons sugar, and 1 cup vanilla yogurt in a small bowl. Use as a topping over fresh fruit or gingerbread.

PUMPKIN PIE

3 eggs
1 unbaked 9-inch pie pastry
  shell
1½ cups canned or mashed
  cooked pumpkin
¾ cup granulated sugar

½ teaspoon salt
1¼ teaspoons ground cinnamon
1 teaspoon ground ginger
½ teaspoon ground cloves
¼ cup milk
¾ cup evaporated milk

> **Serves 8**
>
> Serve as dessert for
> a traditional
> Thanksgiving meal
> or for a fall dessert
> at any meal.

1. Preheat oven to 400°. Lightly beat the eggs and set aside.
2. Line the pie pan with the pastry shell, forming a high edge by crimping the pastry in a tall, thick layer.
3. In a large bowl, combine the pumpkin, sugar, salt, and spices to taste. Stir in the eggs, milk, and evaporated milk until well blended. Pour into the pastry shell.
4. Bake for 50 minutes or until a knife inserted halfway between the edge and the center of the filling comes out clean. Let cool completely on a rack.

Problems with Cinnamon

While it tastes wonderful, cinnamon is a tricky spice. It can kill yeast, causing bread not to rise. It also does not permeate a soup or stew but tends to remain on top of the liquid.

PECAN PIE

Serves 8

Serve as a final course after Roast Turkey with Fruit Stuffing (page 11) and Oven-Roasted Asparagus (page 15).

1 unbaked 9-inch pie pastry
  shell
3 large eggs
1 cup dark corn syrup
½ cup granulated sugar

1 teaspoon vanilla extract
½ teaspoon salt
1 cup coarsely chopped
  toasted pecan pieces

1. Preheat oven to 350°.
2. Place the pie shell in a greased pie pan. Put in the oven and brown slightly, about 5 to 10 minutes. Remove.
3. In a large bowl, beat the eggs until foamy. Add the corn syrup, sugar, vanilla, salt, and pecans; mix well. Pour into the prepared crust.
4. Bake for 40 to 45 minutes or until the top is set. Transfer the pan to a wire rack to cool.

SPICED CRANBERRY GLOGG

Makes 6 servings

You can leave the raisins in for a special treat at the bottom of the glass. Or, remove the raisins and use them in spiced muffins.

1 orange
1 teaspoon whole cloves
1 cinnamon stick
½ cup raisins

1 (6-ounce) can apple juice
  concentrate
1 (6-ounce) can cranberry juice
  concentrate
4½ cups water

1. With a small knife, cut the orange peel into long strips, about ½-inch wide, so the peel begins to spiral. Poke the cloves into the orange peel. Break the cinnamon stick in half.
2. Squeeze the juice from the orange into a medium-sized saucepan. Add the studded orange peel, cinnamon stick, raisins, juice concentrates, and water; heat on medium until simmering.
3. Remove the orange peel and cinnamon stick. Serve promptly or refrigerate and reheat before serving.

APPLE BLOSSOM

2 ounces brandy
2 ounces apple juice
1 teaspoon lemon juice

Ice
Apple slice, for garnish

1. Pour the brandy, apple juice, and lemon juice into a mixing glass nearly filled with ice. Stir.
2. Strain into an old-fashioned glass over ice. Garnish with an apple slice.

Serves 1

This makes a perfect after-dinner drink to help settle stomachs that might have taken in just a little too much!

CRANBERRY CREAM COCKTAIL

3 ounces cranberry juice
2 ounces apple juice
1 ounce lime juice
1 ounce heavy cream

Dash grenadine
2 cups crushed ice or ice
    cubes

Combine all the ingredients in a blender; blend thoroughly. Pour into a large wineglass.

Serves 1

Kids and adults alike will enjoy this cool after-dinner drink. Make it extra-special by garnishing it with fresh apple slices or even some raspberries.

CRANBERRY GIN SOUR

2 ounces gin
½ ounce Triple Sec
1 ounce lime juice
1 ounce lemon juice

2 ounces light cream
1 teaspoon granulated sugar
2 cups crushed ice or ice cubes

Combine all the ingredients in a blender; blend thoroughly. Pour into a large wineglass.

MAYFLOWER COCKTAIL

1½ ounces sweet vermouth
½ ounce dry vermouth
½ ounce brandy

1 teaspoon Pernod
1 teaspoon orange bitters
Ice

Combine all the ingredients in a shaker half-filled with ice. Shake well. Strain into a cocktail glass.

TURKEY SHOOTER

¾ ounce Wild Turkey Bourbon   Ice
¼ ounce white crème de menthe

Pour all the ingredients into a mixing glass nearly filled with ice. Stir.
Strain into a cordial glass or a brandy snifter.

Serves 1
Serve as an after-dinner drink to calm the nerves during all those football games.

BRANDY COCOA

2 tablespoons unsweetened   1½ cups boiling water
  cocoa powder   4 cups whole milk
⅓ cup granulated sugar   3 teaspoons brandy

1. In a saucepan, scald milk.
2. In another saucepan, mix cocoa, sugar, and enough boiling water to
   make a smooth paste.
3. Add remaining water and boil 1 minute, then add to milk.
4. Mix well; add brandy, then beat mixture with egg beater for 2 minutes.
   Serve in large mugs.

Serves 2–3
This is a mellow and delicious drink for the holidays.

CHAPTER 2

CHRISTMAS MEALS

PECAN-CRUSTED ROAST PORK LOIN	28
CARAMELIZED PEARL ONIONS	29
HOLIDAY GOOSE WITH CRANBERRIES	29
HERBED BEEF RIB-EYE ROAST WITH POTATOES	30
SAUERKRAUT-STUFFED ROAST DUCK	31
POACHED SALMON WITH BEARNAISE SAUCE	32
HONEY-ORANGE BEETS	32
TWICE-BAKED POTATOES WITH CHIVES	33
GINGERED MASHED SWEET POTATOES	34
BRUSSELS SPROUTS WITH MUSTARD CREAM	34
MEXICAN CHRISTMAS EVE SALAD	35
OYSTERS ROCKEFELLER SOUP	36
OVEN-ROASTED WINTER VEGETABLES	37
YORKSHIRE PUDDING	38
CLASSIC BREAD PUDDING	38

PECAN-CRUSTED ROAST PORK LOIN

1 garlic clove
1 teaspoon olive oil
1 teaspoon brown sugar
¼ teaspoon dried thyme
¼ teaspoon dried sage

¼ teaspoon freshly ground black pepper
½ pound boneless pork loin roast
¼ cup chopped or ground pecans

1. Crush the garlic with the side of a large knife. Remove the skin. Put the olive oil, garlic, brown sugar, and seasonings in a resealable plastic bag. Mix well. Add the roast and turn it in the bag to coat the meat. Marinate in the refrigerator for 6 to 12 hours.
2. Preheat oven to 400°.
3. Roll the pork loin in the chopped pecans and place it in a roasting pan. Make a tent of aluminum foil and arrange it over the pork loin, covering the nuts completely so that they won't burn. Roast for 10 minutes, then lower the heat to 350°. Continue to roast for an additional 8 to 15 minutes or until the meat thermometer reads 150° to 170°, depending on how well done you prefer it. Let sit for 10 minutes before serving.
4. Serve with Roasted Garlic Mashed Potatoes (page 10) and freshly steamed asparagus.

Create a Celery Roasting Rack

If you want to bake a roast in a casserole alongside potatoes and carrots, elevate the roast on 2 or 3 stalks of celery. The celery will absorb any fat that drains from the meat so that it's not absorbed by the other vegetables. Discard the celery.

CARAMELIZED PEARL ONIONS

2 cups pearl onions
2 teaspoons brown sugar
¼ teaspoon salt

1 tablespoon butter
1 cup cold water

1. Peel the pearl onions.
2. In a heavy-bottomed skillet over medium heat, combine the onions, sugar, salt, butter, and water. Bring to a simmer. Cook gently until all the water is absorbed and the onions are coated in a light glaze, about 5 minutes. Turn heat to low. Cook slowly until the glaze browns and the onions appear golden brown, about 5 minutes more.

HOLIDAY GOOSE WITH CRANBERRIES

1 wild goose, gutted and skinned
½ teaspoon table salt
½ teaspoon ground black pepper

1 (15-ounce) can whole-berry
  cranberry sauce
1 envelope dry onion soup mix
½ cup orange juice

1. Wash the goose cavity with cold water and sprinkle with salt and pepper. Place the goose in a slow cooker.
2. Combine the cranberry sauce, dry onion soup mix, and orange juice. Pour the mixture over the goose.
3. Cook, covered, on low setting for 8 to 10 hours, depending on the size of the goose.

HERBED BEEF RIB-EYE ROAST
WITH POTATOES

Serves 8

Serve with Oven-Roasted Asparagus (page 15) for a complete, festive meal.

2 large sweet potatoes
2 medium Yukon gold potatoes
4 small red potatoes
2 teaspoons dried rosemary
4 garlic cloves
1 teaspoon dry mustard
1 teaspoon salt
1 teaspoon cracked black pepper
4-pound boneless beef rib-eye roast
2 tablespoons vegetable oil

1. Preheat oven to 350°. Peel all the potatoes and cut them into pieces that are roughly 2 inches square.
2. Combine the rosemary, garlic, mustard, salt, and pepper, and divide in half. Rub or press ½ the mixture into the surface of the meat.
3. Place the meat on a rack in a shallow roasting pan and place a meat thermometer (if using) into the thickest part of the meat. Place the roast in the oven. The total roasting time will be 1½ to 2 hours for medium-rare (135°) or 2 to 3 hours for medium (150°).
4. Mix the remaining seasonings with the oil in a large bowl. Add the potatoes to the oil and herb mixture and toss well to coat.
5. About 1 hour before the meat will be done, place the potatoes in the roasting pan around the rack.

Meat Safety

Store meat unopened for up to 2 days in the refrigerator. Freeze it if it will not be used within 2 days. Meat wrapped in butcher paper should be unwrapped and rewrapped in foil, freezer bags, or freezer paper. Frozen meat is best used within 2 months. Meat in transparent film can be frozen in the package for up to 2 weeks.

SAUERKRAUT-STUFFED ROAST DUCK

1 domestic duck
1 cup distilled white vinegar
¼ teaspoon salt
¼ teaspoon ground black
   pepper

2 Granny Smith apples
1 medium-sized yellow onion
4 cups sauerkraut
1 pound pork spareribs

> **Serves 6**
>
> Serve with Garlic Mashed Potatoes (page 10) and Caramelized Pearl Onions (page 29).

1. Clean and wash the duck, then place it in a large kettle. Cover with water and add the vinegar. Soak for 3 hours. Remove the duck from the liquid, dry it off, and season with salt and pepper. Cover and place in the refrigerator overnight.
2. While the duck is being soaked, core and chop the apples. Peel and chop the onion into ½-inch chunks. Combine the apples, onion, sauerkraut, and spareribs in a slow cooker. Cook for 6 hours or until the meat from the ribs falls from the bones. Discard the bones and refrigerate the slow-cooker mixture.
3. The next day, stuff the spare-rib sauerkraut mixture into the duck. Place the stuffed duck into the slow cooker and cook on medium for 8 hours or until golden and tender.

High-Altitude Slow-Cooking

Since water boils at a lower temperature in high altitudes, you may want to cook most of your slow-cooker dishes on the high setting to ensure they're getting hot enough. You also can easily test the slow cooker by heating water in it and determining the temperature with a thermometer.

POACHED SALMON WITH BEARNAISE SAUCE

½ cup water
¼ cup dry white wine
2 salmon steaks
¼ cup mayonnaise
2 tablespoons lemon juice
1 tablespoon Dijon mustard

1 teaspoon granulated sugar
1 teaspoon tarragon
½ teaspoon salt
1 teaspoon freshly ground
black pepper

1. In a skillet, bring the water and wine to a gentle simmer. Add the salmon and cook without boiling for 8 to 10 minutes or until the fish flakes easily with a fork. Cut the steaks in half and arrange on warmed plates.
2. In a small saucepan, whisk together the mayonnaise, lemon juice, mustard, sugar, and tarragon. Cook over medium-low heat, whisking, for about 3 minutes or until warmed through but not boiling. Season with salt and pepper and spoon the sauce over the salmon.

HONEY-ORANGE BEETS

6 medium-sized fresh beets
1 teaspoon grated orange rind
2 tablespoons orange juice
2 teaspoons butter
1 teaspoon honey

¼ teaspoon ground ginger
½ teaspoon salt
¼ teaspoon ground black
pepper

1. Remove and discard the green tops from the beets. In a pot of boiling water, cook the beets for 40 minutes or until tender.
2. Drain the beets and let cool slightly. Slip off the skins and cut the beets into ¼-inch-thick slices.
3. In a medium-sized saucepan, heat the orange zest, orange juice, butter, honey, and ginger over low heat until the butter melts. Add the beets and toss to coat. Season with salt and pepper.

TWICE-BAKED POTATOES WITH CHIVES

4 medium-sized baking
  potatoes
¼ cup thinly sliced green
  onions
¼ cup fresh chopped chives
¼ cup milk

3 ounces cream cheese,
  softened
¼ cup butter
½ teaspoon (or to taste) salt
½ teaspoon (or to taste)
  ground black pepper

> **Serves 4**
>
> Although they look complicated, twice-baked potatoes are an easy way to create an elegant side dish for holiday meals.

1. Bake the potatoes in a 350° oven. Remove from oven and let cool. Thinly slice the green onions. Chop chives.
2. Combine the milk and cream cheese. Cut the potatoes in half lengthwise and scoop out the flesh, being careful to leave a shell of at least ¼ inch.
3. In a medium-sized bowl, combine the potato, cream cheese, and butter. Mash them together thoroughly, then whip by hand or with an electric mixer. Stir in the chives, onions, salt, and pepper.
4. Mound the mixture in the potato shells and place them on an ungreased baking sheet. Bake at 350° for about 30 minutes, or microwave on high for about 10 minutes until well heated.

Potato Peelings

Whenever you cook potatoes, try not to peel them if there is a choice. Potato skins can add a nice crunch to the overall texture of a dish, plus they carry valuable dietary fiber and vitamins.

GINGERED MASHED SWEET POTATOES

Serves 6

Serve as a side dish to traditional holiday turkey or, for a unique taste, serve with Poached Salmon with Bearnaise Sauce (page32).

4 medium-sized sweet potatoes or yams
1/4 cup milk

2 tablespoons butter
1 tablespoon brown sugar
1/2 teaspoon ground ginger

1. Peel and quarter the sweet potatoes. Cook in boiling, salted water until tender, about 20 minutes. Drain and return to the pan.
2. In a small pan or in the microwave, heat the milk and butter. Add to the potatoes along with the brown sugar and ginger. Mash by hand or whip with an electric mixer. (The texture will be thicker than mashed white potatoes.)

BRUSSELS SPROUTS WITH MUSTARD CREAM

Serves 6

For more even cooking, crosshatch the bottom of the Brussels sprouts before placing them in the boiling water.

1 1/2 pounds Brussels sprouts
2 tablespoons unsalted butter
1 large shallot
1/2 cup whipping cream
1/2 teaspoon dried tarragon

3/4 teaspoon Dijon mustard
1/4 teaspoon salt
1/4 teaspoon freshly ground pepper

1. Trim the Brussels sprouts. Peel and mince the shallot.
2. Cook the Brussels sprouts in boiling water until tender, 5 to 6 minutes. Drain well.
3. Melt the butter in the same pan and add the shallot. Cook over medium-high heat until the shallot softens, about 2 minutes. Add the Brussels sprouts and toss gently.
4. Add all the remaining ingredients. Cook just until the cream thickens slightly, about 1 minute.

MEXICAN CHRISTMAS EVE SALAD

2 medium-sized sweet apples
1 medium-sized banana
2 cups pineapple chunks
1 (1-pound) can sliced beets
2 navel oranges

1 pomegranate
Several fresh lettuce leaves
Lemon juice
⅓ cup unsalted peanuts
Nondairy whipped topping

Serves 4

This salad is a Christmas Eve tradition in many Mexican homes but it's enjoyable in even the coldest climates.

1. Peel, core, and thinly slice the apples. Peel and slice the banana into ¼-inch rounds. Drain the pineapples and beets. Peel and section the oranges. Scoop out the pomegranate seeds.
2. Line a large serving platter with the lettuce leaves.
3. In a large bowl, mix together the sliced apples and bananas. Sprinkle with a little lemon juice to keep them from turning brown.
4. Arrange the apples, bananas, pineapple chunks, beets, and orange sections on the platter. Sprinkle peanuts and pomegranate seeds over the fruit.
5. Serve nondairy whipped topping on the side.

Fruit Compote

Nearly any combination of fresh fruits makes a wonderful fruit compote in a slow cooker. Add 1 cup of sugar for every 8 cups of fruit and cook on low until the sauce is thick.

OYSTERS ROCKEFELLER SOUP

5 celery stalks
2 large white onions
3 cups thinly sliced green onions
3 cups spinach
1¼ cups fresh flat-leaf parsley
1 garlic clove
½ teaspoon dried oregano
2 tablespoons butter
1 bay leaf
1 teaspoon dried thyme leaves
2 teaspoons salt

⅛ teaspoon freshly ground black pepper
⅛ teaspoon ground red pepper
⅛ teaspoon ground white pepper
1 tablespoon all-purpose flour
2 cups fresh oysters
Chicken stock, as needed
¾ cup Pernod (French anise-flavored cordial)
6 cups whipping cream

1. Peel the onions and finely chop the onions, celery, spinach, and parsley. Peel and mince the garlic. Crush the dried oregano.

2. Heat the butter in a Dutch oven over medium-high heat. When the butter starts to foam, add the celery, white onions, and bay leaf. Cook for 4 to 5 minutes or until the vegetables are tender. Reduce the heat to low. Add the spinach, green onions, and parsley. Cook, stirring constantly, for 3 to 4 minutes. Remove the bay leaf.

3. Add the garlic, thyme, oregano, salt, and peppers. Cook, stirring constantly, for 4 to 5 minutes. Add the flour and cook for 2 minutes, stirring constantly, and scraping the sides and bottom of the pan.

4. Drain the oysters, reserving the liquid. Add enough chicken stock to the oyster liquid, if necessary, to make 1 cup total. Set aside.

5. Increase the heat to medium-high and carefully add the Pernod to the vegetable mixture. Cook, stirring constantly, for 4 to 5 minutes. Add the oyster and stock liquid mixture, and cook for another 3 to 4 minutes. Let cool slightly. Transfer the vegetable mixture to a blender or food processor. Cover and blend or process to a smooth consistency.

6. Return the mixture to the Dutch oven. Stir in the whipping cream and cook over medium heat for 4 to 5 minutes or until heated through, whisking occasionally. Add the oysters and cook for about 5 minutes or until the oyster edges curl. Serve immediately.

OVEN-ROASTED WINTER VEGETABLES

½ pound rutabaga
½ pound carrots
½ pound parsnips
½ pound Brussels sprouts
1 tablespoon unsalted butter
1 tablespoon extra-virgin
  olive oil

2 teaspoons fresh thyme
2 teaspoons fresh sage
⅛ teaspoon freshly grated
  nutmeg
½ cup Marsala wine

Serves 6

This is the perfect complement to prime rib, turkey, or any winter holiday meal.

1. Preheat oven to 450°. Peel the rutabaga, carrots, and parsnips, and cut into 1-inch pieces.
2. Bring a large pot of salted water to a boil. Add the rutabagas, carrots, and parsnips, and simmer until they are somewhat tender when pierced with a fork, about 5 to 8 minutes. Drain well.
3. Place the rutabagas, carrots, parsnips, and Brussels sprouts in a large roasting pan. Melt the butter in a small saucepan and stir in the oil, thyme, sage, and nutmeg. Drizzle the butter mixture over the vegetables to coat them completely. Pour the Marsala into the bottom of the roasting pan.
4. Cover tightly with foil and bake in the oven for 40 minutes. Remove the foil, toss the vegetables, and continue to cook, uncovered, until the Marsala is evaporated and the vegetables can easily be pierced with a knife, about 20 to 30 minutes. Place on a platter and serve immediately.

Cleaning Roots
Clean root vegetables thoroughly by scrubbing them with a nail brush or scouring pad designated for that purpose. Because they grow in fertilized soil, they can harbor bacteria on their skins.

YORKSHIRE PUDDING

1 cup milk

2 large eggs

1 cup all-purpose flour

1/4 teaspoon salt

1/2 cup fresh beef fat from a roast

1. Preheat oven to 350°. Place a 9" × 9" pan in the oven.
2. Mix together the milk and eggs.
3. In a large mixing bowl, mix together the flour and salt. Stir the milk mixture into the flour mixture so that it forms a smooth paste.
4. Cover the bottom of the hot pan with the beef fat. Pour the batter over the beef fat.
5. Bake the pudding until golden, about 20 minutes.

CLASSIC BREAD PUDDING

2 cups day-old bread

2 eggs

1 1/4 cups milk

1/2 packed cup brown sugar

1 teaspoon ground cinnamon

1 teaspoon vanilla extract

1/4 teaspoon salt

1/2 cup raisins

1. Preheat oven to 350°. Grease an 8-inch square baking dish.
2. Tear the bread into 1-inch cubes. Place the bread cubes in a large bowl. Lightly beat the eggs in a small bowl. Stir in the milk.
3. Pour the milk mixture over the bread cubes. Add the brown sugar, cinnamon, vanilla, salt, and raisins. Toss lightly to blend.
4. Spread the mixture in the prepared baking dish. Place the dish in a baking pan and pour hot water into the pan to a depth of 1 inch.
5. Bake for 35 to 40 minutes or until a knife inserted halfway between the center and the outside edge comes out clean. Serve warm or cold.

CHAPTER 3

CHRISTMAS TREATS

ANISE OVAL COOKIES	40
PFEFFERNUSSE	41
CHRISTMAS THEME SUGAR COOKIES	42
COCONUT WREATH COOKIES	43
CRÈME BRÛLÉE	44
GINGERBREAD MEN	45
PLUM PUDDING PIE	46
PEPPERMINT-FLAVORED CANDY CANE COOKIES	47
MINCEMEAT PIE	48
CHRISTMAS TEACAKES	48
PEPPERMINT BAKED ALASKA	49
GINGERBREAD WITH LEMON TOPPING	50
HOLIDAY PUNCH	51
IRISH COFFEE	51
NONALCOHOLIC WASSAIL	52
HOT CINNAMON STOCKING	52
PERFECT EGGNOG	53
TOM AND JERRY	53

ANISE OVAL COOKIES

4 large eggs
1¾ cups confectioners' sugar
⅛ teaspoon salt

2 cups all-purpose flour
2 teaspoons anise seeds
¼ teaspoon baking powder

1. Separate the egg yolks from the whites.
2. Beat together the confectioners' sugar, egg yolks, and salt in a large bowl until creamy.
3. In a separate bowl, beat the egg whites until very stiff. Fold into the sugar mixture.
4. In another bowl, combine the flour, anise seed, and baking powder. Fold into the creamed mixture thoroughly.
5. Place the dough into a pastry bag fitted with a plain nozzle. Pipe small ovals onto ungreased baking sheets. Let stand overnight to dry.
6. Preheat oven to 325°. Bake the cookies for 18 to 20 minutes or until set. Let cool on a wire rack.

A Dessert Buffet

If you're looking for a fun way to celebrate a holiday, try having a dessert buffet. You can even turn it into a potluck event. Serve a nice mix of beverages to complement the buffet.

PFEFFERNUSSE

3 large eggs
½ packed cup dark brown sugar
3 cups all-purpose flour
½ teaspoon baking powder
½ teaspoon freshly ground black pepper
½ teaspoon ground cloves

½ teaspoon ground cardamom seeds
¼ cup finely ground almonds
¼ teaspoon salt
2 tablespoons lemon juice
Zest of 1 lemon
1 cup confectioners' sugar

Makes 3 to 4 dozen

These are traditional at holiday buffets and parties. However, they also are a popular gift. Place a few in a coffee mug, cover with plastic wrap, and add a red bow!

1. Preheat oven to 350°.
2. Break the eggs in a large bowl and beat with a fork until frothy. Add the sugar and beat until well mixed.
3. In a small bowl, mix the flour with the rest of the dry ingredients, except the confectioners' sugar. Slowly combine the dry mixture with the egg mixture. Blend in the lemon juice and zest. Cover the bowl with plastic wrap and place in the refrigerator for 1 hour.
4. With floured palms, roll the dough into 1-inch balls. Place on a greased or nonstick baking sheet and bake for 10 to 15 minutes or until the bottoms are just beginning to brown.
5. As each batch comes out of the oven, roll immediately in confectioners' sugar and let cool on a wire rack.
6. To keep the cookies soft, as soon as they are cool, place them in an airtight container with an apple slice. Replace the apple slice every 3 days. After 3 weeks, the flavors in the cookies will have blended and the cookies will be ready to eat.

CHRISTMAS THEME SUGAR COOKIES

Makes 1 to 3 dozen

These cookies are a traditional Christmas favorite.

1 cup granulated sugar
1 cup margarine
1 large egg
½ teaspoon almond or vanilla extract
1½ teaspoons baking powder

½ teaspoon salt
2½ cups all-purpose flour
Red and green sugar crystals
Colored jimmies
Small silver ball candies

1. Preheat oven to 350°. Grease a baking sheet.
2. In a large mixing bowl, beat together the sugar and margarine.
3. Beat in the egg, extract, baking powder, and salt. Gradually add in the flour. Mix well.
4. On a floured surface, knead the dough by hand and shape into a large ball. Wrap in plastic wrap and chill for up to 2 hours, until firm.
5. Roll out the dough on a floured surface to ¼-inch thick. Cut out shapes with Christmas theme cookie cutters. Decorate with trimmings.
6. Place on a baking sheet and bake for 10 to 12 minutes or until lightly browned on the edges.

Using Skim Milk

If a recipe calls for whole milk, half-and-half, or cream, you can easily substitute skim milk. You will get all the nutrition and most of the creamy taste with much less fat.

COCONUT WREATH COOKIES

½ cup butter or margarine,
   softened
½ cup granulated sugar
1 large egg

1 (3½-ounce) package
   shredded sweetened coconut
1¾ cups all-purpose flour
Red and green candied
   cherries, sliced

1. Preheat oven to 375°. Grease and flour a baking sheet.
2. In a large bowl, beat together the butter and sugar. Blend in the egg and coconut. On low speed, add the flour, ½ cup at a time, until blended.
3. Wrap the dough in plastic wrap and chill for several hours.
4. On a floured surface, roll out ⅓ of the dough at a time to ¼-inch thickness. Using a 2½-inch doughnut cutter, cut the dough into rings. Remove excess coconut from the edges of the cookies.
5. Place the cherry slices on the cookies to resemble flower petals. Press into the cookies. Place on a baking sheet and bake in batches for about 10 minutes, until brown.

Pretty Presentation

For a spectacular gift presentation, line the bottom of a container with gold foil gift wrap and place each cookie in gold foil candy cups (available at cooking specialty stores).

CRÈME BRÛLÉE

3 eggs
2 cups light cream
1 cup granulated sugar
¼ teaspoon salt

1 teaspoon vanilla extract
½ packed cup brown sugar
½ cup fresh raspberries

1. Lightly beat the eggs. Scald the cream by cooking it over medium heat in a medium-sized saucepan until a light blister forms on top. Do not let the cream boil.
2. In the top pan of a double boiler, combine the eggs, granulated sugar, and salt. Slowly stir in the hot cream and vanilla. Cook over hot (not boiling) water for about 8 minutes or until the custard coats a metal spoon. Continue cooking about 2 minutes longer, or until the custard thickens slightly. Pour into an 8-inch round baking dish with 3-inch-high sides. Cover and chill well.
3. Preheat broiler.
4. Sift the brown sugar evenly over the surface of the custard. Set in a shallow pan and surround the dish with ice cubes and a little cold water. Slip under the broiler about 8 inches from the heat and broil for about 5 minutes or until the custard has a bubbly brown crust.
5. Serve either hot or chilled. Decorate with fresh raspberries right before serving.

Chocolate Curls

Use a swivel vegetable peeler to make attractive shavings and curls from a block of chocolate. Just start with a large flat surface of chocolate, like the edge of a bar or the side of a hunk, and shave away, letting the curls fall onto whatever food you're garnishing. Don't pick them up with your fingers, though, because they melt very fast.

GINGERBREAD MEN

½ cup granulated sugar
½ cup solid vegetable shortening
1 large egg
½ teaspoon salt
1 teaspoon baking powder
½ teaspoon baking soda
1 teaspoon ground ginger

1½ teaspoons ground cinnamon
1 teaspoon ground cloves
½ cup light molasses
2¼ cups all-purpose flour
Prepared frostings
Candies for trimmings

Makes 1 to 3 dozen

If baking with toddlers in the house, be sure to make a big show of locking the door so the Gingerbread Man can't run away!

1. Preheat oven to 350°.
2. In a large mixing bowl, beat together the sugar and shortening. Add the egg, salt, baking powder, baking soda, ginger, cinnamon, cloves, and molasses. Add the flour ½ cup at a time, beating until dough forms.
3. Shape the dough into a ball, wrap in plastic wrap, and chill until firm, at least 1 hour.
4. On a floured surface, roll out the dough to ¼-inch thickness. Using a gingerbread man cookie cutter, cut out the cookies. Place on an ungreased cookie sheet at least 1 inch apart.
5. Bake the cookies in batches for 8 to 10 minutes for small cookies, 12 to 15 minutes for larger cookies. Transfer the baking sheet to a wire rack to cool.
6. Spread frosting over the cookies. Decorate with candies.

Easy Frosting

Put ½ cup confectioners' sugar into 3 different soup bowls. Add 2 drops of food coloring and 1 drop of vanilla flavoring to each bowl. Drizzle milk into the bowls while stirring with a spoon. It will take less than 1 tablespoon of milk to make a good, fairly stiff frosting.

PLUM PUDDING PIE

1 cup pitted dates
1 cup crystallized plums
1 unbaked 9-inch pie pastry
  shell
2 large eggs
1 cup orange marmalade
1 cup shredded sweetened
  coconut

1 cup walnuts
1/4 cup slivers of ginger-
  preserved watermelon rind
  (if available, or any dried
  fruit cut into slivers)
2 tablespoons milk
1 tablespoon butter

1. Preheat oven to 425°. Chop the dates and crystallized plums into 1/4-inch pieces.
2. In a mixing bowl, beat the eggs. Add the dates, plums, marmalade, coconut, walnuts, watermelon rind, and milk, in that order. Blend well.
3. Place the pie crust in a greased pie pan. Pour the filling into the prepared crust. Dot the top with the butter. Bake for 25 minutes or until the crust is golden brown.

Prevent Overbrowning

Whether it's a turkey or a pie, you can prevent overbrowning on the top while baking by covering it with foil halfway through the cooking time.

PEPPERMINT-FLAVORED CANDY CANE COOKIES

1¼ cups margarine
1 cup confectioners' sugar
1 teaspoon vanilla extract
¼ teaspoon salt

1 large egg
3½ cups all-purpose flour
¼ teaspoon peppermint extract
3 drops red food coloring

Makes 2 to 3 dozen

Perfect with Minty Hot Chocolate (page 220) for the kids and with Irish Coffee (page 51) for the adults.

1. Preheat oven to 350°. Grease a baking sheet.
2. Beat together the margarine and sugar on medium speed until light and fluffy. Mix in the vanilla, salt, and egg. On low speed, beat in the flour ½ cup at a time until dough forms. Shape into a ball and divide in half.
3. In a small bowl, mix together the peppermint extract and red food coloring. Knead the food coloring mixture into 1 of the dough halves.
4. With lightly floured hands, roll 1 teaspoon of plain dough into a 4-inch rope. Repeat the process with 1 teaspoon of the red dough. Braid the ropes together and shape as a candy cane. Pinch together the ends to seal. Repeat with the remaining dough.
5. Place the cookies at least 1 inch apart on the prepared baking sheet. Bake in batches for 10 minutes or until golden brown. Transfer the baking sheet to a wire rack to cool.

Making Cookies Different Sizes?

Bake large cookies with large ones and small cookies with small ones for best results. Placing cookies of unlike sizes on the same sheet will result in uneven cooking.

MINCEMEAT PIE

2 eggs
1 (9-ounce) package mincemeat
1¼ cups water
1 cup granulated sugar

2 heaping tablespoons all-purpose flour
⅛ teaspoon salt
½ teaspoon vanilla extract
1 baked 9-inch pie pastry shell

1. Beat the eggs and set aside. Crumble the mincemeat into a bowl. Add the water and let soak for 30 minutes or until swollen.
2. Transfer the mincemeat to a medium-sized saucepan and add the sugar, flour, eggs, salt, and vanilla. Place over low heat and bring to a simmer. Stirring constantly, simmer for about 10 minutes or until thick.
3. Spread the mixture in the pastry shell. Let cool before serving.

CHRISTMAS TEACAKES

1 cup granulated sugar
1 cup margarine
3 large eggs
1 teaspoon nutmeg

3½ cups all-purpose flour
½ cup walnuts
1 cup confectioners' sugar

1. Preheat oven to 350°. Grease a baking sheet. Finely chop the walnuts.
2. In a large bowl, beat together the sugar and margarine until light and fluffy. Beat in the eggs and nutmeg. Beat in the flour ½ cup at a time.
3. Stir in the walnuts until well mixed.
4. Using 1 tablespoon of batter at a time, form cakes about ¼-inch thick. Place the cakes 1 inch apart on the prepared baking sheet. Bake the cakes in batches until golden and set, about 10 minutes.
5. When cool enough to handle but still warm, roll each cake in confectioners' sugar.

PEPPERMINT BAKED ALASKA

1 sponge, angel food, or loaf
   pound cake
4 egg whites
⅛ teaspoon cream of tartar
⅛ teaspoon salt

½ cup granulated sugar
½ teaspoon vanilla extract
1 quart peppermint ice cream

> **Serves 8**
>
> Baked Alaska may be prepared ahead and frozen, unwrapped, for up to 2 days. Brown just before serving.

1. Stack 2 pieces of corrugated 8" × 6" cardboard on top of each other and cover with aluminum foil. Cut the cake into ½-inch-thick slices and arrange the slices on the covered cardboard in a 7" × 5" rectangle. (You may not need all the cake.) Place in the freezer until frozen solid.
2. Let the egg whites stand at room temperature for 1 hour, then beat until frothy with a handheld electric mixer. Add the cream of tartar and salt, and continue beating until soft peaks form when the beaters are slowly raised.
3. Gradually beat in the sugar 2 tablespoons at a time, beating well after each addition. Continue beating for about 3 minutes until glossy. Mix in the vanilla.
4. Preheat oven to 500°.
5. Spoon the ice cream onto the frozen cake base. Quickly spread the ice cream evenly over the top and sides of the cake. Spoon the egg whites on top, spreading them over the top and down the sides onto the foil to seal completely. Make swirls in the egg whites on the top and sides.
6. Place on a baking sheet and bake for 3 minutes or until the meringue is light brown. Remove to a chilled platter and serve at once.

GINGERBREAD WITH LEMON TOPPING

Serves 9

Serve with Perfect Eggnog (page 53) or Hot Cinnamon Stocking (page 52).

½ cup water
½ firmly packed cup light brown sugar
⅓ cup butter
½ cup light molasses
1 teaspoon baking soda
1¼ cups all-purpose flour

1 teaspoon ground cinnamon
½ teaspoon ground ginger
1 large egg
2 tablespoons grated lemon rind
1 tablespoon lemon juice
1 cup confectioners' sugar

1. Preheat oven to 325°. Grease and flour an 8-inch square baking pan. Put the water in small saucepan on high heat and heat until boiling.
2. In a large bowl, mix together the brown sugar and butter. Mix in the molasses and baking soda. Add the flour, cinnamon, and ginger. Mix well.
3. Beat the egg, then add and mix. Add the boiling water and mix well.
4. Pour the batter into the prepared pan. Smooth the top.
5. Bake the gingerbread until a toothpick inserted into the center comes out clean, approximately 40 minutes.
6. While the gingerbread is cooling, mix together the lemon rind, lemon juice, and confectioners' sugar. Drizzle over the gingerbread pieces before serving.

Individual Portions

Foods bake faster in individual portions rather than in one large pan or dish. For example, use individual serving dishes for casseroles rather than one large casserole pan.

HOLIDAY PUNCH

½ medium-sized orange
1 quart apple juice
1 quart cranberry juice cocktail

1 cup brown sugar
4 whole cinnamon sticks
4 whole cloves

1. Peel and cut the orange into ¼-inch-thick slices.
2. Add the apple juice, cranberry juice, and brown sugar to a slow cooker. Cook on low setting, stirring occasionally, until the brown sugar is dissolved.
3. Add the cinnamon sticks and cloves. Cook, covered, for 1 hour on low setting.
4. Right before guests arrive, add the orange slices.

Serves 8

Keep this punch warm by keeping it in the slow cooker. Use a soup ladle to let guests serve themselves.

IRISH COFFEE

1½ ounces Irish whiskey
1 teaspoon granulated sugar
1 cup very hot coffee

2 tablespoons whipped cream
1 ounce Irish Cream or Kahlua liqueur

1. Pour the whiskey into a glass or mug. Mix with the liqueur.
2. Stir in the sugar and add the hot coffee.
3. Top with whipped cream and serve immediately.

Serves 1

This mellow alcoholic drink is equally good alone or served as a dessert coffee. For a different twist, add a dollop of peppermint ice cream instead of whipped cream.

NONALCOHOLIC WASSAIL

2 quarts apple cider
2 cups orange juice
1 cup fresh lemon juice

1 teaspoon cloves
10 cinnamon sticks

1. Put the apple cider, orange juice, and lemon juice into a large saucepan. Add the cloves and 2 of the cinnamon sticks. Warm over medium heat for 20 minutes.
2. When ready to serve, strain off the cloves and cinnamon sticks and pour the liquid into mugs. Place a new cinnamon stick in each mug and serve.

HOT CINNAMON STOCKING

2 cups prepared hot cocoa
2 tablespoons (or to taste)
   cinnamon-flavor liqueur
Whipped cream

2 red maraschino cherries,
   halved
2 green maraschino cherries,
   halved

Pour hot cocoa into 2 large mugs. Add 1 tablespoon of the cinnamon-flavored liqueur to each mug. Top each with whipped cream and red and green maraschino cherries.

PERFECT EGGNOG

6 large eggs
½ cup granulated sugar
1 pint heavy cream
1 pint milk

1 pint whiskey
2 ounces rum
1 tablespoon grated nutmeg

1. Separate the egg yolks and whites, and place the yolks in a large bowl.
2. Add the sugar to the yolks, beating at medium speed until the yolks are stiff.
3. Mix the egg whites into the yolk mixture. Stir in the cream and milk.
4. Add the whiskey and rum. Stir thoroughly.
5. Chill for 2 hours. Serve with grated nutmeg on top.

Makes 6 to 8 cups

Fresh eggnog is so much better than the store-bought varieties that you likely will never go back. Remember to keep some alcohol-free eggnog in the refrigerator for children and guests who don't imbibe.

TOM AND JERRY

1 egg
2 tablespoons granulated sugar
2 ounces light rum

1 ounce brandy
¾ cup hot milk
Nutmeg

1. Separate the egg white and yolk. Beat the egg white and yolk separately. Mix them together in a mug.
2. Add the sugar and mix vigorously. Pour in the rum and brandy. Fill with milk. Stir gently and sprinkle with nutmeg.

Serves 1

Here's something to lift your spirits on a cold holiday night!

NEW YEAR'S

STUFFED MUSHROOMS	56
VEGETABLE GADO-GADO	57
BROCCOLI DIP	58
CREAMY GARLIC AND RED PEPPER DIP	58
PARMESAN CRISPS	59
ARTICHOKE BOTTOMS WITH HERBED CHEESE	59
HERBED CLAM DIP	60
LOUISIANA HOT WINGS	60
PEARS WRAPPED IN PROSCIUTTO ON A BED OF MIXED GREENS	61
EGGPLANT CAVIAR	62
FRIED GREEN TOMATO BRUSCHETTA	63
HOT ARTICHOKE DIP	64
SPINACH AND RICOTTA DIP	64
HOT DUNGENESS CRAB APPETIZER	65
PEANUT POPCORN FUDGE	65
IRISH CREAM	66
CRUNCHY NUT TREATS	66
PEANUTTY OATMEAL CANDY	67
SCOTCH MILK PUNCH	67
CHAMPAGNE COCKTAIL	68
CHAMPAGNE CHARISMA	68
CHAMPAGNE MINT	69
CHAMPAGNE FIZZ	69
NONALCOHOLIC CHAMPAGNE PUNCH	70

STUFFED MUSHROOMS

1 pound fresh button
  mushrooms
1 small yellow onion
2 tablespoons fresh parsley
3 tablespoons butter
¾ cup bread crumbs

½ teaspoon salt
¼ teaspoon ground black pepper
1 teaspoon dried thyme
¼ cup half-and-half
¼ cup grated Parmesan cheese

1. Wash the mushrooms with a damp cloth and remove the stems. Set aside the caps. Chop the mushroom stems into ¼-inch pieces. Peel and finely chop the onion. Roughly chop the parsley.
2. Preheat oven broiler.
3. Heat the butter in a medium-sized skillet over medium heat. Add the onion and cook for 2 minutes, until translucent. Add the mushroom stems and cook for 2 to 3 minutes more. Stir in the bread crumbs, salt, pepper, and thyme. Cook for 1 minute more. Remove from heat and stir in the half-and-half and grated cheese.
4. Using a small spoon, fill each mushroom cap with the mushroom mixture. Place the filled mushrooms on a baking sheet and put under the preheated oven broiler for 5 to 7 minutes, until the tops are browned and the caps have softened and become juicy. Sprinkle the tops with chopped parsley and serve hot or warm.
5. Drizzle with garlic butter or top with an olive slice if desired to add a little extra flavor to these favorite hors d'ouvres.

Dried Mushrooms

Dried wild mushrooms are an excellent way to bring passionate flavors from forests to your dining table. Soak them for a few hours or overnight in room temperature water, then use them as you would fresh mushrooms. The soaking liquid acquires a wonderful flavor; use it in soups or stocks. Pour the water into a clear container and discard any sediment.

VEGETABLE GADO-GADO

16–24 carrot sticks or baby
   carrots
16–24 broccoli florets
16–24 trimmed green beans
16–24 yellow bell pepper strips
16–24 zucchini rounds
Assorted other vegetables
   according to availability

½ cup smooth peanut butter
¼ cup honey
¼ teaspoon salt
⅛ teaspoon cayenne pepper
1 tablespoon lime juice
¾ cup coconut milk

> **Serves 8**
>
> This appetizer has its origins in Indonesia. It can make a wonderful summer sampler when served with several dipping sauces.

1. Blanch all the vegetables quickly in lightly salted boiling water. Plunge immediately into ice-cold water to stop the cooking process. Drain and arrange in an attractive pattern on a serving platter.
2. Combine the peanut butter, honey, salt, cayenne pepper, and lime juice in a food processor or mixing bowl; Pulse or whisk together until smooth. Gradually work in the coconut milk until a saucy consistency is reached. Adjust consistency with hot water, if needed. Serve as a dipping sauce with the blanched vegetables.

Time-Saving Tip

You can purchase precleaned and precut vegetables in plastic bags or even prearranged on a platter. Just add a special dip for quick appetizers.

BROCCOLI DIP

1 small yellow onion
2 celery ribs
1 cup sliced fresh mushrooms
2 garlic cloves

2 cups chopped fresh broccoli
¼ cup butter
1 (10¾-ounce) can cream of
    mushroom condensed soup

1. Peel the onion and chop into ¼-inch pieces. Chop the celery into ¼-inch pieces. Clean the mushrooms by wiping with a damp cloth, then slice paper-thin. Peel the garlic and chop into ⅛-inch pieces. Chop the broccoli into ¼-inch pieces.
2. Combine all the ingredients in a slow cooker. Cover and cook on low setting for 3 to 4 hours.

CREAMY GARLIC AND RED PEPPER DIP

1 fresh red pepper
1 large garlic clove
1 teaspoon dried basil leaves

1 teaspoon hot pepper sauce
   of your choice
1 cup cottage cheese

1. Preheat oven to 350°. Cut the red pepper into ½-inch-wide strips. Place skin-side down on a baking sheet and spread cooking oil on top of the pepper strips. Bake for 1 hour or until well browned. Remove from the oven and cut into 1-inch pieces. Remove the peel from the garlic and crush the clove with the side of a large kitchen knife.
2. In a food processor, blend the red pepper strips, garlic, dried basil, and hot pepper sauce until chopped. Add the cottage cheese and blend well.
3. Chill for at least 1 hour before serving.

PARMESAN CRISPS

1 cup shredded (not grated)
  Parmesan cheese
1 teaspoon salt

1 teaspoon freshly ground
  white pepper

1. Preheat oven to 325°. Line a baking sheet with parchment paper.
2. Place rounded teaspoons of the shredded cheese on the parchment, equally spaced with about 2 inches between each mound.
3. Lightly flatten each mound with your fingertips to a circle about 1½ inches across. Sprinkle with salt and pepper.
4. Place in the oven and remove when the cheese just starts to melt and very lightly begins to brown, about 3 to 5 minutes. Remove immediately.

Serves 15

Use instead of traditional crackers or bread with Hot Artichoke Dip (page 64) or Eggplant Caviar (page 52).

ARTICHOKE BOTTOMS WITH HERBED CHEESE

1 can artichoke bottoms
2 tablespoons mix of fresh
  parsley, basil, and chives
6 fresh radishes

8 ounces cream cheese, softened
½ teaspoon salt
½ teaspoon freshly ground
  black pepper

1. Drain and rinse the artichoke bottoms, then slice into 30 neatly trimmed slices. Chop the herbs. Clean the radishes and slice into 30 rounds.
2. Mix together the cream cheese, herbs, salt, and pepper in a small bowl until smooth.
3. Use a pastry bag to pipe a small rosette of the cream cheese mixture (about 1 rounded tablespoon each) onto each artichoke slice.
4. Top with a radish slice and serve immediately.

Serves 15

Canned artichoke bottoms are a great item to have on hand when you need a quick appetizer with an elegant look.

HERBED CLAM DIP

Makes 1 cup

Use low-fat cottage cheese and low-fat yogurt for a low-fat, low-carb snack.

1 cup cottage cheese
1 (10-ounce) can minced
   clams, liquid reserved
⅓ cup chopped fresh parsley
3 tablespoons plain yogurt

1 tablespoon dried basil
1 tablespoon minced onion
1 tablespoon lemon juice
¼ teaspoon Tabasco sauce

1. Process the cottage cheese in a food processor until smooth. Transfer to a bowl.
2. Drain the clams, reserving 1 tablespoon of the liquid. Add the clams and 1 tablespoon of the liquid to the cottage cheese. Add the remaining ingredients and mix well.
3. Cover and chill well before serving.

LOUISIANA HOT WINGS

Serves 8

If you're going to an evening-long party, add a little water and stir the wings every hour or so; then they won't dry out.

1 small onion
1 jalapeño pepper
1 cup Louisiana red pepper
   sauce
2 tablespoons Worcestershire sauce

2 tablespoons powdered Cajun
   spice, divided
1 cup barbecue sauce
5 pounds thawed chicken wings,
   disjointed with tips removed

1. Preheat slow cooker on high setting. Peel the onion and chop it into ¼-inch pieces. Remove the stem and seeds from the jalapeño pepper and dice the pepper.
2. Add the onion, jalapeño pepper, red pepper sauce, Worcestershire sauce, Cajun spice, and barbecue sauce to the slow cooker and stir well.
3. Add the chicken wings and stir until all the wings are covered.
4. Cover and cook on high setting for 4 hours. Uncover and turn heat to low while serving.

PEARS WRAPPED IN PROSCIUTTO ON A BED OF MIXED GREENS

6 slices prosciutto

2 ripe pears

3 tablespoons extra-virgin olive oil

½ teaspoon salt

½ teaspoon ground black pepper

4 cups mixed salad greens

½ cup prepared vinaigrette salad dressing

½ cup fresh-grated Parmesan cheese

Serves 4

Use a good quality Parmesan cheese from the deli counter to enhance the flavor of this dish.

1. Cut each slice of prosciutto in half lengthwise. Cut each pear into 6 wedges and remove the core.
2. Toss the pear wedges in about 2 tablespoons of the olive oil until evenly coated, and season with the salt and pepper.
3. Heat a grill pan until very hot, almost smoking. Mark the pear slices with dark brown grill marks on each side, using tongs to turn the pears. This should take only a few minutes on each side.
4. Preheat broiler to low. Wrap a piece of prosciutto around the middle of each pear. Place all the wrapped pears on a lightly oiled baking sheet and cook for about 2 to 3 minutes on each side.
5. Toss the salad greens with the vinaigrette. Top with the Parmesan cheese and sprinkle with salt and pepper. Drizzle with the remaining olive oil and serve immediately.

Freezing Cheese

Placing a leftover hunk of cheese into the freezer not only conserves all those odd bits that are too small to use in another recipe, but also hardens up the soft cheeses enough for grating. Be sure to freeze soft cheeses when they have ripened. Semisoft and harder cheeses can be frozen as is, or sliced or grated beforehand.

EGGPLANT CAVIAR

Serves 4

Serve with crackers,
French bread, or
Parmesan Crisps
(page 59).

1 large white onion
3 garlic cloves
1 large eggplant
2 tablespoons olive oil

1 tablespoon tomato paste
1 teaspoon salt
½ teaspoon ground white pepper

1. Preheat oven to 400°. Peel and finely chop the onion and garlic.
2. Place the eggplant in a baking dish and roast on the middle rack of the oven until very well done, about 1 hour. Let cool. Cut the eggplant in half and scoop out the soft pulp with a serving spoon. Place on a cutting board and chop thoroughly, until it has the consistency of oatmeal.
3. Heat the olive oil in a large skillet over medium heat for 1 minute. Add the onions and cook until they are very soft but not brown, about 10 minutes. Add the garlic and cook 1 minute more. Stir in the tomato paste and cook for 1 minute.
4. Add the chopped eggplant and cook until the mixture is thickened. An indentation should remain when a spoon is depressed into the mixture. Season with salt and pepper.

About Eggplant

Eggplants vary widely in flavor and intensity, and some types' delicate bitter edge helps define this beautiful vegetable's character. Long, slender, violet-hued Japanese eggplants contain none of the bitterness of America's large black variety. Pear-sized Italian-style eggplants are similar to our regular ones, but white-skinned varieties are milder. When sliced eggplant is sprinkled with salt it sheds some of its bitterness along with the salty droplets that form along its surface.

FRIED GREEN TOMATO BRUSCHETTA

4 medium-sized green tomatoes
¼ cup fresh basil leaves
12 pimiento-stuffed green olives
1 loaf crusty country bread
1 cup olive oil

2 eggs
1 cup all-purpose flour
1 cup bread crumbs
1 tablespoon balsamic vinegar
¼ cup extra-virgin olive oil

Makes 12

This recipe combines the best of Italy with the best of the deep South. Serve it with champagne for a New Year's treat.

1. Cut the tomatoes into ½-inch-thick slices. Roughly chop the basil leaves. Cut the olives in half lengthwise. Cut the bread into slices about 1-inch thick. Pour the olive oil into a frying pan and preheat to about 325° (medium-low).
2. Lightly beat the eggs in a shallow bowl. Dredge the tomato slices in the flour, dip them in the eggs, and then in the bread crumbs, shaking off excess after each dip. Fry at low heat until golden and mostly tender. Place the still-hot tomatoes flat on a cutting board and dice them into ½-inch pieces.
3. In a large mixing bowl, gently toss the diced tomatoes with the vinegar, basil, and olives. Set aside.
4. Preheat oven to 400°.
5. Brush the bread slices with the extra-virgin oil and place on a baking sheet. Toast in the oven until lightly browned. Remove and top each of 6 slices with the tomato mixture. Cut each in half.

Tomato Types

All tomatoes are not alike. Substitute plum tomatoes for a more robust flavor. Choose golden tomatoes for a more mellow taste. Reserve pricier hot-house tomatoes for salads and recipes in which tomatoes are the main ingredient.

HOT ARTICHOKE DIP

Serves 10

This is excellent served with pita bread, Parmesan Crisps (page 59), or even crisp vegetables such as carrots and celery.

1 (10½-ounce) can artichoke
  hearts
2 garlic cloves
¼ cup mayonnaise
½ teaspoon Worcestershire sauce

½ cup grated Parmesan cheese
½ teaspoon salt
½ teaspoon ground white
  pepper

1. Preheat oven to 350°.
2. Drain and rinse the artichoke hearts. Chop into ¼-inch pieces. Peel and mince the garlic.
3. Combine all the ingredients in a 2-quart ovenproof glass dish. Mix well. Bake, uncovered, for 25 minutes.

SPINACH AND RICOTTA DIP

Serves 12

Serve with fresh trimmed vegetables, Parmesan Crisps (page 59), or toasted bread rounds. No one will guess how easy this was to make!

1 (10-ounce) package frozen,
  chopped spinach
4 green onions
1 small white onion
½ cup ricotta cheese
⅓ cup mayonnaise
¼ cup sour cream

3 tablespoons lemon juice
¼ teaspoon Worcestershire
  sauce
½ teaspoon salt
½ teaspoon ground black
  pepper

1. Thaw and drain the spinach. Peel and chop the green onions. Peel and grate the white onion, reserving the juice.
2. Combine all the ingredients in a food processor and pulse until smooth.
3. Transfer to a bowl and chill thoroughly.

HOT DUNGENESS CRAB APPETIZER

1 (14-ounce) can artichoke
 hearts
½ pound fresh Dungeness
 crabmeat
2 cups mayonnaise

1 small yellow onion
1 cup shredded Parmesan
 cheese
1 bunch fresh parsley

Makes 2 cups

When making this dish ahead of time, do not cover with aluminum foil, as the crab will discolor.

1. Preheat oven to 350°. Drain the artichoke hearts and chop into ¼-inch pieces. Drain the crabmeat and chop. Peel the onion and chop thinly. Chop the parsley.
2. Combine all the ingredients *except* the parsley and mix well. Place in a shallow baking dish and heat in the oven for 6 to 8 minutes or until the internal temperature is at least 140°.
3. Garnish with minced parsley. Serve with assorted breads.

PEANUT POPCORN FUDGE

2 cups granulated sugar
½ cup smooth peanut butter
½ cup milk
1 tablespoon margarine

1 heaping cup of coarsely
 chopped popped popcorn
1 teaspoon vanilla extract

Serves 12

This recipe calls for experimentation. Try adding peanuts, coconut, or crispy rice cereal until you find the perfect "fudge" for your family and friends.

1. Grease a medium-sized baking dish.
2. In a medium-sized saucepan, combine the sugar, peanut butter, and milk, and warm over low heat until smooth. Add the margarine, popcorn, and vanilla.
3. Beat until all the ingredients are well distributed and the mixture is of an even consistency.
4. Pour onto the prepared baking dish. Chill well.

IRISH CREAM

Makes about 4 drinks

To make an elegant-looking drink, top with whipped cream and drizzled chocolate syrup.

1 (12-ounce) can condensed
  milk
8 ounces Irish whiskey
4 large eggs

1 tablespoon chocolate syrup
1 teaspoon vanilla extract
1 teaspoon coconut extract

Mix together all the ingredients in a blender. Chill for 1 hour and serve.

CRUNCHY NUT TREATS

Makes about 3 dozen

These are a wonderful complement to those meat and cheese appetizers so prevalent at New Year's Eve parties.

1 cup solid vegetable shortening
¼ cup confectioners' sugar,
  plus extra for dusting
1 teaspoon vanilla extract

2 cups sifted all-purpose flour
½ cup chopped almonds
½ cup chopped walnuts

1. Preheat oven to 300°.
2. In a large bowl, beat together the shortening, confectioners' sugar, and vanilla extract. Beat in the flour at low speed. Stir in the nuts.
3. Shape the dough into round balls and place several inches apart on an ungreased baking sheet. Bake in batches for 15 to 18 minutes. Check frequently during the last 5 minutes to ensure they don't scorch.
4. Transfer cookies to a wire rack. Roll the warm cookies in confectioners' sugar. Let stand until cool.

PEANUTTY OATMEAL CANDY

1 cup granulated sugar
½ cup evaporated milk
¼ cup margarine
¼ cup crunchy peanut butter

½ teaspoon vanilla extract
1 cup old-fashioned dry oats
½ cup peanuts

1. In a saucepan, bring the sugar, evaporated milk, and margarine to a boil, stirring frequently.
2. When the sugar is dissolved, remove from heat and stir in the peanut butter and vanilla.
3. Mix in the oats and peanuts. Drop the mixture by rounded teaspoon onto wax paper so that each morsel has a peak. (If the mixture is too stiff, add a few drops of milk.) Chill until firm.

Makes 2 dozen

Try experimenting with this recipe by replacing the peanuts with coconut and the peanut butter with melted milk chocolate. Or use almonds instead of peanuts.

SCOTCH MILK PUNCH

2 ounces scotch
6 ounces milk

1 teaspoon sugar
⅛ teaspoon nutmeg

Pour the scotch into a highball glass. Add the milk and sugar. Stir well. Dust with nutmeg.

Serves 1

This is a traditional cure for New Year's Day hangovers, although it's pretty tasty during the party, too.

CHAMPAGNE COCKTAIL

Serves 1

A traditional treat to help ring in the New Year.

1 teaspoon fine sugar
3 dashes bitters

6 ounces chilled champagne
Lemon twist

Dissolve the sugar in the bitters in the bottom of a champagne flute. Add the champagne and stir. Top with a lemon twist.

CHAMPAGNE CHARISMA

Serves 1

It's just as good without the sherbet. Or try a different flavor of sherbet for a unique taste.

1 ounce vodka
½ ounce peach-flavored brandy
1 ounce cranberry juice

1–2 scoops raspberry sherbet
2 ounces chilled champagne

Combine all the ingredients *except* the champagne in a blender. Blend well. Pour into a large red wine goblet. Add the champagne and stir.

CHAMPAGNE MINT

½ ounce green crème de menthe   Chilled champagne to fill glass

Pour the crème de menthe into a champagne flute. Add the champagne and stir gently.

Serves 1
What a wonderful, mellow drink to complement all those appetizers!

CHAMPAGNE FIZZ

2 ounces gin   *Ice*
1 ounce lemon juice   *4 ounces champagne*
1 teaspoon granulated sugar

1. Combine the gin, lemon juice, and sugar in a shaker half-filled with ice. Shake well.
2. Strain into a highball glass over ice. Add the champagne and stir gently.

Serves 1
A fun twist on the traditional treat.

NONALCOHOLIC CHAMPAGNE PUNCH

1 cup fine sugar
1 cup water
2 cups grapefruit juice

Juice of 1 lemon
1½ quarts ginger ale

1. Dissolve the sugar in the water in a punch bowl.
2. Add the grapefruit and lemon juices to the sugar water and mix well.
3. Add the ginger ale to the punch bowl just before serving.

Serving Tips

Pouring a cold drink into a warm glass is not a crime, but it should be. It robs the drink of its chill and the pleasure of its proper temperature. Chilling glasses is not hard, of course—just difficult to remember. If refrigerator or freezer space allows, squeeze the glass in along with the ice cream. If not, fill a glass with ice just before serving, stir it a bit, and discard the ice.

Chapter 5

VALENTINE'S DAY

ARTICHOKES IN COURT BOUILLON WITH LEMON BUTTER	72
SCALLOPS AND SHRIMP WITH WHITE BEAN SAUCE	73
CHEESE FONDUE	74
SWEET FENNEL WITH LEMON AND SHAVED PARMIGIANO	75
PASTA WITH ARTICHOKES	76
SPINACH-WRAPPED ZUCCHINI FLAN	77
FRENCH ONION SOUP	78
COQUILLES ST. JACQUES PROVENÇAL	79
GRILLED LOBSTER WITH LEMON AND TARRAGON	80
GAME HENS IN RED WINE	81
CARAMEL RUM FONDUE	82
SALMON IN WHITE WINE WITH DRIED PEACHES	82
HERB LINGUINE WITH SALMON, CREAM, AND PISTACHIOS	83
PEARS POACHED IN WHITE WINE WITH STRAWBERRY SAUCE	84
CHOCOLATE SOUFFLÉ	85
AMARETTO CAKE	86
APPLE-BUTTERED RUM PUDDING WITH APPLE TOPPING	87
BISHOP	88
VALENTINE	88
SANGRIA	89
MIDORI MIMOSA	89
BELLINI	90

ARTICHOKES IN COURT BOUILLON
WITH LEMON BUTTER

Serves 4

Serve as the first course to a romantic menu including Scallops and Shrimp with White Bean Sauce (page 73).

4 whole artichokes

4 lemons

2 tablespoons whole coriander seeds

2 tablespoons salt

1 cup butter

1. Trim the stems of the artichokes to about 2 inches. Bring 5 quarts water to a rapid boil. Halve 3 of the lemons, squeeze them into the boiling water, and toss the squeezed lemon fruits into the water along with the coriander seeds and salt. Boil for 5 minutes.

2. Place the artichokes in the cooking liquid and cover with a heavy plate or other object to keep them from floating. Boil until a paring knife inserted where the stem meets the bottom comes out easily, about 15 minutes. Meanwhile, melt the butter in the microwave for 30 seconds on high, then mix with the juice of the remaining lemon.

3. Serve each person a whole artichoke accompanied by a ramekin of butter sauce and a large bowl for discarded leaves.

How to Eat an Artichoke

Eat the artichoke leaf by leaf, dipping them in butter and nibbling at the tender bits at the bottoms of the outer leaves first and gradually reaching the fully edible inner leaves. When you reach the hairlike "choke," scoop it out with a spoon, discard it, and carve the prized "heart" at the bottom into pieces for easy consumption.

SCALLOPS AND SHRIMP WITH WHITE BEAN SAUCE

1 small white onion
2 garlic cloves
1⅓ cups canned white beans
½ pound medium-sized shrimp
2 teaspoons olive oil, divided
¼ cup dry white wine

¼ tightly packed cup fresh parsley leaves
¼ lightly packed cup fresh basil leaves
¼ cup chicken broth
½ pound scallops

> **Serves 4**
>
> Add 1 pound of crab-meat instead of the shrimp and scallops for a smoother texture. Mix with the bean purée and serve over egg noodles.

1. Remove the skins from the onion and garlic. Chop the onion into ¼-inch pieces. Mince the garlic. Drain and rinse the beans. Parboil the shrimp. Remove the shells and devein the shrimp.

2. In a medium-sized saucepan, sauté the onion and garlic in 1 teaspoon of the olive oil over moderately low heat until the onion is soft. Add the wine and simmer the mixture until the wine is reduced by half. Add the parsley, basil, ⅓ cup of the beans, and the chicken broth. Simmer the mixture for 1 minute, stirring constantly.

3. Transfer the bean mixture to a blender or food processor and purée it. Pour the purée back into the saucepan and add the remaining beans. Simmer for 2 minutes.

4. Heat the remaining 1 teaspoon of oil over moderately high heat in a medium-sized skillet until it is hot but not smoking. Sauté the shrimp for 2 minutes on each side, or until they are cooked through.

5. Using a slotted spoon, transfer the shrimp to a plate and cover to keep warm. Add the scallops to the skillet and sauté them for 1 minute on each side, or until they are cooked through. To serve, divide the bean sauce between 4 shallow bowls and arrange the shellfish over the top.

How to Parboil

The key to effective parboiling is not to let the shrimp cook for too long. Bring a large pot of water to boil (more than enough to cover the shrimp when added). Add the shrimp and boil for 2 to 3 minutes. Immediately drain and rinse in cold water.

CHEESE FONDUE

Serves 6

Turn down the lights, add a few candles, and let the conversation flow as people assemble their own meals.

1 garlic clove
¾ pound Swiss cheese
¾ pound Gruyère cheese
1 loaf French bread
Assorted bite-sized vegetables
    such as carrot sticks, broccoli,
    cauliflower, and green beans

2 cups dry white wine
1 tablespoon cornstarch
2 tablespoons kirsch

1. Cut the end off the garlic clove and remove the skin. Shred the cheeses. Cut the French bread into 1-inch cubes.
2. Put the vegetables in a vegetable steamer and cook until soft but not mushy.
3. Rub the inside of a medium-sized saucepot with the cut-side of the garlic. Leave the clove in the bottom of the pot. Add the wine and cook over medium heat until it simmers. Whisk in the cheese in small handfuls, making sure that the last addition has completely melted before adding the next.
4. Combine the cornstarch and kirsch to form a paste; whisk into the cheese mixture. Simmer the fondue gently for 5 to 7 minutes to allow the cornstarch to thicken.
5. Transfer the cheese mixture to a fondue pot and set a low flame under it, just hot enough to keep it at the border of simmering. Assemble a platter with the vegetables and bread cubes and set the table with either long fondue forks or long wooden skewers.

Making Your Own Pasta

Use semolina flour to make homemade noodles. It is made from high-gluten wheat and is more finely ground. The pasta is slightly stiffer than that made from regular flour so it also holds up better in slow-cooked casseroles.

SWEET FENNEL WITH LEMON AND SHAVED PARMIGIANO

2 bulbs fresh fennel
½ fresh lemon
1 wedge (at least 4 inches long) Parmigiano Reggiano cheese

1 tablespoon extra-virgin olive oil
Pinch of salt

Serves 4

This is the perfect hors d'oeuvres for an Italian meal, but it also makes an interesting treat for any dinner.

1. Trim the stems and hairlike fronds from the fennel tops. Break the bulbs apart, layer by layer, using your hands to make long, bite-sized pieces. Discard the core. Arrange the pieces in a pyramid-shape on a small, attractive serving plate.
2. Squeeze the lemon over the fennel. Using a peeler, shave curls of the cheese over the fennel, allowing them to fall where they may. Make about 10 curls. Drizzle the olive oil over the plate and sprinkle with salt.
3. Serve at room temperature.

Even-Seasoning Secret

To avoid salty patches in some parts of your food, and bland, unseasoned patches on other parts, take a cue from pro chefs: Season from a great height. Most chefs pinch salt between their thumb and forefinger and sprinkle it down onto food from about head height. It tends to shower broadly over the food this way, covering evenly.

PASTA WITH ARTICHOKES

Serves 4

Serve with garlic toast and antipasto salad for a romantic Italian dinner.

1 (10-ounce) package frozen
   artichoke hearts
1¼ cups water
1 tablespoon lemon juice
¼ cup sun-dried tomatoes
   packed in oil
2 garlic cloves

1½ cups uncooked linguine
4 teaspoons olive oil
¼ teaspoon red pepper flakes
2 teaspoons dried parsley
¼ cup grated Parmesan cheese
½ teaspoon freshly grated
   black pepper

1. Cook the artichokes in the water and lemon juice according to package directions. Drain, reserving ¼ cup of the liquid. Let the artichokes cool, then cut into quarters. Drain the tomatoes and chop into ¼-inch pieces. Peel and finely mince the garlic. Cook the pasta according to package directions.

2. Heat the olive oil in a nonstick skillet over medium heat. Add the garlic and sauté for 1 minute. Reduce heat to low and stir in the artichokes and tomatoes. Simmer for 1 minute. Stir in the reserved artichoke liquid, the red pepper flakes, and parsley. Simmer for 5 minutes.

3. Pour the artichoke sauce over the pasta in a large bowl. Toss gently to coat. Sprinkle with cheese and top with pepper.

Low-Fat Garlic Toast

Instead of smearing the bread with butter before toasting, give it a light spritz of olive oil and bake in a 350° oven for 6 to 8 minutes. Rub a cut garlic clove across the top of each slice. The flavor is great and the fat is near zero.

SPINACH-WRAPPED ZUCCHINI FLAN

1 small zucchini (about
 ¾ pound)
4–6 large leaves flat-leaf
 spinach
½ cup heavy cream
2 eggs
1 egg yolk

1 teaspoon fresh-grated nutmeg
⅛ teaspoon curry powder
⅛ teaspoon cayenne powder
½ teaspoon salt
½ teaspoon ground black
 pepper
1 teaspoon butter, softened

Serves 4

The flan can be made the day before and gently reheated just before serving.

1. Preheat oven to 300°. Trim the zucchini and cut into 2-inch pieces. Wash the spinach thoroughly and remove the stems.
2. Bring salted water to a boil in a medium-sized saucepan. Using a steamer insert, steam the zucchini, covered, until tender. Add the spinach leaves to the steamer when the zucchini is just about done. When the leaves just start to wilt, remove them from the water. Spread them out flat on paper towels and pat dray. Remove the zucchini and let cool.
3. Squeeze the zucchini with your hands to remove as much water as possible. Transfer the zucchini to a food processor and process for about 30 seconds. Add the cream, eggs, egg yolk, nutmeg, curry powder, cayenne, salt, and pepper; process until very smooth.
4. Lightly butter four 4-ounce ramekins. Use the spinach to line each ramekin, positioning the leaves with the ribbed side facing inward. Leave a little spinach overhanging the edges of the ramekins.
5. Pour the custard into the spinach-lined ramekins. Fold the overhanging spinach leaves over the custard.
6. Place the ramekins in a baking dish. Fill the pan with boiling water ⅔ of the way up the sides of the ramekins. Bake for about 45 minutes or until just set. Remove the ramekins from the water and let rest for at least 5 minutes before unmolding.

FRENCH ONION SOUP

4 large yellow onions
1 garlic clove
¼ cup butter, plus extra for buttering
3 cups rich beef stock
1 cup dry white wine

¼ cup medium-dry sherry
1 teaspoon Worcestershire sauce
1 loaf French bread
¼ cup fresh grated Romano cheese

1. Peel and thinly slice the onions. Peel and mince the garlic clove.
2. In a large frying pan, slowly sauté the onions in the butter until limp and glazed. Transfer to a slow cooker. Add the beef stock, white wine, sherry, Worcestershire, and garlic. Cover and cook on low for 6 to 8 hours.
3. Preheat broiler. Cut 6 slices of French bread about 1-inch thick, and butter the slices. (Reserve the remaining bread to serve with the meal.) Grate the cheese if necessary. Place the buttered French bread on a baking sheet. Sprinkle with the cheese. Place under the broiler until lightly toasted.
4. To serve, ladle the soup into 6 bowls. Float a slice of toasted French bread on top of each serving.

Cry for Onions?

If onions make you cry, try storing them in the refrigerator in a tightly sealed container. Peel them under cold, running water as needed and chop them in a food processor.

COQUILLES ST. JACQUES PROVENÇAL

2 pounds fresh scallops
½ teaspoon salt
½ teaspoon ground white pepper
1 small yellow onion
½ pound fresh mushrooms

2 large red tomatoes
1 tablespoon chives
1 garlic clove
6 tablespoons butter, divided
½ cup dry white wine

Serves 6

This also can be made with shrimp or crabmeat. It is best served with a dry white wine.

1. Pat the scallops dry. If they are large, cut them into smaller pieces about the size of a nickel. Sprinkle the scallops lightly with salt and pepper. Peel and mince the onion. Wash the mushrooms with a damp cloth and slice. Peel the tomatoes and chop into ¼-inch pieces. Mince the chives. Peel and mince the garlic clove.

2. Sauté the scallops along with the minced onion in 4 tablespoons of the butter until the onions look transparent, about 5 minutes, turning the scallops to brown all sides lightly. Remove the scallops and onions. Keep warm.

3. Add the remaining butter to the pan and sauté the mushrooms for 2 minutes. Add the tomatoes, wine, chives, and garlic. Simmer for 5 minutes. Pour over the scallops and serve.

Sautéing with Water

For a healthy alternative, sauté onions and garlic in a few tablespoons of water instead of oil or butter. They tend to get a little crisper this way, but this cooking method saves many grams of fat.

GRILLED LOBSTER WITH LEMON AND TARRAGON

Serves 2

Serve with Oven-Roasted Asparagus (page 15) and Champagne Charisma (page 68).

2 uncooked lobster tails
2 tablespoons fresh lemon juice
1½ teaspoons grated lemon zest
2 tablespoons chopped fresh chives
1 tablespoon chopped fresh tarragon
½ cup butter
½ teaspoon salt
½ teaspoon freshly ground black pepper

1. Thaw the lobster tails if necessary. Create lemon zest by grating the peel of a fresh lemon. Chop the chives and tarragon.
2. Preheat a charcoal or gas grill to high heat.
3. In a small saucepan over low heat, melt the butter and add the lemon zest, lemon juice, chives, tarragon, salt, and pepper. Set aside and keep warm.
4. Use heavy kitchen shears to split the lobster tails by cutting the length of the underside. Brush the cut-side of the tails with 1 tablespoon of the butter sauce.
5. Grill the lobsters cut-side down for about 4 minutes. Turn them and grill for another 4 minutes. Turn them again to the cut-side and grill until the lobster meat is just opaque but still juicy, about 2 minutes. Transfer to plates.
6. Brush the lobster with the butter sauce and serve the remaining sauce in a small ramekin on the side.

Serving Lobster Graciously

Provide your guests with a clean towel and small bowl of warm water with a floating lemon slice for use as a finger bowl. Another alternative is to remove the meat from the shell before serving. Use kitchen shears to split the shell. Brush the meat with the seasoned butter before serving.

GAME HENS IN RED WINE

2 game hens, fresh or thawed
1 cup all-purpose flour
½ teaspoon salt
¼ teaspoon ground black
    pepper

⅓ cup vegetable oil
1½ cups dry red wine
1 cup sour cream

> **Serves 2**
>
> Don't have a slow cooker? Use a covered casserole at 300° in your oven and cut the cooking time in half.

1. Clean the game hens by running them under cold water. Combine the flour, salt, and ground black pepper. Roll the game hens in the mixture until lightly coated.
2. Heat the vegetable oil at medium temperature in a medium-sized frying pan. Place the game hens in the frying pan and brown on all sides.
3. Place the game hens in the slow cooker on low setting. Pour the red wine on top of the game hens. Cover and cook on low setting for 5 hours.
4. Add the sour cream and cook for another hour.

To Prevent Curdling

To prevent curdling of milk, yogurt, or sour cream in long-cooking dishes, mix it with an equal amount of cooking liquid from the dish being prepared. Add the milk products during the last hour of the cooking process and always cook them on low heat.

CARAMEL RUM FONDUE

Serves 2 to 8

Serve with apple wedges, fresh strawberries, marshmallows, or walnuts.

1 (14-ounce) package caramels
2/3 cup cream

1/2 cup miniature marshmallows
1 tablespoon rum

1. Combine the caramels and cream in a slow cooker. Cover and cook on low setting for 2 to 3 hours or until the caramels are completely melted.
2. Stir in the marshmallows and rum. Continue cooking, covered, on low setting for 1 hour.
3. Transfer to a traditional fondue pot before serving.

SALMON IN WHITE WINE WITH DRIED PEACHES

Serves 4

Serve with fresh steamed broccoli drizzled with fresh-squeezed lime juice.

1½ pounds salmon fillets
¼ cup all-purpose flour
2 tablespoons extra-virgin olive oil
1 cup dry white wine

½ cup vegetable stock
1 cup dried peaches
½ teaspoon freshly ground black pepper

1. Preheat oven to 350°. Pat the salmon dry with the paper towels. Coat the salmon with a light layer of the flour.
2. Heat the olive oil in a frying pan at medium heat. Add the salmon and brown on all sides. Discard the oil and place the salmon fillets on paper towels to soak up additional oil.
3. Add the wine and vegetable stock to an oven-proof casserole. Place the salmon fillets in the bottom of the casserole. Quarter the dried peaches and place them on top of the salmon. Sprinkle with pepper. Cover and bake for 30 minutes.

HERB LINGUINE WITH SALMON, CREAM, AND PISTACHIOS

2 tablespoons chopped pistachio nuts

¼ red bell pepper

2 garlic cloves

¾ pound salmon fillet

2 teaspoons lemon zest

¼ cup freshly grated Parmesan
   cheese

¼ cup unsalted butter

1½ cups heavy cream

½ teaspoon, plus 1 tablespoon
   salt

½ teaspoon ground white
   pepper

12 ounces fresh herb linguine

Serves 4

Serve with a light,
sweet white or
blush wine.

---

1. Preheat oven to 300°. Chop the pistachio nuts, if necessary. Seed and dice the red bell pepper. Peel and mince the garlic. Dice the salmon fillet. Create the lemon zest by grating a fresh lemon peel. Grate the Parmesan cheese, if necessary.

2. Place the pistachios on a baking sheet and toast in the oven for about 5 minutes. Set aside to cool.

3. In a large, deep skillet, melt the butter over medium-low heat. Add the bell pepper and garlic. Raise the heat to medium and sauté for 1 minute. Add the salmon and sauté for 1 minute. Add the cream, lemon zest, the ½ teaspoon salt, and the pepper. Cook until reduced and thickened, stirring frequently.

4. Meanwhile, in a large pot, bring at least 4 quarts water to a rolling boil. Add the 1 tablespoon salt. Add the pasta, stir to separate, and cook until al dente. Drain.

5. Transfer the linguine to a large, warm bowl. Add the sauce and toss well. Sprinkle with the pistachios and Parmesan cheese.

Resist the Urge to Precook Pasta

Pasta that has been precooked will continue cooking from the heat it generates long after it's removed from the pan. The result will be a gooey, mushy, untasty mess. Even if it means keeping the sauce warm, make your pasta as fresh as possible.

PEARS POACHED IN WHITE WINE
WITH STRAWBERRY SAUCE

4 Bosc pears
1 pint strawberries
1 lemon
1 bottle white wine
　(Chardonnay or Riesling)
8 whole cloves

2 whole cinnamon sticks
1 cup granulated sugar,
　divided
1 teaspoon vanilla extract
8 sprigs fresh mint

1. Cut the pears in half lengthwise and scoop out the seeds. Hull the strawberries and cut in half. Create zest from the lemon peel by shaving off with a vegetable peeler in strips.
2. Combine the wine, lemon zest, cloves, cinnamon sticks, and ½ cup of the sugar in a large (4- to 5-quart) pot. Bring to a boil.
3. Reduce heat to a simmer and add the pears, arranging them so they are mostly submerged. Cover tightly and cook slowly for 5 minutes. Remove from heat and leave to steep for 20 minutes. Chill in the refrigerator.
4. In a blender or food processor, combine the strawberries, remaining ½ cup sugar, and vanilla. Purée until smooth, adding a few drops of water if necessary to get things started.
5. Spoon the sauce onto dessert plates to forms small pools midplate. Serve the pears cut-side down atop the sauce. Garnish with mint sprigs at the stem end.

Balancing Your Menu

If you're leafing through this book in order to design a balanced meal, keep in mind that opposites attract. In other words, if your entrée is rich, go for a light, fruit-based dessert. Or, if you are serving a light salad, choose a calorie-laden, chocolate dessert.

CHOCOLATE SOUFFLÉ

2 ounces unsweetened chocolate
8 eggs
¾ cup granulated sugar
4 drops vanilla extract

1 cup all-purpose flour
2 cups milk
Confectioners' sugar
Sweetened whipped cream

> **Serves 12**
>
> Soufflés can be easy to make as long as you follow directions carefully. The egg whites and yolks cannot meet until they are folded gently together. Note that a soufflé typically falls somewhat while cooling.

1. Melt the chocolate and let cool. Separate the egg yolks from the whites, placing 5 of the yolks in a medium-sized bowl and discarding the remaining 3 yolks. Divide the egg whites into 3 portions as designated in step 6, following. Make sure no yolk is in the whites. (Even a tiny amount will cause the soufflé not to rise.)

2. Beat the egg yolks with ½ cup of the granulated sugar and the vanilla until light and fluffy. Gradually beat in the flour until a paste forms.

3. Scald the milk in a saucepan by heating it until a thin film appears on top. Add the egg yolk mixture to the milk and bring to a boil. With a wire whisk, quickly and vigorously beat the mixture until the paste is well incorporated into the milk and the mixture is smooth. Continue to stir with a wooden spoon until the mixture is thick.

4. Add the melted chocolate, stirring to blend. Let cool.

5. Preheat oven to 350°. Grease 12 individual soufflé dishes or custard cups, each 2 inches in diameter.

6. Gradually add the remaining ¼ cup granulated sugar to the egg whites and beat in 3 stages as follows: Beat 3 egg whites, then add another 3 egg whites and beat them. Finally, add the remaining 2 egg whites and beat until stiff and shiny but not dry. (The egg whites should not slide when the bowl is tipped.)

7. Fold the egg whites into the soufflé batter just until no white streaks remain. Do not stir or mix well. Evenly divide the batter among the prepared dishes.

8. Bake for 30 minutes or until the tops are firm. Dust with confectioners' sugar and serve topped with whipped cream.

AMARETTO CAKE

1 yellow sheet cake in 2 layers
2 eggs
½ cup cornstarch
½ cup granulated sugar
2 cups milk
1 teaspoon vanilla extract
1 teaspoon rum extract

1 cup amaretto liqueur, divided
1 (10-ounce) jar apricot preserves
2 cups whipping cream
Fresh strawberries

1. The cake should be cooled completely. It can be baked a day ahead of time, if necessary.
2. Beat the eggs well. Combine the eggs, cornstarch, sugar, milk, vanilla extract, rum extract, and ¾ cup of the amaretto liqueur in a saucepan over low heat. Cook, stirring constantly, for 15 minutes or until a skin begins to form. Remove from heat and let cool.
3. Using a serrated knife, cut each cake layer in half horizontally, to yield 4 layers. Place a layer on a serving plate. Spread with ⅓ of the preserves and top with ⅓ of the pudding. Repeat with the remaining layers.
4. Make the frosting by whipping together the cream and remaining ¼ cup amaretto until soft peaks form. Frost the top and sides of the cake with the cream. Arrange the strawberries on top.

Make Condensed Milk

To make your own sweetened condensed milk, use 1 cup powdered milk, ⅔ cup granulated sugar, ⅓ cup boiling water, and 3 tablespoons melted butter. Mix everything in the blender and you have the equivalent of a 14-ounce can of condensed milk.

APPLE-BUTTERED RUM PUDDING
WITH APPLE TOPPING

For the pudding:
2 cups light cream
1 cup cooked white rice
⅓ cup granulated sugar
½ teaspoon salt
1 tablespoon unflavored gelatin
¼ cup water
2 tablespoons rum or
   1 teaspoon rum flavoring
1 cup sour cream

For the apple topping:
½ packed cup light brown
   sugar
2 tablespoons cornstarch
¼ teaspoon salt
½ teaspoon ground cinnamon
½ cup water
1 (20-ounce) can pie-sliced
   apples
1 tablespoon butter
2 tablespoons rum or
   1 teaspoon rum flavoring

Serves 6 to 8

This is delicious hot or cold. Serve it as the finale to a meal of Cheese Fondue (page 74).

1. To make the pudding, combine the cream, rice, sugar, and salt in a saucepan and bring to a boil. Reduce heat to low and simmer for 20 minutes, stirring occasionally.
2. Meanwhile, in a bowl, soften the gelatin in the water for 5 minutes. Remove the rice mixture from the heat and stir in the gelatin mixture until the gelatin dissolves. Let cool until thickened but not set.
3. Fold in the rum and sour cream. Spoon into individual molds (about 1 cup in size) and chill until firm.
4. To make the topping, combine the brown sugar, cornstarch, salt, cinnamon, butter, rum flavoring, and water in a saucepan and stir well. Add the apples and bring to a boil. Reduce heat to low and simmer for 15 to 20 minutes, or until the apples are tender, stirring occasionally.
5. Release puddings from the molds and place on individual plates. Spoon warm topping over them right before serving.

BISHOP

2 ounces orange juice
1 ounce lemon juice
1 teaspoon fine sugar

Ice
4 ounces red wine (such as Merlot)

1. Pour the juices and sugar into a mixing glass nearly filled with ice. Stir. Strain into a highball glass over ice.
2. Fill with red wine. Garnish with a fruit slice, if desired.

VALENTINE

4 ounces Beaujolais
1 teaspoon cranberry liqueur

2 ounces cranberry juice
Ice

Combine all the ingredients in a shaker half-filled with ice. Shake well. Strain into a wineglass.

SANGRIA

1 lemon
1 orange
1 bottle dry red wine
2 ounces Triple Sec
1 ounce brandy

2 ounces orange juice
1 ounce lemon juice
¼ cup fine sugar
10 ounces club soda
Ice

1. Cut the orange and lemon into slices. Do not peel.
2. Combine red wine, Triple Sec, brandy, orange juice, lemon juice, and sugar; mix well. Add the orange and lemon slices. Chill for at least 1 hour.
3. Add the club soda. Add ice and stir.

> **Serves 10**
>
> This traditional romantic drink is wonderful with pasta or heavier dishes.

MIDORI MIMOSA

2 ounces Midori
1 teaspoon lime juice

4 ounces chilled champagne

Combine all the ingredients in a champagne flute or white wine glass. Stir gently.

> **Serves 1**
>
> The Midori turns this from a brunch drink to a light evening drink perfect with salads or seafood.

BELLINI

2 ounces peach nectar
½ ounce lemon juice

Chilled champagne to fill glass

Pour the juices into a champagne flute and stir to mix. Fill with champagne. Stir gently.

Fresh Lemon Juice

Fresher is always better. The acid zing of lemon juice is a catalyst for the successful mingling of flavors. A convenient way to use fresh juice is to use a small hand reamer or electric citrus reamer.

Chapter 6
EASTER

BAKED ORANGE ROUGHY WITH ORANGE-RICE DRESSING	92
WHITE WINE AND LEMON PORK ROAST	93
SCENTED ESCAROLE WITH FENNEL	94
GLAZED CARROTS WITH BALSAMIC VINEGAR	95
GLAZED BAKED HAM WITH ROSEMARY	95
APRICOT-STUFFED PORK TENDERLOIN	96
CAULIFLOWER VICHYSSOISE	97
YOGURT AND CUCUMBER SOUP WITH MINT AND DILL	98
BAKED PEAR CRISP	99
NEW ORLEANS PRALINES	100
LIGHT LEMON PUDDING	101
EASTER COOKIES	102
PINEAPPLE-PEAR MOLD	103
ALMOND COOKIES	104
MINT MERINGUE COOKIES	104
CREAMY PEACH DRINK	105
LEMONY APPLE DRINK	105
APRICOT SPARKLER	106
PEACH BUNNY	106

BAKED ORANGE ROUGHY WITH ORANGE-RICE DRESSING

Serves 4

Steamed carrots and zucchini rounds are the perfect color and nutritional complement to this meal.

2 celery ribs
1 medium-sized yellow onion
1 teaspoon orange zest
1⅓ cups cooked white rice
2 tablespoons ground cashews
½ cup fresh-squeezed orange juice

1 tablespoon lemon juice
1 pound orange roughy fillets
1 teaspoon sea salt
½ teaspoon ground white pepper
2 teaspoons butter

1. Preheat oven to 350°. Chop the celery into ¼-inch pieces. Peel the onion and chop into ¼-inch pieces. Grate orange peel to create zest. Cook the rice according to package directions. Grind the cashews.
2. In a microwave-safe bowl, mix the celery and onion with the citrus juices and orange zest. Microwave on high for 2 minutes or until the mixture comes to a boil. Add the rice and stir to moisten. Add water 1 tablespoon at a time if necessary so that the rice is thoroughly coated with liquid. Cover and let stand for 5 to 10 minutes.
3. Rinse the fillets and pat dry between paper towels. Prepare a baking dish with nonstick spray. Spread the rice mixture in the dish and arrange the fillets on top. Season the fillets with the salt and pepper.
4. Combine the butter and cashews in a microwave-safe bowl and microwave on high for 30 seconds, or until the butter is melted. Stir and spoon over the top of the fillets. Cover and bake for 10 minutes.
5. Remove the cover and bake for an additional 5 to 10 minutes or until the fish flakes easily when tested with a fork. The cashews should be lightly browned.

WHITE WINE AND LEMON PORK ROAST

1 garlic clove
3 shallots
½ cup dry white wine
1 tablespoon lemon juice
1 teaspoon olive oil

¼ teaspoon dried thyme
⅛ teaspoon ground black
  pepper
½ pound pork loin roast

> **Serves 4**
>
> Variation: Instead of white wine and lemon juice, use 1 teaspoon Dijon mustard and 1 tablespoon orange marmalade in the marinade.

1. Crush the garlic with the side of a large knife. Remove the skin and roughly chop the clove. Remove the skin from the shallots and roughly chop the shallots.
2. Combine the garlic, shallots, white wine, lemon juice, olive oil, thyme, and black pepper in a small mixing bowl. Mix well and transfer to a large sealable plastic bag. Add the pork loin and place in the refrigerator for 1 to 12 hours.
3. Preheat oven to 350°. Remove the meat from the marinade and place the roast on a rack in a roasting pan. Roast for 20 to 30 minutes or until the meat thermometer reads 150° to 170°, depending on how well done you like pork.

Flavorful Marinades

Prepare dishes that must marinate the night before. The extra hours marinating will impart even more flavor to the dish.

SCENTED ESCAROLE WITH FENNEL

2 garlic cloves
1 small yellow onion
12 cups escarole
1½ teaspoons fennel seeds
2 tablespoons extra-virgin olive oil

½ teaspoon salt
¼ teaspoon freshly ground black pepper
1 tablespoon freshly grated Parmesan cheese

1. Peel and mince the garlic cloves. Peel and finely chop the onion. Coarsely chop the escarole. Lightly toast the fennel seeds over medium heat in a dry skillet.
2. Heat the olive oil on medium in a medium-sized skillet. Add the garlic and cook for about 1 minute, until it starts to brown. Add the onion and cook until translucent, about 5 minutes.
3. Add the escarole and fennel seeds, season with salt and pepper, and cover. Cook until the escarole is wilted and simmering in its own juices.
4. Remove the cover and raise heat to medium-high; cook until most of the liquid has evaporated, about 5 minutes. Serve garnished with the grated cheese.

Bulgar Wheat

Bulgar is a crunchy, nutty wheat grain that can be substituted for rice or pasta in most dishes. To prepare, just pour boiling water over the bulgur and let it sit until the liquid is absorbed.

GLAZED CARROTS WITH BALSAMIC VINEGAR

3½ pounds baby carrots
¼ cup chopped chives
½ cup butter
6 tablespoons granulated sugar

⅓ cup balsamic vinegar
½ teaspoon salt
½ teaspoon freshly ground
  black pepper

Serves 10

This is a colorful and flavorful side for any holiday meal but complements Easter ham perhaps best of all.

1. Peel the carrots and cut into 2-inch pieces. Cut in half lengthwise. Chop the chives and set aside.
2. Melt the butter in a large sauté pan over medium heat. Add the carrots and cook for about 5 minutes. Cover and cook for another 7 minutes or until slightly tender.
3. Stir in the sugar and vinegar. Cook, uncovered, until the carrots are tender and glazed and the liquid has reduced. Season with the salt and pepper.
4. Serve in a warm bowl and garnish with fresh chives.

GLAZED BAKED HAM WITH ROSEMARY

4-pound boneless ham
30 whole cloves
3 tablespoons chutney of your
  choice

1 packed tablespoon dark brown
  sugar
2 tablespoons prepared horseradish mustard
2 teaspoons fresh rosemary leaves

Serves 12

This ham tastes great served either hot or cold. Serve it the next day as sandwiches.

1. Preheat oven to 325°. Place the ham in a roasting pan set on a rack. Insert the whole cloves all over the ham and bake for about 1½ hours or until the internal temperature reads 130°.
2. Meanwhile, in a small saucepan, combine the chutney, brown sugar, mustard, and rosemary. Cook over low heat until warm and liquefied.
3. Drizzle the glaze over the ham and bake for an additional 30 minutes or until the internal temperature reads 140°. The outside of the ham should be crusty and sugary brown.

APRICOT-STUFFED PORK TENDERLOIN

Serves 3–4

Serve with Glazed
Carrots with Balsamic
Vinegar (page 95).

6 dried apricots
1 cup red wine (such as Merlot)
1½-pound pork tenderloin
1 shallot
3 garlic cloves

½ cup pecans
3 fresh sage leaves
½ teaspoon salt
½ teaspoon fresh-cracked black
pepper

1. Soak the dried apricots in the red wine for at least 1 hour to rehy-drate. Preheat oven to 375°.
2. Butterfly the tenderloin by making a lengthwise slice down the middle, making certain not to cut completely through.
3. Mince the shallot and garlic. Chop the pecans and sage. Slice the apricots into quarters.
4. Lay out the tenderloin. Layer all the ingredients over the tenderloin and season with salt and pepper. Carefully roll up the loin and tie securely.
5. Place the tenderloin on a rack and roast for 1 to 1½ hours. Let cool slightly before slicing.

The Other White Meat

Although pork is not really "the other white meat," today's pigs are not fat. In fact, pork tends to be leaner than beef. Substitute pork for beef in any recipe but remember to remove the fat from around the edges.

CAULIFLOWER VICHYSSOISE

2 medium-sized leeks
1 medium-sized white onion
1 large head cauliflower
1 tablespoon vegetable oil

4 cups chicken stock
½ teaspoon salt
½ teaspoon freshly ground
   white pepper

> **Serves 4**
>
> Serve the soup in warm soup bowls and garnish with a drizzle of extra-virgin olive oil and a sprinkling of freshly minced chives.

1. Remove the green part of the leeks and discard. Peel and thinly slice the leeks. Peel and dice the onion. Cut the cauliflower into florets.
2. Heat the oil in a large soup pot over medium heat. Cook the leeks and onions for 3 to 4 minutes, stirring, until tender. Be careful not to overcook the leeks and onions; they should retain their original color.
3. Add the cauliflower and stock, and bring to a boil. Reduce the heat and simmer, covered, for about 20 minutes or until the cauliflower is tender.
4. Transfer the soup to a blender and purée until smooth. Return the soup to the pot to warm. Season with salt and pepper.

Food Processor Safety

When puréeing hot mixtures, leave the vent uncovered on your food processor. If using a blender, either remove the vent cover from the lid or leave the lid ajar so the steam can escape.

YOGURT AND CUCUMBER SOUP WITH MINT AND DILL

3 cups yogurt
1 large cucumber
2 garlic cloves
2½ tablespoons chopped fresh dill weed, divided
1 tablespoon finely chopped fresh mint

2 cups milk
2 tablespoons olive oil
2 tablespoons fresh lemon juice
½ teaspoon salt
½ teaspoon freshly ground white pepper
4 drops hot pepper sauce

1. Put the yogurt into a cheesecloth-lined strainer and let drip over a bowl for 2 hours at room temperature, or overnight in the refrigerator.
2. Peel the cucumber and cut 6 paper-thin slices. Set aside for garnish. Seed and coarsely grate the remaining cucumber. Peel the garlic cloves and put through a garlic press. Finely chop the dill weed. Finely chop the fresh mint.
3. Discard the water from the yogurt and place the yogurt in a medium-sized bowl. Whisk the milk into the yogurt until smooth. Stir in the cucumber, garlic, 2 tablespoons of the dill, the mint, olive oil, lemon juice, salt, pepper, and hot pepper sauce. Refrigerate for 1 to 2 hours, until ice cold.
4. Garnish each serving with a little of the remaining dill and a slice of cucumber.

Buying Garlic
When buying fresh garlic, look for heads that are plump, firm, and heavy for their size. Any green shoots or sprouts indicate that the garlic is old and will have an off flavor. Store whole bulbs in an open plastic bag in the vegetable drawer of your refrigerator.

BAKED PEAR CRISP

2 fresh pears
2 tablespoons frozen, unsweet-
    ened pineapple juice concen-
    trate
1 teaspoon vanilla extract
1 teaspoon rum (or ½ tea-
    spoon rum extract)

1 tablespoon butter
⅛ cup whole-wheat flour
⅓ firmly packed cup brown
    sugar
½ cup oat bran flakes

> **Serves 4**
>
> This dish has endless varieties. Use peaches, plums, or apples. Mix your fruits by adding a few berries.

1. Preheat oven to 375°. Treat a 9" × 12" baking dish with nonstick cooking spray. Core and cut up the pears into the baking dish (leave the skins on).
2. In a glass measuring cup, microwave the frozen juice concentrate for 1 minute. Stir in the vanilla and rum, then pour over the pears.
3. Using the same measuring cup, microwave the butter for 30 to 40 seconds, until melted.
4. Toss together the remaining ingredients in a bowl, being careful not to crush the cereal. Spread uniformly over the pears and dribble the melted butter over the top of the cereal.
5. Bake for 35 minutes or until the mixture is bubbling and the top is just beginning to brown. Serve hot or cold.

Using Canned Fruit

If substituting canned fruit for fresh in a dessert recipe, choose fruit in a water base, not syrup. Syrup bases tend to draw the sugar out of the fruit while in the can.

NEW ORLEANS PRALINES

1½ packed cups light brown sugar

½ cup granulated sugar

½ cup evaporated milk

¼ cup light corn syrup

1 tablespoon margarine

1 teaspoon vanilla extract

1½ cups pecans

1. Line baking sheets with wax paper.
2. Stir together the sugars, evaporated milk, and corn syrup in a heavy 3-quart saucepan. Cook over very low heat, stirring frequently, for about 1 hour or until the mixture registers 236° on a candy thermometer. Test by dropping a nugget of the mixture into cold water; it should form a soft ball that flattens when removed from the water. Do not cook the mixture too fast, as it will curdle.
3. Remove from heat. Add the margarine and vanilla, and beat for about 1 minute or until well blended.
4. Add the nuts and stir until coated. Quickly drop by tablespoonfuls onto the prepared baking sheets. When cool and set, remove from the paper.

Fatty Oils

All oils are 100 percent fat, including butter and margarine. For a healthy diet, use them sparingly and substitute unsaturated vegetable oil or extra-virgin olive oil whenever possible.

LIGHT LEMON PUDDING

1 tablespoon unflavored gelatin
½ cup, plus 1 tablespoon cold
  water
1 cup boiling water
½ cup granulated sugar
¼ cup, plus ¼ teaspoon lemon
  juice

1 teaspoon lemon zest
½ cup regular nonfat dry milk
  powder
½ cup ice water

Serves 6

This makes a wonderful light dessert after a meal of Apricot-Stuffed Pork Tenderloin (page 96).

1. In a small bowl, soften the gelatin in the 1 tablespoon cold water. Add the boiling water to dissolve.
2. Add the sugar, the ½ cup cold water, the ¼ cup lemon juice, and the lemon zest. Chill until very thick, about 90 minutes.
3. Chill a deep mixing bowl and beaters. Add the dry milk, ice water, and the ¼ teaspoon lemon juice to the chilled bowl. Beat until fluffy, then cover and chill.
4. Break up the gelatin lemon mixture with a fork. Add to the whipped milk mixture. Using an electric mixer, beat until fluffy but not too soft. Cover and chill until firm before serving, about ½ hour.

Full-Flavor Herbs

Crushing dried herbs before you add them to a recipe will result in a stronger flavor. You can pinch them between your fingers or use a spoon to crush them on a plate before adding them to the dish.

EASTER COOKIES

½ pound butter, softened
1½ cups granulated sugar
3 eggs
½ cup orange juice
6 cups all-purpose flour
2 teaspoons baking powder
½ teaspoon baking soda
1½ teaspoons vanilla extract
1½ teaspoons anise flavoring
Sesame seeds
60 whole cloves

For the glaze:
1 egg
5 tablespoons milk

1. Preheat oven to 375°. Grease 2 baking sheets.
2. In a large bowl, cream the butter until soft. Add the sugar and mix thoroughly. Add the eggs 1 at a time, mixing well after each addition. Add the orange juice and mix well.
3. Add the flour, baking powder, and baking soda; beat to combine. Add the vanilla and anise flavorings; mix thoroughly. The mixture will be stiff and you will have to knead it by hand in order to mix thoroughly.
4. Shape it into desired forms—figure 8s are traditional—and place on the prepared baking sheets.
5. To create the glaze, beat the egg and milk together. Brush each cookie with the glaze, sprinkle with sesame seeds, and place a whole clove in the center of each cookie.

PINEAPPLE-PEAR MOLD

2 medium pears
2 tablespoons unflavored
  gelatin
2½ cups orange juice, divided

1 (20-ounce) can crushed
  pineapple

Serves 6

Gelatin molds are a traditional salad at many Easter dinners. Add your favorite fresh fruits or even some grated carrots to complement the meal.

1. Peel, core, and dice the pears.
2. In a small saucepan, soften the gelatin in ½ cup of the orange juice for 5 minutes. Place over low heat and stir until the gelatin dissolves.
3. Stir in the undrained crushed pineapple and the remaining 2 cups orange juice. Cover and chill until partially set, about 30 minutes.
4. Fold the pears into the pineapple mixture and transfer to a 6-cup mold.
5. Cover and chill until firm, about 30 minutes. To unmold, dip the bottom of the mold in hot water for 10 seconds, then invert onto a plate.

Broiled Grapefruit

Try this fun fruit as an elegant dessert. Cut a grapefruit in half and loosen the sections with a knife. Sprinkle a little brown sugar on the halves and top with a pat of butter. Broil a few minutes until heated through.

ALMOND COOKIES

Makes 2 dozen

Many families serve these with coffee and orange juice as a light breakfast before Easter morning church services.

½ cup butter or margarine
½ cup superfine sugar
½ teaspoon salt
¼ teaspoon almond extract

1 egg yolk
1 cup unsifted flour
Blanched almonds

1. Preheat oven to 350°. In a large bowl, cream together the butter, sugar, salt, and almond flavoring until light and fluffy. Thoroughly beat in the egg yolk. Stir in the flour. Cover and chill for 1 hour before shaping.
2. Using a level tablespoon for each, shape the dough into small balls and place them 1 inch apart on an ungreased baking sheet. Press an almond onto the center of each cookie. The sides will crack slightly.
3. Bake for 15 to 18 minutes or until the bottoms of the cookies are browned but the tops are still light. The edges will turn tan. Carefully remove to a rack to cool.

MINT MERINGUE COOKIES

Makes about 1 dozen

These are the perfect Easter morning surprise. Perhaps the Easter Bunny left them there for the adults to find?

2 egg whites
½ teaspoon cream of tartar
¾ cup granulated sugar
¼ teaspoon peppermint flavoring

3 drops green food coloring
1 cup semisweet chocolate
    morsels

1. Preheat oven to 350°. In a medium-sized bowl, beat together the egg whites and cream of tartar until fluffy.
2. Add the sugar and beat until very stiff. Add the flavoring and the food coloring.
3. Fold in the chocolate morsels.
4. Drop by teaspoonfuls onto an ungreased baking sheet. The cookies will not spread during cooking, so they can be placed close together.
5. Turn off the oven and place the cookies inside. Leave the cookies in the oven overnight or until the oven cools.

CREAMY PEACH DRINK

2 ounces frozen peaches *1 ounce light cream*
1 teaspoon granulated sugar *Lemonade to fill glass*

1. Put the peaches and sugar in blender and blend well.
2. Pour into a tumbler. Add the cream and lemonade. Stir well. Garnish with a peach slice, if desired.

Serves 1

Serve with Yogurt and Cucumber Soup with Mint and Dill (page 98) for a true spring treat.

LEMONY APPLE DRINK

3 ounces apple juice *8 ounces ginger ale*
1 ounce lemon juice *1 ounce grenadine*

Pour the apple and lemon juice into a tumbler. Stir. Add the ginger ale. Drizzle in the grenadine.

Serves 1

This is a wonderful complement to Baked Orange Roughy with Orange-Rice Dressing (page 92).

APRICOT SPARKLER

Serves 1

Serve this to comple-
ment Apricot-Stuffed
Pork Tenderloin
(page 96).

2 ounces apricot nectar
1 ounce lemon juice
Ice

Club soda to fill glass
Lemon twist

1. Combine the apricot nectar and lemon juice in a shaker half-filled with ice. Shake well.
2. Strain into an old-fashioned glass with a few ice cubes. Add the club soda and stir gently. Add a lemon twist.

PEACH BUNNY

Serves 1

This is a good after-
dinner drink or end-
of-day tummy settler.
It also complements
desserts such as
Amaretto Cake
(page86).

1 ounce peach-flavored brandy
¾ ounce white crème de cacao

¾ ounce light cream
Ice

1. Combine all the ingredients in a shaker half-filled with ice. Shake well.
2. Strain into a cordial glass.

Chapter 7
PASSOVER FOODS

ZUCCHINI-STUFFED CHICKEN   108
BRAISED LAMB WITH A SOUR ORANGE MARINADE 109
FISH IN RED SAUCE   110
LEEK AND MEAT FRITTERS   111
GEFILTE FISH   112
WHITE BEAN AND ARTICHOKE SALAD   113
MATZO BREI   114
APPLE HAROSET   114
PASSOVER BROWNIES   115
APPLE-CINNAMON FARFEL KUGEL   115
SPINACH FRITATTA   116
CHOCOLATE RASPBERRY TORTE   117

ZUCCHINI-STUFFED CHICKEN

Serves 8

Serve with Chocolate Raspberry Torte (page 117) for dessert.

8 bone-in, skin-on chicken breasts
2 medium zucchini
1 small yellow onion
2 eggs
3 cups matzo farfel
2 tablespoons chicken bouillon
   powder

¼ teaspoon garlic powder
¼ teaspoon onion powder
½ teaspoon salt
½ teaspoon ground black
   pepper

1. Preheat oven to 375°. Grease a 9" × 13" baking pan.
2. Rinse the chicken breasts under cold, running water. Pat dry. Shred the zucchini using a vegetable grater. Peel and chop the onion. Beat the eggs and set aside.
3. Place the farfel in a bowl and cover with hot water for 5 minutes. Drain and squeeze out water.
4. In a medium-sized mixing bowl, combine the zucchini, farfel, eggs, chicken bouillon, onion, garlic powder, onion powder, salt, and pepper.
5. Place 2 to 3 tablespoons of the stuffing under the skin of each chicken breast and arrange them in the baking pan.
6. Bake for 40 to 50 minutes. Drain off excess fat and serve.

Onion Varieties
Onions vary in sweetness. Vidalia tend to be the sweetest, followed by red, then yellow. White onions are the least sweet and are better in meat dishes than in soups.

BRAISED LAMB WITH A SOUR ORANGE MARINADE

4 sour oranges
4 garlic cloves
1 large white onion
1 tablespoon dried oregano
2 bay leaves

1 cup dry white wine
6 pounds deboned leg of lamb
1 teaspoon salt
1 teaspoon ground black pepper
2 tablespoons vegetable oil

16 servings

If you are unable to find sour oranges, substitute a combination of orange and lemon juice.

1. Juice the sour oranges. Peel and mince the garlic. Peel the onion and slice thinly. Combine the orange juice with the garlic, onion, oregano, bay leaves, and white wine in a large bowl.
2. Place the meat in the marinade. Make sure all the meat is covered. Cover the bowl and refrigerate for 2 to 4 hours.
3. Remove the meat from the marinade, reserving the marinade. Sprinkle the meat with the salt and pepper. In a large pot, heat the oil on medium-high. Place the meat in the pan and sear on all sides.
4. Decrease heat to low. Pour the reserved marinade over the meat in the pan and cover. Cook until the meat is fork-tender, about 3 hours. Add water to the pot if necessary to keep the meat from scorching.

Cooking with Lamb

Lamb is underused in North America, yet it has a wonderful flavor. Substitute it for pork in your next slow-cooker recipe for an unexpected treat.

FISH IN RED SAUCE

Serves 6

This traditional dish is reminiscent of foods shepherds would have eaten centuries ago.

¼ cup minced fresh parsley

8 ounces pimientos

3 red tomatoes

2 carrots

2 celery ribs

2 garlic cloves

½ teaspoon salt

½ teaspoon ground black pepper

1 (28-ounce) can tomato purée

¼ cup water

3 tablespoons fresh lemon juice

6 (3-ounce) cod fillets

1 teaspoon white granulated sugar

1. Mince the parsley. Chop the pimientos into ¼-inch pieces. Chop the tomatoes into ¼-inch pieces. Peel and slice the carrots. Slice the celery. Peel and mince the garlic.

2. In a large saucepan, combine the parsley, pimientos, tomatoes, salt, pepper, and tomato purée. Bring to a boil. Add the carrots, celery, and garlic. Cook until the carrots can easily be pierced with a fork but are still firm.

3. Stir in the water and lemon juice. Place the fish into the pan without stirring. Baste the fish with the liquid. Sprinkle the sugar on top of the fish but do not stir. Continue basting periodically.

4. When the fish is opaque and warmed through, remove from heat. Let cool and serve cold.

Grilling Fish

When grilling fish, place the fish steaks or fillets on a hot, well-oiled grill. Grill for about 10 minutes per inch of thickness of the fillet, measured at its thickest part. Turn once during grilling. Thoroughly brush the fish with vegetable oil or basting sauce several times during grilling. Grill until the fish flakes when tested with a fork at its thickest part.

LEEK AND MEAT FRITTERS

1 garlic clove
4 leeks
1 pound ground lamb
2 eggs

1 teaspoon salt
½ teaspoon white pepper
1 cup matzo meal
½ cup vegetable oil

Makes 30 fritters

These are a fun treat served with fresh fruit and vegetables.

1. Peel and crush the garlic. Cut the white part of the leek stalks into 4 or 5 pieces each and cook uncovered in boiling water until tender. Drain and grind in a meat grinder.
2. In a large bowl, mix together the ground leeks, lamb, and eggs. Add the salt, pepper, and garlic; mix well. Add the matzo meal until the mixture is stable but not too hard. (If the mixture is too firm, add another egg.)
3. Form small, bite-sized patties. Heat the oil in a frying pan to medium temperature. Fry the patties until golden.

Skillet Sense

When using a greased griddle or skillet, it is hot enough for cooking when a drop of water "skitters" across it. Do not allow oil or butter to brown. The griddle or skillet is ready just before the oil or butter begins to sizzle.

GEFILTE FISH

Serves 8

This traditional Passover dish is excellent served with White Bean and Artichoke Salad (page 113).

1½ pounds salmon fillets
1½ pounds red snapper fillets
1 pound black cod fillets
1 pound ling cod fillets
4 large onions
6 carrots
5 eggs
½ cup white granulated sugar, divided

4 teaspoons salt, divided into 3 teaspoons and 1 teaspoon
4 teaspoons ground white pepper
3–4 cups ice water
¾ cup matzo meal
½ teaspoon paprika
½ teaspoon ground black pepper

1. Clean the fish fillets, reserving the skins. Peel the onions and carrots. Slice 2 of the onions and 2 of the carrots, and set aside.

2. In a meat grinder, grind together the fish, the 2 whole onions, and the 4 whole carrots. Place the fish mixture in a wooden bowl. Using a hand-held chopper (a mallet with several dull knives on the end), add the eggs 1 at a time. Add ¼ cup of the sugar, 3 teaspoons of the salt, and white pepper. Continue to chop until very well blended.

3. Stir in the ice water a little at a time throughout this process. Add the matzo meal and chop again. If the mixture is not thick enough to bind together to make an oval gefilte fish ball, add more matzo meal.

4. Fill 2 large, heavy stockpots halfway with water. Add the sliced onions, sliced carrots, fish skins (if desired), paprika, the remaining salt, the black pepper, and the remaining sugar, dividing each ingredient evenly between the 2 pots. Bring to a boil over medium heat and let boil for 10 minutes.

5. With wet hands, shape the fish balls and carefully drop into the boiling stock. Cover slightly and cook over medium-low heat for 2 hours.

6. When done, let the fish sit in the pot for 10 minutes, then carefully transfer the pieces to containers. Strain the remaining stock over the fish balls until covered. Chill and serve.

WHITE BEAN AND ARTICHOKE SALAD

3 cups cooked white beans
1 cup canned artichoke hearts
⅔ cup diced green bell pepper
⅓ cup black olives
¼ cup chopped red onion
¼ cup fresh chopped parsley
¼ ounce chopped fresh mint leaves
¾ teaspoon dried basil
⅓ cup olive oil
¼ cup red wine vinegar

8 servings
This dish is so flavorful it can be served simply with matzo crackers.

1. Drain the white beans. Drain the artichoke hearts and quarter. Dice the green bell pepper. Chop the black olives, red onion, parsley, and mint leaves.
2. In a large bowl, combine the beans, artichoke hearts, bell peppers, olives, onion, parsley, mint, and basil; mix well.
3. In a small container with a lid, combine the oil and vinegar. Cover and shake well.
4. Pour the oil and vinegar over the salad and toss to coat.
5. Cover and chill in the refrigerator for several hours or overnight, stirring occasionally, to let the flavors blend.

Fresh Versus Dry

If you don't have fresh herbs, you can always use dry ones. Just make sure to experiment with the proper amount. Some dry herbs have a more concentrated flavor while others have a weaker one.

MATZO BREI

Serves 1

This traditional Passover dish can be served many different ways. Try it with sugar or jelly. Or experiment by adding a little left-over White Bean and Artichoke Salad (page 113) to the top.

1 matzo cracker
1 egg
¼ teaspoon salt
¼ teaspoon ground black pepper
2 tablespoons vegetable oil

1. Break the matzo cracker into small pieces in a medium-sized bowl. Cover with hot water for 1 minute , then squeeze out the water.
2. In a small bowl, beat the egg with the s alt and pepper. Add to the matzo and mix well.
3. Heat the oil to medium in a medium frying pan. Pour the mixture into the pan. Brown 1 side and turn over.

APPLE HAROSET

Serves 4

Try a variation of this by using tarter Granny Smith apples and almonds.

2 large Red Delicious or other
  sweet apples
1 cup walnuts
1 teaspoon granulated sugar
1 teaspoon ground cinnamon
2 tablespoons kosher red wine

1. Peel, core, and finely chop the apples. Finely chop the walnuts.
2. Mix together the apples, nuts, sugar, and cinnamon in a bowl. Add the wine and thoroughly blend. Refrigerate.

Hold the Salt

Resist the urge to salt. Salt draws flavors and juices out of meat and vegetables. Let the flavors release on their own time for the best result. Guests can salt their own dishes if they prefer. They'll also use less than if you add it while cooking.

PASSOVER BROWNIES

5 eggs
2½ cups granulated sugar
1¼ cups vegetable oil
1¼ cups matzo cake meal

1½ cups unsweetened cocoa
  powder
1¼ cups chopped walnuts

1. Preheat oven to 325°. Grease a 9" × 13" pan.
2. Beat together the eggs and sugar. Add the oil. Mix in the cake meal and cocoa. Add 1 cup of the nuts, and mix. Pour into the prepared baking pan. Top with the remaining nuts.
3. Bake for 30 to 35 minutes. If doing the toothpick test, the toothpick will not come out completely clean even though the brownies are done.

Makes 2 dozen

The secret to moist brownies is to under-bake them. Check these after 25 minutes and every couple minutes afterward.

APPLE-CINNAMON FARFEL KUGEL

Nonstick cooking spray
2 large Red Delicious or other
  sweet apples
3 egg whites

1 cup hot water
1 cup matzo farfel
½ cup granulated sugar
2 teaspoons ground cinnamon

1. Preheat oven to 375°. Spray an 8" × 8" baking dish with nonstick cooking spray.
2. Peel, core, and shred the apples. Stiffly beat the egg whites and set aside.
3. In a large bowl, combine the water and farfel. Add the sugar, apple, and 1 to 1½ teaspoons of the cinnamon. Fold in the egg whites. Pour the mixture into the prepared baking dish and dust the top with the remaining cinnamon.
4. Bake for 45 minutes.

Serves 6

Serve this kugel as a dessert with Gefilte Fish (page 112).

SPINACH FRITATTA

3 servings

Serve with Apple-
Cinnamon Farfel Kugel
(page 115).

2 (10-ounce) packages frozen
  chopped spinach
½ cup water
4 eggs
3 matzo crackers
½ teaspoon salt

½ teaspoon ground black
  pepper
¼ teaspoon ground nutmeg
2 tablespoons grated Parmesan
  cheese, plus extra for garnish
3 tablespoons butter

1. Heat the spinach in a saucepan with the water until completely thawed. Strain the spinach, reserving ½ the liquid.
2. Beat the eggs and set aside. Crumble the matzo into a medium-sized mixing bowl and pour the spinach and the remaining liquid over them. Mix thoroughly until the matzo are softened. Add the eggs, salt, pepper, nutmeg, and cheese.
3. Heat the butter in a medium-sized skillet to medium temperature. Add the spinach mixture. Cook, uncovered, for 5 minutes on each side. Garnish with a sprinkling of grated Parmesan and serve immediately.

Frozen Vegetables

Frozen vegetables will quickly separate if you place them in a colander and run hot water over them.

CHOCOLATE RASPBERRY TORTE

16 ounces semisweet chocolate
2 cups unsalted butter
1 cup cola-flavored carbonated
  beverage
1/3 cup raspberry jam
1 teaspoon lemon juice
8 eggs, at room temperature
1 cup granulated sugar
2 tablespoons vanilla sugar

For the glaze:
1 cup semisweet chocolate
  chips
2 tablespoons unsalted butter

Serves 16

Dress up this cake by trimming it with fresh whole raspberries, chocolate leaves, or cocoa powder.

---

1. Preheat oven to 350°. Line the bottom of a 10-inch springform pan with parchment paper. Chop the semisweet chocolate.
2. In a heavy saucepan over low heat, mix together butter and cola, and heat through. Remove the pan from the stove and add the chocolate, stirring to melt the chocolate. When melted, set aside and let the mixture cool completely.
3. In a small mixing bowl, blend the raspberry preserves and lemon juice together. Set aside.
4. In another bowl, whip the eggs with the sugar and vanilla sugar for 10 minutes on high speed. Whisk the cooled, melted chocolate into the egg mixture until thoroughly incorporated. (The mixture will deflate.) Stir in the raspberry preserve mixture. Pour into the prepared springform pan.
5. Place the springform pan on a baking sheet in the oven and reduce the oven's heat to 325°. Bake for 55 to 60 minutes, until the cake is done. (The top will have a slight crust and the middle will seem set.) The cake may rise and fall, but that is fine. Remove the cake and refrigerate for several hours.
6. To make the glaze, melt the chocolate chips with the butter. Stir to melt evenly. Pour over the chilled cake before serving.

CHAPTER 8

CINCO DE MAYO

CARNE ASADA	120
TOTOPOS	121
MEXICAN CHICKEN ROLL-UPS	122
BAJA LOBSTER TAILS	123
MEXICALI SHRIMP ON THE GRILL	124
GAZPACHO	125
GUACAMOLE	126
CHURROS	127
ORANGE LIQUEUR MOUSSE	128
MARGARITA PIE	128
PEPITA BALLS	129
ENCHILADAS	129
MOLASSES CANDY	130
MEXICAN COFFEE	130
SPARKLING FRUIT DRINK	131
CLASSIC MARGARITA	131
FRUITY MARGARITA	132

CARNE ASADA

4 garlic cloves
1 medium-sized white onion
½ cup tequila
¼ cup lime juice
¼ cup lemon juice
¼ cup orange juice

1 teaspoon Tabasco sauce
1 teaspoon ground black pepper
2 pounds flank steak
1 dozen corn tortillas
1 cup tomato salsa
1 cup guacamole

1. Peel and crush the garlic. Peel the onion and chop into ¼-inch pieces.
2. Mix together the garlic, onion, tequila, juices, Tabasco sauce, and pepper in a bowl. Add the meat, turning to coat. Cover and marinate in the refrigerator for 4 to 12 hours, turning occasionally.
3. Preheat grill to medium heat. Wrap the tortillas in aluminum foil and place on the grill.
4. Remove the meat from the marinade, reserving the marinade. Grill the steak for 12 to 18 minutes, turning and basting halfway through with the reserved marinade. Turn the tortillas occasionally.
5. Remove the meat from the grill and cut into thin slices. Serve the steak slices on the tortillas. Garnish with salsa and guacamole.

What Is a Tomatillo?

Tomatillo is a fruit and is also known as a Mexican green tomato. Tomatillos should be used while they are green and still quite firm. They come with a parchmentlike covering. To use tomatillos, remove the covering and wash. Tomatillos have a flavor with hints of lemon, apples, and herbs. Cooking enhances the tomatillo's flavor and softens its thick skin.

TOTOPOS

1 small yellow onion
2 avocados
¼ head lettuce, shredded
3 dill pickles
1 fresh red tomato
2 cups Carne Asada meat
  (page 112)
1 tablespoon butter
2 cups canned kidney beans,
  undrained

1 teaspoon salt
½ teaspoon ground black
  pepper
1⅓ cups vegetable oil, divided
12 corn tortillas
2 tablespoons white wine
  vinegar
1½ teaspoons granulated sugar
¼ teaspoon garlic salt
¾ cup crumbled goat cheese

> **Serves 6**
>
> Change the ingredients to suit your whims. Hot peppers, spicy chicken, and guacamole also make good toppings.

1. Peel the onion and chop finely. Peel and pit the avocados and slice into crescents ⅓-inch thick. Shred the lettuce. Slice the pickles into ¼-inch rounds. Remove the stem from the tomato and cut into ¼-inch slices. Cut the beef into ½-inch pieces and warm in a small pan on low heat.

2. Melt the butter in a medium-sized frying pan on medium heat. Add the onion and sauté until limp but not brown. Add the kidney beans, with their liquid, and the salt and pepper. Cook until the liquid is reduced by half.

3. In a large skillet, heat 1 cup of the vegetable oil to medium-high. Fry the tortillas 1 at a time, turning when first side is lightly browned. Transfer to paper towels to drain and cool.

4. Mix together the vinegar, sugar, garlic salt, and the ⅓ cup remaining vegetable oil in a small container with a cover. Cover and shake until well mixed.

5. Combine the lettuce, avocado, pickles, and meat in a medium-sized bowl. Mix with the vinegar and oil dressing.

6. Spread the beans about ½-inch thick on the tortillas. Pile the salad mixture on top. Add the tomato slices and sprinkle with the cheese.

MEXICAN CHICKEN ROLL-UPS

1 green bell pepper
1 red bell pepper
1 medium-sized yellow onion
3 cups chopped red tomatoes
4 cups shredded lettuce
2 garlic cloves
4 scallions

1 skinless, boneless whole
  chicken breast
1 tablespoon olive oil
4 large flour tortillas
¼ cup shredded Cheddar
  cheese
¼ cup salsa of your choice

1. Chop the green and red peppers, onion, and tomatoes into ¼-inch pieces. Shred the lettuce. Peel the garlic and scallions, and chop into ⅛-inch pieces. Dice the chicken breast. Set oven to 250°. Wrap the tortillas in aluminum foil, and place in the oven to warm.

2. In a large skillet, heat the oil on high. Add the bell peppers, onion, and garlic; sauté until soft, about 7 minutes. Add the chicken, cover, and reduce heat to low; cook until the chicken is tender, about 8 minutes.

3. Transfer the chicken mixture to a serving bowl. Set out the warmed tortillas. Place the lettuce, scallions, cheese, and salsa in separate small bowls. Let diners make their own roll-ups.

Anaheim Peppers

The Anaheim, also known as the New Mexico chili pepper, can range from 3 to 6 inches long. Its shade of green is a little lighter than either the jalapeño or poblano, and it is also the chili with the least bite.

BAJA LOBSTER TAILS

6 shallots
2 garlic cloves
3 fresh jalapeño peppers
3 fresh limes
4 medium-sized lobster tails
3 tablespoons olive oil
2 teaspoons ground cumin

2 teaspoons paprika
½ teaspoon cayenne pepper
2 tablespoons unsalted butter
1 teaspoon sea salt
1 teaspoon freshly ground
   black pepper

Serves 4

Serve with Gazpacho
(page 125) and
Margarita Pie
(page 128).

1. Peel the shallots and chop into ¼-inch pieces. Peel and mince the garlic. Seed the jalapeño peppers and chop into ¼-inch pieces. Juice 2 of the limes and cut the third lime into wedges.
2. Preheat grill to medium.
3. Cut the lobster tails in half lengthwise. Sprinkle lightly with salt and black pepper.
4. Heat the olive oil in a medium-sized skillet to medium temperature. Add the shallot and sauté until golden, about 4 minutes. Add the garlic and jalapeños; sauté for another 1 to 2 minutes. Add the cumin, paprika, and cayenne pepper; cook, stirring, for another 1 to 2 minutes.
5. Remove from the heat. Stir in the lime juice, butter, the 1 teaspoon salt, and 1 teaspoon black pepper.
6. Place the lobsters on the grill, shell-side down, approximately 4 inches from the heat source. Grill for 8 to 9 minutes, occasionally turning the tails onto their sides to cook through. Spoon the butter mixture over the lobsters during cooking. Garnish with fresh lime wedges.

MEXICALI SHRIMP ON THE GRILL

Serves 4

This recipe also can be used with baby shrimp, cooked in the oven for ½ hour, then put into Enchiladas (page 129) or served as Totopos (page 121).

2 pounds large shrimp
½ cup fresh cilantro
2 jalapeño peppers
2 garlic cloves
¼ cup white wine vinegar
3 tablespoons lemon juice
¾ cup olive oil

½ teaspoon ground cayenne pepper
½ teaspoon red pepper flakes
½ teaspoon salt
½ teaspoon ground black pepper

1. Peel and devein the shrimp but leave on the tails. Finely chop the cilantro. Remove the stems and seeds from the jalapeño peppers and mince the peppers. Peel and mince the garlic.
2. Combine all the ingredients except the shrimp in a large bowl. Whisk together. Add the shrimp and toss lightly, coating on all sides.
3. Lay the shrimp flat in a large glass or ceramic pan. Pour the remaining sauce over the shrimp and cover with plastic wrap. Refrigerate for 3 to 12 hours, stirring occasionally.
4. Preheat grill to medium. Place the shrimp in a vegetable basket and place on the grill. Turn frequently to cook thoroughly, about 5 minutes.

Poblano Peppers

Like the jalapeño, the poblano is dark green, but shaped like a cone and has a milder flavor. The flavor comes out when roasted.

GAZPACHO

4 large red tomatoes
1 small yellow onion
1 green bell pepper
2 medium carrots
2 celery stalks
4 cups canned condensed
  tomato soup

2 tablespoons olive oil
2 tablespoons white wine vinegar
2 teaspoons salt
1 teaspoon ground black
  pepper
1 medium cucumber

Serves 8

Gazpacho makes an excellent first course to a heavier beef or chicken meal. It also makes a good lunch served with white bread and cheese.

1. Peel the tomatoes and cut into quarters. Remove the skin from the onion and cut into quarters. Remove the stem and seeds from the green pepper and cut into quarters. Peel the carrots and cut into quarters. Remove the leaves from the celery and cut the stalks into quarters.
2. Combine 2 cups of the tomato soup, the olive oil, wine vinegar, salt, pepper, and ½ of the vegetables in a blender. Blend until liquefied, about 1 minute. Pour into a bowl. Repeat with the remaining tomato soup and vegetables. Combine with the previous mixture.
3. Cover and chill in the refrigerator for at least 2 hours before serving.
4. Cut the cucumbers into thin slices and place on top right before serving.

Bell Peppers

Bell peppers have different flavors depending on their color. Green is the most acidic and sour tasting. Red has the most peppery flavor. Yellow and orange have a gentle flavor. Combine them to create unique flavors and a beautiful dish.

GUACAMOLE

2 garlic cloves
1 small red onion
1 small jalapeño pepper
4 ripe Hass avocados
1 plum tomato

¼ cup fresh cilantro
2 tablespoons lime juice
½ teaspoon salt
½ teaspoon freshly ground
  black pepper

1. Peel the garlic and chop into ⅛-inch pieces. Peel the onion and chop into ¼-inch pieces. Remove the stem and seeds from the jalapeño pepper and chop into ⅛-inch pieces. Halve, pit, and scoop the meat from the avocados. Seed and chop the tomato into ¼-inch pieces. Chop the cilantro.
2. In a medium-sized mixing bowl, mash together the garlic, onion, and jalapeño with a fork.
3. Add the avocado and mix until it forms a chunky paste.
4. Add the lime juice, salt, pepper, tomato, and cilantro. Stir to combine.

Pitting an Avocado

To remove the pit of an avocado, start by cutting through the skin, down to the pit, and scoring the fruit lengthwise. Gripping both halves, give a quick twist to separate 1 half from the pit, leaving the other half holding that large nut. If you plan to use only ½ of the avocado, it's best to leave the pit in the unused portion, since it prevents the fruit from turning brown overnight. To remove the pit, hack into the middle of it with the blade of your knife, gripping the fruit in the palm of your other hand. Twist the knife clockwise to loosen the pit. It should fall right out of a ripe avocado.

CHURROS

3 cups vegetable oil
1 cup water
½ cup butter
1 cup all-purpose flour

¼ teaspoon salt
3 eggs
1 cup confectioners' sugar
¼ cup ground cinnamon

Serves 12

These traditional treats also can be formed into small patties and served with jam.

1. Pour the oil into a medium-sized frying pan. The oil should be 1 to 2 inches deep. Heat to 375°.
2. Heat the water to a rolling boil in a medium-sized saucepan. Add the butter and continue to boil.
3. Quickly stir in the flour and salt. Reduce heat to low and stir vigorously until the mixture forms a ball.
4. Remove from heat and beat in the eggs 1 at a time, until the mixture is smooth and glossy.
5. Form the dough into round sticks about 10 inches long and 1-inch thick.
6. Fry the sticks 2 or 3 at a time until light brown. Place the sticks on paper towels and let cool.
7. Mix together the confectioners' sugar and cinnamon on a large plate. As soon as the churros are cool, roll them in the mixture. Set aside until completely cool.

Frying Food

Although it seems easy, frying food is a great art. The oil must be hot enough to cook the food without soaking into the food. At the same time, if the oil is too hot, it will cook the outside of the food before the inside is completely cooked.

ORANGE LIQUEUR MOUSSE

Serves 4

If serving a light meal, try using this as a dessert for Gazpacho (page 125).

1 (3-ounce) package orange-flavored gelatin
1 cup boiling water
1/4 cup cold water

1/4 cup orange liqueur
1 cup whipping cream
1/2 teaspoon ground cinnamon
1/2 cup shredded coconut

1. Dissolve the gelatin in the boiling water. Add the cold water and cool the mixture to room temperature. Stir in the orange liqueur. Chill in the refrigerator until the mixture starts to thicken, about 30 minutes.
2. Whip the cream until it piles softly. Gradually add the gelatin mixture and cinnamon, stirring gently until evenly blended. Pour into a mold. Chill until set, about 1 hour.
3. Turn the mold onto a serving plate and top with the shredded coconut.

MARGARITA PIE

Serves 8

For a low-fat version of this recipe, use egg substitute and nonfat whipped topping. It tastes the same and has very few calories.

1 tablespoon unflavored gelatin
2/3 cup granulated sugar
1/4 teaspoon salt
2 eggs
1/2 cup lime juice

1 teaspoon fresh lime zest
1/4 cup tequila
1 1/2 cups whipped cream
1 prebaked 9-inch pie shell

1. In a small saucepan, combine the gelatin, sugar, and salt. In a bowl, beat together the eggs and lime juice until blended.
2. Add the gelatin mixture to the egg mixture. Cook in a medium-sized saucepan over medium heat, stirring until the gelatin dissolves, about 5 minutes.
3. Stir in the lime zest and tequila. Cover and chill until the mixture thickens to a pudding consistency.
4. Fold the whipped cream into the tequila mixture. Spoon into the pie shell and chill well.

PEPITA BALLS

*1 pound unsalted, hulled
   pepitas (pumpkin seeds).*

*1 cup sweetened condensed
   milk*
3½ cups confectioners' sugar

1. Grind the pepitas finely.
2. Mix the pepitas with the condensed milk and 3 cups of the confectioners' sugar.
3. Shape into 1-inch balls and roll in the remaining sugar. Place on wax paper on a baking sheet.
4. Refrigerate for 2 to 3 hours or until set.

ENCHILADAS

3 cups refried beans
12 corn tortillas
*2 cups shredded Monterey jack
   cheese*

*2 cups canned red or green
   chili sauce*

1. Preheat oven to 375°. Shred the cheese.
2. Ladle ½ cup of the chili sauce into a 9" × 12" baking pan.
3. Put ¼ cup of the beans in the center of each tortilla. Add 2 tablespoons shredded cheese to each tortilla. Roll up and place in a baking pan.
4. When all the enchiladas are in the baking pan, cover with the remaining sauce and cheese. Bake for 15 to 20 minutes.

MOLASSES CANDY

1 cup light molasses
1 firmly packed cup brown sugar
2 tablespoons butter
1 teaspoon cider vinegar
¼ teaspoon almond extract
1½ cups toasted, slivered almonds

1. Combine the molasses, brown sugar, butter, and vinegar into a heavy saucepan. Bring to a boil. Boil hard for 7 to 12 minutes or until the mixture reaches 260° on a candy thermometer. The mixture should form a firm ball when a small amount is dropped in cold water.
2. Remove from heat. Add the almond extract and almonds. Stir well.
3. Pour onto a greased baking sheet. Spread out in as thin a layer as possible. Let cool. Break into 2-inch pieces.

MEXICAN COFFEE

6 cups water
¼ packed cup brown sugar
3-inch stick cinnamon
6 whole cloves
¾ cup regular grind, roasted coffee

1. In a medium-sized saucepan, combine the water, brown sugar, cinnamon, and cloves. Heat at medium temperature, stirring periodically, until the sugar is dissolved.
2. Add the coffee and bring to a boil. Reduce heat and simmer, uncovered, for 1 to 2 minutes. Remove from the heat.
3. Cover and let stand for 15 minutes. Strain before serving.

SPARKLING FRUIT DRINK

4 cups watermelon meat
1 mango
1 papaya
1 pineapple
1 guava

2 cups fresh strawberries
1 cup white granulated sugar
2 gallons sparkling water
2 pounds ice cubes

1. Remove the rind, stems, seeds, and cores from the fruits. Cut the fruit into ½-inch pieces. Reserve all the juices.
2. Stir the sugar into the water until it dissolves.
3. Add the fruit and juices to the water. Stir well.
4. Add the ice cubes and serve immediately.

Serves 12 to 24

This festive drink is often served at parties where children are present. Everyone loves snacking on the fruit once the water is gone.

CLASSIC MARGARITA

1½ ounces tequila
1 ounce lime juice
½ ounce Triple Sec

Ice
Salt and lime wedge to rim glass

1. Combine the tequila, lime juice, and Triple Sec in a shaker half-filled with ice. Shake well.
2. Rim a cocktail glass by running the lime wedge along the top, then dipping the rim in salt.
3. Strain the drink into the glass. Garnish with the lime wedge.

Serves 1

Nothing says Cinco de Mayo like fresh margaritas. Involve your guests in making their own drinks for a truly festive atmosphere.

FRUITY MARGARITA

1½ ounces tequila
1 ounce fruit-flavored liqueur
1 ounce Triple Sec

Ice
Lime wedge and sugar
  to rim glass

1. Combine tequila, liqueur, and Triple Sec in a shaker half-filled with ice. Shake well.
2. Rim a glass by running the lime wedge over the top and dipping the rim into the sugar.
3. Strain the drink into the glass. Garnish with fresh fruit, if desired.

Making It Nonalcoholic

If you want to make uncooked foods calling for liqueur nonalcoholic, simply substitute 1 tablespoon of the flavored extract mixed with half water and half corn syrup. You will get a very similar flavor without the alcohol.

CHAPTER 9

MOTHER'S DAY AND FATHER'S DAY

SMOKED MUSSELS IN CREAM SAUCE WITH PASTA	134
BROCCOLI FLORETS WITH LEMON BUTTER SAUCE	135
HOT DILL PASTA WITH SCALLOPS	136
FIGS WITH BRIE AND PORT WINE REDUCTION	137
BEER SOUP	137
VENISON MEDALLIONS WITH CRANBERRY DIJON CHUTNEY	138
SHRIMP SCAMPI	139
FILET SOUTHWESTERN	140
CLASSIC WALDORF SALAD	141
CHEESY GOLDEN APPLE OMELET	141
BEEF AND HORSERADISH SALAD	142
BAR HARBOR FISH CHOWDER	143
EASY CHICKEN CORDON BLEU	144
QUAIL BAKED IN WHITE WINE	145
CHOCOLATE FONDUE	146
CHOCOLATE MOUSSE	147
ROAST DUCKLING WITH ORANGE GLAZE	148
CHERRIES JUBILEE	148
MIMOSA	149
WHITE WINE COOLER	149

SMOKED MUSSELS IN CREAM SAUCE WITH PASTA

2 garlic cloves
1 large leek
4 cups fresh mushrooms
4 ounces smoked mussels
1 bunch fresh parsley
1⅓ cups uncooked linguine
3 teaspoons extra-virgin olive oil, divided

2 teaspoons butter
½ cup dry white wine
2 cups cottage cheese
1 teaspoon all-purpose flour
½ teaspoon cracked black pepper

1. Crush the garlic with the back of a large knife. Remove the skins. Remove the skin from the leek and chop into ½-inch pieces to yield ½ cup. Thinly slice the mushrooms. Drain any oil from the mussels. Roughly chop the parsley.

2. Place the mushrooms in a vegetable steamer; steam for 5 minutes on medium-high heat. Boil the pasta in 2 quarts water and 1 teaspoon of the olive oil until tender but not mushy.

3. Melt the butter in a deep nonstick skillet. Add the garlic and leeks, and sauté just until transparent. Add the wine and bring to a boil. Cook until reduced by half. Add the mushrooms and toss in the wine mixture.

4. In a blender or food processor, purée the cottage cheese. Add it to the wine-mushroom mixture and bring to serving temperature over low heat. Make sure the mixture does not boil. If the mixture seems too thin, sprinkle flour over the mixture, stir until blended, and cook until thickened.

5. Add the mussels to the cottage cheese mixture just prior to serving. Stir well to bring the mussels to serving temperature. Toss the pasta with the remaining 2 teaspoons olive oil. Divide onto 4 plates. Ladle the mixture over the noodles right before serving. Top with cracked pepper and parsley.

BROCCOLI FLORETS WITH LEMON BUTTER SAUCE

2 small shallots
1 lemon
8 ounces cold unsalted butter
¼ cup white cooking wine
½ teaspoon salt
¼ teaspoon white pepper
1 large head broccoli

Serves 4

This sauce can be used with any vegetable. It is especially good over carrots and zucchini rounds.

1. Remove the skins from the shallots and mince. Juice the lemon. Cut the butter into small pieces. Break the broccoli into bite-sized florets.
2. Place the shallots, ½ of the lemon juice, and the wine in a small saucepan over medium heat. Simmer until almost dry.
3. Reduce heat to very low and stir in a few small pieces of the butter, swirling it in with a wire whisk until it is mostly melted. Gradually add the remaining butter, whisking constantly until all the butter is added and the sauce is smooth. Take care that the sauce does not boil.
4. Season the sauce with the salt, white pepper, and remaining lemon juice. Keep in a warm place but not over a flame.
5. Wash the broccoli and boil in 4 quarts of rapidly boiling, salted water. Drain and serve with the lemon-butter sauce.

Reducing Saltiness
If a dish tastes too salty, add 1 teaspoon each of cider vinegar and sugar to help cut down on the salty flavor in the recipe.

HOT DILL PASTA WITH SCALLOPS

Serves 4

This meal is best accompanied by a slightly sweet white wine.

1 pound sea scallops
2 large carrots
3 garlic cloves
3 green onions
6 ounces fresh snap peas
8 ounces fettuccine
2 tablespoons olive oil, divided
1 tablespoon butter
½ cup dry white wine
⅓ cup water

1 tablespoon fresh dill
1 teaspoon instant chicken
   bouillon granules
¼ teaspoon crushed red
   pepper
2 tablespoons cornstarch
2 tablespoons cold water
¼ cup grated Parmesan cheese
½ teaspoon freshly cracked
   black pepper

1. Thaw the scallops if frozen. Cut any large scallops in half and set aside. Peel and thinly slice the carrots. Peel and mince the garlic cloves. Peel and thinly slice the green onions. Remove the stems from the snap peas.
2. Cook the fettuccine in boiling water with 1 tablespoon of the olive oil until al dente. Drain, toss with the butter, and set aside.
3. Pour the remaining oil into a wok or large skillet. Preheat over medium-high heat. Add the carrots and garlic; stir-fry for 4 minutes. Add the green onions and snap peas; stir-fry for 2 to 3 minutes or until crisp. Remove the vegetables and set aside.
4. Reduce heat to low and let the wok cool for 1 minute. Carefully add the wine, the ⅓ cup water, the dill, bouillon granules, and crushed red pepper to the wok. Add the scallops. Simmer, uncovered, for 1 to 2 minutes or until the scallops are opaque, stirring often.
5. Stir together the cornstarch and 2 tablespoons cold water. Add to the wok. Cook and stir until the mixture is thickened and bubbly. Return the vegetables to the work. Add the pasta and toss to mix. Heat through.
6. Transfer to dinner plates. Sprinkle with Parmesan cheese and cracked black pepper.

FIGS WITH BRIE AND PORT WINE REDUCTION

2 cups port wine
1 tablespoon cold, unsalted
   butter

12 ounces Brie cheese
6 fresh figs
¼ cup confectioners' sugar

1. Heat the wine on medium in a medium-sized saucepan, and let reduce by half. Remove from heat and add the cold butter.
2. Cut the Brie into 6 equal portions. Cut the figs in half.
3. To serve, drizzle the wine reduction on plates, sprinkle with confectioners' sugar, and arrange figs and Brie on top.

> **Serves 6**
>
> A tiny piece of dark chocolate is the perfect addition to this appetizer.

BEER SOUP

1 cup all-purpose flour
1½ tablespoons butter
1 (12-ounce) bottle of your
   favorite beer

1½-inch piece cinnamon
1 teaspoon granulated sugar
2 egg yolks
½ cup milk

1. In a large stockpot, brown the flour in the butter, then add the beer.
2. Add the cinnamon and sugar and bring to a boil.
3. Whisk together the egg yolks and milk, then stir into the hot (but not boiling) beer.
4. Strain and serve with croutons, fresh popcorn, or toasted slices of French bread on top.

> **Serves 4**
>
> Sometimes all Dad, or Mom, wants to do is laze around and watch a game. This is the perfect treat for helping him, or her, do just that.

VENISON MEDALLIONS WITH CRANBERRY DIJON CHUTNEY

2 small shallots
2 cups mushrooms
1 cup fresh cranberries
1 teaspoon honey
1 tablespoon Dijon mustard
2 teaspoons butter, divided
1 teaspoon salt

1 teaspoon ground black pepper
8 (2½-ounce) venison medallions
1 cup dry red wine
¼ cup cider vinegar
½ cup chicken stock
1 tablespoon red currant jelly

1. Peel and mince the shallots. Clean and quarter the mushrooms.
2. In a small sauté pan, combine the cranberries, honey, mustard, and 1 teaspoon of the butter. Season with salt and pepper. Cook over low heat for about 4 minutes until the cranberries just start to pop. Remove from heat and set aside.
3. Season the venison with salt and pepper. Melt the remaining butter in a large sauté pan over high heat until very hot. Add the venison and sear for about 2 minutes or until golden brown. Turn over and sear for another 2 minutes. The meat should be medium-rare at this point. Transfer to a warm platter and keep warm.
4. Return the sauté pan to medium heat. Add the shallots and cook for about 2 minutes or until tender. Stir in the mushrooms and cook until softened. Add the wine, vinegar, and stock, and scrape the bottom of the pan with a wooden spoon to loosen any browned bits. Raise the heat to high and cook for about 10 minutes or until the liquid is reduced to about ½ cup. Stir in the jelly and adjust seasoning to taste.
5. Spoon a small amount of the cranberry sauce on top of each venison medallion. Ladle the sauce on top and around the venison.

Venison Definition

Venison isn't necessarily deer meat. It also is the term used for elk or caribou meat. These meats can vary widely in taste depending on what the animal has eaten. As a result, they are best served in stews or other dishes that blend many flavors.

SHRIMP SCAMPI

16 jumbo shrimp
16 clams
3 garlic cloves
1 pound fettuccine
1 tablespoon olive oil
¼ cup butter

1 cup dry white wine
1 teaspoon dried oregano,
   crumbled
1 teaspoon dried basil,
   crumbled

Serves 6
Serve with a dry white wine or champagne.

1. Peel and devein the shrimp. Split each shrimp along the back from the tail to the head, but not all the way through. Scrub the clams well. Peel and mince the garlic.
2. Cook the fettuccine in boiling salted water until al dente. Drain the fettuccine, place in a warmed bowl, and toss with the olive oil.
3. Meanwhile, melt the butter in a large skillet over medium heat. Add the garlic and sauté until soft and translucent, about 10 minutes.
4. Add the shrimp, clams, wine, oregano, and basil. Cook until the shrimp are pink and the clams have opened, 5 to 10 minutes. Discard any clams that did not open.
5. Toss the shrimp and clams with the pasta and serve.

Preparing Fresh Shrimp

When using fresh shrimp, boil them for 3 minutes. Run under cold water. Remove all of the shell, although you can keep the tail on if you like. Take a small fork and run it along the back of the shrimp to remove the black vein.

FILET SOUTHWESTERN

6 shallots
1 tablespoon cilantro
2 teaspoons chipotle peppers
  in adobo sauce

¼ cup butter, softened
1 tablespoon lime juice
4 (1-inch-thick) filets mignons
1 tablespoon vegetable oil

1. Peel and mince the shallots. Mince the cilantro. Purée the chipotle peppers in adobo sauce in a blender or food processor.
2. Adjust oven rack so the filets will be 4 inches from the heating element, and preheat broiler.
3. Beat the butter and lime juice with an electric mixer until light and fluffy. Mix in the shallots, cilantro, and peppers.
4. Remove the filets from the refrigerator about 15 minutes before you are ready to begin cooking them. Flatten them slightly by pressing with a plate. Oil 1 side of the filets lightly and place on the broiler pan, oiled-side down. Spread about 1 teaspoon of the butter mixture on each fillet. Broil for 4 minutes for rare or 6 minutes for medium.
5. Turn the filets. Top each with another teaspoon of the butter mixture and broil an additional 4 to 6 minutes. To serve, top each filet with a quarter of the remaining butter mixture.

What Fish Tastes Best?

If adding sauces and spices to fish, look for a firm, mild-flavored white-fleshed fish that holds up well to cooking. Bass, flounder, shark, swordfish, and red snapper all work well. Some fish can have surprisingly strong flavors, so if you want to try a new fish, take a small piece home and steam it to see if you like the flavor before putting it in your recipe.

CLASSIC WALDORF SALAD

2 large Red Delicious apples
2 celery stalks
½ cup walnuts
½ cup mayonnaise

1 tablespoon granulated sugar
1 teaspoon lemon juice
½ teaspoon salt

Serves 6
Serve as a salad before Filet Southwestern (page 140).

1. Dice the apples into ½-inch pieces. Finely slice the celery. Coarsely chop the walnuts.
2. Blend the mayonnaise with the sugar, lemon juice, and salt.
3. Combine the apples, celery, and nuts, and fold in the dressing mixture.
4. Chill for at least 1 hour before serving.

CHEESY GOLDEN APPLE OMELET

1 Golden Delicious apple
2 tablespoons butter, divided
4 eggs
1 tablespoon water
¼ teaspoon salt

¼ teaspoon ground black pepper
2 tablespoons crumbled blue cheese
2 tablespoons grated Parmesan cheese

Serves 2
This is the perfect way to greet your Mom or Dad in the morning. Serve with a Mimosa (page 149).

1. Pare, core, and slice the apple. Sauté in 1 tablespoon of the butter in a medium-sized pan on medium heat until barely tender. Set aside.
2. Combine the eggs, water, salt, and pepper until blended. Heat the remaining butter in a skillet. Add the egg mixture. Cook slowly, lifting the edges to allow the uncooked portion to flow under.
3. When the eggs are cooked, arrange the apple slices on half of the omelet. Sprinkle with cheeses. Fold in half.

BEEF AND HORSERADISH SALAD

1 cup fresh green beans

1½ cups fresh baby carrots

¾-pound beef sirloin steak, 1-inch thick

4 cups torn Boston or Bibb lettuce

1 (16-ounce) can julienne-cut beets

For the dressing:

1½ ounces softened cream cheese

2 tablespoons prepared horse-radish sauce

3–4 tablespoons milk

1. Wash the green beans. Remove the ends and strings and cut in half lengthwise. Cook the beans, covered, in boiling water in a medium-sized saucepan for 5 minutes.
2. Add the carrots and cook for 10 to 15 more minutes or until the vegetables are tender. Drain. Cover and chill the vegetables for 4 to 24 hours.
3. Remove broiler pan from the oven. Preheat broiler.
4. Place the steak on unheated rack of broiler pan. Broil 3 inches from the heat for 13 to 15 minutes for medium, turning once.
5. In the meantime, combine the cream cheese, horseradish sauce, and milk in a small container with a cover. Cover and shake until well mixed.
6. Arrange the torn lettuce on plates. Top with steak. Drizzle with dressing.

BAR HARBOR FISH CHOWDER

¼ pound salt pork
4 cups cubed small red
   potatoes
3 medium-sized onions
2 teaspoons salt, divided
3 pounds flounder, haddock,
   or cod

2 cups milk
1 tablespoon butter
¼ teaspoon freshly ground
   black pepper

> **Serves 6**
>
> Although the recipe calls for discarding the salt pork, many people like to add it to the soup at the end to create an interesting array of flavors.

1. Dice the salt pork into ½-inch pieces. Cut the red potatoes into ½-inch pieces. Peel and thinly slice the onions. Scald the milk by heating it in a saucepan on medium heat until a thin film appears on top.
2. Fry the salt pork in a large skillet. Set aside, leaving the drippings in the pan. Add the potatoes, onions, and ½ teaspoon of the salt. Cover with hot water and cook over medium heat, covered, for 15 minutes or until the potatoes are just tender.
3. Meanwhile, cut the fish into large chunks and place in another saucepan. Add boiling water to cover and the remaining 1½ teaspoons salt. Cook slowly, covered, until the fish is fork-tender, about 15 minutes. Remove from heat. Strain and reserve liquid.
4. Remove any bones from the fish. Add the fish and strained liquid to the potato-onion mixture. Pour in the milk and heat through, about 5 minutes. Mix in the butter and pepper. Serve at once.

Selecting Fish

When purchasing fresh fish, check for clear and bright eyes, firm skin that bounces back when touched, and a fresh, clean smell. Try not to keep fresh fish more than a day in your refrigerator before cooking.

EASY CHICKEN CORDON BLEU

2 whole chicken breasts
4 small ham slices
4 small Swiss cheese slices
¼ cup all-purpose flour
¼ cup grated Swiss cheese

½ teaspoon fresh or ¼ teaspoon dried sage
¼ teaspoon ground black pepper
1 (10¾-ounce) can condensed cream of chicken soup

1. Remove the skin and bones from the chicken breasts. Cut each breast in half and pound with a kitchen mallet until about ¼-inch thick.
2. Place a ham slice, then a Swiss cheese slice on each piece of chicken. Roll up and secure with toothpicks.
3. Combine the flour, cheese, sage, and black pepper in a small bowl. Dip the chicken rolls into the mixture. Place in the bottom of a slow cooker. Pour the condensed soup over the chicken rolls. Cook, covered, on low heat for 4 to 6 hours.

Grate Your Own Cheese
As a time and money saver, buy blocks of cheese and grate them yourself. To keep the cheese from sticking together, add a little cornstarch and toss the cheese until mixed through.

QUAIL BAKED IN WHITE WINE

2 quail or game hens (fresh
   or frozen)
2 garlic cloves
1 small yellow onion
1 tablespoon shortening
2 whole cloves
1 teaspoon black peppercorns
1 bay leaf

1 teaspoon fresh-chopped
   chives
1 cup dry white wine
½ teaspoon salt
⅛ teaspoon ground black
   pepper
⅛ teaspoon cayenne pepper
1 cup heavy cream

> **Serves 2**
>
> If you don't have wine handy for your recipe, substitute 1 tablespoon of red or cider vinegar mixed with 1 cup of water.

1. Thaw the quail, if necessary, and clean by running under cold water. Peel and chop the garlic and onion into ¼-inch pieces.
2. Melt the shortening in a medium-sized frying pan on medium heat. Add the garlic, onions, cloves, peppercorns, and bay leaf. Cook for several minutes. Add the quail and brown on all sides.
3. Place the quail and the mixture from the frying pan into a slow cooker. Chop the chives into ¼-inch pieces. Add the chives, wine, salt, pepper, and cayenne pepper to the slow cooker. Cook, covered, on low setting for about 6 hours.
4. Remove the quail and set aside. Remove the bay leaf and discard. Strain the liquid, then add the cream to the liquid. Stir well for 5 minutes. Pour over the quail to serve.

Game Hens

Rock Cornish game hens weigh only 1 to 1½ pounds and are all white meat. They are a separate bread of poultry, unlike capons, which are small male chickens that have been neutered.

CHOCOLATE FONDUE

1 quart water
½ cup granulated sugar
Angel food cake
Canned pineapple chunks
Canned mandarin oranges
Fresh bananas
Fresh strawberries

12 ounces milk chocolate
½ cup whipping cream
3 tablespoons orange-flavored liqueur
½ cup chopped toasted almonds
1 tablespoon honey

1. Mix the sugar into the water and place in a large bowl. Cut the angel food cake into 1-inch squares. Drain the pineapple and mandarin oranges. Slice the bananas and dip them in sugar water to prevent browning. Chill the fruit in the refrigerator. Chop the toasted almonds.
2. Combine the almonds, chocolate, cream, liqueur, and honey in a saucepan. Heat slowly until the chocolate is melted, stirring well. Pour the chocolate into a fondue pot placed over a low flame.
3. Arrange the cake and fruit on a platter.

Melting Chocolate

The easiest way to melt chocolate morsels is to use the microwave. Place the chocolate in an uncovered, microwave-safe container. A cover could cause moisture condensation to build up, ruining the chocolate. Stop the microwave and stir the chocolate every few seconds, because chocolate will be melted without looking melted.

CHOCOLATE MOUSSE

6 eggs
1½ tablespoons kirsch or
   cherry brandy
1½ tablespoons dark rum
1 tablespoon, plus a few
   drops vanilla extract

6 ounces bittersweet chocolate
1½ cups heavy cream
2½ tablespoons confectioners'
   sugar
Whipped cream and chocolate
   shavings, for garnish

> **Serves 8**
>
> This is actually a lighter version of traditional French chocolate mousse, which contains egg yolks. However, it is just as tasty and equally glamorous.

1. Chill eight 8-ounce wineglasses. Separate the egg yolks from the whites. Discard the yolks. Whip the egg whites to medium-soft peaks and refrigerate.

2. Combine the kirsch, dark rum, 1 tablespoon vanilla extract, and the chocolate in a double boiler. Warm, stirring occasionally, until melted and smooth.

3. Whip together the cream, confectioners' sugar, and a few drops of vanilla until it forms soft peaks when the whisk is lifted from it.

4. Gently fold ⅓ of the whipped cream into the chocolate mixture. Fold the chocolate mixture back into the rest of the whipped cream, mixing only as much as is necessary to incorporate it most of the way. (A few streaks of chocolate are okay.) Fold the whipped egg whites very gently into the chocolate cream mixture, just barely enough to incorporate.

5. Put the mousse into a pastry bag with a star tip (or a plastic bag with a corner cut out), and pipe into the prepared wineglasses. Cover the glasses individually with plastic wrap and chill for at least 6 hours until set. Garnish with a spoonful of whipped cream and chocolate shavings.

Don't Have a Double Boiler?

Find a steel mixing bowl that will fit securely into a pot. It shouldn't fit too low but shouldn't be so high that it is not sturdy. Simply fill the pot halfway with water and you have your double boiler.

ROAST DUCKLING WITH ORANGE GLAZE

Serves 2

Fresh steamed asparagus tips give a pleasing complement in both taste and color to this meal.

2 cups prepared poultry
   stuffing
1 duckling, fresh or thawed
½ cup granulated sugar

½ teaspoon salt
1 teaspoon cornstarch
1 (6-ounce) can frozen orange
   juice concentrate, thawed.

1. Prepare the stuffing according to the package directions and stuff into the duckling cavity. Place the duckling, breast-side up, in a slow cooker. Cover and cook on low setting for 6 hours.
2. One hour before serving, combine the sugar, salt, and cornstarch in a medium-sized saucepan. Add the thawed orange juice concentrate. Stir over moderate heat until slightly thickened. Brush the entire surface of the duckling with the glaze. Repeat every 15 minutes for the remaining 1 hour.

CHERRIES JUBILEE

Serves 6

This is a wonderful dessert for Shrimp Scampi (page 139).

1 (16-ounce) can pitted sweet
   cherries
⅓ cup granulated sugar
2 tablespoons cornstarch

1 tablespoon lemon juice
⅓ cup brandy
Vanilla ice cream

1. Drain the cherries, reserving the juice in a measuring cup. Add enough water to the juice to make 1 cup liquid.
2. In a small saucepan, mix together the sugar and cornstarch. Gradually stir in the diluted cherry juice until smooth. Bring to a boil over medium heat, stirring constantly. Boil for 1 minute.
3. Add the cherries and lemon juice. Remove from the heat and keep warm.
4. Just before serving, add the brandy. Ignite while still in the saucepan. After the flame dies down, spoon the cherries over the ice cream.

MIMOSA

3 ounces chilled champagne   *3 ounces orange juice*

Combine in a champagne flute or white wine glass. Stir gently.

Serves 1

Serve this with Cheesy Golden Apple Omelet (page 141) to wake up your Mom or Dad.

WHITE WINE COOLER

4 ounces white wine (such as Chablis)   *Sparkling water to fill glass*
Ice
2 ounces pineapple juice   *1 fresh lime wedge*

1. Pour the wine, juice, and sparkling water over ice into a large wine-glass. Stir gently.
2. Garnish with the lime wedge.

Serves 1

This is the perfect complement to any fish or poultry dish.

CHAPTER 10

MEMORIAL DAY

TEXAS CAVIAR	152
GREEN BEANS IN LEMON HONEY	153
CHICKEN SKEWERS WITH SPICY ISLAND MARINADE	154
LONDON BROIL WITH MUSHROOMS	155
STRAWBERRY CHICKEN SALAD	156
SMOKED SALMON SALAD WITH CILANTRO DRESSING	157
BURGERS WITH LEMON PEPPER	158
MARINATED GINGER CHICKEN	158
CALIFORNIA TRI-TIP	159
BRUSSELS SPROUTS A L'ORANGE	160
GRILLED RIB-EYE STEAKS WITH ONIONS	160
STRAWBERRY SORBET	161
MINT JULEP	162
LEMON-SPIKED PINEAPPLE SMOOTHIE	162

TEXAS CAVIAR

2 ripe, firm avocados
1 bulb fresh garlic
1 small red onion
2 medium-sized red tomatoes
1 bunch fresh cilantro
1 (15-ounce) can whole-kernel corn
1 (15-ounce) can black-eyed peas

1 (15-ounce) can black beans
2 tablespoons vegetable oil
3 tablespoons Tabasco sauce
2 tablespoons red wine vinegar
1 teaspoon coarse ground black pepper

1. Remove the pit and skin from the avocados. Cut the flesh into ½-inch cubes. Peel and mince the garlic cloves. Peel and chop the onion. Remove the stems from the tomatoes and chop the tomatoes into ½-inch pieces. Chop the cilantro. Drain and rinse the corn, black-eyed peas, and black beans.
2. In a small bowl, mix together the vegetable oil, Tabasco sauce, vinegar, pepper, and garlic.
3. Place the avocados in a medium-sized mixing bowl. Pour the vegetable oil mixture over the avocados and stir gently to coat.
4. In a large mixing bowl, mix together the onion, tomatoes, cilantro, corn, peas, and beans. Add the avocado mixture to the large bowl and gently mix with the other ingredients.

Garlic in Jars?

Beware of prepared garlic. While preminced garlic looks like a good buy and certainly sounds easier, chopped garlic releases an oil while stored. This affects both the taste and consistency in your recipes. Fresh garlic is always best.

GREEN BEANS IN LEMON HONEY

½ lemon
2 tablespoons butter
3 tablespoons honey
1 teaspoon cider vinegar
½ teaspoon salt

1 tart apple
1 teaspoon cornstarch
1 tablespoon water
3 cups fresh green beans
1 medium-sized yellow onion

> **Serves 4**
>
> Even vegetable haters will love this combination of sweet and tart flavors. Use this recipe to complement a grilled steak or pork chops.

1. Slice the lemon into wedges no thicker than ⅛ inch. In a small saucepan, combine the lemon slices with the butter, honey, vinegar, and salt. Bring to a boil, stirring constantly, for 5 minutes.
2. Core and dice the apple into pieces about ¼-inch square. Do not remove the peel. Add to the lemon mixture and cook on medium heat for about 5 minutes.
3. Stir together the cornstarch and water until you have a light paste. Stir this into the apple-lemon mixture. Bring to a boil, then cook on low heat for about 3 minutes.
4. Snap off the ends of the green beans and discard. Wash the green beans thoroughly in cold water. Peel and slice the onion into ¼-inch rings. Place the green beans and onions in a large saucepan and pour the apple-lemon mixture over them. Cook, covered, for 15 minutes or until the beans are cooked through but not soggy.

Add Some Tartness

Use lemon juice when cooking casseroles or other slow-cooked dishes. Sprinkle a little juice on top and the vegetables will retain their color better. The lemon juice also adds a tang that is a nice substitute for fatty butter.

CHICKEN SKEWERS WITH
SPICY ISLAND MARINADE

For the marinade:
4 scallions
2 garlic cloves
¼ cup fresh lime juice
2 tablespoons chopped parsley
½ teaspoon dried thyme
½ teaspoon dried rosemary
1 fresh jalapeño pepper
⅛ teaspoon hot sauce
½ teaspoon salt
½ teaspoon ground black pepper

For the skewers:
1 pound boneless, skinless
   chicken breast
8 white mushrooms
4 metal or bamboo skewers
2 tablespoons vegetable oil

1. Peel the scallions and garlic. Remove the seeds and stem from the jalapeño pepper. Trim the stems from the mushrooms and clean the mushrooms with a damp cloth.
2. Combine all the marinade ingredients in a food processor and mix until finely chopped.
3. Slice the chicken into 8 equal pieces. Place the chicken in a plastic storage bag with a leak-proof seal. Pour the marinade over the chicken. Refrigerate for at least 3 hours.
4. Remove the chicken from the marinade. Discard the marinade. Thread a rolled-up strip of chicken on a skewer. Add a mushroom and another strip of chicken. Repeat with the remaining skewers.
5. Prepare a charcoal grill or preheat a gas grill to high heat. Lightly oil the grill rack. Grill the skewers on each side for about 5 minutes or until done. Turn the skewers several times to ensure all sides cook evenly.

Boneless Chicken
Buying chicken breasts that are already deboned and skinned is a great time-saver. They cost more, but one way to save money is to buy larger quantities when they are on sale and freeze them.

LONDON BROIL WITH MUSHROOMS

5 garlic cloves
1 green onion
½ cup dry red wine
¼ cup olive oil
2 tablespoons red wine vinegar
1¼ teaspoon Worcestershire
  sauce

2-pound London broil
1 teaspoon salt
1 teaspoon ground black pepper
1 pound fresh mushrooms
1 tablespoon butter

Serves 4

To serve, slice the meat against the grain. Top with mushrooms.

1. Peel and mince 2 of the garlic cloves. Peel and sliver the remaining 3 garlic cloves. Keep separate. Finely chop the green onion, including the green top.
2. In a small mixing bowl, combine the minced garlic, green onion, red wine, oil, vinegar, and Worcestershire sauce.
3. Poke several small holes in the London Broil and place the garlic slivers in the holes. Place the meat in a shallow baking pan and pour the wine mixture over the meat. Cover and refrigerate, turning once, for several hours.
4. Preheat grill to medium-high. Grill the London broil for 3 minutes. Turn and sprinkle the cooked side with salt and pepper. Cook for another 3 minutes or until cooked to your liking.
5. During the last few minutes of cooking the meat, sauté the sliced mushrooms in butter.

STRAWBERRY CHICKEN SALAD

Serves 4

This is a wonderful luncheon meal. Finish the theme by ending with Strawberry Sorbet (page 161).

2 cups diced cooked chicken
1 cup sliced celery
¼ cup chopped red onion
1½ pints fresh strawberries
½ cup mayonnaise
2 tablespoons chutney of your choice

1 tablespoon lemon juice
1 teaspoon grated lemon zest
1 teaspoon salt
1 teaspoon curry powder
4 lettuce leaves
Fresh mint sprigs

1. If necessary, cook the chicken and cut into ½-inch pieces. Slice the celery into ½-inch pieces. Peel the onion and chop into ¼-inch pieces. Remove the stems from the strawberries.
2. In a large bowl, stir together the mayonnaise, chutney, lemon juice, zest, salt, and curry powder, mixing well.
3. Add the chicken, celery, and onion. Toss well, cover, and chill.
4. Just before serving, slice 1 pint of strawberries. Add to the chicken mixture and toss gently.
5. Line a platter of individual serving plates with the lettuce leaves. Mound the chicken mixture on the lettuce. Garnish with the whole strawberries and mint. Serve at once.

Strawberry Garnish

Using a strawberry with the green cap and stem still on, make thin slices nearly up to the cap, being careful not to cut all the way through. Press gently to create a strawberry fan. The color and flavor complement poultry dishes but it looks beautiful with any meal.

SMOKED SALMON SALAD WITH CILANTRO DRESSING

For the dressing:
2 tablespoons plain yogurt
1 tablespoon fresh lemon juice
1 tablespoon white wine vinegar
1 tablespoon minced fresh cilantro
¼ teaspoon salt
⅛ teaspoon freshly ground black pepper
⅛ teaspoon ground red pepper
½ cup olive oil

For the salad:
1 head romaine lettuce
½ pound smoked salmon
1 cup pitted ripe olives
1 (15-ounce) can chickpeas (garbanzo beans)
½ medium-sized red onion

Serves 4

This is excellent served with crusty French bread and a Lemon-Spiked Pineapple Smoothie (page 162).

1. Combine all the dressing ingredients *except* the olive oil in a small bowl. Set aside.
2. Trim the romaine and discard the stem ends. Slice the remaining inner leaves into 1½-inch pieces. Wash and dry the lettuce pieces. Flake the fish into bite-sized pieces. Cut the olives in half. Drain the chickpeas. Cut the onion into thin slices.
3. In a large bowl, combine lettuce, salmon, olives, chickpeas, and onion. Whisk the olive oil into the dressing and pour over the salad. Toss gently.

Olives

Avoid buying canned supermarket-grade factory-pitted olives. They have usually been overprocessed and retain little or no true olive flavor. It is best to select olives from the delicatessen department, or buy good imported olives in a glass jar and pit them by hand.

BURGERS WITH LEMON PEPPER

Makes 8 large burgers

Serve with potato chips and beans for an authentic American meal.

2 pounds lean hamburger
3 tablespoons lemon pepper
1 tablespoon dried thyme
1 tablespoon paprika
1 teaspoon garlic powder

$1/2$ teaspoon granulated sugar
$1/2$ teaspoon salt
$1/4$ teaspoon ground coriander
$1/8$ teaspoon ground cumin
$1/8$ teaspoon cayenne pepper

1. Form the hamburger into 8 equal-sized patties.
2. Stir together all the ingredients *except* the hamburger in a small mixing bowl. Generously sprinkle the mixture on the raw burgers and let stand for 1 hour in the refrigerator.
3. Cook the burgers on broiler or grill until desired doneness.

MARINATED GINGER CHICKEN

Serves 4

Serve with Green Beans in Lemon Honey (page 153) and Strawberry Sorbet (page 161).

1 (2–3 pound) frying chicken
$1/2$ cup lemon juice
$1/2$ cup vegetable oil
$1/4$ cup soy sauce

1 teaspoon fresh grated ginger-root (or 1 tablespoon ground ginger)
1 teaspoon onion salt
$1/4$ teaspoon garlic powder

1. Cut the chicken into serving pieces. Place in a shallow baking dish.
2. In a small bowl, combine the lemon juice, oil, soy sauce, ginger, onion salt, and garlic powder. Pour over the chicken. Cover and refrigerate at least 4 hours or overnight, turning occasionally.
3. Grill or broil for about 20 minutes, basting frequently with the marinade, and turning after 10 minutes. Cook until the meat is no longer pink and the juices run clear.

CALIFORNIA TRI-TIP

1 tablespoon freshly cracked
  peppercorns
2 teaspoons garlic salt
1 teaspoon dry mustard

¼ teaspoon cayenne pepper
2–3 pound tri-tip roast
Oak, mesquite, or hickory
  chips for grilling

> **Serves 6**
>
> This works equally well hot as a main dish, room temperature over lettuce as a salad, or cold in sandwiches.

1. Mix together the pepper, garlic salt, mustard, and cayenne. Rub into the surface of the tri-tip. Cover with plastic wrap and refrigerate overnight.
2. Soak the wood chips in water for at least 30 minutes. Preheat grill to medium. Add the soaked woods chips to the coals.
3. Sear the tri-tip directly over medium heat, turning once, to seal in juices, about 2 minutes on each side. Then grill the tri-tip indirectly over medium heat, turning once, until the internal temperature is about 140°. Grill an additional 30 minutes.
4. Remove from heat and let stand for 5 minutes. Slice diagonally against the grain.

Meat Grades
The higher the grade of meat, the more marbling (fat) contained in the cut. For a healthy alternative, use a lower grade of meat and cook it slowly to tenderize. "Select" is the least fatty grade.

BRUSSELS SPROUTS A L'ORANGE

Serves 4

Serve with Marinated Ginger Chicken (page 158).

4 cups fresh Brussels sprouts
1¼ cups fresh-squeezed orange juice
½ teaspoon cornstarch
¼ teaspoon ground cinnamon

1. In a slow cooker, combine all the ingredients. Stir until well mixed. Cover and cook on low for 1 hour.
2. Uncover and cook on low for 1 additional hour until the sauce has thickened and the Brussels sprouts are tender.

GRILLED RIB-EYE STEAKS WITH ONIONS

Serves 4

Serve with Brussels Sprouts a l'Orange (page 160).

4 large white onions
4 garlic cloves
2 tablespoons olive oil
4 boneless ribeye steaks, 1-inch thick
½ teaspoon salt
½ teaspoon ground black pepper
4 teaspoons dry vermouth

1. Peel and slice the onions. Peel the garlic cloves and split in half.
2. In a large skillet, heat the olive oil on medium; cook the onions in the oil until golden brown, about 10 to 15 minutes. Cover and keep warm.
3. Rub both sides of the steaks with the cut-side of the garlic and season with salt and pepper. Grill the steaks for 3 to 4 minutes on each side, or to the desired degree of doneness.
4. Pour 1 teaspoon vermouth over each steak immediately before removing from the grill. Serve with grilled onions.

STRAWBERRY SORBET

2 cups fresh strawberries
¾ cup orange juice
½ cup 1% milk

¼ cup, plus 1 tablespoon honey
2 egg whites

Serves 8

This is a perfect dessert for Burgers with Lemon Pepper (page 158).

1. Remove the stems from the strawberries.
2. In a blender, combine the berries, orange juice, milk, and the ¼ cup honey. Blend until smooth, about 1 minute. Pour into a 9-inch square baking pan. Cover and freeze until almost firm, about 3 hours.
3. Beat the egg whites with an electric mixer at medium speed until soft peaks form. Increase the speed to high and gradually add the 1 tablespoon honey, beating until stiff peaks form.
4. Break the frozen mixture into chunks. Transfer the pieces to a chilled large bowl. Beat with an electric mixer until smooth. Fold in the egg whites with a rubber spatula.
5. Return the mixture to the baking pan. Cover and freeze until firm, 6 to 8 hours. To serve, scrape across the surface of the frozen mixture with a spoon and mound in dessert dishes.

Making Nonstick Pans

There is no need to buy special nonstick pots and pans. Just use a bit of vinegar before you cook in a new pan the first time. Pour enough vinegar into the pan to cover the bottom of the pan, and then bring it to a boil. Wipe out the pan. Let cool and wash the pan.

MINT JULEP

4 sprigs fresh mint
1 teaspoon fine sugar
1 teaspoon water

Crushed ice
2½ ounces bourbon

1. In a Collins glass, muddle the mint leaves, sugar, and water.
2. Fill the glass with crushed ice and add the bourbon.
3. Garnish with mint and serve with straws.

LEMON-SPIKED PINEAPPLE SMOOTHIE

1 fresh lemon
1 medium-sized ripe pineapple
6 tablespoons freshly squeezed lemon juice

4 cups cold water
Ice

1. Cut the lemon into thin slices and set aside.
2. Peel the pineapple and cut out the core. Cut the fruit into pieces about 1-inch square. Place in a food processor and process to a somewhat smooth, pulpy consistency. Transfer to a large pitcher.
3. Add the lemon juice and cold water. Stir until mixed. Serve in glasses over ice with a thin slice of lemon for garnish.

Chapter 11
SUMMER PICNICS

ZESTY FETA AND OLIVE SALAD	164
AVOCADO AND PEACH SALAD	165
SPINACH SALAD WITH APPLE-AVOCADO DRESSING	166
HONEY DIJON TUNA SALAD	166
POLYNESIAN BANANA SALAD	167
RISOTTO WITH FRESH SUMMER VEGETABLES	167
SUNSHINE BEAN SALAD WITH GOLDEN GATE DRESSING	168
TRICOLOR PEPPER SALAD	169
CALIFORNIA GARDEN SALAD WITH AVOCADO AND SPROUTS	170
SUMMER VEGETABLE SLAW	171
WILD BLACKBERRY PIE	172
FISH HOUSE PUNCH	173
CAPE COD PUNCH	173

ZESTY FETA AND OLIVE SALAD

1 small red onion
1 celery rib
1 small cucumber
1 garlic clove
1 fresh lemon
1 fresh orange
12 small cherry tomatoes
½ cup kalamata olives
2 tablespoons fresh Italian parsley

2 teaspoons fresh oregano
1 teaspoon fresh mint
1 tablespoon fresh cilantro
2 ounces crumbled feta
1 tablespoon olive oil
12 large romaine or butter lettuce leaves
½ teaspoon freshly ground black pepper

1. Remove the skin from the onion and dice into ⅛-inch pieces. Chop the celery into ⅛-inch pieces. Dice ½ of the cucumber into ⅛-inch pieces and cut the other ½ into slices. Remove the peel from the garlic and mince finely. Use the lemon and orange to create 1 teaspoon each of zest. Peel the lemon and orange and cut into thin slices. Cut the cherry tomatoes in half (or quarters if they are large). Pit the olives and cut each into 8 slices. Mince the parsley, oregano, mint, and cilantro.
2. Place the feta in a large bowl and add the onion, celery, diced cucumber, garlic, lemon and orange zest, cherry tomatoes, and olives; mix gently. Add the fresh herbs and olive oil, and toss.
3. Arrange the lettuce leaves on 4 salad plates. Arrange the cucumber, lemon, and orange slices around the sides. Spoon the feta salad on top. Top with freshly ground pepper.

Cracked Black Pepper
Like many seeds, black pepper's best flavor remains locked inside until it's smashed. Place 10 peppercorns at a time on a flat, hard surface. Using a small saucepot or skillet, apply pressure with the heel of your hand to break the seeds a few at a time.

AVOCADO AND PEACH SALAD

1 garlic clove
1 avocado
1 peach
1 small Vidalia onion
⅛ cup water
⅛ cup frozen orange juice concentrate
1 teaspoon rice wine vinegar
1 tablespoon olive oil

½ teaspoon vanilla
1½ tightly packed cups baby arugula
2 tablespoons fresh tarragon leaves
½ teaspoon sea salt
¼ teaspoon freshly ground black pepper

> **Serves 4**
>
> This is a perfect first course for any summer meal. Use it to complement a heavier dish such as a roast or ribs.

1. Crush the garlic with the side of a large knife. Remove the skin. Peel the avocado and dice into ¼-inch pieces. Peel the peach and dice into ¼-inch pieces. Remove the skin from the onion and slice thinly.

2. In a large measuring cup, whisk together the garlic, water, orange juice concentrate, vinegar, oil, and vanilla until well mixed.

3. Prepare the salad by arranging layers of the arugula and tarragon, then the avocado, peach, and onions. Drizzle the salad with the orange juice vinaigrette. Season with salt and pepper.

Salad Dressing

Greens should be thoroughly dry before adding dressing, to enable it to stick to the leaves. Don't dress a salad until you are ready to serve it. Use only enough to coat the greens lightly. If desired, you can serve additional dressing at the table.

SPINACH SALAD WITH APPLE-AVOCADO DRESSING

Serves 4

This is a wonderful first course for virtually any meal. It complements any meat or pasta meal.

1 ripe avocado
1 garlic clove
1 small red onion
6 radishes
¼ cup unsweetened apple juice
1 teaspoon cider vinegar

1 teaspoon soy sauce
½ teaspoon Worcestershire sauce
2 teaspoons olive oil
2½ tightly packed cups spinach greens
½ cup bean sprouts

1. Remove the skin and pit from the avocado. Peel and mince the garlic. Peel the onion and slice thinly. Clean the radishes and slice thinly.
2. Place the avocado, garlic, apple juice, cider vinegar, soy sauce, Worcestershire sauce, and oil in a food processor or blender; process until smooth.
3. In a large bowl, combine the onion, radishes, spinach greens, and bean sprouts; mix well. Pour the dressing over the salad and toss.

HONEY DIJON TUNA SALAD

Serves 2

Variation: To make a complete meal, add 1 cup cooked pasta to the salad before placing on the greens. Serve with fresh melon cubes.

½ cup water-packed tuna
2 celery ribs
1 small yellow onion
1 small red pepper
8 ounces nonfat plain yogurt

2 teaspoons Dijon mustard
2 teaspoons lemon juice
½ teaspoon honey
2 tablespoons raisins
2 cups iceberg lettuce

1. Drain the tuna and flake with a fork. Cut the celery into ¼-inch pieces. Remove the skin from the onion and cut into ¼-inch pieces. Remove the stem and core from the red pepper. Chop ½ of the red pepper into ¼-inch pieces. Slice the other ½ into ¼-inch strips.
2. Add the tuna, celery, onion, chopped red pepper, yogurt, mustard, lemon juice, honey, and raisins to a medium-sized bowl; mix well.
3. Arrange lettuce leaves on plates and top with the tuna salad. Use the red pepper strips for garnish.

POLYNESIAN BANANA SALAD

4 bananas
1 cup coconut cream
2 tablespoons curry powder

1 cup soft raisins
4 teaspoons shredded coconut

Serves 4

Excellent with spicy food and rice, this rich, sweet salad can be part of a meal, snack, or dessert.

1. Slice the bananas about ½-inch thick on a slight diagonal.
2. Whisk together the coconut cream and curry powder. Add the bananas and raisins. Toss gently to coat.
3. Transfer to a serving dish and sprinkle with the shredded coconut.

Plump Raisins

If you find your raisins are a bit too dry, soak them in a light white wine for an hour or so. They will plump up nicely while the wine will add extra flavor to your dish.

RISOTTO WITH FRESH SUMMER VEGETABLES

1 tablespoon butter
1 large white onion
1 cup chopped fresh zucchini
1 cup uncooked white rice
4 cups chicken broth

1 cup fresh green beans
½ teaspoon salt
½ teaspoon ground black pepper
1 cup fresh snow peas
⅓ cup chopped fresh parsley

Serves 8

While it is excellent served warm, this is a great dish to make 1 or 2 days ahead of time and serve cold at your picnic. Bring assorted gourmet crackers and cheeses as well as a light white wine.

1. Melt the butter in a small skillet on medium-high heat. Peel and chop the onion into ¼-inch pieces. Sauté the onions in the butter for 3 to 5 minutes, until translucent. Drain.
2. Chop the zucchini into 1-inch pieces. Place the onions, zucchini, uncooked white rice, chicken broth, green beans, salt, and pepper in a slow cooker. Mix well. Cover and cook on low setting for 7 to 8 hours or until the rice is soft. Add the peas and cook for 1 to 2 hours more.
3. Chop the parsley into ¼-inch lengths, add it to the slow cooker, and stir well. Cook, uncovered, for 15 to 30 minutes.

SUNSHINE BEAN SALAD
WITH GOLDEN GATE DRESSING

Serves 8

Perfect as a first course
with fried chicken
or hamburgers.

For the dressing:
⅓ cup granulated sugar
½ teaspoon dry mustard
1 teaspoon salt
2 tablespoons all-purpose flour
1 egg
½ cup white wine vinegar
1½ cups water
1 tablespoon butter

For the salad:
1 (16-ounce) can chickpeas
   (garbanzo beans)
1 (8-ounce) can corn kernels
1 cup diced celery
½ cup chopped red onion
2 tablespoons diced pimientos
¼ cup diced green bell peppers

1. To make the dressing, stir together the sugar, mustard, salt, and flour in a small bowl. In another small bowl, beat the egg with a fork, then beat into the dry mixture.
2. In a small saucepan, combine the vinegar, water, and butter; cook over low heat until the mixture simmers. Remove from the heat and gradually add the egg mixture, stirring vigorously.
3. Return to heat and cook, stirring constantly, until smooth and thick, 2 or 3 minutes.
4. Drain the chickpeas and corn kernels. Dice the celery. Peel and chop the onion into ¼-inch pieces. Dice the pimientos into ⅛-inch pieces. Remove the seeds and stem from the green pepper and chop into ¼-inch pieces.
5. Combine the chickpeas, corn, celery, onion, pimiento, and green pepper in a large glass bowl. Moisten to taste with the dressing. Chill before serving.

TRICOLOR PEPPER SALAD

2 red bell peppers
2 green bell peppers
2 yellow bell peppers
2 celery stalks
2 large cucumbers
1 large red onion
2 cups cherry tomatoes
4 garlic cloves

¼ cup chopped fresh parsley
3 tablespoons lime juice
1 tablespoon lemon juice
2 tablespoons white wine
   vinegar
1 tablespoon olive oil
½ teaspoon salt
¼ teaspoon cayenne pepper

Serves 8

Serve with hot dogs,
hamburgers,
or grilled chicken.

1. Remove the stems and seeds from the bell peppers and chop into ½-inch pieces. Chop the celery into ¼-inch pieces. Peel the cucumbers and dice into ¼-inch pieces. Peel the onion and chop into ½-inch pieces. Halve the cherry tomatoes. Peel and mince the garlic cloves. Roughly chop the parsley.
2. In a large salad bowl, combine the bell peppers, celery, cucumbers, onion, and tomatoes; mix well.
3. In a small bowl, stir together the garlic, parsley, lime and lemon juices, vinegar, oil, salt, and cayenne pepper. Add the dressing to the salad and toss well to combine.
4. Cover and chill for 1 hour, tossing occasionally before serving.

Seedless Cucumbers

If slippery cucumber seeds bother you, look for specifically grown seedless cucumbers in the grocery store. These longer, thin cucumbers taste just as good.

CALIFORNIA GARDEN SALAD WITH AVOCADO AND SPROUTS

Serves 4

The fruity taste of large, green Florida avocados gives this salad a lighter, more summer flavor, although the smaller Haas avocadoes are more authentic for this California salad.

For the dressing:

1 tablespoon fresh-squeezed
   lemon juice
3 tablespoons extra-virgin
   olive oil
1 tablespoon chopped shallots
½ teaspoon salt
¼ teaspoon freshly ground
   black pepper

For the salad:

2 heads Boston or
   Bibb lettuce
2 large red tomatoes
1 ripe avocado
1 cup alfalfa sprouts

1. Peel and mince the shallots. Combine all the dressing ingredients in a small bowl, mixing well.
2. Wash the lettuce and trim away outside leaves. Core the tomatoes and cut into 8 wedges each. Remove the skin and pit from the avocado. Cut the avocado into 8 wedges.
3. Arrange the lettuce leaves, stem-end in, on 4 plates, making a flower-petal pattern. You don't need to use the smallest inner leaves.
4. Toss the tomatoes in 1 tablespoon of the dressing. Place 4 onto each salad. Toss the avocado pieces with 1 tablespoon dressing and place 2 wedges on each salad. Divide the sprouts into 4 bunches and place a bunch in the center of each salad. Drizzle the salads with the remaining dressing.

Avocados

Avocados are one of the few vegetables high in fat. Substitute cucumber for avocado for a fresh flavor with none of the fat grams. Choose a seedless cucumber and remove the skin before dicing it.

SUMMER VEGETABLE SLAW

1 small head green cabbage
2 medium carrots
1 red bell pepper
1 green bell pepper
1 yellow bell pepper
1 small red onion
2 ears fresh sweet corn
1/4 pound snow peas

12 fresh green beans
1/2 teaspoon granulated sugar
1/4 cup cider vinegar
1 tablespoon peanut oil
1/2 teaspoon celery seeds
1/2 teaspoon salt
1/2 teaspoon ground black
  pepper

Serves 8

This is an excellent accompaniment to crispy fried foods like chicken and onion rings.

1. Quarter and core the cabbage. Slice as thinly as possible. Peel the carrots, then shave as thinly as possible. (Discard the small amount that can't be shaved.) Remove the stems and seeds from the bell peppers and cut into fine julienne strips. Peel the onion and cut into julienne strips. Cut the corn kernels from the cob.
2. Combine all the vegetables in a large mixing bowl. Mix together the sugar, vinegar, oil, celery seeds, salt, and pepper. Toss the vegetables with the dressing. Allow to sit for at least 10 minutes before serving.

Wilted Spinach Salad

Stir-fry fresh spinach in a little butter or olive oil until wilted. Sprinkle with allspice, onion powder, or a splash of lemon juice. Add a little crumbled bacon and chopped, hard-boiled egg. Serve with simple oil and vinegar for dressing.

WILD BLACKBERRY PIE

Serves 12

This recipe also can be used to create a mixed berry pie. Use a combination of black raspberries, blueberries, and blackberries.

Uncooked pastry for a double-crust, 9-inch pie
½ cup black walnuts
4 cups blackberries
1 tablespoon lemon juice

½ cup granulated sugar
½ packed cup brown sugar
½ teaspoon ground cinnamon
3 tablespoons all-purpose flour
5 tablespoons butter

1. Preheat oven to 350°. Line a deep-dish 9-inch pie plate with ½ of the pastry, leaving 1 inch of the pastry hanging over the edge of the plate. Chop the nuts.
2. In a large bowl, combine the nuts, blackberries, lemon juice, sugars, cinnamon, and flour; mix lightly. Spoon into the prepared shell. Dot with 3 tablespoons of the butter cut into small pieces.
3. On a lightly floured work surface, roll out the remaining pastry into a thin round and cut into ½-inch-wide strips. Moisten the edge of the bottom pastry with water. Arrange the pastry strips on top of the pie, forming a lattice top. Trim the ends of the strips as necessary and press the ends together with the bottom crust.
4. Turn the edge of the bottom crust and strips under and flute to make an attractive rim. Melt the 2 remaining tablespoons of butter over a low heat in a small saucepan. Brush the lattice and edges with the melted butter. Sprinkle lightly with cinnamon and sugar, if desired.
5. Bake for 45 minutes or until the top crust is golden.

Freeze Nuts

Squirrels know to freeze their nuts under the cold ground in winter. The reason is that nuts go rancid within a couple of months at room temperature. Store them in the freezer in airtight containers.

FISH HOUSE PUNCH

½ cup fine sugar
1½ cups lemon juice
1 pint peach brandy
1 pint light rum

2 bottles dry white wine
1 quart sparkling water
Ice

Makes 24 servings

The perfect punch for an outdoor summer gathering with fresh fruit and light hors d'oeuvres.

1. Dissolve the sugar in the lemon juice and brandy. Add the rum and wine. Stir well. Refrigerate.
2. Pour into a punch bowl over ice. Add the club soda just before serving.

CAPE COD PUNCH

½ cup fine sugar
2 quarts cranberry juice
1 quart orange juice
½ cup lemon juice

3 cups vodka
Ice
1 quart sparkling water

Makes 24 servings

Serve with Risotto with Fresh Summer Vegetables (page 167).

1. Dissolve the sugar in the juices in a large bowl. Add the vodka and stir well.
2. Pour over ice in a punch bowl. Add the water just before serving.

Chilled Cups

For a delightful drink presentation for a summer party, chill the drink glasses and keep them in a cooler outside. As you fill drinks, grab an ice-cold glass and give people a frosty treat on a steamy day.

CHAPTER 12

FOURTH OF JULY

GRILLED CINNAMON PORK TENDERLOINS	176
ORANGE-AVOCADO SLAW	176
CLASSIC AMERICAN POTATO SALAD	177
JUMBO BEER-BATTERED ONION RINGS	177
THREE-BEAN SALAD	178
FRIED GREEN TOMATOES	178
DEVILED EGGS	179
FRIED CHICKEN	180
GRILLED ZUCCHINI WITH BALSAMIC VINEGAR	181
ALL-AMERICAN BARBECUED CHICKEN	182
BARBECUED PORK AND BEANS	183
HAM BARBECUE	183
SUMMERTIME STRAWBERRY SOUP	184
BUBBLY BERRY BLAST	185
STRAWBERRY PIE	186
CLASSIC APPLE PIE	187
KEY LIME PIE	188

GRILLED CINNAMON PORK TENDERLOINS

4 teaspoons soy sauce
4 teaspoons burgundy wine
2 teaspoons brown sugar
¼ teaspoon honey

¼ teaspoon garlic powder
¼ teaspoon ground cinnamon
4 (8-ounce) pork tenderloins

1. Combine the soy sauce, burgundy wine, brown sugar, honey, garlic powder, and ground cinnamon in a sealable plastic bag; shake well. Add the tenderloins and shake gently until the meat is well coated. Place in the refrigerator for at least 1 hour.
2. Heat coals or gas grill until moderately hot. Grill the tenderloins on both sides until meat thermometer hits 160°. Allow the meat to rest for 10 minutes in its juices.

ORANGE-AVOCADO SLAW

1 avocado
¼ cup orange juice
½ teaspoon curry powder
⅛ teaspoon ground cumin
¼ teaspoon granulated sugar
1 teaspoon white wine vinegar

1 tablespoon olive oil
5 cups broccoli slaw mix
½ teaspoon sea salt
¼ teaspoon freshly ground black pepper

1. Peel the avocado, remove the pit, and chop the meat into ¼-inch pieces.
2. In a medium-sized bowl, whisk together the orange juice, curry powder, cumin, sugar, and vinegar. Add the oil in a stream, whisking until emulsified.
3. In a large bowl, toss the avocado with the slaw mix. Drizzle with the vinaigrette. Chill until ready to serve, and season with the salt and pepper.

CLASSIC AMERICAN POTATO SALAD

2 pounds potatoes (any variety)
1 small carrot
¾ cup mayonnaise
2 teaspoons Dijon mustard
1 teaspoon granulated sugar
½ teaspoon salt
¼ teaspoon ground black pepper
1 tablespoon Italian parsley

Serves 8

For a fun treat, try making this potato salad with one of the specialty potatoes such as the purple or Yukon gold varieties.

1. Peel and cut the potatoes into ½-inch cubes. Boil in salted water until soft. Drain. Peel and grate the carrot. Roughly chop the parsley.
2. Whisk together the mayonnaise, mustard, sugar, salt, and pepper. Add the potatoes and carrot. Toss gently until the potatoes are all coated. Garnish with chopped parsley.

JUMBO BEER-BATTERED ONION RINGS

Peanut oil, for frying
2 extra-large eggs
1 (12-ounce) bottle pilsner or lager beer
½ cup peanut oil
3 cups cornstarch
½ teaspoon salt
2 extra-large Spanish or Bermuda onions

Serves 4

Who can resist this all-American treat? They are a must-have for any kid's party or backyard barbecue.

1. Heat oil to 360° in a medium-sized deep fryer or deep skillet.
2. Beat the eggs. Whisk together the eggs, beer, ½ cup oil, 2 cups of the cornstarch, and the salt until it makes a thick batter.
3. Remove the skin from the onions. Cut them into 1-inch-thick slices. Separate into rings. Dredge the onion rings in the remaining 1 cup cornstarch, dip into the batter, and add to the pot 1 at a time, making sure the first has started to sizzle before adding the next. Flip each ring so it cooks evenly on both sides. Drain on paper towels.

THREE-BEAN SALAD

1 (16-ounce) can green beans
1 (16-ounce) can yellow wax
   beans
1 (16-ounce) can red kidney
   beans
1 medium-sized red onion

½ cup granulated sugar
⅔ cup vinegar
⅓ cup vegetable oil
½ teaspoon salt
⅛ teaspoon ground black
   pepper

1. Drain the beans. Peel the onion and slice thinly, then cut the slices into quarters.
2. Whisk together the sugar, vinegar, oil, salt, and pepper.
3. In a large bowl, combine the beans, onion, and dressing; mix well. Chill for at least 4 hours, mixing occasionally. Drain before serving.

FRIED GREEN TOMATOES

2 large green tomatoes
1 teaspoon salt
1 teaspoon freshly ground
   black pepper

1 cup yellow cornmeal
1 cup extra-virgin olive oil

1. Slice the tomatoes about ¼-inch thick. Season both sides with salt and pepper. Dredge the tomato slices in the cornmeal, coating well on both sides.
2. Heat the oil in a medium-sized skillet over medium heat. Fry the tomatoes in the oil until golden brown, turning them only once. Drain excess oil on paper towels. Serve immediately.

DEVILED EGGS

4 large eggs
2½ tablespoons mayonnaise
1½ teaspoons Dijon mustard
½ teaspoon hot red pepper
  sauce
½ teaspoon salt

½ teaspoon ground white
  pepper
2 tablespoons minced fresh
  chives
1 teaspoon paprika

Makes 8

This update of a summer tradition is sure to appeal to traditionalists as well as newcomers to the deviled egg scene.

1. Place the eggs in a medium-sized saucepan and cover with water. Bring to boil, reduce to a simmer, and cook for 9 minutes. Plunge the eggs into a bowl filled with ice water. Allow the eggs to cool completely.
2. Carefully peel the shells from the eggs. Cut the eggs in half and remove the yolks from the whites. Place the yolks in a bowl and add the mayonnaise, mustard, hot pepper sauce, salt, pepper, and chives. With the back of a fork, mash all of the ingredients until blended.
3. Fill the egg whites with the yolk mixture using a teaspoon or a pastry bag fitted with a star tip. Dust with paprika. Chill until served.

Raw Eggs

Raw eggs can be harmful to some people, especially pregnant women, infants, and people with immune disorders. Although foods such as eggnog and mayonnaise contain raw eggs, these foods are pasteurized so they pose no risk. You can find pasteurized eggs at most large grocery stores.

FRIED CHICKEN

Serves 4

Serve with Three-Bean
Salad (page 178) and
Strawberry Pie
(page 186).

3-pound fryer chicken
1½ cups buttermilk
½ cup all-purpose flour
1½ teaspoons salt
½ teaspoon black pepper

1 teaspoon paprika
½ teaspoon garlic powder
½ teaspoon grated nutmeg
3 cups vegetable oil

1. Wash the chicken and cut into 8 serving pieces.
2. Pour the buttermilk into a large nonmetallic bowl. Add the chicken pieces and turn to coat. Cover and refrigerate, turning occasionally, for 2 to 3 hours.
3. In a large bowl, combine the flour with the salt, pepper, paprika, garlic powder, and nutmeg. Remove the chicken pieces from the buttermilk and shake off any excess liquid. Allow to drain. Toss the chicken pieces in a plastic food storage bag with the flour mixture to ensure the pieces are evenly coated.
4. Pour ¾ inch of oil into a deep skillet and heat to 350°.
5. Fry the chicken in batches to avoid overcrowding the pan. Cook for about 10 to 15 minutes, turning occasionally so the pieces cook to an even crispy golden brown. Drain the chicken on paper towels.

Roasting Chickens
Roasting chickens are older and larger than broiler-fryers, usually weighing from 4 to 6 pounds. They are not as tender as broiler-fryers but when cooked by a slow method, like roasting, they become tender and flavorful.

GRILLED ZUCCHINI WITH BALSAMIC VINEGAR

3 garlic cloves
4 medium zucchini
¼ cup extra-virgin olive oil
½ teaspoon salt
¼ teaspoon ground black pepper

2 tablespoons balsamic vinegar
¼ cup coarsely chopped fresh herbs (mint, basil, chives, parsley, etc.)

Serves 6

Serve with Fried Chicken (page 180) or Grilled Cinnamon Pork Tenderloins (page 176).

1. Peel the garlic and chop finely. Scrub the zucchini and cut in half lengthwise.
2. Heat the oil in a small saucepan over low heat. Add the garlic and cook until just fragrant. Remove from the heat.
3. Preheat the grill to high temperature. Brush the zucchini with the garlic oil and season with salt and pepper. Grill the zucchini, skin-side down, until it begins to soften, about 3 minutes. Turn, and cook the other side until tender.
4. Cut each piece of zucchini in half at an angle into 2 or 3 pieces and place in a bowl. Drizzle the vinegar over the zucchini and add the chopped herbs and the remaining garlic oil. Toss well and season with salt and pepper.

Chopping Fresh Herbs

Although recipes might call for chopping leafy herbs, it's best to bunch gentle leaves like basil, oregano, or mint into small stacks, then slice them against the cutting board with the sharpest knife you can find. Chopping can result in unattractive black edges, clumps, and rapid spoilage.

ALL-AMERICAN BARBECUED CHICKEN

Serves 8

This sauce is equally good used for ribs or pork chops.

2 (3-pound) roasting chickens
1 medium-sized yellow onion
2 tablespoons vegetable oil
2 (15-ounce) cans tomato sauce
1 cup red wine vinegar

1 teaspoon prepared mustard
½ cup dark molasses
¼ cup Worcestershire sauce
⅓ packed cup brown sugar
¾ teaspoon cayenne pepper

1. Split the chickens in half. Peel the onion and chop into ¼-inch pieces. Preheat grill to medium temperature.
2. Heat the oil in a skillet over medium heat. Add the onion and sauté until tender, about 10 minutes.
3. Mix in the tomato sauce, vinegar, mustard, molasses, Worcestershire sauce, brown sugar, and cayenne. Heat to boiling over high heat, stirring frequently. Reduce heat and simmer, uncovered, for 30 to 45 minutes or until the sauce thickens slightly. Reserve 1½ cups of the mixture to serve as a sauce.
4. Place the chicken on the grill over medium heat. Cook for 25 to 30 minutes. Turn and baste generously with sauce. Cook for 25 minutes more, turning the pieces often and basting frequently. To test for doneness, pierce the chicken with a fork. The juices will run clear when the chicken is fully cooked.

Adding Smoky Flavor to Vegetarian Dishes

For a smoky flavor, most nonvegetarian recipes call for smoked pork bones or bacon. Vegetarians can achieve a similar result by adding smoked chilies, such as chipotles (smoked jalapeños) to those dishes.

BARBECUED PORK AND BEANS

2 tablespoons chopped yellow
  onion
1 pound canned or fresh
  baked beans
½ cup prepared mustard

½ cup prepared ketchup
4 lean pork chops
¼ cup lemon juice
¼ cup granulated sugar

Serves 4

Serve with Classic Apple Pie (page 187) for dessert.

1. Chop the onion into ¼-inch pieces. Mix with the beans and place in the bottom of a slow cooker.
2. Spread the mustard and ketchup over both sides of the pork chops. Sprinkle both sides with the lemon juice and sugar.
3. Lay the pork chops on top of the beans. If possible, do not layer them. Cook on low heat for 4 to 6 hours.

HAM BARBECUE

2 pounds chopped ham
1 bottle chili sauce
½ cup ketchup

½ cup water
¼ cup corn syrup
8 whole-wheat bulky rolls

Serves 8

This is the perfect meal for those not-quite-perfect summer days. Cold temperatures and rain won't take the fun out of this summer meal.

1. Mix together all the ingredients in a slow cooker. Cover and cook on low setting for 1 to 2 hours, stirring occasionally.
2. Serve on the whole-wheat rolls.

Make-Ahead Meals
Cooked meats can be refrigerated for up to 3 months. Freeze in 1- or 2-cup measures. Thaw in the refrigerator or microwave. Do not refreeze thawed meats that have not been cooked.

SUMMERTIME STRAWBERRY SOUP

Serves 6

Serve as a dessert
for Fried Chicken
(page 180).

3 cups strawberries
½ teaspoon ground cinnamon
4 ounces frozen orange juice
   concentrate
½ cup water
¼ cup dry red wine

¼ teaspoon ground cloves
2 tablespoons cornstarch
2 tablespoons water
1 pint vanilla frozen yogurt
1 pint plain yogurt

1. Clean the strawberries and remove the stems. Mix the strawberries, cinnamon, orange juice concentrate, water, wine, and cloves in a large saucepan. Bring to a boil, reduce heat to medium-low, and simmer for 10 minutes.
2. Mix together the cornstarch and water in a small bowl. Stir ⅓ cup of the strawberry mixture into the cornstarch mixture until smooth and then add to the saucepan. Bring to a boil, stirring until thick, about 5 minutes.
3. Remove from the heat, let cool for 1 hour or longer, and then add both yogurts. Stir until the frozen yogurt melts. Cover and refrigerate for 1 hour before serving.

Freezing Soups and Stews

Label all items and use within 3 months. When freezing stews, leave the potatoes out. Undercook the vegetables so they don't become mushy when reheated.

BUBBLY BERRY BLAST

1 cup fresh strawberries
1 cup fresh blueberries
2 tablespoons unflavored
 gelatin

½ cup frozen, unsweetened
 apple juice concentrate
3 cups unsweetened sparkling
 water

Serves 6

A delicious treat on a hot summer day.

1. Wash the blueberries and strawberries. Slice the strawberries into eighths.
2. Mix the gelatin and apple juice in a small saucepan. Stir and let stand for 1 minute. Place the mixture over low heat and stir until completely dissolved, about 3 minutes.
3. Stir in the sparkling water. Refrigerate until the mixture begins to gel or is the consistency of unbeaten egg whites.
4. Fold the fruit into the partially thickened gelatin mixture. Pour into a 6-cup mold. Refrigerate for 4 hours or until firm.

Microwave It

Try this in the microwave: Blend the gelatin and apple juice. Let stand for 1 minute, then heat in a microwave-safe bowl on high setting for 45 seconds. Stir the mixture until the gelatin is completely dissolved. Continue with steps 3 and 4.

STRAWBERRY PIE

Serves 8

Serve with Fried
Chicken (page 180).

2 pints fresh strawberries
1 prebaked 9-inch pie shell
1 pound cream cheese, softened
¼ cup granulated sugar
2 teaspoons grated lemon rind
4 tablespoons lemon juice,
   divided

2 tablespoons cornstarch
¼ cup water
1 (12-ounce) jar strawberry
   preserves
1 container whipped cream

1. Clean the strawberries, remove the hulls, and slice. Put the pie shell into a 9-inch pie pan.
2. In a medium-sized bowl, combine the cream cheese, sugar, lemon rind, and 2 tablespoons of the lemon juice; mix well. Spread in the bottom of the prebaked pie shell. Top with the fresh strawberries.
3. In a small saucepan, combine the cornstarch and water. Stir well to dissolve the cornstarch, then stir in the preserves. Bring to a boil, stirring constantly. Cook and stir for about 5 minutes, or until thick and clear.
4. Remove from heat and stir in the remaining 2 tablespoons lemon juice. Let cool to room temperature. Pour the cooled preserves over the berries. Chill well.
5. Garnish with whipped cream right before serving.

Fat Facts

Unsaturated fats are better for your body than saturated fats. Animal fats are saturated fats and most vegetable fats are unsaturated fats. But remember, coconut and palm oil are saturated vegetable fats and are used in most bakery and processed snack foods.

CLASSIC APPLE PIE

1 prepared 9-inch graham
   cracker pie crust
6 medium-sized tart apples
   such as Granny Smith
½ cup granulated sugar
1 teaspoon ground cinnamon

¼ teaspoon ground nutmeg
¼ teaspoon salt
¾ cup water
1 tablespoon lemon juice
2 tablespoons cornstarch
1 tablespoon butter

> **Serves 8**
>
> Tradition says this must be served with a huge scoop of vanilla ice cream, preferably 1 or 2 hours before the Fourth of July fireworks begin.

1. Put the pie crust in the pie pan. Peel the apples and slice thinly. Preheat oven to 350°.
2. Combine the sugar, cinnamon, nutmeg, and salt in a large saucepan. Stir in ½ cup of the water, the lemon juice, and apples. Place over medium heat and stir gently until the mixture comes to a boil. Cover and simmer for 13 to 20 minutes or until the apples are almost tender, stirring occasionally.
3. Meanwhile, in a small bowl, dissolve the cornstarch in the remaining ¼ cup water. When the apples are done cooking, stir in the cornstarch until thickened and clear. Stir in the butter.
4. Pour the apple filling into the pie crust. Bake for 30 minutes or until bubbling hot and the apples are tender.

Blender or Food Processor

They seem interchangeable sometimes, but they're not. Blenders and food processors are different tools with different strengths. For ultra-smooth purées, a blender is the first choice. For rougher purées or chopping jobs with drier ingredients, use a processor.

KEY LIME PIE

½ cup key lime juice
1 teaspoon key lime zest
4 eggs
1 tablespoon unflavored gelatin
1 cup granulated sugar, divided
¼ teaspoon salt

¼ cup water
3 drops green food coloring
1 cup whipped cream
1 prebaked 9-inch pastry shell
1 tablespoon pistachio nuts
1 key lime

1. Juice key limes to yield ½ cup of juice. Grate the rind of a key lime to yield 1 teaspoon zest. Separate the egg yolks from the egg whites.
2. In a saucepan, combine the gelatin, ½ cup of the sugar, and the salt; mix well.
3. In a bowl, beat together the lime juice, egg yolks, and water until well blended; stir into the gelatin mixture. Place over medium heat and cook, stirring, just until the mixture comes to a boil.
4. Remove from the heat. Stir in the 1 teaspoon grated rind. Add the food coloring. Chill, stirring occasionally, until the mixture mounds slightly when dropped from a spoon.
5. Whip the cream until stiff.
6. In a large bowl, beat the egg whites until soft peaks form. Gradually add the remaining ½ cup sugar, beating until stiff peaks form. Fold the gelatin mixture into the egg whites. Fold in ½ of the whipped cream. Pile into the pastry shell and chill until firm.
7. Grate the pistachio nuts and thinly slice the remaining key lime. Use the remaining whipped cream, the nuts, and lime slices for garnish.

SWEET CORN PUDDING	190
ITALIAN BEETS	190
SPICY CHILLED SHRIMP	191
FENNEL- AND GARLIC-CRUSTED PORK ROAST	192
GRILLED BEEF AND ONION KEBABS	193
BABY BACK RIBS WITH SAUERKRAUT	194
BALSAMIC-MARINATED BEEF TENDERLOIN	195
SPICY COLD PEARS	196
ORANGE CUPS WITH LEMON CREAM	196
CHAMPAGNE-MARINATED SUMMER BERRIES	197
CHEERY CHERRY CRISPY	197
PLANTER'S PUNCH	198
CARIBBEAN SUNSET	198

SWEET CORN PUDDING

Serves 8

Serve to complement
Baby Back Ribs with
Sauerkraut
(page 194).

2 (10-ounce) cans whole-kernel
   corn with juice
3 (10-ounce) cans creamed corn

2 cups corn muffin mix
½ pound margarine, softened
1 cup sour cream

Mix together all the ingredients in a medium-sized mixing bowl. Pour into a slow cooker. Cover and heat on low setting for 2 to 3 hours.

ITALIAN BEETS

Serves 8

Serve this to comple-
ment Grilled Beef and
Onion Kebabs
(page 193).

4 medium beets
3 cups water

1 cup Italian salad dressing
¼ cup balsamic vinegar

Remove the tops and stems from the beets. Peel the beets and slice into ¼-inch-thick rounds. Mix together with the water, dressing, and vinegar in a slow cooker. Add the beets to the mixture. Cover and cook on low setting for 9 to 10 hours.

SPICY CHILLED SHRIMP

3 pounds fresh shrimp
3 fresh jalapeño chilies
3 garlic cloves
½ cup chopped fresh cilantro
3 fresh lemons
1 large red onion
¾ cup olive oil

¼ cup white wine vinegar
3 tablespoons fresh lemon juice
¼ teaspoon cayenne pepper
1 teaspoon salt
½ teaspoon ground white
   pepper

Serves 12

Keep the shrimp chilled and put the serving bowl on ice while serving.

1. Peel and devein the shrimp, leaving the tails on. Remove the stem and seeds from the jalapeño peppers and mince the peppers. Peel and mince the garlic cloves. Chop the cilantro. Slice the lemons. Peel and slice the onion.
2. Boil the shrimp in fresh water in a large pot until pink and opaque, about 3 minutes. When done, chill the shrimp in ice water. Drain and place in the refrigerator.
3. Whisk together the chilies, garlic, cilantro, olive oil, vinegar, lemon juice, cayenne pepper, salt, and white pepper until well blended. Pour over the shrimp. Toss to coat.
4. Layer the shrimp, lemon slices, and onion in a large glass bowl. Cover and refrigerate for 4 hours.

Flavor Your Oil

To infuse oil with flavor and complexity, stuff herbs, spices, and garlic cloves into a bottle of it, and steep for at least 3 days. Fine olive oil becomes a transcendent condiment when perfumed by rosemary, thyme, savory, garlic, peppercorns, dried mushrooms, or truffles.

FENNEL- AND GARLIC-CRUSTED PORK ROAST

Serves 6

Serve with Italian Beets (page 190).

1 small head fennel
½ cup coarsely chopped onion
6 garlic cloves
¼ cup chopped assorted fresh herbs (thyme, sage, rosemary, parsley, oregano, etc.)

4½-pound pork rib roast, tied
2 tablespoons olive oil
2 teaspoons fennel seeds
1 teaspoon freshly ground black pepper
Salt to cover meat

1. Coarsely chop the fennel. Peel the onion and garlic, and chop roughly. Roughly chop the herbs.
2. In a blender or food processor, combine the fennel, onion, garlic, and olive oil; purée into a paste. Add the herbs, fennel seeds, and pepper; pulse to combine.
3. With a small, sharp knife, make shallow diamond cuts in the skin of the pork roast. Season the meat all over with salt, rubbing it in well. Rub the garlic-fennel paste over the roast to cover it with a layer about ¼-inch thick. Cover and refrigerate for up to 8 hours. Remove from the refrigerator and let stand at room temperature for about 20 minutes.
4. Preheat oven to 375°.
5. Transfer the roast to a roasting pan with a rack. Roast for about 1 hour and 15 minutes or until the internal temperature reads 150° on a meat thermometer. Remove the roast from the oven and allow to rest for at least 20 minutes. Slice the roast into thick chops.

What Is Fennel?

Fennel is a broad bulblike vegetable cultivated in the Mediterranean and the United States. In many cultures, it has long been believed to have medicinal qualities. Both the base and stems can be eaten raw as a flavorful addition to salads. Fennel can be cooked in a variety of ways, including braising, grilling, roasting, and sautéing. Fennel is often mislabeled as "sweet anise." The flavor of fennel is much lighter and sweeter than licorice-tasting anise.

GRILLED BEEF AND ONION KEBABS

1½ pounds boneless sirloin
   steak
12 pearl onions
1 tablespoon minced garlic
4 teaspoons finely ground
   whole coriander seeds
4 teaspoons finely ground
   anise seeds

1 tablespoon ground paprika
¼ teaspoon cayenne pepper
1 teaspoon salt, divided
½ teaspoon ground black
   pepper, divided
½ cup olive oil, divided

Serves 4

Serve with Strawberry
Sorbet (page 161)
for dessert.

1. Trim excess fat from the steak and cut the meat into 1-inch cubes. Peel and mince the garlic. Peel the pearl onions. Preheat grill to medium heat.
2. Place the ground coriander and anise seeds in a medium-sized bowl. Add the garlic, paprika, cayenne pepper, ½ of the salt, ½ of the black pepper, and ¼ cup of the olive oil; stir until combined. Add the sirloin cubes and stir to coat. Set aside.
3. In a medium-sized bowl, combine the onions, the rest of the salt and pepper, and the remaining olive oil. Toss to coat.
4. Divide the steaks cubes and onions among 8 skewers. Thread the meat and onions on the skewers, alternating a steak cube with an onion.
5. Grill the kebabs until well browned and medium-rare, 5 to 7 minutes.

Preparing Pearl Onions

When using pearl onions, cook them first in boiling water for 3 minutes. Plunge them into cold water. Remove them from the water and cut off the ends before easily removing the stems.

BABY BACK RIBS WITH SAUERKRAUT

Serves 4

Serve with Italian Beets (page 190) to add color.

3 pounds baby back ribs
1 (32-ounce) container sauerkraut
3 cups shredded red cabbage
4 garlic cloves
1 (14½-ounce) can stewed tomatoes

2 tablespoons, plus 1 teaspoon paprika
1 teaspoon salt
1 teaspoon ground black pepper

1. Trim the ribs of excess fat. Drain and rinse the sauerkraut. Shred the red cabbage. Peel and mince the garlic.
2. Preheat oven to 375°.
3. In a medium-sized bowl, combine the sauerkraut, cabbage, garlic, tomatoes, and 1 teaspoon of the paprika; stir well to mix. Spread this mixture into the bottom of a large, oiled baking dish.
4. Arrange the ribs on top of the sauerkraut mixture, curved side up. Season with salt and pepper and the rest of the paprika. Bake in the oven, covered, for about 1 to 1½ hours or until the meat is tender. Uncover the pan, turn the ribs over, and bake uncovered for another 20 minutes. To serve, cut the ribs apart from the bones and serve over the sauerkraut.

Sauerkraut

Always thought of as a German creation, sauerkraut was eaten by Chinese laborers on the Great Wall of China more than 2,000 years ago. Chinese sauerkraut was made from shredded cabbage fermented in rice wine.

BALSAMIC-MARINATED BEEF TENDERLOIN

6 (10-ounce) beef tenderloin
   filets, 1-inch thick
½ cup extra-virgin olive oil,
   plus extra for grilling
½ cup, plus 2 tablespoons balsamic vinegar

2 tablespoons finely chopped
   fresh rosemary
1 teaspoon salt
1 teaspoon coarsely ground
   black pepper

> **Serves 6**
>
> Serve with
> Champagne-Marinated
> Summer Berries (page
> 197) for dessert.

1. Place the meat in a shallow casserole dish. Mix together the ½ cup olive oil, the 2 tablespoons balsamic vinegar, and the rosemary in a small bowl. Pour over the filets, turning the meat to ensure the steaks are evenly coated. Let marinate in the refrigerator, covered, for 2 hours. Turn after 1 hour.
2. Preheat grill to medium-high. Coat a grill pan or sauté pan lightly with oil and preheat until very hot, almost smoking. Turn down heat to medium.
3. Remove the filets from the marinade. Sprinkle salt and pepper on both sides. Place filets in preheated pan and cook for 3 to 4 minutes on each side for medium-rare.
4. Place the remaining balsamic vinegar in a small saucepan and cook over medium heat until reduced to about half. Let the filets sit for a few minutes after they are done cooking, then drizzle with a little of the reduced balsamic vinegar. Serve immediately.

Olive Oil

The difference between extra-virgin olive oil and other types of olive oil is mostly in the taste. Extra-virgin olive oil is from the first pressing of the olives. It is fruitier and more intense in flavor than other olive oils. It is best in vinaigrettes, chilled soups, or drizzled over any dish. Other olive oils are usually better to cook with because they have a higher smoking point.

SPICY COLD PEARS

4 fresh pears
1 teaspoon orange zest
1 teaspoon lemon zest
2 cups cranberry juice

2 tablespoons granulated sugar
½ teaspoon ground cinnamon
½ teaspoon ground cloves

1. Peel, core, and halve the pears lengthwise. Grate the rind of an orange and a lemon to create the zest.
2. In a medium-sized saucepan, combine all the ingredients. Bring to a boil, cover, and reduce heat to low; simmer until tender, about 15 minutes. Serve the pears warm or chilled.

ORANGE CUPS WITH LEMON CREAM

Serves 6

This dish must be served the same day it is prepared or the filling will start to separate.

4 large oranges
Zest of 1 lemon

⅓ cup whipping cream
½ cup vanilla yogurt

1. With a sharp knife, cut each orange in half crosswise. Remove the flesh (with a grapefruit spoon) and chop finely, then place the flesh in a bowl. Set the peels aside.
2. Mix the lemon zest with the chopped orange flesh. In a separate bowl, whip the cream until it is stiff. With a rubber spatula, fold the yogurt into the whipped cream. Add the cream mixture to the chopped oranges and stir gently to mix.
3. Very thinly slice off the bottom of each orange shell so they sit level on a plate. Fill all the shells with the orange mixture, then place on a serving plate. Refrigerate the filled shells until ready to serve.

CHAMPAGNE-MARINATED SUMMER BERRIES

1 cup fresh strawberries
1 cup fresh raspberries
½ cup red currants
½ cup fresh blueberries
2 tablespoons granulated sugar

⅛ cup fresh lemon juice, divided
1 cup chilled champagne
1 bunch fresh mint sprigs

Serves 4

Serve as dessert for Grilled Beef and Onion Kebabs (page 193).

1. Hull the strawberries and cut in half. Wash all the fruit in cold water.
2. Mix together all the fruit in a glass bowl and sprinkle with the sugar and the lemon juice. Set aside for 10 minutes.
3. To serve, spoon the fruit into glass dishes. At the table, pour the chilled champagne over the fruit and decorate with mint sprigs.

CHEERY CHERRY CRISPY

⅓ cup butter or margarine, divided
2 pounds fresh cherries
⅓ cup water

⅔ packed cup brown sugar
½ cup quick-cooking oats
½ cup all-purpose flour
1 teaspoon cinnamon

Serves 8

This dish works equally well with blueberries or raspberries.

1. Lightly grease a slow cooker with ½ teaspoon of the butter. Remove the stems and pits from the cherries and put the cherries in the slow cooker. Add the water.
2. In a bowl, mix together the brown sugar, oats, flour, and cinnamon. Cut in the remaining butter by using a fork and slicing the butter into small pieces. Continue doing this until the mixture is crumbly.
3. Sprinkle the crumbs over the cherries. Cook, uncovered, on low setting for 3 to 4 hours.

PLANTER'S PUNCH

2 ounces light rum
1 ounce dark rum
1 ounce lime juice
1 ounce lemon juice
2 ounces orange juice

1 ounce pineapple juice
Ice
1 dash Triple Sec
Grenadine
Fresh fruit, for garnish

1. Combine rums and juices in a shaker half-filled with ice. Shake well.
2. Pour into a highball glass nearly filled with ice. Top with Triple Sec and grenadine. Garish with slices of fresh fruit.

CARIBBEAN SUNSET

4 ounces red wine (such as
   Merlot)
2 teaspoons Cointreau

Dash bitters
Club soda
Lemon twist

Combine ingredients in a large wineglass. Stir. Add a lemon twist.

CHAPTER 14

FALL FAVORITES

FRUITED PORK LOIN CASSEROLE	200
ROASTED BUTTERNUT SQUASH PASTA	201
WARM POTATO SALAD WITH BALSAMIC VINEGAR AND ONIONS	202
CARROT TIMBALES	203
WILD RICE WITH APPLES AND ALMONDS	204
VENISON WITH DRIED CRANBERRY VINEGAR SAUCE	205
NEW ENGLAND BOILED DINNER	206
CHOCOLATE CHIP COOKIES	207
APPLE CRISP	208
CARROT CAKE	208
FRUITY CITRUS SPICE TEA	209
CIDER PUNCH	210
NONALCOHOLIC MULLED CIDER PUNCH	210

FRUITED PORK LOIN CASSEROLE

Serves 4

For a change of pace, use small red potatoes sliced in half. Add some green grapes and dried pears to the recipe, too.

4 small Yukon Gold potatoes
2 (2-ounce) pieces pork loin
1 teaspoon olive oil
1 tablespoon grated Parmesan cheese
½ teaspoon salt
¼ teaspoon freshly ground black pepper
1 Red Delicious apple
2 fresh apricots
1 small red onion
⅛ cup apple cider

1. Preheat oven to 350°. Spread olive oil on the bottom and sides of a medium-sized casserole dish.
2. Peel the potatoes and slice thinly. Trim the pork loins and pound flat. Rub the olive oil over the entire surface of the loins. Sprinkle each side of the pork loins with the Parmesan cheese, salt, and pepper. Peel, core, and thinly slice the apple. Cut the apricots in half and remove the seeds. Peel the onion and chop into ⅛-inch pieces.
3. Layer ½ the potato slices across the bottom of the dish. Top with the first piece of flattened pork loin. Arrange the apple slices over the top of the loin and place the apricot halves on top of the apple. Sprinkle the red onion over the apricots and apples. Add the second flattened pork loin and layer the remaining potatoes atop the loin. Drizzle the apple cider over the top of the casserole.
4. Cover the casserole and bake for 45 to 60 minutes or until the potatoes are tender. Remove the casserole and keep it covered for 10 minutes.

Casseroles

Food placed in a deep casserole dish will take more time to cook than food placed in a shallow casserole dish. Try to match the size of the dish to the quantity of the food being placed in it.

ROASTED BUTTERNUT SQUASH PASTA

1 butternut squash
1 garlic clove
1 medium-sized red onion
4 teaspoons olive oil
2 teaspoons red wine vinegar

¼ teaspoon dried oregano
2 cups cooked linguine
½ teaspoon freshly ground
    black pepper

Serves 4

For added flavor, use roasted instead of raw garlic in this recipe. Roasting the garlic causes it to caramelize, adding a natural sweetness.

1. Preheat oven to 400°. Cut the squash in half and scoop out the seeds. Remove the skin from the garlic and mince finely. Remove the skin from the onion and chop into ¼-inch pieces.
2. Using nonstick spray, coat 1 side of each of 2 pieces of heavy-duty foil large enough to wrap the squash halves. Wrap the squash in the foil and place on a baking sheet. Bake for 1 hour or until tender.
3. Scoop out the baked squash flesh and discard the rind. Roughly chop the squash. Add the olive oil, garlic, and onion to a nonstick skillet and sauté until the onion is transparent.
4. Remove pan from heat and stir in the vinegar and oregano. Add the squash and stir to coat it in the onion mixture. Add the pasta and toss to mix. Season with freshly ground black pepper.

Stir Pasta Early

To prevent pasta from clumping and cooking unevenly, wait until water is boiling rapidly before adding dried pasta, and stir the pasta immediately to separate the pieces or strands. Pasta should boil vigorously in a large amount of water, uncovered.

WARM POTATO SALAD WITH BALSAMIC VINEGAR AND ONIONS

2 medium-sized yellow onions
1 pound small white "boiling" potatoes
2 tablespoons extra-virgin olive oil
3 sprigs fresh thyme leaves

½ teaspoon granulated sugar
1 tablespoon balsamic vinegar
½ teaspoon salt
¼ teaspoon pepper
Pinch of chopped fresh Italian parsley

1. Remove the skin from the onions and slice thinly. Halve the potatoes and boil in salted water until very tender. Drain water and discard.
2. Heat the olive oil on medium in a medium-sized skillet for 1 minute. Add the onions, thyme, and sugar. Cook slowly, stirring regularly with a wooden spoon until the onions are very soft and browned to the color of caramel, about 10 minutes.
3. Stir in the balsamic vinegar. Remove from heat. Toss gently with the warm cooked potatoes and season with salt and pepper. Allow to rest 10 minutes before serving, garnished with the chopped parsley.

Testing Potatoes for Doneness
To check a potato for doneness, poke the tip of a knife into the thickest part, then lift the knife up, handle first. If the potato falls off, it's done. If it hangs on, it needs more cooking time.

CARROT TIMBALES

2 cups fresh carrots
¼ cup shallots
½ cup chopped fresh tarragon
1 tablespoon unsalted butter,
    plus extra for buttering
2 tablespoons port wine
½ teaspoon salt

⅛ teaspoon freshly grated
    nutmeg
¼ teaspoon black pepper
1 cup cream
3 large eggs
¼ cup grated Parmesan cheese

Serves 4

Other vegetables may be substituted for carrots in this timbales recipe. Try cauliflower, broccoli, zucchini, or fresh sweet corn.

1. Peel and slice the carrots. Cook in boiling water until they can be easily cut with a butter knife but are not mushy. Drain off water and discard. Chop roughly in a food processor. Remove the peels from the shallots and chop finely. Chop the tarragon.

2. Preheat oven to 375°. Butter 4 6-ounce ramekins or custard cups.

3. In a small skillet over medium heat, melt the 1 tablespoon butter. Add the carrots and cook about 3 minutes. Add the shallots to the carrots, along with the Port, salt, nutmeg, and pepper. In a small saucepan, heat the cream until steaming but not boiling. Whisk the eggs into the vegetable mixture, then gradually whisk in the cream.

4. Divide the mixture into the prepared cups and line them up in a shallow casserole or roasting pan. Add enough hot tap water to come ⅔ of the way up the sides of the custard cups. Cover the pan with foil and bake in the center of the oven for 25 to 30 minutes or until almost set.

5. Open the oven door. Loosen but do not remove the foil and bake for 10 minutes more. Let rest at room temperature for 10 minutes before loosening with a knife, inverting, and unmolding. Garnish with the chopped tarragon and grated cheese.

WILD RICE WITH APPLES AND ALMONDS

½ cup uncooked wild rice
1 large white onion
1 Rome or Golden Delicious apple
½ cup almond slivers
¼ cup chopped parsley

1 tablespoon vegetable oil
¼ cup golden raisins
½ teaspoon salt
¼ teaspoon black pepper
1 tablespoon olive oil

1. Boil the rice in 2½ quarts salted water until tender, about 40 minutes. Drain, saving the cooking liquid. Set aside.
2. Remove the skin from the onion and chop into ¼-inch pieces. Peel the apple, remove the core, and dice into ¼-inch cubes. Toast the almond slivers in a small, dry skillet on medium heat until they are visibly shiny. Roughly chop the parsley.
3. Heat the oil in a large skillet over medium heat for 1 minute. Add the onions and cook until softened, about 5 minutes. Add the apples, raisins, and a splash of the rice cooking liquid. Cook for 5 more minutes until the apples are translucent.
4. Combine the cooked rice, the apple mixture, almonds, salt, and pepper. Stir in olive oil. Serve garnished with the parsley.

Preventing Boil-Over

A lump of butter or a few teaspoons of cooking oil added to water when boiling rice, noodles, macaroni, or spaghetti will prevent the liquid from boiling over.

VENISON WITH DRIED CRANBERRY VINEGAR SAUCE

½-pound venison roast
1 garlic clove
1 small red onion
2 tablespoons dried cranberries
1 tablespoon granulated sugar
3 tablespoons water
2 tablespoons white wine
  vinegar
2 teaspoons olive oil
2 tablespoons dry red wine
½ cup chicken broth
½ teaspoon cracked black
  pepper
1 teaspoon all-purpose flour
1 tablespoon water
2 teaspoons butter

Serves 4

This is excellent served with wild rice and roasted butternut squash.

1. Slice the meat thinly. Crush the garlic with the side of a large knife. Remove the skin from the red onion and cut into eighths.

2. Add the cranberries, sugar, water, and vinegar to a saucepan and bring to a boil. Reduce heat to a simmer for 5 minutes. Remove from heat and transfer to a food processor or blender. Process until the cranberries are chopped but not puréed. Set aside.

3. Pour the olive oil into nonstick skillet heated to medium-high. Add the garlic and onion, and sauté for 30 seconds. Deglaze the plan with the red wine, and cook, stirring occasionally, until the wine is reduced by half. Add the cranberry mixture and the chicken broth, and bring to a boil.

4. Reduce heat to medium-low, season with the pepper, and add the venison; simmer for 10 minutes, or until the meat is cooked. Remove the meat and set aside.

5. Whisk together the flour and water to form a smooth paste. Whisk the slurry into the sauce and simmer until the sauce thickens. Remove from the heat, add the butter, and whisk to incorporate the butter into the sauce. Drizzle the sauce over the meat before serving.

Slicing Meat

To slice meat thinly, freeze it first and let it thaw slightly. The meat will slice as easily as cheese when it is semi-thawed.

NEW ENGLAND BOILED DINNER

Serves 6

Serve with Apple Crisp (page 208) for dessert on a blustery fall day.

3-pound corned beef brisket
6 medium carrots
3 medium potatoes
3 medium parsnips
6 small yellow onions
½ medium head cabbage
1½ teaspoons whole black
 peppercorns
2 bay leaves
1½ cups milk
4 teaspoons cornstarch
2 tablespoons horseradish mustard

1. Trim excess fat from the meat. Peel the carrots and cut into chunks. Peel the potatoes and cut into quarters. Peel the parsnips and cut into chunks. Peel the onions and cut in half. Shred the cabbage.
2. Place the meat in a Dutch oven. Add the juices and spices from the package included with meat. Add enough water to cover the meat. Add the peppercorns and bay leaves. Bring to a boil. Reduce heat and simmer, covered, for 2 hours.
3. Add the carrots, potatoes, parsnips, and onions to the Dutch oven. Return to boiling. Reduce heat and simmer, covered, for 10 minutes. Add the cabbage and cook for 20 minutes or until the vegetables are tender.
4. Remove the meat and vegetables from the liquid. Discard the liquid and bay leaves. Slice the meat across the grain.
5. Make the mustard sauce by stirring together the milk and cornstarch in a small saucepan. Cook and stir until thickened and bubbly. Cook and stir for 2 minutes more. Stir in the mustard. Heat through.
6. Put the meat and vegetables on a platter and drizzle with the mustard sauce.

CHOCOLATE CHIP COOKIES

1 cup butter
¾ cup granulated sugar
¾ packed cup light brown
   sugar
1 teaspoon vanilla extract
2 large eggs

2½ cups all-purpose flour
1 teaspoon baking soda
1 teaspoon salt
2 cups semisweet chocolate
   chips

Makes 24

They might not be elegant, but they certainly are a comfort food. Who can imagine a family celebration that doesn't incorporate this all-time favorite?

1. Preheat oven to 375°. Soften the butter by leaving at room temperature for 1 to 2 hours or by microwaving for 10 seconds on high.
2. In a large mixing bowl, use a wooden spoon to cream together the butter, granulated sugar, brown sugar, and vanilla. Add the eggs 1 at a time, mixing until incorporated before adding the next egg.
3. In a separate mixing bowl, whisk together the flour, baking soda, and salt.
4. Add the flour mixture to the egg mixture in 3 additions, mixing just enough to incorporate after each addition. Stir in the chocolate chips.
5. Drop the dough in tablespoon-sized drops onto ungreased baking sheets. Bake until golden, about 10 minutes. Cool the pans for a few minutes before transferring the cookies to a wire rack to cool completely.

Warm Chocolate

Heat releases the flavor of chocolate and nutmeats. Try reheating chocolate chip cookies in your microwave or oven for a few seconds just before serving.

APPLE CRISP

4 medium-sized tart cooking
   apples such as Granny
   Smith
¾ packed cup light brown sugar
½ cup all-purpose flour

¾ teaspoon ground nutmeg
¾ teaspoon ground cinnamon
½ cup quick-cooking rolled
   oats
¾ cup margarine or butter

1. Preheat oven to 375°. Grease an 8-inch square baking pan.
2. Peel, core, and slice the apples thinly. Arrange the apples in the prepared pan.
3. In a medium-sized bowl, combine the sugar, flour, nutmeg, cinnamon, and oats; stir well. Add the butter and cut in with a pastry blender or 2 knives until crumbly. Sprinkle over the apples.
4. Bake for about 30 minutes or until the topping is golden brown and the apples are tender. Let cool slightly on a rack.

CARROT CAKE

3 cups grated carrots
½ cup chopped walnuts
3 cups all-purpose flour
2 teaspoons baking powder
2 teaspoons salt
1 teaspoon baking soda

2 teaspoons ground cinnamon
1½ cups vegetable oil
2 cups granulated sugar
2 eggs
1 cup raisins

1. Preheat oven to 350°. Peel, then grate the carrots. Chop the walnuts.
2. Sift together the flour, baking powder, salt, baking soda, and cinnamon in a medium-sized bowl. In a large bowl, mix together the carrots, oil, and sugar. Add the eggs 1 at a time, beating well after each addition.
3. Gradually beat the flour mixture into the carrot mixture, mixing well. Fold in the nuts and raisins. Pour into an ungreased 9-inch tube pan.
4. Bake for 1 hour or until a knife inserted into the center of the cake comes out clean. Let cool on a rack.

FRUITY CITRUS SPICE TEA

3-inch cinnamon stick
2 tablespoons fresh orange peel
6 whole cloves
¼ cup fresh cranberries

2 cups water
2 (1-serving) bags black tea
1 cup fresh orange juice
1 tablespoon brown sugar

Makes 4 servings

Create your own variations on this drink by adding raisins, apple chunks, or even fresh pineapple pieces.

1. Break the cinnamon stick into ¼-inch pieces. Cut the orange peel into ½-inch pieces.
2. In a medium-sized saucepan, combine the cinnamon stick, orange peel, cranberries, cloves, and water. Bring to a boil.
3. Remove from heat and add the tea bags. Let stand for 5 minutes.
4. Remove the tea bags. Stir in the orange juice and brown sugar. Heat through but do not boil. Pour the mixture through a strainer before serving.

Creating a Cheese Board

Cheese boards are an easy and elegant entertaining style. A cheese board should include a mix of goat, cow, and sheep's milk cheese. Use a variety of textures including soft cheeses such as Brie or Camembert; smoked cheeses such as mozzarella, Gouda, or provolone; hard cheeses such as manchego; and blue cheeses such as Roquefort or Gorgonzola.

CIDER PUNCH

Serves 15

Serve for any fall gathering such as birthdays, anniversaries, and even Halloween parties.

2 quarts hard cider
6 ounces Drambuie
6 ounces dry sherry
¼ cup granulated sugar

2 ounces lemon juice
2 cups sparkling water
1 block of ice
4 apples

1. Add the liquid ingredients to a punch bowl with the block of ice.
2. Slice the apples and add to the punch bowl right before guests arrive.

NONALCOHOLIC MULLED CIDER PUNCH

Serves 20

The perfect drink after a chilly fall walk or a day raking leaves. Serve with Carrot Cake (page 208).

2 gallons apple cider
2 lemons
2 oranges
5 cinnamon sticks

1 tablespoon cinnamon
1 tablespoon nutmeg
6 whole cloves

Combine all the ingredients in a large pot. Heat just to boiling. Reduce heat and serve warm.

CHAPTER 15
KIDS' CELEBRATIONS

SLOPPY JOES	212
PIZZA MEATBALLS	213
EASY CHILI	214
MADHOUSE SPAGHETTI	215
PARTY SNACK MIX	216
RED DEVIL CHOCOLATE CAKE	217
OOEY, GOOEY S'MORES	218
OLD-FASHIONED BAKED APPLES	218
STRAWBERRIES IN BUTTERSCOTCH SAUCE	219
SPARKLING CITRUS PUNCH	219
MINTY HOT CHOCOLATE	220

SLOPPY JOES

1 medium-sized yellow onion
2 celery ribs
2 pounds extra-lean hamburger
½ cup canned tomato paste
¼ cup white vinegar
3 teaspoons Worcestershire sauce

2 tablespoons brown sugar
1 teaspoon garlic salt
½ teaspoon ground black pepper

1. Peel the onion and chop into ¼-inch pieces. Chop the celery into ¼-inch pieces.
2. Put the onion, celery, and hamburger in a medium-sized skillet on medium-high heat. Cook until the hamburger is brown and no pink remains. Drain off the grease.
3. Combine all the ingredients in a slow cooker. Cover and cook on low setting for 2 to 3 hours.

Mini-Bakery

Use a slow cooker as a mini-bakery for young children. Let them mix up a batch of chocolate chip cookies and watch through the glass lid as 1 or 2 cookies at a time bake right before their eyes.

PIZZA MEATBALLS

For the meatballs:
½ pound Swiss cheese
1 medium-sized yellow onion
½ green bell pepper
2 pounds extra-lean hamburger
2¾ cups bread crumbs
1 teaspoon salt
¼ teaspoon dried basil
¼ teaspoon ground black pepper
1 cup canned condensed vegetable soup
¼ cup skim milk

For the sauce:
1 garlic clove
1 medium-sized yellow onion
6 large ripe tomatoes
1 cup beef broth
½ cup (4 ounces) tomato paste
1 teaspoon salt
1 teaspoon dried oregano

Serves 8
Make these ahead of time and freeze them. They can be thawed in the microwave for those last-minute lunch demands or as an after-school snack.

1. To make the meatballs, cut the cheese into ¼-inch cubes. Peel and chop the onion into ¼-inch pieces. Remove the stem and seeds from the green pepper and chop the pepper into ¼-inch pieces.
2. Mix all the meatball ingredients together well and form into firm balls no larger than 2 inches in diameter. Lay the meatballs in the bottom of a slow cooker.
3. To make the sauce, peel the garlic and slice thinly with a paring knife. Peel and chop the onions into ½-inch pieces. Peel the tomatoes with a sharp paring knife, gently lifting the skin off; quarter the tomatoes, and mix in a blender on low speed for 2 minutes. Combine all the sauce ingredients and pour over the meatballs.
4. Cover and cook on low setting for 2 hours.

Replacing Fresh Tomatoes

You can substitute a 28-ounce can of peeled tomatoes for 3 fresh tomatoes in any slow-cooked recipe. Be sure to include the juice from the can when adding it to the recipe.

EASY CHILI

1 large yellow onion
2 celery ribs
1 pound lean ground beef
1½ teaspoons granulated sugar
½ teaspoon salt
¾ teaspoon garlic powder
1½ tablespoons chili powder

¾ teaspoon oregano leaves
¼ teaspoon pepper
1 (15-ounce) can tomato sauce
1 (6-ounce) can tomato paste
2½ cups water
1 (15½-ounce) can kidney
   beans

1. Peel and chop the onion into ¼-inch pieces. Chop the celery into ¼-inch pieces.
2. In a large, heavy skillet, cook the beef and onions until the beef is browned. Drain off the juices.
3. Add all the remaining ingredients *except* the kidney beans; mix well. Bring the mixture to a boil. Reduce heat and simmer, covered, for 30 minutes.
4. Drain the kidney beans and add them to the skillet; simmer, uncovered, for 10 minutes to heat the beans. Add more water if needed.

Cooking Beans

Any bean recipe gives you 2 options. Cook it longer and let the beans dissolve for a creamy texture. Serve it earlier in the cooking process, as soon as the beans are completely soft, for more distinct flavors in every bite.

MADHOUSE SPAGHETTI

2 medium-sized yellow onions
12 Spanish olives with
    pimientos
1 pound spaghetti
1 teaspoon salt

2 pounds lean ground beef
1 (28-ounce) can tomatoes
1 (6-ounce) can tomato paste
¼ cup grated Parmesan cheese

> **Serves 8**
>
> Serve with a lettuce salad and Strawberries in Butterscotch Sauce (page 219) for dessert.

1. Peel the onions and chop into ¼-inch pieces. Slice the olives. Boil the spaghetti noodles until al dente.
2. Sprinkle a Dutch oven with the salt. Add the beef and onions, and cook until the beef is browned. Pour off the fat.
3. Remove from heat and add the tomatoes and their liquid, chopping the tomatoes as you add them. Add the tomato paste and sliced olives. Return the mixture to the stovetop. Bring to a boil and reduce to a simmer. Simmer for 45 to 60 minutes, stirring occasionally.
4. Add the cooked spaghetti and mix well. Place in a large serving bowl. Sprinkle with the Parmesan cheese.

Buying Pasta

There are many types of exotic pastas on the market today, but once the sauce is added, you frequently can't taste the difference. Unless you are making plain buttered noodles, regular old pasta is the economical choice.

PARTY SNACK MIX

Serves 12

This nutritious, low-fat treat keeps for weeks in airtight containers, making it the ideal after-school snack.

½ teaspoon vegetable oil
4 tablespoons butter or margarine
1 teaspoon garlic salt
½ teaspoon onion salt
4 teaspoons Worcestershire sauce

3 cups Corn Chex cereal
3 cups Wheat Chex cereal
3 cups Rice Chex cereal
1 cup shelled, skinless peanuts
2 cups mini pretzel sticks
½ cup grated Parmesan cheese

1. Preheat oven to 250°. Put the vegetable oil on a paper towel and spread the oil over the bottom and sides of a large baking pan.
2. Combine the butter, garlic salt, onion salt, and Worcestershire sauce in the pan and place it in the oven until the butter is melted, about 5 minutes.
3. In the meantime, in a large bowl, combine the Corn Chex, Wheat Chex, Rice Chex, peanuts, and pretzel sticks. Add to the baking pan and stir until the mix is covered with the butter mixture.
4. Cook for 45 minutes, stirring after every 15 minutes. Spread the mixture on paper towels and lightly sprinkle with the Parmesan cheese.

No Breakfast?

If you have a child who doesn't like to eat breakfast, serve a snack mix such as this with a slice of cheese. Your child will get all the nutrition of a good breakfast and not even know it!

RED DEVIL CHOCOLATE CAKE

2 packed cups brown sugar, divided
1 cup milk, divided
3 squares (3 ounces) unsweetened chocolate
½ cup vegetable shortening
1 teaspoon vanilla
1 teaspoon red food coloring
3 eggs
2 cups sifted all-purpose flour
2 teaspoons baking soda
½ teaspoon salt

> **Serves 8**
>
> Serve with Minty Hot Chocolate (page 220).

1. Preheat oven to 350°. Line the bottom of 2 8-inch cake pans with wax paper and grease the sides.
2. In a small saucepan, combine 1 cup of the brown sugar, ½ cup of the milk, and the chocolate over very low heat until the chocolate melts. Remove from heat and let cool.
3. In a large bowl, stir the shortening to soften. Gradually add the remaining 1 cup brown sugar and cream until light and fluffy. Add the vanilla and red food coloring, mixing well. Beat in the eggs 1 at a time, beating well after each addition. Blend in the chocolate mixture.
4. In another bowl, sift together the flour, baking soda, and salt. Add the flour mixture to the creamed mixture alternately with the remaining ½ cup milk, beginning and ending with the flour mixture. Beat well after each addition. Pour into the prepared pans.
5. Bake for about 25 minutes, or until a knife inserted into the center of the cakes comes out clean. Cool on racks.

Try Different Flavors

The next time a recipe says vanilla extract, reach for a bottle of different flavored extract instead. In the grocery store, you will see almond extract as well as lemon, orange, mint, and even coconut.

OOEY, GOOEY S'MORES

Makes 8

For a different yet still scrumptious treat, use half of a chocolate bar with almonds or half of a Mounds bar instead of the half all-chocolate candy.

16 graham cracker squares
4 Hershey's chocolate bars
(without almonds)

4 large marshmallows

1. Preheat oven to 450°.
2. Place 8 graham cracker squares on a baking sheet. Top each with ½ of a chocolate bar. Top each with 1 marshmallow.
3. Cook for 10 minutes or until the chocolate is beginning to melt. Remove and add 1 graham cracker square to the top of each "sandwich." Press down until the chocolate and marshmallow begin to ooze out of the sandwich.

OLD-FASHIONED BAKED APPLES

Serves 4

Add raisins or dried cranberries to the filling ingredients for another tasty treat.

4 baking apples (Romes or
Cortlands are best)
8 whole cloves

2 ounces butter
⅓ cup light brown sugar
½ teaspoon ground cinnamon

1. Preheat oven to 350°.
2. Wash and dry the apples thoroughly. Using a small knife, cut a divot from the top of the apples, leaving the stem intact. This "cover" will be replaced when baking. Scoop out the seeds and core from the apples with a melonballer or small spoon. Drop 2 cloves into each apple.
3. Knead together the butter, brown sugar, and cinnamon. Divide equally into the apples, leaving enough space to replace the tops.
4. Place the apples in a 9" × 9" baking dish with ½ cup water in the bottom. Bake for 1 hour. Sprinkle with cinnamon or confectioners' sugar before serving.

STRAWBERRIES IN BUTTERSCOTCH SAUCE

¼ pound fresh strawberries
1 cup brown sugar
1 cup light corn syrup
½ cup heavy cream
4 drops vanilla extract

1. Wash and hull the strawberries.
2. Combine the sugar and corn syrup in a saucepan. Stir over low heat until the sugar dissolves. Cook for 5 minutes.
3. Remove from heat. Stir in the cream and vanilla. Beat for about 2 minutes, until the sauce is smooth. Pour the warm sauce over the strawberries.

Serves 4

This is the perfect dessert for any kids' party, whether you're serving Sloppy Joes (page 212) or Madhouse Spaghetti (page 215).

SPARKLING CITRUS PUNCH

1 (6-ounce) can tangerine juice concentrate
1 (6-ounce) can frozen grapefruit juice concentrate
1 pint fresh strawberries
2 cups cold water
1 liter sparkling water
Ice
Fresh mint sprigs

1. Thaw the tangerine and grapefruit juice concentrates. Wash and hull the strawberries, and cut them in half.
2. Mix together the tangerine juice, grapefruit juice, cold water, and sparkling water. Pour into a punch bowl and stir to mix. Add ice.
3. Add the strawberries and a few sprigs of mint.

Serves 12

Any fruit juices can be used to make this a special treat. Add blueberries or blackberries instead of strawberries when they are in season.

MINTY HOT CHOCOLATE

Serves 12

Use a soup ladle to let kids serve them-selves right from the slow cooker.

12 cups whole milk
1 cup chocolate syrup

1 teaspoon peppermint extract

Combine all the ingredients in a slow cooker. Cook, uncovered, on high setting for 30 minutes, stirring every 5 minutes until the chocolate syrup is dissolved.

Little Slow Cookers
Pint-sized slow cookers are available at many household department stores. These are ideal for hot appetizers because they can keep them warm for an entire evening. If the appetizer starts to dry out, simply add a little water and stir.

CARAWAY-RUBBED CHICKEN	222
YAM LATKES WITH MUSTARD SEEDS AND CURRY	223
BRAISED LAMB IN POMEGRANATE SAUCE	224
HUNGARIAN CABBAGE AND NOODLES	225
PURIM RAVIOLI	226
SALMON HASH	227
QUICHE IN A LOAF	228
MOCK CHOPPED LIVER	229
MOSCARDINI	229
GORGONZOLA AND APPLE SALAD	230
HAMANTASCHEN	231
HONEY CAKE LEKACH	232
PURIM POPPY SEED CANDY	233

CARAWAY-RUBBED CHICKEN

Serve this Hanukkah meal with fresh green vegetables and yams.

2 tablespoons caraway seeds
¼ teaspoon whole black peppercorns
1 teaspoon finely shredded
   lemon peel

½ teaspoon salt
3–4 pound broiler-fryer chicken
2 tablespoons lemon juice
1 fresh lemon

1. Preheat oven to 375°.
2. With a mortar and pestle, slightly crush the caraway seeds and whole black pepper. Shred the lemon peel. Stir in the lemon peel and salt.
3. Rub the caraway mixture over the entire bird and under the skin of the breast.
4. Place the chicken, breast-side up, on a rack in a shallow pan. Roast, uncovered, for 1 to 2 hours or until the meat is no longer pink. Remove from oven, cover, and let stand for 10 minutes.
5. Drizzle the lemon juice over the chicken before carving. Cut the lemon into slices. Serve the chicken with the lemon slices.

Safe Chicken Handling

To prevent the transmission of salmonella and other bacteria from raw chicken, always wash your hands before and after handling raw chicken. Thoroughly wash all cutting boards and utensils you have used to prepare raw chicken. Also make sure chicken is cooked to at least 170°. If the chicken smells funny, throw it out.

YAM LATKES WITH MUSTARD SEEDS AND CURRY

2 packed cups coarsely grated, peeled yams
½ cup chopped red bell pepper
1 (15-ounce) can chickpeas (garbanzo beans)
¼ cup chopped cilantro

3 tablespoons cornstarch
1 egg
2 teaspoons curry powder
1 teaspoon salt
2 teaspoons mustard seeds
8 tablespoons vegetable oil

Makes 12
This Hanukkah dish can be served as a side dish or entrée. Serve with chutney or jam.

1. Peel and grate the yams. Chop the bell pepper into ¼-inch pieces. Drain the chickpeas. Chop the cilantro.
2. Place a baking sheet in the oven. Preheat oven to 325°.
3. Combine the yams and bell pepper in large bowl. Add the cornstarch. Toss to coat.
4. In a food processor, purée the chickpeas to coarse paste. Add the egg, curry powder, and salt; blend well. Transfer the mixture to a small bowl. Mix in the cilantro and mustard seeds. Stir the chickpea mixture into the yam mixture.
5. Heat 6 tablespoons oil in large skillet on medium. Working in batches, drop 1 heaping tablespoon batter per pancake into the hot oil. Using the back of a spoon, spread to 3-inch rounds. Cook until brown, about 3 minutes per side. Transfer to the baking sheet in the oven to keep warm before serving.

Toasting Seeds

Toast seeds, from cumin to pumpkin, in a dry pan until they give off a slight smoke and brown slightly, about 2 minutes over medium heat. You can then pulverize them in a coffee grinder, if the recipe calls for it.

BRAISED LAMB IN POMEGRANATE SAUCE

Serves 8

This Hanukkah meal is wonderful served with Yam Latkes with Mustard Seeds and Curry (page 223).

7-pound lamb shoulder
2 medium-sized yellow onions
10 garlic cloves
¼ cup olive oil
1 tablespoon salt
½ tablespoon ground black pepper
2 cups, plus 1½ tablespoons all-purpose flour
2 cups chicken stock
1 cup dry red wine

1 cup unsweetened pomegranate juice
½ cup tomato paste
2 firmly packed tablespoons light brown sugar
1 tablespoon dried oregano
1 teaspoon ground cinnamon
¾ teaspoon ground allspice
1½ tablespoons margarine
1 bunch fresh parsley

1. Debone the lamb shoulder but reserve the bones. Trim excess fat from the meat. Roll the meat and tie it with butcher's twine. Peel the onions and chop into ¼-inch pieces. Peel the garlic and smash with the side of a large knife.
2. Position a rack in the lowest third of oven and preheat to 325°.
3. Heat the oil in heavy, large pot or Dutch oven over high heat. Add all the lamb bones and cook until brown, turning often, about 15 minutes.
4. Transfer the bones to a plate. Season the lamb meat with some of the salt and pepper, and dredge thoroughly in the 2 cups flour. Add to the pot and cook until brown on all sides, about 10 minutes. Transfer the lamb to the plate with the bones.
5. Add the onions and garlic to the pot and cook until the onions are just golden, about 5 minutes. Return the lamb meat to the pot. Arrange the bones around the lamb. Stir in the stock, red wine, pomegranate juice, tomato paste, brown sugar, oregano, cinnamon, and allspice. Bring to a boil. Baste the lamb with the stock mixture.
6. Cover and transfer to the oven. Bake, turning once, until the lamb is tender when pierced with long, sharp knife, about 2½ hours. Remove from oven and let cool. Cover and chill overnight.

7. Preheat oven to 325°.

8. Remove the fat from surface of the lamb and cooking liquid. Transfer the lamb to a platter. Remove the string from the lamb. Cut the meat into ½-inch-thick slices. Arrange in a shallow baking dish.

9. Bring the pan juices to a boil. Remove and discard the bones. Strain the pan juices, pressing hard on the solids to extract as much liquid as possible. Melt the margarine in the same pot over medium heat. Add the 1½ tablespoons flour and stir until the mixture begins to brown, about 2 minutes.

10. Whisk in the pan juices and boil until the sauce is reduced to 2 cups, about 15 minutes. Season with salt and pepper. Pour over the lamb. Cover with foil and bake until the lamb is heated through, about 25 minutes.

11. Arrange the lamb on a platter. Spoon the sauce over the top. Garnish with parsley.

If You Substitute Lamb or Veal . . .

Since lamb and veal are inherently tender meats, they need less cooking time than their grown-up counterparts. Decrease the time by half and add the meat later in the cooking cycle.

HUNGARIAN CABBAGE AND NOODLES

1 large cabbage
1 medium-sized yellow onion
1 teaspoon salt
3 tablespoons vegetable oil
1 tablespoon granulated sugar

1 teaspoon freshly ground
  black pepper
12 ounces egg noodles
1 tablespoon poppy seeds

1. Core the cabbage and thinly slice until you have about 8 cups. Peel the onion and chop into 1/4-inch pieces.
2. Sprinkle the cabbage with the salt. Let stand for 30 minutes, then squeeze dry. Lay on paper towels to soak up excess moisture.
3. Heat the oil in a large skillet. Add the sugar and heat until the sugar browns. Add the onions and cook until they start to wilt. Stir in the cabbage. Sauté, stirring frequently, until the cabbage is tender, about 20 minutes. Season with the pepper. Transfer the cabbage and juices to a large bowl and keep warm.
4. Cook the noodles in boiling salted water until tender. Drain. Quickly toss the noodles with the cabbage mixture and the poppy seeds. Serve immediately.

Spicy Substitutions

Anytime a recipe calls for a basic spice, try substituting something more fun. In place of pepper flakes, for example, substitute toasted cumin seeds, fennel seeds, anise, or chopped fresh ginger.

PURIM RAVIOLI

For the pasta:
4 eggs
2½ cups all-purpose flour
½ teaspoon salt

For the filling:
2 pounds spinach
1 small yellow onion
1 small carrot

½ cooked chicken breast
3 tablespoons, plus 1 teaspoon
 and 1 pinch salt
2 tablespoons olive oil
1 teaspoon freshly ground
 black pepper
1 tablespoon unbleached flour
6 quarts water
3 cups prepared marinara sauce

Makes 8 dozen

Spinach ravioli is a traditional Purim treat.

1. Make the pasta by combining the eggs, flour, and salt; blend well.
2. Remove the stems from the spinach and rinse the leaves in cold water. Peel the onion and cut into quarters. Peel the carrot and chop coarsely. Cube the chicken breast.
3. Place the spinach in a pot with no water other than that retained from washing. Add a pinch of salt and cook, covered, for 5 minutes. Drain in a colander.
4. In a large skillet, combine the spinach, onion, carrot, chicken, and oil. Add 1 teaspoon of the salt and ⅛ teaspoon of the pepper; cook over moderate heat for 4 to 5 minutes or until most of the liquid has evaporated. Add the flour and stir for 1 minute. Remove from heat. Cool for 5 or 6 minutes, then very finely chop the mixture.
5. Roll half the pasta dough into a paper-thin sheet and place over a floured board. With a feather brush dipped in cold water, lightly brush the top to maintain moisture. Place mounds of the spinach mixture on the dough in straight lines about 2 inches apart.
6. Roll out the other half of the dough into a paper-thin sheet and place loosely over the sheet with the filling. With an Italian pastry wheel, press along the furrows, cutting and sealing at the same time.
7. Bring the water to a boil. Add the ravioli and the 3 tablespoons salt. Stir until boiling resumes. Cook for 4 to 5 minutes, uncovered. Drain and serve with the marinara sauce.

SALMON HASH

¾ pound fresh salmon fillet
½ teaspoon salt
½ teaspoon ground black pepper
2–3 medium-sized russet potatoes
¾ cup sliced yellow bell pepper
¾ cup sliced red bell pepper
1 large yellow onion
¾ cup sliced leeks (white part only)

1 tablespoon chopped Italian flat-leaf parsley
2 tablespoons fresh-squeezed lemon juice
2 cups cold water
6 tablespoons clarified butter
½ teaspoon chopped thyme
½ teaspoon minced savory
½ teaspoon minced tarragon
2 tablespoons unsalted butter

1. Remove the skin from the salmon fillet and cut the fish into 12 pieces. Season with salt and pepper, and refrigerate. Peel and shred the potatoes. Thinly slice the peppers, onion, and leek. Chop the parsley.

2. Combine the lemon juice and cold water in a large bowl. Place the potatoes in the lemon water. Just before frying, drain and squeeze out excess liquid from the potatoes.

3. In a large skillet, heat the clarified butter and spread the potatoes loosely and evenly on the bottom of the pan. Brown the potatoes and drain on paper towels. Set aside and keep warm.

4. Pour out all but 1 tablespoon of the butter from the pan. Add the bell peppers, onion, and leek. Sauté for 3 to 4 minutes or until the vegetables are softened. Stir in the herbs. Stir in the potatoes. Keep warm.

5. Melt the unsalted butter in a skillet over high heat and sauté the salmon until golden brown, about 2 minutes. Do not allow the pieces of salmon to touch or they will steam and not sear. Turn the salmon over and add the potato mixture to the skillet. Cook for an additional 1 to 2 minutes.

QUICHE IN A LOAF

½ cup minced scallions
½ cup minced green olives
½ cup minced sun-dried tomatoes
2 tablespoons minced flat-leaf
Italian parsley
2 teaspoons minced fresh dill
2 cups shredded white
Cheddar cheese
1 cup shredded Swiss cheese
¼ cup grated Parmesan cheese,
plus extra for garnish

6 eggs
1¾ cups all-purpose flour
1¾ teaspoons baking powder
¾ cup dry white wine
½ cup vegetable oil
½ cup light cream
1½ teaspoons salt
1 teaspoon garlic powder
¼ teaspoon pepper
1 teaspoon paprika, plus extra
for garnish

Serves 8

This Yom Kippur meal is great served with salsa or yogurt. It also can be served as an appetizer.

1. Mince the scallions, green olives, sun-dried tomatoes, parsley, and dill. Shred the cheeses. Lightly beat the eggs.
2. Preheat oven to 350°. Lightly grease a 9" × 5" loaf pan.
3. In a large bowl, blend the flour and baking powder. Make a well in the center of the dry ingredients and add the wine, the oil, cream, and eggs; stir to mix. Fold in the remaining ingredients. Pour or spoon the mixture into the prepared pan. Sprinkle the top with extra Parmesan cheese and dust with paprika.
4. Bake for 40 to 45 minutes, until set. Allow to cool before serving.

Break an Egg

Always break eggs 1 at a time into a small bowl before adding them to the pan or bowl. This way, if you get a bit of shell, a spoiled egg, or a broken egg for a dish calling for whole eggs, you won't ruin the entire item with 1 bad egg.

MOCK CHOPPED LIVER

Serves 8

Serve this Rosh Hashanah dish with matzo crackers and fresh vegetables.

2 shallots
1 pound button mushrooms
2 tablespoons unsalted margarine

½ teaspoon salt
½ teaspoon ground black pepper

1. Peel and finely chop the shallots. Clean the mushrooms and chop finely.
2. Melt the margarine in a large skillet over medium heat. Add the shallots and sauté until softened, about 2 minutes.
3. Add the mushrooms and sauté until the moisture is evaporated, about 10 minutes.
4. Purée the mushroom mixture in a blender or food processor. Season with the salt and pepper.

MOSCARDINI

Makes 30

This is a classic Purim recipe. Instead of almonds, try hazelnuts for a different flavor.

1¼ cups ground toasted almonds
1¼ cup granulated sugar
¼ cup unsweetened cocoa

¼ cup unbleached flour
⅓ teaspoon cinnamon
1 egg
1 egg yolk

1. Preheat oven to 350°.
2. Combine the ground almonds, sugar, cocoa, flour, and cinnamon in a small bowl. Add the egg and egg yolk, and mix well.
3. Place on an oiled and floured baking sheet, about 2½ inches apart. Flatten with a fork.
4. Bake for 10 minutes, then transfer to a cooling rack.

GORGONZOLA AND APPLE SALAD

1 tablespoon Dijon mustard
3 tablespoons balsamic vinegar
1 tablespoon lemon juice
1 tablespoon honey
½ cup olive oil
½ teaspoon salt

½ teaspoon ground black pepper
2 heads romaine lettuce
½ pound Gorgonzola cheese
2 Red Delicious apples
1 cup toasted pecans

Serves 8
This is perfect for Rosh Hashanah, but it is good any time of year.

1. Process the mustard, vinegar, lemon juice, and honey in a blender. Gradually add the olive oil until well blended. Season with salt and pepper. Cover and refrigerate for at least 1 hour.
2. Tear the lettuce into bite-sized pieces. Crumble the Gorgonzola cheese. Core the apples and slice thinly. (Do not peel the apples.) Chop the pecans.
3. Mix the lettuce and apples in a large bowl. Put large helpings on individual plates. Top with Gorgonzola and pecans. Drizzle the dressing on top.

Blanching Vegetables

Quickly parboiling green vegetables, or "blanching" them, locks in nutrition, flavor, and especially bright color. The key is to bring the vegetables immediately up to a boil, cook them only enough to tenderize them, and stop the cooking by plunging them immediately into ice-cold water, a step known as "shocking" the vegetables. Blanche only small amounts at a time so the water never stops boiling. Salt plays an important role in keeping green vegetables green, and it is recommended in both the blanching and shocking waters.

HAMANTASCHEN

Makes 30

This dish is a must for Purim. Try different fillings to see which your family likes best.

½ pound margarine
8 teaspoons granulated sugar
3¼ cups all-purpose flour
2 teaspoons baking powder
¼ teaspoon salt

2 eggs
3 teaspoons orange juice
2 teaspoons vanilla
1 jar jam or poppy seed filling

1. Cream together the margarine and sugar. Sift the dry ingredients and add to the margarine mixture; mix well. Add the eggs, orange juice, and vanilla. Knead until the dough forms and divide into 6 sections. Refrigerate until chilled, about 1 hour.
2. Preheat oven to 325°.
3. Roll out each section on a floured board. Use a glass as a cutter for forming circles for the hamantaschen shape. Place 1 teaspoon of filling into each circle and fold into a triangle by pinching the edges together. Bake on a baking sheet for 25 minutes.

How Many Carbs in Wine?

A bottle of wine will yield 4 to 5 servings. A 5-ounce serving of white wine contains 1.2 grams of carbohydrates; 5 ounces of red wine contains 2.4 grams of carbohydrates; and a 5-ounce glass of champagne contains 4.3 grams of carbohydrates.

HONEY CAKE LEKACH

2 tablespoons canola oil
½ cup plum/apple baby food
6 large eggs, at room temperature
1 cup honey
1½ firmly packed cups light
brown sugar
3 cups all-purpose flour
1 teaspoon baking soda

2 teaspoons baking powder
⅛ teaspoon salt
2 teaspoons cinnamon
1 teaspoon ground nutmeg
½ cup finely chopped almonds
½ cup brewed coffee, at room
temperature
¼ cup sliced almonds

Serves 20

These Rosh Hashanah
cakes may be frozen
for up to 3 months.

1. Preheat oven to 350° with a rack set in the lower third of the oven. Grease two 9" × 5" loaf pans. Separate egg whites from yolks.
2. Combine the oil, baby food, egg whites, honey, and brown sugar in a large mixing bowl. Beat with an electric mixer on medium speed for 3 minutes.
3. In a small mixing bowl, thoroughly mix together the flour, baking soda, baking powder, salt, cinnamon, nutmeg, and chopped almonds. Alternately, stir the flour mixture and the coffee into the sugar mixture, beginning and ending with the flour. *Do not overmix.* The batter will be very thin.
4. Pour the batter into the prepared pans. Rap the pans sharply on the counter several times to break any large bubbles. Sprinkle ⅛ cup of the sliced almonds on top of each loaf.
5. Place the cakes in the oven and bake for about 1 hour, until a toothpick inserted into the center of the cake comes out clean. Set the pans on a rack to cool. For best flavor, make the cakes 1 day ahead.

PURIM POPPY SEED CANDY

1 pound poppy seeds
2 cups chopped pecans
2 cups honey

½ cup granulated sugar
½ teaspoon powdered ginger

1. Grind the poppy seeds in a coffee grinder or with a mortar and pestle. Chop the pecans, if necessary.
2. In a medium-sized saucepan, cook the honey and sugar until syrupy. Stir in the poppy seeds and cook until the mixture is thick, about 20 minutes. Stir frequently. The mixture should not run when a small amount is dropped on a wet surface.
3. Stir in the nuts and ginger.
4. Moisten your hands with water and pat out the mixture onto a wet board or counter. It should be about ½-inch thick. Let cool for 5 minutes, then score into diamond shapes with a sharp knife. When cool, lift from the board with a spatula.

Sautéing Tip

For a light taste, sauté onions and garlic in extra-virgin olive oil, canola oil, or vegetable oil. For a richer flavor, use a darker olive oil or butter.

CHAPTER 17

FANCY FOODS FOR A DIABETIC DIET

CUCUMBER SLICES WITH SMOKED SALMON CREAM	236
WALNUT CHICKEN WITH PLUM SAUCE	236
CHICKEN THIGHS CACCIATORE	237
CRAB CAKES WITH SESAME CRUST	238
MOCK STUFFED GRAPE LEAVES	239
FILLETS OF FISH WITH LIME AND CUMIN	239
BROCCOLI AND CARROT CASSEROLE	240
BERRY PUFF PANCAKES	241
BANANAS FOSTER	242

CUCUMBER SLICES WITH SMOKED SALMON CREAM

2–3 medium cucumbers
1 ounce smoked salmon
8 ounces Neufchâtel cheese,
  at room temperature

½ tablespoon lemon juice
½ teaspoon freshly ground
  pepper
Chopped dill (optional)

1. Cut the cumbers into slices about ¼-inch thick. Place the slices on paper towels to drain while you prepare the salmon cream.
2. Combine the smoked salmon, Neufchâtel cheese, lemon juice, and pepper in a food processor; blend until smooth.
3. Fit a pasty bag with the tip of your choice and spoon the salmon cream into the bag. Pipe 1 teaspoon of the salmon cream atop each cucumber slice.
4. Garnish with dill, if desired.

WALNUT CHICKEN WITH PLUM SAUCE

¾ pound boneless, skinless
  chicken breast
1 teaspoon cooking sherry
1 egg white

2 teaspoons peanut oil
2 drops toasted sesame oil
  (optional)
⅓ cup ground walnuts

1. Preheat oven to 350°. Cut the chicken into bite-sized pieces and sprinkle with the sherry; set aside.
2. In a small bowl, beat the egg white and oils until frothy. Fold the chicken pieces into the egg mixture, then roll them individually in the chopped walnuts.
3. Spray a baking sheet with nonstick cooking spray. Arrange the chicken pieces on the baking sheet. Bake for 10 to 15 minutes or until the walnuts are lightly browned and the chicken juices run clear.

CHICKEN THIGHS CACCIATORE

½ cup chopped onion
2 garlic cloves
4 chicken thighs
1 (14½-ounce) can unsalted,
    diced tomatoes
2 teaspoons olive oil
½ cup dry red wine
1 teaspoon dried parsley

½ teaspoon dried oregano
¼ teaspoon ground black pepper
⅛ teaspoon granulated sugar
¼ cup grated Parmesan cheese
4 cups cooked spaghetti
    noodles
2 teaspoons extra-virgin
    olive oil

Serves 4

To add more flavor to this recipe, substitute beef broth for ½ of the red wine.

1. Remove the peel from the onion and chop into ¼-inch pieces. Peel and mince the garlic. Remove the skin from the chicken thighs. Drain the tomatoes.
2. Heat a deep, nonstick skillet over medium-high heat and add the 2 teaspoons olive oil. Add the onion and sauté until transparent. Add the garlic and chicken thighs. Sauté the chicken for 3 minutes on each side, or until lightly browned.
3. Remove the chicken from the pan and add the wine, tomatoes, parsley, oregano, pepper, and sugar. Stir well and bring to a boil.
4. Add the chicken back to the pan and sprinkle with the Parmesan cheese. Cover, reduce heat to low, and simmer for 10 minutes. Uncover and simmer for 10 more minutes.
5. Put 1 cup cooked pasta on each of 4 plates. Top each with a chicken thigh and then divide the sauce between the dishes. Drizzle ½ teaspoon olive oil over the top of each dish.

Fat-Free Flavor

To add the flavor of sautéed mushrooms or onions without the added fat of butter or oil, roast or grill them first. Thinly slice the mushrooms, then simply spread them on a baking sheet treated with nonstick spray. Bake for 5 minutes in a 350° oven.

CRAB CAKES WITH SESAME CRUST

1 small scallion
1 pound lump crabmeat
1 large egg
1 tablespoon minced fresh ginger
1 tablespoon dry white cooking sherry
1 tablespoon freshly squeezed lemon juice
6 tablespoons mayonnaise
½ teaspoon sea salt
½ teaspoon ground white pepper
¼ cup lightly toasted sesame seeds

1. Preheat oven to 375°. Treat a baking sheet with nonstick cooking spray. Remove the skin from the scallion and chop finely.
2. In a large bowl, mix together the scallion, crab, egg, ginger, sherry, lemon juice, mayonnaise, salt, and pepper.
3. Form the mixture into 10 equal cakes. Spread out the sesame seeds on a plate and dip both sides of the cakes in the seeds to coat the cakes evenly.
4. Arrange the cakes on the prepared baking sheet and bake for 8 to 10 minutes or until thoroughly warmed.

Proper Fish Handling
Always wash your hands after handling raw fish. Also wash all surfaces and utensils that the raw fish has touched.

MOCK STUFFED GRAPE LEAVES

1 cup cooked white rice
¾ cup golden raisins
½ cup apple jelly
⅛ teaspoon saffron
½ teaspoon salt
1 bunch fresh Swiss chard
*   leaves*

1. Combine the cooked white rice, ½ cup of the golden raisins, ¼ cup of the apple jelly, the saffron, and salt. Mix with a spoon until all the ingredients are evenly distributed.
2. Wash the Swiss chard leaves in cold water. Using a large melon scooper, place 1 scoop of the rice mixture in the center of each leaf. Fold in the ends and roll up tightly, as you would an egg roll. Place them in layers in a slow cooker.
3. Cover and cook on low setting for 2 to 4 hours.

> **Makes about 24**
>
> Add a small dollop of apple jelly and a raisin on the top of each appetizer for a sweeter taste.

FILLETS OF FISH WITH LIME AND CUMIN

12 fish fillets (such as haddock)
2 tablespoons lime juice
1 teaspoon ground cumin
¼ cup plain yogurt
½ teaspoon salt
½ teaspoon ground black
*   pepper*

1. Preheat oven to 350°.
2. Arrange the fish in a single layer in a baking dish. Combine the lime juice and cumin, and pour over the fish, turning to coat. Bake, uncovered, for 10 to 15 minutes or until the fish flakes easily when tested with a fork.
3. In a bowl, combine the yogurt with 1 tablespoon of the juice from the baking dish. Season with the salt and pepper and serve over the fish.

> **Serves 4**
>
> Serve with whole-grain rice and Bananas Foster (page 242) for dessert.

BROCCOLI AND CARROT CASSEROLE

Serves 6

Serve with Walnut Chicken with Plum Sauce (page 236).

1 cup fresh broccoli
3 medium carrots
1 small yellow onion
½ green bell pepper
1 cup unsalted tomato juice
⅛ teaspoon dried basil

⅛ teaspoon dried oregano
⅛ teaspoon dried parsley
¼ teaspoon garlic powder
3 tablespoons grated Parmesan cheese, divided

1. Cut the broccoli into florets. Peel the carrots and slice into ¼-inch rounds. Peel the onion and chop into ¼-inch pieces. Chop the bell pepper into ¼-inch pieces.
2. Preheat oven to 350°. Treat a large casserole dish with nonstick spray.
3. Layer the broccoli, carrots, onion, and pepper in the prepared casserole dish.
4. Mix together the tomato juice, seasonings, and 2 tablespoons of the Parmesan cheese; pour the mixture over the vegetables. Cover and bake for 1 hour.
5. Uncover, sprinkle with the remaining Parmesan cheese, and continue to bake for 10 minutes, or until the liquid thickens and the mixture bubbles.

Season First

When you ready vegetables for steaming, add fresh or dried herbs, spices, sliced onions, minced garlic, grated ginger, or just about any other seasoning you'd normally use. The seasonings will cook into the vegetables during steaming.

BERRY PUFF PANCAKES

2 large whole eggs
1 large egg white
½ cup skim milk
½ cup all-purpose flour
1 tablespoon granulated sugar

⅛ teaspoon sea salt
2 cups fresh berries of your
  choice
1 tablespoon confectioners' sugar

Serves 6

While perfect for breakfast or brunch, this also makes a wonderful dessert.

1. Preheat oven to 450°. Treat a 10-inch ovenproof skillet or deep pie pan with nonstick spray. Once the oven is heated, place the pan in the oven for a few minutes until it is hot.
2. In a medium-sized mixing bowl, beat the eggs and egg white until mixed. Whisk in the milk. Slowly whisk in the flour, sugar, and salt.
3. Remove the preheated pan from the oven and pour the batter into it. Bake for 15 minutes.
4. Reduce the heat to 350° and bake for an additional 10 minutes or until the batter is puffed and brown. Remove from the oven and slide the puffed pancake onto a serving plate.
5. Cover the pancake with the fruit and sift the confectioners' sugar over the top. Cut into 6 equal wedges, and serve.

Syrup Substitutes

Spreading 2 teaspoons of your favorite low-sugar jam or jelly on a waffle or pancake gives you a sweet topping while counting as a fruit for the day.

BANANAS FOSTER

Serves 4

Serve as dessert for Chicken Thighs Cacciatore (page 237).

4 bananas
½ cup apple juice concentrate
Grated zest of 1 orange
¼ cup fresh orange juice

1 tablespoon ground cinnamon
12 ounces nonfat frozen vanilla yogurt

1. Slice the bananas about ¼-inch thick.
2. Combine all the ingredients *except* the yogurt in a nonstick skillet. Bring to a boil and cook until the bananas are tender.
3. Put 3 ounces of the yogurt in each dessert bowl or stemmed glass and spoon the heated banana sauce over the top.

Ripe Bananas

Overripe bananas are higher in sugar and therefore can adversely affect your blood glucose levels. You can freeze bananas in the skins until ready to use. Doing so makes them perfect additions for fruit smoothies or fruit cups. Remove them from the freezer and run a little water over the peel to remove any frost. Peel them using a paring knife and slice according to the recipe directions. Frozen bananas can be added directly to smoothies and other recipes.

CHAPTER 18

LOW-CARB CELEBRATIONS

CRABMEAT ON RED PEPPER STRIPS	244
PORK AND VEAL PÂTÉ	245
STILTON AND CHEDDAR CHEESE SOUP	246
MUSTARD-GLAZED MONKFISH WRAPPED IN BACON	247
LOBSTER AND ASPARAGUS SALAD	248
SEAFOOD ROLL-UPS	249
RED SNAPPER WITH CAYENNE TOMATO SAUCE	249
PORTOBELLOS STUFFED WITH BASIL AND SALMON ON ARUGULA LEAVES	250
SAGE- AND PANCETTA-WRAPPED SHRIMP	251
CHICKEN WITH NECTARINE SALSA	252
REFRIGERATOR PUMPKIN PIE WITH MACADAMIA NUT CRUST	253

CRABMEAT ON RED PEPPER STRIPS

Makes about 16

Serve with white wine as an appetizer before a beef meal.

2 green onions
½ plum tomato
1 tablespoon chopped fresh parsley
1 tablespoon chopped fresh tarragon
2 large red bell peppers
⅓ cup mayonnaise
2 teaspoons fresh-squeezed lemon juice

½ teaspoon grated fresh lemon zest
⅛ teaspoon cayenne pepper
8 ounces flaked crabmeat
½ teaspoon salt
½ teaspoon ground black pepper
1 bunch fresh chervil sprigs

1. Peel and finely chop the green onion. Seed and mince the tomato. Chop the fresh parsley and tarragon. Remove the stem and seeds from the red peppers and cut into 1-by-2-inch strips.
2. Mix together the green onions, tomato, parsley, tarragon, mayonnaise, lemon juice, lemon zest, and cayenne in a medium-sized bowl until blended.
3. Add the crabmeat and toss lightly to coat. Season with salt and pepper.
4. Spoon 1 or 2 teaspoons of the crab mixture onto each bell pepper strip. Garnish with chervil sprigs.

Fresh Seafood

While fresh seafood can be easier to find than ever before, small Midwestern towns still have trouble importing it in time. If you can't find fresh, look for seafood that has been flash frozen and thawed by the grocery.

PORK AND VEAL PÂTÉ

1¼ pounds pork shoulder or
   rump
½ pound veal shoulder
½ pound salt pork
1 small yellow onion
1½ cups water

¼ teaspoon ground cloves
¼ teaspoon ground cinnamon
½ teaspoon salt
½ teaspoon freshly ground
   black pepper

Serves 6
A French classic, this low-carb pâté has a crumbly texture because it is not weighted during the cooling and setting process.

1. If not available precut, cut the pork and veal into 1-inch cubes. Peel the onion and chop into ¼-inch pieces. Finely chop the salt pork.

2. With a sharp knife, finely chop the pork and veal pieces to the texture of ground meat. Put the pork and veal, onions, and water in a large pot. Cook over medium heat, uncovered, until the liquid has evaporated and the meat begins to brown, about 30 minutes.

3. Put the salt pork into a small saucepan. Cook, uncovered, over medium heat, stirring often, until the fat has been rendered and the pork is golden brown, about 30 minutes.

4. Add the salt pork and the rendered fat to the meat mixture along with the remaining ingredients. Transfer to a container with a cover and set aside to cool to room temperature. Cover and refrigerate for at least 3 hours before serving.

An Appetizer-Making Party

Consider asking some of your guests to assist in preparing appetizers for your party. People enjoy the chance to "do something" while they are getting to know everyone else. It also helps break the ice if many of your guests don't know each other. Most people gravitate to the kitchen to talk anyway, so put them to good use!

STILTON AND CHEDDAR CHEESE SOUP

Serves 8

Serve with Lobster
and Asparagus Salad
(page 248).

1 small white onion
1 medium carrot
1 celery rib
3 garlic cloves
2 tablespoons butter
3 cups chicken stock
½ cup crumbled Stilton cheese
½ cup diced Cheddar cheese
⅛ teaspoon baking soda

1 cup heavy cream
⅓ cup dry white wine
1 bay leaf
½ teaspoon salt
½ teaspoon freshly ground
   black pepper
¼ teaspoon cayenne pepper
¼ cup chopped fresh parsley,
   for garnish

1. Peel the onion and chop into ⅛-inch pieces. Peel the carrot and chop into ⅛-inch pieces. Chop the celery into ⅛-inch pieces. Peel and mince the garlic.
2. Melt the butter in a large saucepan over medium-high heat. Add the onion, carrot, celery, and garlic; sauté for about 8 minutes or until soft.
3. Add the stock, cheeses, baking soda, cream, wine, bay leaf, salt, pepper, and cayenne pepper; stir well to combine. Bring to a boil, reduce heat to low, and simmer for about 10 minutes. Remove and discard the bay leaf.
4. In a food processor or blender, purée the soup until smooth. Add milk to the soup if it is too thick. Garnish with fresh parsley.

Don't Eat Bay Leaves

Remember, bay leaves add lots of flavor, but you should always remove them before serving a dish. Bay leaves are sharp and dangerous to eat.

MUSTARD-GLAZED MONKFISH WRAPPED IN BACON

12 slices apple-wood-smoked or other high-quality bacon
6 (6-ounce) monkfish fillets
½ teaspoon salt

½ teaspoon black pepper
⅔ cup Dijon mustard
2 tablespoons chopped tarragon

Serves 6
Serve with Refrigerator Pumpkin Pie with Macadamia Nut Crust for dessert (page 253).

1. Preheat oven to 350°.
2. Place the bacon on a nonstick baking sheet and precook for about 8 minutes. The bacon should be almost fully cooked but still pliable. Drain the bacon on paper towels. Discard the fat from the baking sheet.
3. Make sure the monkfish is trimmed of all membranes and dark spots. Season the monkfish with salt and pepper. Rub each fillet with 2 tablespoons of the mustard to coat completely.
4. Wrap each fillet with 2 slices of bacon, making sure the bacon doesn't overlap. Secure the bacon with toothpicks if necessary. Wrap each fillet tightly in plastic wrap, twisting the ends closed, and refrigerate for about 1 hour.
5. Preheat oven to 375°.
6. Unwrap the fish and place on an oiled baking sheet. Bake for about 20 to 25 minutes until the fish is almost cooked. Increase the oven temperature to low broil. To finish, place the fish under the broiler for just about 30 seconds to crisp the bacon.
7. Drizzle a bit of the natural pan juices over the fish and sprinkle with chopped tarragon. Serve immediately.

Poor Man's Lobster?

Monkfish has been described as the poor man's lobster even though it has no resemblance to lobster whatsoever. Cooked properly, it has the texture of shellfish and does not have the "flakiness" of most fish. Mild in flavor and moderately firm in texture, it is a hearty fish.

LOBSTER AND ASPARAGUS SALAD

Serves 2

Serve with Stilton and Cheddar Cheese Soup (page 244).

1 garlic clove
2 anchovies, well drained
1 tablespoon snipped fresh chives
1 tablespoon chopped fresh parsley
1 teaspoon chopped fresh tarragon
½ cup mayonnaise
1 teaspoon tarragon vinegar

½ teaspoon salt
½ teaspoon ground black pepper
2 tablespoons sour cream
1 pound (16–20 spears) asparagus spears
2 precooked lobsters, claw and tail meat removed, shells discarded
2 cups mixed salad leaves

1. Peel and crush the garlic clove. To make the dressing, combine the garlic, anchovies, and herbs in a food processor or blender; process until smooth. Add the mayonnaise; process to mix. Add the vinegar, salt, and pepper. Transfer to a bowl or other container, cover, and chill for at least 1 hour. Before serving, stir in the sour cream.

2. Trim off and discard the ends off the asparagus spears, making all the spears the same length. Use a vegetable peeler to peel off any tough outer layer on the stalks if necessary. Start about 1½ inches from the top when peeling. Cook the asparagus in a pan of salted, boiling water for 4 to 8 minutes, depending on the size, or until tender but still somewhat crisp and a vibrant green. Drain and rinse immediately under cold, running water, then drain again.

3. Slice the lobster tail meat into ½-inch rounds. Leave the claw meat intact. Arrange the asparagus spears and lobster meat on a bed of the salad leaves on a chilled salad plate. Spoon a little of the dressing over the salad and serve immediately.

Substituting Seafood

Most shellfish can readily be substituted for another in any recipe. Simply use the weight of the meat as the guide, not the weight with the shell on it. Remember that scallops and shrimp are shellfish, too.

SEAFOOD ROLL-UPS

8 ounces canned or fresh crabmeat and/or baby shrimp
¼ red bell pepper
2 tablespoons chopped fresh
   chives

1 (8-ounce) package cream
   cheese, softened
¼ cup mayonnaise
5 (9-inch) flour tortillas, at room
   temperature

> **Makes 24**
>
> For an extra treat, serve with tomato salsa as a dipping sauce.

1. Chop the seafood into ¼-inch pieces. Chop the red pepper into ¼-inch pieces. Roughly chop the chives.
2. Combine the cream cheese and mayonnaise. Blend in the seafood.
3. Spread on the tortillas, dividing evenly. Sprinkle the red pepper and chives evenly over the tortillas.
4. Roll up each tortilla, tightly wrap with plastic wrap, and refrigerate at least 3 hours. Cut into ¾-inch pieces before serving.

RED SNAPPER WITH CAYENNE TOMATO SAUCE

1 tablespoon olive oil
5 ounces red snapper fillet, skin on
2 tablespoons sour cream
1 tablespoon minced chives
½ teaspoon sun-dried tomato paste

½ teaspoon cayenne pepper
1 teaspoon lemon juice
½ teaspoon salt
½ teaspoon ground white pepper

> **Serves 1**
>
> You can also heat the sauce for a nice touch.

1. Preheat oven to 375°. Add the olive oil to a small ovenproof nonstick sauté pan over medium-high heat. Place the snapper fillet, skin-side down, in the pan and cook until golden brown. Carefully flip the fillet and place in the oven. Bake the snapper for about 6 minutes or until cooked through. To check for doneness, insert a thin-bladed knife into the thickest part of the fillet. The flesh should be flaky with no translucence.
2. In a small bowl, mix together the sour cream, minced chives, tomato paste, cayenne pepper, and lemon juice. Season with salt and white pepper.
3. Serve the sauce over the snapper fillet.

PORTOBELLOS STUFFED WITH BASIL AND SALMON ON ARUGULA LEAVES

Serves 2

Serve as an appetizer before Sage- and Pancetta-Wrapped Shrimp (page 251).

2 large portobello mushroom
   caps
4 scallions
2 garlic cloves
¼ cup fresh basil leaves
½ pound salmon

10 ounces fresh arugula leaves
3 teaspoons light olive oil
½ teaspoon salt
½ teaspoon ground black
   pepper
3 tablespoons cream cheese

1. Preheat oven to 375°. Clean the mushroom caps by wiping with a damp cloth. Peel and mince the scallions and garlic cloves. Cut the basil leaves into julienne strips. Skin, debone, and chop the salmon into 1-inch cubes. Steam the arugula leaves until limp.

2. Brush the mushrooms with the oil and season with salt and pepper. Place the mushrooms on a foil-covered baking sheet, lightly oiled, stem-side up. Roast for about 20 to 30 minutes, until tender when pierced with a fork, but not shriveled.

3. Mix together the scallion, garlic, basil, and cream cheese in a small bowl. Split the salmon into 2 equal portions and place ½ on each mushroom cap. Top with the cream cheese mixture. Season with salt and freshly ground black pepper.

4. Bake the stuffed mushrooms, uncovered, for 20 to 25 minutes, until the cream cheese is bubbly and starting to brown on top and the salmon is cooked through. Serve each mushroom cap on a bed of arugula leaves.

Arugula

Arugula is also known as rocket. The tender baby leaves are best, featuring a peppery bite. The larger leaves are somewhat bitter. Fresh arugula contains a fair amount of grit, so the leaves should be rinsed several times before using. Arugula is a good source of iron as well as vitamins A and C.

SAGE- AND PANCETTA-WRAPPED SHRIMP

1½ pounds uncooked large shrimp

6 ounces thinly sliced pancetta

28 fresh sage leaves (about 2 bunches)

½ cup sherry vinegar

Serves 4

This also makes an excellent appetizer when served just 1 per guest.

1. Remove the shells and tails from the shrimp. Devein the shrimp. Cut the slices of pancetta in half. Tear the sage leaves from the stems.
2. On a flat surface, lay out a half slice of pancetta. Place 1 large or 2 small leaves of sage on top, then place 1 shrimp across the pancetta and sage. Roll the pancetta around the shrimp and secure it closed with a toothpick, exposing the tail and head ends of the shrimp. Repeat with the rest of the shrimp.
3. Heat a medium-sized nonstick skillet on medium-high flame. Cook the rolled shrimp in 2 batches (to avoid overcrowding the pan) until the pancetta is light brown and crispy on each side. Place the shrimp on paper towels to drain, and cover to keep warm.
4. Immediately after all the shrimp have been cooked, keeping the pan on the flame, pour in the sherry vinegar and cook down to a syrup-like consistency. Place the shrimp on a platter and pour the hot reduced vinegar over the shrimp. Serve immediately.

What Size Shrimp?

Shrimp is sold in the following categories:

Colossal:	less than 10 pieces per pound
Jumbo:	11–15 pieces per pound
Extra-large:	16–20 pieces per pound
Large:	21–30 pieces per pound
Medium:	31–35 pieces per pound
Small:	36–45 pieces per pound
Miniature:	100 pieces per pound

CHICKEN WITH NECTARINE SALSA

Serves 4

Serve with a fresh green salad and a side of fresh fruit.

4 (4-ounce) boneless, skinless chicken breasts
1 tablespoon lime juice
1½ teaspoons ground cumin
½ teaspoon salt
½ teaspoon ground black pepper

1 fresh nectarine
1 jalapeño pepper
2 garlic cloves
2 tablespoons chopped fresh cilantro
½ cup chunky salsa
Lime wedges, for garnish

1. Preheat grill or broiler.
2. Rinse the chicken and pat dry. Brush the chicken with the lime juice and sprinkle evenly with the cumin, salt, and pepper. Grill the chicken on the rack of an uncovered grill directly over medium heat or broil for 12 to 15 minutes, until the chicken is tender and no longer pink, turning once.
3. Meanwhile, prepare the nectarine salsa: Chop the nectarine into ¼-inch pieces. Seed and finely chop the jalapeño pepper. Peel and mince the garlic. Chop the cilantro. Stir together the nectarine, jalapeño, garlic, cilantro, and salsa in a small bowl. Spoon over the chicken and serve with the lime wedges on the side for garnish.

Cooking Chicken

Chicken should be cooked to the following temperatures for safety:

Boneless chicken:	165°
Bone-in pieces:	170°
Ground chicken:	165°
Bone-in whole chicken:	180°

REFRIGERATOR PUMPKIN PIE WITH MACADAMIA NUT CRUST

1½ cups finely chopped
  macadamia nuts
16 packets sugar substitute
2 tablespoons butter, softened,
  plus extra for greasing
1 packet unflavored gelatin

¼ cup water
1 teaspoon pumpkin pie spice
1 (25-ounce) can pumpkin purée
2 teaspoons grated orange zest
1½ cups heavy cream
2 teaspoons vanilla extract

Serves 8

This medium-carbohy-drate dish is excellent served as dessert for the very low-carb Mustard-Glazed Monkfish Wrapped in Bacon (page 247).

1. Heat oven to 400°. Butter the bottom and sides of a 9-inch spring-form pan.
2. In a medium-sized bowl, combine the macadamia nuts, 4 packets of the sugar substitute, and the butter; mix well. Press the mixture onto the bottom and 1 inch up the sides of the prepared pan. Bake for 10 minutes, until golden brown. Cool on a wire rack.
3. In a small bowl, sprinkle the gelatin over the water. Let sit for 5 minutes until the gelatin softens.
4. Heat a small skillet over medium heat and toast the pumpkin pie spice for 1 to 2 minutes, until fragrant, stirring frequently. Reduce heat to low, stir in the gelatin mixture, and cook for 1 to 2 minutes until the gelatin melts. Remove from heat and let cool to room temperature.
5. Place the pumpkin purée in a large bowl and mash with a fork to loosen. Mix in the orange zest. In another large bowl, using an electric mixer on high speed, beat the cream with the remaining 12 packets of sugar substitute and the vanilla until soft peaks form. With a rubber spatula, slowly fold in the gelatin mixture.
6. In 3 parts, gently fold the whipped cream mixture into the pumpkin purée. Pour the filling into the cooled pie shell and smooth the top. Refrigerate for at least 3 hours before serving.

Chapter 19

LOW-FAT CELEBRATIONS

PASTA AND SMOKED TROUT WITH LEMON PESTO	256
BAKED RED SNAPPER ALMANDINE	257
SALMON TORTELLINI SALAD	258
FUSILLI WITH CHICKEN AND CORIANDER PESTO	259
SAVORY PASTITSIO	260
CHEESE COINS	262
ORECCHIETTE WITH SUMMER TOMATO SAUCE AND OLIVES	263
PEARS IN ORANGE SAUCE	264
LEMON BLUEBERRY ICE "CREAM"	265

PASTA AND SMOKED TROUT
WITH LEMON PESTO

2 garlic cloves

2 tightly packed cups fresh basil leaves

⅛ cup toasted pine nuts

2 teaspoons fresh-squeezed lemon juice

2 teaspoons water

5 teaspoons extra-virgin olive oil, divided

4 tablespoons grated Parmesan cheese, divided

4 ounces uncooked linguini

2 ounces boneless smoked trout

1 teaspoon freshly ground black pepper

1. Place the pasta in 1 quart boiling water and 1 teaspoon olive oil. Boil until the pasta is soft but firm. Drain and set aside.
2. Peel the garlic. In a food processor, pulse the garlic until finely chopped. Add the basil, pine nuts, lemon juice, and water; process until puréed. Add the remaining 4 teaspoons of the olive oil and 3 tablespoons of the Parmesan cheese; pulse until the pesto is smooth. Set aside.
3. Flake the smoked trout and add to the pesto mixture. Add the pasta and toss. Divide onto 4 plates and sprinkle each serving with Parmesan cheese.

Smoked Fish

Smoking is not just a way to add flavor to meat. Native Americans would smoke fish over their fires in the fall as a way to preserve it through the winter. Unlike other preservation methods, a well-smoked fish will remain flaky and tender for months.

BAKED RED SNAPPER ALMANDINE

1 pound red snapper fillets
1 teaspoon sea salt
½ teaspoon freshly ground
   white pepper
4 teaspoons all-purpose flour

1 teaspoon olive oil
2 tablespoons raw almonds
1 teaspoon unsalted butter
1 tablespoon lemon juice

Serves 4

Serve with rice pilaf
and fresh fruit for a
festive yet light meal.

1. Preheat oven to 375°. Rinse the fish fillets and pat dry between layers
   of paper towels. Season with salt and pepper. Sprinkle the front and
   back of the fillets with the flour.
2. In an ovenproof, nonstick skillet on medium-high heat, sauté the fillets
   in the olive oil until they are nicely browned on both sides.
3. Finely grind the almonds and combine with the butter in a microwave-
   safe dish. Microwave on high for 30 seconds, or until the butter is
   melted. Stir.
4. Pour the almond-butter mixture and the lemon juice over the fillets.
5. Bake for 3 to 5 minutes, or until the almonds are nicely browned.

Lemon Juice at Hand
Squeeze juice from lemons when you have time or when lemons are
on sale and freeze the juice so it's ready to use when you need it.

SALMON TORTELLINI SALAD

Serves 4

Serve with fresh fruit
and a green salad.

8 ounces frozen or fresh cheese
   tortellini
4 carrots
1 zucchini
1 red bell pepper
2 (6½-ounce) cans salmon

1 cup plain low-fat yogurt
¼ cup grated Parmesan cheese
¼ cup chopped parsley
1 tablespoon low-fat milk
1 teaspoon dried oregano

1. Cook the tortellini according to package directions. Drain, rinse under cold water, and drain again. Peel and slice the carrots thinly. Slice the zucchini. Remove the seeds and stem from bell pepper and cut into narrow strips. Drain the salmon and flake with a fork.
2. In medium-sized bowl, gently toss together the pasta, carrots, zucchini, and bell pepper. Add the salmon and mix.
3. In a small bowl, stir together the yogurt, cheese, parsley, milk, and oregano until well mixed. Add to the pasta mixture and toss gently to coat evenly.
4. Cover and refrigerate for several hours before serving.

Moldy Cheese

Chances are your mother probably told you that you just had to scrape off the mold before you ate cheese because cheese is just mold anyway. That is definitely an oversimplification. The mold on the outside of cheese comes from bacteria in the air and while it likely won't make you sick if you scrape it off, it is a sign that the cheese is not in perfect form.

FUSILLI WITH CHICKEN AND CORIANDER PESTO

2 whole chicken breasts, halved
1 pound fusilli pasta
4 garlic cloves
4 serrano chile peppers

½ cup slivered blanched almonds
3 ounces cilantro
2 tablespoons olive oil
1 cup low-fat mayonnaise

Serves 4

Serve with a green salad and fresh fruit for a traditional Italian dinner.

1. Preheat oven to 375°. Cook the pasta in boiling water until al dente.
2. Place the chicken breasts in a baking pan. Bake until cooked through and tender, 15 to 20 minutes. Remove from the oven and let cool. Remove and discard the skin and bones and shred the meat. Place the meat in a medium-sized bowl, cover, and chill.
3. Meanwhile, peel the garlic and cut into ¼-inch pieces. Remove the stems and seeds from the chili peppers. In a food processor or blender, combine the garlic, chilies, almonds, and cilantro; process until finely chopped. With the motor running, add the oil in a thin, steady stream, processing until the pesto is the consistency of a thick paste.
4. Place the pesto in a bowl. Whisk in the mayonnaise.
5. In a large bowl, combine the chilled pasta, shredded chicken, and the pesto; stir to mix well. Cover and chill for 1 hour before serving.

Releasing Garlic's Potential

Get the most out of garlic by "popping" the clove before adding it to a dish. Hold a large knife on its side and place the peeled clove under it. Push down until you hear the clove pop. You'll release all the wonderful oils without having to chop.

SAVORY PASTITSIO

Serves 10

This is a perfect cold-weather dish. Serve with Pears in Orange Sauce (page 264) for dessert.

2 teaspoons olive oil

1 large white onion, peeled and finely chopped

1½ pounds lean ground beef

1 cup water

¾ cup dry white whine

1 (6-ounce) can tomato paste

½ cup bulgur

¾ teaspoon cinnamon

¾ teaspoon nutmeg

¾ teaspoon allspice

1½ teaspoons salt

½ teaspoon ground black pepper

2 cups 1% cottage cheese

2 tablespoons all-purpose flour

1 cup fat-free chicken broth, divided

1 (12-ounce) can evaporated skim milk

¾ cup, plus 2 tablespoons freshly grated Parmesan cheese

1 pound elbow macaroni

2 tablespoons chopped fresh parsley

1. In a large nonstick skillet, heat 1 teaspoon of the oil over medium heat. Add the chopped onion and sauté until softened, about 5 minutes. Add the ground beef and cook, breaking it up with a wooden spoon, until no longer pink, about 5 minutes. Drain off fat.

2. Add the water, wine, tomato paste, bulgur, spices, 1 teaspoon of the salt, and the pepper. Simmer uncovered over low heat, stirring occasionally, until the bulgur is tender, about 20 minutes.

3. In a food processor or blender, purée the cottage cheese until completely smooth. Set aside.

4. In a small bowl, stir together the flour and ¼ cup of the chicken broth until smooth.

5. In a medium-sized heavy saucepan, combine the evaporated skim milk and the remaining chicken broth. Heat over medium heat until scalded (a thick film forms on top). Stir the flour mixture into the hot milk mixture and cook, stirring constantly, until thickened, about 2 minutes. Remove from the heat and whisk in the puréed cottage cheese and the ½ cup of grated cheese. Season with salt and pepper. To prevent

a skin from forming, place wax paper or plastic wrap directly over the surface and set aside.

6. In a large pot of boiling salted water, cook the macaroni until al dente, 8 to 10 minutes. Drain and return to the pot. Toss with ¼ cup of the grated cheese, the remaining 1 teaspoon oil, and ½ teaspoon of the salt.

7. Preheat oven to 350°. Spray a 9" × 13" baking dish with nonstick cooking spray.

8. Spread ½ of the pasta mixture over the bottom of the prepared dish. Top with ⅓ of the cream sauce. Spoon all of the meat sauce over the top, spreading evenly. Cover with another ⅓ of the cream sauce. Top with the remaining pasta mixture and cover with the remaining cream sauce. Sprinkle with the remaining 2 tablespoons of grated cheese.

9. Bake for 40 to 50 minutes, or until bubbling and golden. Sprinkle with parsley before serving.

Parsley Facts

While lots of dishes look nicer with a sprig of parsley, the problem is that you have to buy it in such big bunches. However, parsley will stay crisp and fresh for up to a week if you store it standing in a glass of ice water in the refrigerator. Change the water every couple of days. If you still haven't used it up, give it to the dog to help freshen his breath.

CHEESE COINS

24 coins

A perfect appetizer for Fusilli with Chicken and Coriander Pesto (page 259).

¼ cup reduced-fat margarine, at room temperature
2 cups shredded low-fat Cheddar cheese
½ teaspoon dry mustard
½ teaspoon seasoned salt

2 teaspoons minced canned green chili peppers
2 teaspoons minced pimientos
½ teaspoon Worcestershire sauce
1¼ cups all-purpose flour

1. Preheat oven to 350°.
2. In a bowl, using a mixer, beat together the margarine, cheese, mustard, seasoned salt, green chilies, pimientos, and Worcestershire sauce until blended.
3. Add the flour, beating it until a stiff dough forms. Shape into small balls (about ½ inch in diameter) and place well spaced on ungreased baking sheets. Press each ball lightly with the tines of a fork.
4. Bake until lightly browned, about 15 minutes. Remove from the oven and serve piping hot. Store in an airtight container at room temperature for up to 2 weeks.

Ovens

Even today's modern ovens can vary widely in temperature. Gas ovens are especially prone to variations. Before you begin using a new oven, buy an inexpensive food thermometer and determine the temperature your oven really cooks at when it's set at various temperatures.

ORECCHIETTE WITH SUMMER TOMATO SAUCE AND OLIVES

1½ pounds tomatoes
2 garlic cloves
2 tablespoons basil leaves
⅓ cup kalamata olives, pitted

3 tablespoons olive oil
½ teaspoon ground black pepper
1 pound orecchiette pasta

Serves 4

Serve with Lemon Blueberry Ice "Cream" (page 265) for dessert.

1. Peel, seed, and chop the tomatoes into ½-inch pieces. Peel and mince the garlic. Shred the basil leaves. Pit the olives, if necessary.
2. In a large bowl, combine the tomatoes, garlic, basil, oil, and pepper; stir to mix well. Set aside at room temperature for at least 30 minutes.
3. Cook the pasta in boiling salted water until al dente. Drain and place in a large warmed bowl.
4. Pour the tomato mixture into a food processor or blender and blend on medium speed until well mixed. Expect a few chunks of tomatoes to remain. (You likely will have to divide the mixture in half to do this.)
5. Put the tomato sauce in a large saucepan and heat on medium heat until it begins to bubble. Serve over pasta. Garnish with the olives.

Pitting Olives

Pitting olives is easy. The key is to use a tool that's as hard as the pits to get them out. Try the bottom of a small pot or pan. Put the olives on a cutting board in groups of 3 or 4 and put the bottom of the pan flat on top of them. With the heel of your hand, smash the olives between the pan and the board, using the curved edge of the pan for leverage. Once flattened, the olives will easily give up their pits.

PEARS IN ORANGE SAUCE

2 Bartlett pears
1 cup water
⅔ cup orange juice
2 tablespoons lemon juice
1 tablespoon cornstarch

3 tablespoons honey
¼ teaspoon orange zest
¼ teaspoon salt
1 bunch fresh mint leaves

1. Halve the pears lengthwise and core.
2. In a medium-sized skillet, bring the water to boil. Add the pear halves, cover, and simmer gently over low heat until tender when pierced with a knife, about 10 minutes. Set aside.
3. In a small saucepan, mix together the orange juice, lemon juice, and cornstarch. Stir until the cornstarch is dissolved. Add the honey, orange zest, and salt; mix well.
4. Place over medium heat and cook until thickened and bubbly, about 10 minutes.
5. To serve, spoon the sauce over the pears and garnish with mint leaves.

Ripening Fruit
If you find you must buy unripe fruit, put it in a paper bag and store it in a cool place for a day or two. Before you know it, the fruit will ripen. This works for any kind of fruit, including berries and tomatoes.

LEMON BLUEBERRY ICE "CREAM"

1 pint fresh blueberries
½ cup granulated sugar, divided
1 tablespoon cornstarch
1 (12-ounce) can evaporated
   skim milk

2 egg whites
1 teaspoon lemon zest
2 tablespoons lemon juice
1 teaspoon pure vanilla extract

> **Serves 4**
>
> If you don't have an ice cream maker, take the mixture out of the refrigerator before it is solid and serve by scraping the top.

1. In a medium-sized saucepan, combine the blueberries with ¼ cup of the sugar. Place over medium heat, stirring constantly, until the sugar dissolves, about 5 minutes. Remove from heat.

2. Place a colander over a bowl and pour the blueberry mixture into the colander. Press the berries through the colander with the back of a spoon. Scrape the mashed berries from the outside of the colander into the bowl with the blueberry juice. Place the bowl in the refrigerator.

3. Add the remaining ¼ cup sugar and the cornstarch to the saucepan. Stir in about ⅔ of the evaporated milk. Place over medium heat and bring to a boil, stirring constantly. Cook the mixture until it is the consistency of pudding.

4. Remove from the heat and add the egg whites and the remaining evaporated milk, mixing well. Stir the milk mixture into the blueberry mixture. Add the lemon zest, lemon juice, and vanilla; stir until blended. Chill for 20 minutes.

5. Pour into an ice cream maker and freeze according to the manufacturer's instructions.

Add a Little Zest
Citrus goes great with seafood of all kinds. Try squeezing some lemon or lime on any of your favorite fish recipes.

CHAPTER 20

WORLD FAVORITES

SCANDINAVIAN BAKED COD WITH SPICY PLUM SAUCE	268
CHRISTMAS PIGLET	269
COCONUT TURKEY CURRY	269
VIETNAMESE CRAB AND PINEAPPLE SOUP	270
BRAZILIAN PAELLA	271
FRENCH COUNTRY MUSSELS	272
NORTH AFRICAN EGGPLANT	273
NATIVE AMERICAN PUDDING	274
GERMAN COFFEE CAKE	275
MINTED MIDDLE EASTERN BUTTERMILK SHAKE	276

SCANDINAVIAN BAKED COD
WITH SPICY PLUM SAUCE

Serves 4

Add fresh-steamed broccoli and carrots to create a colorful, wholesome meal.

1 garlic clove
1 medium Granny Smith apple
1 small red onion
1 pound cod fillets
1 teaspoon paprika
1 teaspoon grated fresh ginger
1 bay leaf
2 teaspoons soy sauce

1 teaspoon olive oil
¼ cup plum sauce
¼ teaspoon frozen unsweetened apple juice concentrate
¼ teaspoon dark molasses
¼ teaspoon Chinese five-spice powder
1⅓ cups cooked brown rice

1. Preheat oven to 400°. Treat a baking dish with nonstick spray. Crush the garlic clove with the side of a large knife and remove the skin. Peel, core, and chop the apple into ½-inch cubes. Remove the skin from the onion and chop into ¼-inch pieces.

2. Rinse the cod and pat dry between paper towels. Rub both sides of the fish with paprika and set in the prepared baking dish.

3. In a covered, microwave-safe bowl, mix together the garlic, apple, onion, ginger, bay leaf, and soy sauce in the oil and microwave on high for 3 minutes or until the apple is tender and the onion is transparent. Stir, discard the bay leaf, and top the fillets with the apple mixture. Bake, uncovered, for 10 to 15 minutes or until the fish is opaque.

4. While the fish bakes, add the plum sauce to a microwave-safe bowl. Add the apple juice concentrate, molasses, and five-spice powder. Microwave on high for 30 seconds. Stir, add a little water if needed to thin the mixture, and microwave for another 15 seconds. Cover until ready to serve.

5. To serve, equally divide the cooked rice among 4 serving plates. Top each with an equal amount of the baked fish mixture and plum sauce mixture, drizzling the sauce atop the fish.

CHRISTMAS PIGLET

1 (12- to 15-pound) piglet
1 teaspoon salt
½ cup sour cream

½ cup melted butter
¼ cup water

Serves 8

For a traditional Russian meal, serve with baked apples and Roasted Garlic Mashed Potatoes (page 10).

1. Preheat oven to 350°.
2. Scald the piglet and dry with paper towels. Rub the inside with salt and place, back-side up, on a baking sheet.
3. Brush the sides with the sour cream and pour the melted butter over the piglet. Pour the water on the baking sheet. Bake for 1½ hours, basting with the juice that drips onto the baking sheet.

COCONUT TURKEY CURRY

1 medium-sized yellow onion
1 garlic clove
5 cups cubed cooked turkey
½ teaspoon ground ginger
2 teaspoons curry powder
⅓ cup all-purpose flour

2 cups chicken or turkey broth, divided
1 teaspoon salt
1 teaspoon ground black pepper
1 (16-ounce) can coconut cream, unsweetened
1 cup skim milk

Serves 6

Serve with white rice and small dishes of raisins, peanuts, chutney, coconut, bacon, and green onions on the side.

1. Peel the onion and garlic and cut into quarters. Cut the turkey into 1-inch cubes.
2. Purée the onions, garlic, ginger, curry powder, flour, and ½ cup of the broth until smooth.
3. In a large saucepan, combine the puréed mixture and all the remaining ingredients *except* the turkey. Cook, stirring often, until thickened. Add the meat and heat gently.

VIETNAMESE CRAB AND PINEAPPLE SOUP

1 cooked Dungeness crab
15 medium-sized raw shrimp
15 medium-sized steamer clams
1 cup cubed fresh pineapple
½ small yellow onion
4 garlic cloves
½ pound ripe tomatoes
2 scallions
4 cilantro sprigs
5 basil leaves
3 dill sprigs
6 mint leaves

3 tablespoons olive oil
10 cups water
1 stalk lemongrass
3 tablespoons Vietnamese fish sauce
2 tablespoons granulated sugar
½ teaspoon chili sauce
1 teaspoon salt
2 tablespoons fresh-squeezed lime juice
⅛ teaspoon saffron
1 bay leaf

1. Remove the meat from the crab. Peel and devein the shrimp (leaving the tails on). Scrub the clamshells. Cut the pineapple into bite-sized chunks. Peel the onion and garlic, and chop into ¼-inch pieces. Seed and chop the tomatoes into ½-inch pieces. Chop the scallions, cilantro, basil leaves, dill, and mint.

2. Heat the oil in a soup pot. Add the onion and sauté on medium for 3 minutes. Add the garlic and tomatoes; cook for 3 more minutes. Add the pineapple, water, and lemongrass, bringing everything to a boil. Reduce to a simmer and cook for 20 minutes.

3. Add the fish sauce, sugar, chili sauce, salt, and lime juice. Bring to a boil. Add the crab, and the clams in their shells, cooking for about 5 minutes, until the clams are open.

4. Add the shrimp, scallions, cilantro, basil, dill, mint, saffron, and bay leaf; simmer for 2 to 3 more minutes, until the shrimp turn pink. Discard the bay leaf and lemongrass stalk, and serve.

BRAZILIAN PAELLA

½ pound spicy pork sausage
1 (2–3-pound) chicken
2 large yellow onions
1 pound canned tomatoes
½ teaspoon salt

½ teaspoon ground black pepper
1½ cups uncooked long-grain
   brown rice
3 chicken bouillon cubes
2 cups hot water

Serves 8

Serve with fresh-sliced oranges and bananas sprinkled with coconut to achieve a true Brazilian flavor.

1. Form the sausage into balls about the size of large marbles. Clean and cut the chicken into serving-sized pieces. Peel and chop the onions into ¼-inch pieces. Drain the tomatoes, retaining the liquid, and cut into 1-inch pieces.
2. Using a large skillet on medium-high heat, fry the sausage balls until they are well browned and crisp. Place them on paper towels to absorb the grease. Sprinkle the chicken with salt and pepper. Without emptying the grease from the skillet, fry the chicken pieces for about 10 minutes. Place the chicken on paper towels to absorb the grease.
3. Drain all but 3 tablespoons of grease from the skillet. Sauté the onions on medium heat in the skillet until translucent. Add the rice to the skillet and continue to sauté, stirring constantly for 10 minutes.
4. Place the sausage balls, chicken, onion and rice mixture, tomato juice, and tomatoes in a slow cooker. Mix the bouillon in the hot water. Add to the slow cooker. Cover and cook on low setting for 8 to 9 hours.

Freezing Cooked Rice

Cooked rice can be frozen up to 6 months. The next time you make some for a meal, make twice what you need and freeze the rest in an airtight container. It needs virtually no thawing when added to a casserole.

FRENCH COUNTRY MUSSELS

Serves 6

Serve with white rice and fresh-steamed asparagus.

1 large white onion
4 garlic cloves
1 (16-ounce) can peeled tomatoes
½ cup minced fresh parsley

4 pounds mussels
1 tablespoon olive oil
1 cup dry white wine
½ teaspoon ground black pepper

1. Peel the onion and chop into ¼-inch pieces. Peel and mince the garlic. Drain the tomatoes. Mince the parsley. Scrub and debeard the mussels.
2. In an 8-quart pot, heat the oil over medium heat. Add the onion and garlic, and sauté until browned, about 10 minutes.
3. Add the tomatoes, breaking them up with a wooden spoon. Add the parsley and pepper. Raise the heat to high and cook for about 2 minutes.
4. Add the wine and cook for another 2 minutes.
5. Add the mussels, tossing them to coat well with the tomato mixture. Cover and cook, stirring occasionally, until the mussels open, about 5 minutes. Discard any mussels that did not open. Serve immediately.

What Is Clarified Butter?

Clarified butter is also known as drawn butter. Clarifying butter separates the milk solids and evaporates the water, leaving a clear golden liquid. Clarified butter has a higher heating point before smoking and also has a longer shelf life than regular butter. Clarified butter is used to sauté where a high heating point is needed.

NORTH AFRICAN EGGPLANT

2 medium eggplants
3 tablespoons olive oil, divided
1 large ripe tomato
4 garlic cloves
1 tablespoon dried marjoram

1 teaspoon coriander seeds
¼ teaspoon salt
½ teaspoon crushed red pepper
1 tablespoon toasted pine nuts

Serves 6

This side dish is perfect with seafood or other light main dishes.

1. Preheat oven to 425°.
2. Peel the eggplants and cut into 1-inch cubes. Toss with half of the olive oil and place in a shallow roasting pan. Roast, uncovered, for 10 minutes, stirring once.
3. Meanwhile, chop the tomato. Peel and mince the garlic.
4. Heat the remaining oil in a large skillet. Cook the tomato, garlic, marjoram, coriander, salt, and red pepper until the tomato is soft. Add the eggplant and reduce heat to low.
5. Cook, covered, for 10 minutes. Stir in the pine nuts during the last 5 minutes of cooking.

What to Brown In

For browning and crispness, clarified butter achieves the best results. This may be because residual proteins in the butter caramelize on foods, or it may simply be the high temperatures that clarified butter can reach without burning. Start with a neutral oil, such as peanut oil, and add a nugget of whole butter to get a better brown.

NATIVE AMERICAN PUDDING

2 tablespoons butter, plus ¼
    tablespoon for greasing
3 cups 1% milk
½ cup cornmeal
½ teaspoon salt

3 large eggs, beaten
¼ packed cup light brown sugar
⅓ cup molasses
½ teaspoon allspice
½ teaspoon ginger

1. Lightly grease a 3- to 6-quart slow cooker with the ¼ tablespoon butter. Preheat the slow cooker on high for 15 minutes.
2. In a medium-sized saucepan, bring the milk, cornmeal, and salt to a boil. Boil, stirring constantly, for 5 minutes. Cover and simmer on low for 10 minutes.
3. In a large bowl, combine the remaining ingredients. Gradually whisk the cornmeal mixture into the combined ingredients until thoroughly mixed and smooth. Pour into slow cooker. Cover and cook on low setting for 4 to 5 hours.

Stocking Up on Ethnic Staples
If your local grocery store doesn't carry certain ethnic spices or ingredients, you may be able to find them on the Internet or at specialty shops. Just make sure to stock up on shelf-stable necessities so you can make these dishes whenever you like.

GERMAN COFFEE CAKE

½ cup butter
1¼ cups granulated sugar,
   divided
2 eggs
1 cup sour cream
1 teaspoon vanilla extract

1 teaspoon baking soda
1 teaspoon baking powder
½ teaspoon salt
2 cups all-purpose flour
½ cup chopped walnuts
1 teaspoon cinnamon

10 servings
This Bavarian treat often is served as a Sunday morning treat with strong black coffee.

1. Preheat oven to 350°. Grease a 13" × 9" baking pan.
2. Cream together the butter and 1 cup of the sugar thoroughly. Add the eggs, sour cream, vanilla, baking soda, baking powder, salt, and flour; beat well. Pour into the prepared baking pan.
3. Combine the remaining ¼ cup sugar, the nuts, and cinnamon to make the topping. Lightly stir 2 tablespoons of the topping into the batter. Pour patter into baking pan and sprinkle remaining topping on top.
4. Bake for 35 to 40 minutes.

Where'd They Get That Stuff?

Coffee, nuts, coconut, and cinnamon. Not exactly foods you think of being native to Germany, so how did these dishes become synonymous with this cool-weather country? Most likely, they were brought to Germany when Marco Polo followed Genghis Khan from eastern China through Russia and into Europe.

MINTED MIDDLE EASTERN BUTTERMILK SHAKE

Serves 1

Serve with red meat or chicken dishes.

Handful ice cubes
1 cup nonfat buttermilk
⅛ teaspoon salt

¼ cup fresh mint leaves, plus
extra for garnish

Combine all of the ingredients in a blender. Cover and blend until the ice becomes blended. Pour into a tall mug and garnish with more mint leaves.

Fresh Mint

For the freshest mint, try growing your own. You can start them from seeds or from young seedlings that have already been started. Put them in an enclosed space or pots or they will spread. If you want to grow mint indoors, put it in a window that gets a lot of sunlight.

Introduction to Gourmet Entertaining

▶ What does "gourmet" mean? When you think of the word, you probably have a sense of what it refers to, but you may find it difficult to explain. Some people associate gourmet with fancy ingredients, or an exacting recipe. Sometimes it is synonymous for French, and impossible to pronounce. We often ascribe "gourmet" to that which is both delicious and unfamiliar. Or it could be the thing adorning the plate that simply looks too beautiful to eat. And, of course, it can refer to the meal that cost as much as a home mortgage.

Today, the mystique of gourmet cooking has been replaced by something far more useful: knowledge. Gourmet cuisine is no longer reserved for celebrity chefs or the French. It can come in the form of a solitary ingredient that is not readily available, such as quail eggs or galanga root. It can be taking the extra time to think of presentation when you put a dish together. For instance, rather than throwing salad in a bowl, you can drizzle the dressing on the side of the plate, build a tower of mixed greens, and finish it with a chive garnish. It takes five minutes, but looks far more dramatic on the plate.

In this part of the book, you'll see that planning your next meal for your dinner party or holiday family dinner is easier than you might think.

Chapter 21

Going Gourmet

Food. It's perhaps life's most universal necessity, as well as joy. Whether it is a mother preparing dinner for her family, a husband throwing prime rib on the grill, or a chef showcasing his or her skill at a fabulous restaurant, eating is about family and community. You use it to celebrate positive events, such as a new job or a raise, or even as a way to propose marriage. Sitting around the table together in the evening to share details about your day is a way to use the custom of dinner to bring your family closer together. You rely on food for nourishment, though it goes far beyond simple sustenance.

Small Beginnings

Over the years Americans have gained access to a rainbow of cuisines. *The Round-the-World Cookbook,* a collection of recipes compiled by Pan American Airways, spoke to wives in the 1950s as if they were on the culinary cutting edge by introducing the food of other cultures. The average housewife, suddenly armed with recipes from lands she had probably only caught pictures of in magazines, had a newfound sense of running an "international" kitchen, a far cry from today's traveled career woman, mother, and wife.

Another way of learning about food came from the diversity of people who make up the United States. You need only look to our own cultural melting pot to see how it overflows into your kitchens: countless immigrants brought with them a taste of their own cultures. If you grew up in California, Mexican food was de rigueur, and no one can live in New Orleans without reveling in French cuisine. Of course, the United States has its own unique culinary traditions, from good ol' Texas barbecue, to the hearty flavors of Soul Food, to the birth of the almighty California Cuisine.

There are many characteristics that can distinguish gourmet food from what is not considered to be gourmet, such as:

- Always using the freshest ingredients available.
- Daring to incorporate unique or hard-to-find ingredients.
- Not being afraid of unusual combinations, but never sacrificing taste for the sake of complexity.
- Concentrating on presentation, remembering that you eat with your eyes.
- Realizing that a great meal is an investment, and being willing to sometimes spend a bit extra for special ingredients.
- Cooking with enthusiasm, which is always infectious.

Food from Afar

Perhaps most influential of all on the education of the American palate, at least in recent years, has been travel. With the radical expansion of airline routes and lower prices, it's a good bet the average household has journeyed abroad, tasting foods that made firsthand impressions on their palates. Americans are opening their minds (and mouths) across the globe. Part of the excitement of travel is having the chance to eat beyond our usual menus. Memorable travel is often synonymous with great food. How many times do you, when recalling a destination, think back to an awe-inspiring meal, the pungent scents wafting through a food market, or even an explosively fresh fruit drink served on the side of the road?

Yet even with today's travel opportunities, a shocking number of people still do not journey beyond the borders of the United States. Only a small percentage of American citizens carry current passports. They may know of various cultures, but they have not experienced them firsthand. Food provides that opportunity. One way may be to visit a local international restaurant. Mexican, Italian, French, Thai, Japanese, and Chinese are all common restaurant choices, but now America is experiencing an upswing in even more exotic foods—Ethiopian, Persian, and so on—including a growing number of upscale fusion restaurants, such as Sushi Samba in New York City, which seamlessly blends Japanese and Latin flavors. These establishments boast eclectic cuisine that defies one simple geographical reference.

Food as Art

Over the years, cooking has developed into an art. Through the introduction of culinary shows (starting with Julia Child, now an entire network—the Food Network—is dedicated to the cause), through magazines, Internet sites, and books, American tastes are becoming more educated. Instead of simply following recipes in rote fashion, many cooks want to feel as though the kitchen is a place where they can experiment, learn, and create. Today's average cook wants the key to feeling innovative in the kitchen.

These vast sources and opportunities for learning about food gave birth to a new generation of "foodies." Baby boomers, one of the world's best-fed generations, went from frequenting exotic restaurants and lands to taking these experiences directly into their own kitchens. And why not? Today's average kitchen is well suited to inquisitive palates. Even markets play an important role in this global culinary education. The average upscale market, such as

Whole Foods or Trader Joe's, nurtures this newborn culinary enthusiasm by stocking shelves with an ever-growing list of international staples and hard-to-find gourmet items.

Getting Organized

Professional chefs have a philosophy called *mise en place,* which means "everything in its place." Quite simply, it's organization. Before you go shopping, it always wise to write a list of the things you'll need to purchase, and it's helpful to consider the best places to buy the ingredients you'll be using. You have a lot of options to explore these days with so many specialty food stores opening. You'll also want to take into account the before and after of making a meal—setting up your workspace and serving the meal.

Shopping

Read a recipe in its entirety at least once before starting your shopping list. Write your list to take advantage of items at the salad bar for prepped produce, the deli counter for sliced meats and cheeses, the produce counter for cleaned greens, the freezer section for prepped vegetables, and the dairy counter for specialty cheeses. As you get more familiar with your grocery store, you can begin to write your shopping list in the same organization of the store, grouping dairy together, produce together, deli together, and other categories.

Know your stores. There are many specialty stores out there, including gourmet shops, cheese shops, ethnic markets, butchers, restaurant supply houses, and local supermarkets. Plan to stop at one new store on shopping expeditions when you have time, and you'll be amazed at the different foods and products that are designed to save you time.

Never shop on an empty stomach. While shopping can be fun, the goal is to buy what you need and not have leftovers, and shopping while hungry is a recipe for buying more than you need.

Setup

A clean work area is a pleasure to be in. Give yourself counter space. Make sure your sink and dishwasher are clean, have a couple of clean cutting boards on hand, and you're set. Your products should be arranged in the order listed in the recipe—this is also the order in which you'll use them. Pre-measure where possible, prepare baking pans if specified, preheat your oven when needed, and bring refrigerated items to room temperature if required. Now take a step back and put away anything that you're not going to be using, including spice jars, dairy containers, canisters, pans, or bowls. Trimmings and scraps should go into the garbage and dirty dishes should go into the sink, preferably in hot, soapy water to make cleanup easy. Good planning may seem like work, but it's actually a way to establish good habits that save time in the long run. Now is also a good time to think ahead and chill salad plates and warm serving platters.

Cooking

Your area is clean and your ingredients are prepared and you're ready to start. Take a minute and read the recipe in its entirety one more time. The worst time to realize you forgot something is in the middle of cooking. Have a few extra tasting spoons available and make sure there are paper towels and dishcloths easily accessible—just in case.

It's always a good idea to wash a few pots and pans when you have a minute, but don't let yourself become distracted from your priority, which is cooking. Follow the steps in the recipe and the suggested times provided for each step, but always keep in mind that the visual indicators noted in the recipe supersede the suggested times: if your fish is golden brown and cooked through in 6 minutes even though the recipe says 9 minutes, take it off the heat. Each oven and stovetop cook differently, pans cook differently, and meats, poultry, fishes, and vegetables each cook differently depending on age. Let your senses—not the clock—guide you.

Serving and Presentation

Even if you're cooking for just yourself, use a plate and sit at the table to enjoy your meal. It's just no fun to stand at the stove and eat your food from the pan. You deserve to be served, even if you're the one serving. Take a minute to chill salad plates and soup cups, if appropriate, and warm your dinner plates and serving platters.

> Make sure you have a spot in the kitchen or a clean dishwasher so you have somewhere to put dirty dishes if you're serving a multicourse meal. It's better to have a place to put them temporarily than to leave them on the table.

Cleanup

Cleanup is a necessary evil. Try not to leave everything for the end; put dirty dishes in the dishwasher as you use them. If you're going to leave a dirty pot on the stove to save sink space, fill it partway with hot soapy water so it can soak while you're enjoying your meal.

Restaurant supply houses, many of which are now open to the public, and larger discount chains sell a variety of aluminum disposable pans at a reasonable cost. Use these pans for any dishes that will be messy due to sauces, broiling, or roasting. You can run them through the dishwasher, and if they don't come out clean, toss them in the garbage. Place your broiler rack on a small rimmed baking sheet with sides or a small baking pan filled halfway with water—the drippings will fall into the pan, reducing your broiler cleaning time by at least half. Clean your broiler and grill after each use; it's disheartening to start preparing dinner and realize the broiler or grill was never cleaned from the previous use.

Kitchen Essentials

Your kitchen is where quality outweighs quantity when it comes to equipment. Your kitchen equipment will determine the efficiency of your workspace, which saves time in prepping, cooking, and cleanup. Having the right appliances makes your cooking experience efficient and easy. The right utensils for the right job also play a big role in how smoothly everything goes. Everything from what you use to cook to how you get rid of the scraps shapes the outcome of your cooking.

Basic Equipment

Freezer containers, food storage bags, freezer bags, and refrigerator bags in a variety of sizes, parchment paper, plastic film, and aluminum foil are staples that you should not be without. Ideal for storing leftovers for short or long periods of time, these items make it easy to handle any food that doesn't get eaten and provide versatility for storing depending on the type of food you're working with. For strainers and colanders, buy two different sizes of the metal type and you won't need to worry about heat resistance. A metal steamer basket is perfect for preparing vegetables, and the quality is usually consistent from brand to brand. Cutting boards are also helpful tools. Ideally, you should have two or three on hand. It's good to have one board for fruits, one for onions, garlic, etc., and one for meat and poultry. You can also have one for fish. Proper maintenance is mandatory, so be sure to follow the manufacturer's directions. They're available in wood and plastic, but the difference is simply one of personal preference.

A good cookware store will work with you to explain the pros and cons of each type of cookware for pots, pans, and ovenware. There are many manufacturers and each brand has its advantages. You'll know the types of foods you'll be preparing most and your style of cooking—braising, broiling, stovetop grilling, and sautéing. Invest in the cookware that you'll be using most.

There are many cost-effective cookware sets on the market, but make sure you analyze your storage space before bringing home that twenty-two-piece set that was just too good to pass up. Check with people you know who cook—ask what they use and what their likes and dislikes are and what they would do differently if purchasing a cookware set again.

Food Processors

Mini–food processors are huge timesavers for mincing garlic, shallots, herbs, and a number of other items. Many are now under $25, and if you watch for sale specials, you can get an extra work-bowl at no charge. You can also use a full-size food processor. Prices have come down on these appliances, so research before you buy to get the most for your money. Simple is better than complex—pay only for the accessories that you'll actually use. These appliances come with helpful manuals that provide tips for using them to get certain desired results. It's worth taking the time to get acquainted with the different ways you can use these products so that you know different ways to prepare food. In the end, these tips will make cooking much easier and save you time!

Handy Gadgets

One tool that every kitchen and cook should have is a hand mixer. Invest in a quality mixer with good motor speed. Several models also include a number of accessories including "wands" that are invaluable for puréeing soups, sauces, and fruit smoothies.

Citrus graters, which are also called *rasps,* are incredibly efficient tools that are excellent for grating the rinds of fruits for zest, and the larger version can be used for cheeses. Vegetable peelers are helpful, too. Buy two—you'll be glad you did (especially when you forget to run the dishwasher!). Can openers, whether manual or electric, are another must-have for any kitchen. A quality manual one is just as easy to use an electric one, and does the job all the same—it just depends on your preference. Pick one that's easy to hold and has rubberized handles. Instant-read thermometers are a sure way to test temperatures and doneness. Many thermometers now have the proper temperatures for meat and poultry printed right on them or their cover. Timers are also a must-have—it's just too easy to get distracted and a timer can save you from making countless mistakes.

Useful Equipment

When it comes to what you use to measure your ingredients, what you'll cook them in, and where you'll store them, there are some basic items that you'll need. Liquid measuring cups are essential. Don't count on just one big glass measuring cup to do everything. Have a variety of sizes and use the size that fits the job. There are several sets that nest, which saves on storage space. There is a difference between dry and wet measuring equipment, too. Dry measuring cups are available in plastic or metal. One advantage to plastic is that it's microwavable, but it will eventually stain. Metal cups are more durable, but lack the convenience of being microwavable.

In addition to measuring cups, you'll need measuring spoons. One set works for both liquid and dry measures and the metal spoons are worth the investment.

Utensils

It's important to have a variety of different spoons available when you cook. There are many different types, such wooden and metal, slotted and nonslotted, big and little. Using the right tool makes everything easier and potentially saves on spills and accidents.

Knives are also a personal preference. Check out several different manufacturers, and test them for weight and balance. A good cookware store will let you try out several types by cutting a potato or other vegetable to see if you like the feel. Paring knives are invaluable, as are a good midsize (8 to 10 inches) chef's knife, an 8-inch serrated knife, and an 8- to 10-inch carving knife for slicing roasts. Your choice of knife sizes and types is truly a personal preference. Knives can be quite costly, so take time to do the research before investing. The most important part of your knife kit is a sharpener. Learn how to use it, and have your knives professionally sharpened a few times a year. Dull knives cause accidents.

Also necessary, but less commonly considered, are tools such as ladles, spatulas, tongs, and whisks. It's nice to have a small (2-ounce) and a medium-sized (6-ounce) ladle on hand for hot liquids and skimming. There are two different types of spatulas available—the mixing type and the turning type. For the mixing type, have several sizes of heat-resistant quality. That way you can use your spatulas for any application, hot or cold. Use good-quality metal spatulas for the turning type. Make sure the handle is heat resistant so it won't melt when you rest it on the edge of a hot skillet. There is also a specialty spatula called a *fish-turner*. This tool is very helpful if you prepare a fair amount of fish. You should also have a few heat-resistant plastic spatulas to protect the surface of nonstick pans, if you own them. For tongs, purchase two or three good-quality aluminum ones in different sizes. Check the locking mechanism before purchasing—some of the mechanisms are cumbersome. Wire whisks come in handy when making sauces and homemade vinaigrettes. You should have at least one good whisk on hand.

Chapter 22

Vive La France

288   Brome Lake Duck Suprême

288   Salmon Fillets in Sweet Wine with Orange and Fennel

289   Escargots in Chablis

290   Rabbit with Wild Thyme

291   Corn Clam Chowder with Mulard Duck–Pan Seare
Foie Gras

292   Truffle Oil and Brie Soufflé

293   French Onion Soup with Port

294   Bouillabaisse

295   Chocolate Mousse with Goat Cheese Cream

296   Goat Cheese Cream

296   Moules Mariniere (Mussels in White Wine)

297   Crepes with Curaçao Strawberries and Oranges

298   Raclette (Melted Cheese with Potatoes)

299   Shrimp and Melon Salad

299   Pesto Beurre Blanc

300   Foie Gras–Stuffed Cornish Hens

301   Left Bank's Chocolate Fondant

Brome Lake Duck Suprême

Serves 4

The following four recipes all come from Executive Chef Mélanie Gagnon, at the Auberg Ste-Catherine de Hatley in Québec.

1½ cup Mistral du Cep d'Argent (or another sweet wine such as Banyuls or Pineau de Charente)

⅓ cup sugar

½ cup fresh cranberries

1 grapefruit, zested and juice squeezed

1 orange, zested and juice squeezed

4 duck breasts

Salt and pepper, to taste

1. Combine the sweet wine, sugar, cranberries, grapefruit, and orange zest and juice together in a medium saucepan.
2. Simmer over medium heat for 7 minutes. If you prefer a thicker sauce, dissolve 1 tablespoon cornstarch in 1 tablespoon of cold water and add to the sauce when hot.
3. Cook duck breast in a sauté pan for 6 minutes on the skin side, 3 minutes on the other side. Finish in the oven for 10 minutes at 350°. Slice the duck breast and serve with the sauce.

Salmon Fillets in Sweet Wine with Orange and Fennel

Serves 4

This sweet twist on salmon is another recipe by Chef Executif Mélanie Gagnon, Auberge Ste-Catherine-de-Hatley in Quebec.

4 salmon fillets (approximately 7 ounces each)

Salt and pepper, to taste

2 tablespoons butter

¼ cup of Mistral du Cep d'Argent, or another sweet wine

¼ cup fish broth

1 orange, peeled and cut in fine, round slices

⅓ cup fennel bulb, finely chopped

1 teaspoon garlic, chopped

1. Season salmon with salt and pepper. Melt butter in frying pan. When butter starts to foam, fry fillets until they are golden and pink, approximately 3 minutes on each side. Finish in the oven for 5 minutes at 200°.
2. Splash fillets with 2 tablespoons of wine and flambé. Quickly transfer salmon to a plate and put near oven to keep warm.
3. Pour the remainder of the wine, fish broth, orange slices, fennel, and garlic into the pan. Bring to a boil and reduce by half. Season to taste with salt and pepper. Dress salmon on the plates and surround with sauce.

Escargots in Chablis

1 ounce garlic, chopped
½ ounce salt
½ ounce pepper
1½ ounces parsley, chopped
¾ cup butter
64 snails (8 per person)
4 cups Chablis (white wine)
2 cups water

Pinch nutmeg
2 onions, chopped
1 carrot, chopped
3 garlic cloves, minced
2 ounces shallots, finely
   chopped
1 bouquet garni

Serves 8

Chef Executif Mélanie Gagnon of Auberge Ste-Catherine de Hatley in Québec says you should soak the snails for 2 hours in salt water (4 cups of water plus 2 tablespoons ocean salt) before cooking them. Wash them thoroughly after they soak.

1. For the escargot butter, combine the garlic, salt, pepper, parsley, and butter.
2. Boil the presoaked and washed snails for 10 minutes, then remove them from their shells and wash several times under running water.
3. Place the snails in a saucepan with half of the Chablis and 2 cups of water. Add salt, pepper, nutmeg, onions, carrot, garlic, and bouquet garni. Cook at 250° for 1½ hours. Leave to cool in water, then drain.
4. Sauté the snails with the shallots, then add ½ cup of Chablis. Leave them to absorb the wine vapors for a few minutes.
5. Replace the snails in their shell and butter on top with the escargot butter. Line the snails one against another in a heatproof pan. Pour the rest of the Chablis in the bottom of the pan and leave to cook until the wine has totally evaporated. Serve very hot!

One Flavorful Bouquet

A bouquet garni can be used in many dishes and is an easy way to impart flavor. To make, combine enough dried parsley, thyme, and rosemary to fit into the center of a small square of cheesecloth. Crackle a dried bay leaf on top of the mixture, then gather the cheesecloth and tie it together with a string. This way you can remove it easily when the dish is done.

Rabbit with Wild Thyme

Serves 4

In this rabbit recipe, Mélanie Gagnon, of Auberge Ste-Catherine de Hatley, uses wild thyme for added flavor. Wild thyme is more commonly found in Europe, and ordinary thyme can work equally well.

3 pounds rabbit, cut into pieces
4 cups Cuvée Louis de Montfort
   (or another red wine)
2 tablespoons thyme
1 bay leaf
2 tablespoons flour
1 ounce fatty bacon, chopped
18 pearl onions
3 small shallots, chopped

3 garlic cloves, crushed
3 sprigs wild thyme, chopped
1 pinch tarragon, chopped
1 ounce butter
1 rabbit liver (reserve the one in
   the rabbit), finely chopped
1 tablespoon cognac
Salt and pepper, to taste

1. Marinate the rabbit overnight in the red wine, thyme, and bay leaf (reserving the liver). Take the rabbit out of the marinade and sprinkle with flour.
2. Heat the bacon in a casserole dish for 5 minutes, then brown the rabbit in it. Add the onions, shallots, and garlic cloves. Allow to brown, stirring continuously, for 6 to 7 minutes.
3. Pour in half the marinade. Add the wild thyme and the tarragon. Season with salt and pepper and leave to cook over a medium heat for 1½ hours.
4. In a small pan melt the butter, then add the chopped raw rabbit liver and cognac. Add to the casserole and leave to simmer for 5 minutes. Serve.

The First Step Toward a Great Sauce

One of the most important steps in making a sauce is deglazing. Once your meat (pork, beef, chicken, etc.) has been seared or cooked in a pan, remove it and pour out any excess fat or oil. Then use a liquid such as wine or stock and pour it into the pan, scraping the bottom to remove all the tasty bits of meat. You can then add other things to the sauce, such as cream to give it body, or butter to give a rich flavor and sheen.

Corn Clam Chowder with Mulard Duck–Pan Seared Foie Gras

Serves 6

This recipe is provided by Chef Jean-François Méthot of Les Trois Tilleuls, in Québec. For this recipe, first soak the clams in a bowl of cold salt water for 24 hours to rid the mussels of any impurities.

6 shallots, minced
1 sprig thyme
1 ounce olive oil
2 pounds small clams
5 ounces white wine
1 ounce butter
2 ears of corn, sliced off the cob
16 ounces heavy cream

1 white leek
3 carrots
3 celery stalks
2 tablespoons flour
6 slices of foie gras
   (approximately 2 ounces
   per person)
6 chives, as garnish

1. Sauté 5 minced shallots with the sprig of thyme in the olive oil. Add the clams and the white wine. Cook covered for 2 or 3 minutes, stirring from time to time with a wooden spoon, until the clams open. Remove the clams; drain and reserve the cooking liquid.
2. Sweat the remaining shallot in the butter. Add the corn and the cooking juice of the clams. Add 4 ounces of water and reduce it to ¼, then add the cream. Let it cook for several more minutes, then mix it and check seasoning. Remove the clams from their shells, but reserve a few shells for decoration of the plates.
3. Cut a julienne of white leeks, carrots, and celery. Drop them in boiling water for about 20 seconds (this is called blanching). Then plunge them in cold water to stop the cooking and retain the bright color.
4. Flour the foie gras and pan sear it by itself in a nonstick pan on high flame. In 6 prewarmed bowls, place some clams and the vegetable julienne in the middle and add the seared foie gras on top. Pour the clam chowder all around. Garnish with some chives and an open clam shell.

Shallots and Leeks

Many French recipes call for both shallots and leeks. Members of the Allium family (which includes onions, garlic, chives, and scallions), leeks are perfect for sautéing, as well as steaming and being treated like a vegetable. Shallots, which are like small, teardrop-shaped onions, are used in soups, sauces, and braised and stewed dishes when a mild onion flavor is desired. Because they are small, they require some patience to peel and chop, but they are well worth the extra effort.

Truffle Oil and Brie Soufflé

Serves 4

This recipe is provided by Chef Roland Ménard, of Hovey Manor, North Hatley, Québec. The addition of truffle oil to this soufflé is an easy way to impart a gourmet flavor.

1 teaspoon unsalted butter

½ cup milk

2 drops truffle oil

1 tablespoon white flour

1 pinch salt

2 egg yolks

2 ounces Brie cheese

2 egg whites

Pinch freshly ground white pepper

1. Melt butter in a saucepan, add milk, truffle oil, flour, and salt. Cook it at a low temperature until it gets thick (a few minutes).
2. Remove the saucepan from the burner. Add the egg yolks and cheese, mixing well.
3. Whisk egg whites with the white pepper and add it to the truffle oil mixture.
4. Pour in 4 buttered ramekins and bake at 350° for approximately 15 minutes, until it has risen. Serve immediately.

Le Diamant Noir

Known as *le diamant noir,* or "the black diamond," a truffle is a fungus that grows underground. Only a small amount is needed to impart flavor, as truffles are very strong. You can also infuse oils with truffles to use in many dishes—to liven up salad dressings, add some depth to sautéed vegetables, and turn a simple egg dish into something gourmet.

French Onion Soup with Port

4 ounces unsalted butter
3 tablespoons olive oil
3 pounds Spanish onions,
    sliced
2 garlic cloves, chopped
1 pinch thyme
2 bay leaves
1 tablespoon sugar

1 teaspoon salt, or to taste
2 tablespoons flour
2 pints veal stock
1½ cup of port
1 teaspoon pepper, to taste
16 slices toasted French bread
1 cup grated Gruyere cheese,
    to taste

> **Serves 8**
>
> In this recipe Chef Roland Ménard of Hovey Manor in North Hatley, Québec, shares his variation of French onion soup, using port.

1. Melt butter and olive oil in a large heavy pot over medium heat. Add onions, garlic, thyme, and bay leaves and continue stirring until lightly browned. Reduce the heat to low, cover, and cook, stirring occasionally until onions turn golden, about 15 minutes.
2. Uncover, sprinkle with the sugar and ½ teaspoon salt. Raise heat to medium and continue cooking uncovered approximately 30 minutes, stirring often.
3. Sprinkle flour over onions and cook until flour is browned, 2 to 3 minutes. Pour in stock, a bit at a time, while stirring. Raise heat to high and bring to boil. Stir in port, ½ teaspoon salt, and pepper. Reduce heat to low and cover. Cook until onions start to dissolve, about 45 minutes.
4. Preheat broiler. Ladle soup into ovenproof bowls. Top each bowl with two slices of toasted French bread. Sprinkle with grated cheese.
5. Broil until cheese melts. Serve immediately.

Foods of the South of France

All manner of French gourmet treats come from the south of France: truffles from the Périgord region, foie gras from the Dordogne region, and cassoulet from Toulouse. Once you enter the Languedoc, Provence, and Pay Basque regions, there is a Mediterranean touch to the cuisine, using olive oil, tomatoes, eggplant, many types of wild mushrooms, and garlic.

Bouillabaisse

Serves 6

There are countless variations of this famous dish. Here is a very straightforward version, offered by Chef Executif Maro Patry, of Château Bromont in Québec.

1 large onion, diced
4 tomatoes, diced
3 garlic cloves, chopped
1 medium-sized carrot
1 piece celery
¼ cup olive oil
2 cod filets, cut into medium-sized pieces
2 pike filets, cut into medium-sized pieces

¼ pound mussels
18 black tiger shrimp, deveined
14 scallops
½ teaspoon saffron
½ bottle dry white wine
1 cup water
1 sprig fresh thyme
½ sprig rosemary
Salt and pepper, to taste

1. Preheat the oven to 350°.
2. Place all the vegetables with the olive oil in a large heavy-bottomed pot. Then put the cut pieces of fish and shellfish on top of the vegetables. Sprinkle in the saffron, add white wine, water, thyme and rosemary.
3. Place pot in the oven for 45 minutes. Season with salt and pepper to taste. Serve.

Central France: From Escargots to Boeuf Bourguignon

Many famed French dishes come from central France: Escargot à la Bourguignon (escargot stuffed with garlic butter), Boeuf Bourguignon (beef cooked in red wine), and Coq au Vin (Bresse chicken in red wine), to name a few. Burgundy wine is another world-famous product from the center of France, which has inspired countless chefs. Lyon, which consideres itself the gastronomic capital of France, boasts an impressive number of three-star Michelin chefs.

Chocolate Mousse with Goat Cheese Cream

3 ounces sweet chocolate
4 egg yolks
¼ cup sugar
4 egg whites
1½ cup heavy cream, whipped
1 recipe of Goat Cheese Cream
(page 296)

½ pint of fresh raspberries,
for garnish
A few sprigs of mint leaves,
for garnish

Serves 4–6
This recipe, by Executive Chef Jacques Poulin, Chef of Lion D'or in Québec, combines a chocolate French classic with the unexpected taste of goat cheese.

1. Place the chocolate on a double boiler. (If you do not have one, put the chocolate in a medium-sized stainless steel bowl and set it over a simmering pot of water, being careful that no water splashes inside the bowl.) Stir until chocolate is melted. Remove from heat and set aside to cool.

2. Beat egg yolks until light in color. Add sugar and continue beating until light and fluffy. Stir in cooled chocolate.

3. Beat egg whites until stiff, slowly fold into chocolate mixture using a spatula.

4. Fold the whipped cream into the chocolate mixture. Pour mousse into 4 to 6 individual ramekins or small serving bowls. Chill in refrigerator for 2 hours.

5. Using two large service spoons, fill one with a scoop of the Goat Cheese Cream and push them against one another (rotating the spoons as needed) so that the cheese takes the shape of a miniature football (this is called a "quenelle"). Place 1 or 2 quenelles atop the mousse, and garnish with fresh raspberries and mint.

Goat Cheese Cream

Serves 4–6

Serve this delicious combination with Chocolate Mousse (page 295).

2 cups heavy cream
½ cup Chèvre des Neiges, or
    another mild goat cheese

1 tablespoon Mistral wine
1 tablespoon maple syrup

Blend all ingredients together. Use immediately.

Moules Mariniere (Mussels in White Wine)

Serves 4

One of the best parts of this dish is the broth, so be sure to serve it with some fresh French bread. Soaking up the remaining liquid is not impolite— it's part of the fun.

1 tablespoon unsalted butter
1 tablespoon extra-virgin olive
    oil
¾ small yellow onion, chopped
1 clove garlic, minced
½ teaspoon freshly ground
    pepper

5 pounds mussels, scrubbed
    and debearded
1¾ cups dry white wine
3 tablespoons minced fresh flat-
    leaf parsley

1. In a deep pot melt the butter with the olive oil over medium-high heat. Add the onion, and sauté 2 to 3 minutes, until translucent.
2. Add garlic, pepper, and mussels. Pour in wine, then sprinkle with half the parsley. Cover, cook on low heat until mussels just start to open, 10 to 12 minutes.
3. Uncover and stir in remaining parsley.
4. Using slotted spoon, scoop mussels into individual bowl, throwing away any that did not open. Ladle in a good portion of broth. Serve.

Crepes with Curaçao Strawberries and Oranges

4 large eggs
1¾ to 2 cups milk, as needed
⅓ cup all-purpose flour
1 teaspoon sugar
1 teaspoon salt
2 pints of fresh strawberries,
    sliced, plus extras for garnish
2 oranges, cut into segments

2 tablespoons brown sugar
4 tablespoons Curaçao
¼ cup butter
1 cup whipped cream
8 fresh mint sprigs

Serves 8

This is a delicious recipe created by Jacques Poulin, Executive Chef of Auberge au Lion D'or in Orford, Québec. If you find lumps when making the batter, pass it through a sieve lined with several pieces of cheesecloth. If your batter is too thick, just add a bit of milk.

1. To make the batter: In a large bowl whisk together eggs and 1¾ cups milk. Whisk in flour, sugar, salt, a bit at a time, until there are no more lumps. Cover and refrigerate for 2 hours.

2. In a medium bowl mix together the strawberries, orange segments, brown sugar, and Curaçao. Refrigerate for 30 minutes.

3. Place a 12-inch frying pan over medium-high heat (when you spatter a bit of water and it sizzles, it is ready). Drop in 1 teaspoon butter, tipping the pan so it distributes evenly on bottom. Pour in only ¼ cup batter and distribute evenly on bottom by tipping and rotating pan. When the batter bubbles and the sides appear cooked, approximately 20 to 30 seconds, flip with a spatula. Cook very briefly on second side, transfer to another plate, stacking crepes, one at a time.

4. To serve, place a heaping spoonful of the strawberry-orange mixture, inside the crepes. Add a dollop of whipped cream, and then roll up the crepe. Garnish with a small spoon of whipped cream, a few slices of strawberries, and a sprig of mint.

Raclette (Melted Cheese with Potatoes)

Serves 4

Raclette is also the name of a Savoyard cheese and is so common in France that many families own electric raclette grills, which have eight squares that can be filled with cheese to melt.

12 boiling potatoes, such as Yukon gold, Yellow Finn, or White Rose
1 teaspoon salt
1½ pounds raclette cheese, cut into 4 equal portions

1 pound prosciutto
4 gherkins, sliced
Freshly ground pepper to taste
2 sweet red peppers
1 cup Archer Porto wine, or any other port

1. In a large saucepan combine the potatoes, 1 teaspoon salt, and water to just cover.
2. Bring to a boil over high heat, reduce to medium and cook uncovered until potatoes can be easily pierced with a sharp knife (approximately 20 minutes). Drain, and then mash them. (You can use a food processor, but be sure to let them cool off a bit first.) Cover, and set aside.
3. Put a slice of prosciutto in a raclette cheese tray, add a scoop of mashed potatoes in the middle, and fold the prosciutto over. Put a slice of gherkin and a slice of cheese on top of each piece of prosciutto, sprinkle the pepper on top, and then put the cheese tray on the raclette grill.
4. Cut the sweet peppers into 1-inch cubes and place them in a medium pot over a medium-low heat along with the port wine, until the port has evaporated (approximately 15 minutes). Serve with the raclette.

The Story of Raclette

Long ago in the Swiss Alps, cowherds would carry potatoes and gherkin pickles up the mountainsides to eat with their cheese and milk. They'd bake the potatoes in the campfire and melt the cheese on a rock near the fire. As it melted, they scraped the cheese onto the potatoes and pickles. The word *raclette* comes from the French word "to scrape."

Shrimp and Melon Salad

2 tablespoons fresh lemon juice
1 teaspoon minced fresh baby
dill, plus a few sprigs for
garnish
½ cup mayonnaise
½ cup white wine

3 cups mixed honeydew and
cantaloupe, ¼-inch cubed
1 pound baby shrimps, lightly
chopped
Few leaves of Boston hearth
lettuce, for garnish

In a medium-sized bowl stir together lemon juice, minced baby dill, mayonnaise, and wine. Add melon and shrimps. Cover and refrigerate for at least 1 hour. To serve, scoop a generous portion of shrimp and melon salad onto Boston hearth lettuce in a large pasta plate.

Pesto Beurre Blanc

¼ cup shallots, minced
¼ cup red wine vinegar
¼ pound butter, softened

⅛ cup heavy cream
1 tablespoon pesto (can be
store-bought)

Put the shallots in a pan with vinegar and cook over medium heat until the liquid is evaporated. Whisk in butter until a smooth emulsion is formed. Continue mixing and add cream. Continue cooking on low-medium heat for 1 minute. Add pesto. Serve with a fresh white fish of your choosing.

Foie Gras–Stuffed Cornish Hens

12 ounces foie gras
24 ounces bread (no crust)
1 celery root
¼ cup chopped shallots
2 tablespoons garlic
Salt and pepper, to taste

4 ounces chopped cilantro
4 ounces chopped chives
6 Cornish hens
18 ounces Cornish hen jus
1 quart chicken stock

1. In a large, hot sauté pan add the foie gras and disburse evenly in the pan. Let cook for about 20 seconds. Add the bread. After the bread has absorbed the fat from the foie gras (about 30 seconds), add the celery root, shallots, and garlic. Allow the stuffing to cook for five minutes. Take stuffing off heat. Season with salt and pepper. Place on tray and sprinkle chopped cilantro and chives on top while still hot. Let the stuffing cool and mix thoroughly.

2. Bone the hen from the spine forward leaving the skin intact, and only half the wing bone and the leg from the knee down. Open the hen with the skin side to the cutting board and the wings at the top. (You can also ask your butcher to prepare the birds.) Season the inside of the hen with salt and pepper.

3. Place ⅙ of the stuffing on each hen. Using three toothpicks, close the hen beginning with the bottom working up the spine. Rest the hen on its legs and replace any stuffing that has fallen out. Close up the top with the final toothpick. Truss the hen with butcher's twine. Fold the legs around the front and wrap twine around the entire hen, tucking the wings under the string.

4. Sear the hen on every side in a hot sauté pan until dark golden brown. Deglaze the pan with Cornish hen jus and thin with chicken stock. Place the pan in a 350° oven using the sauce to baste the hen. Cook until the hen is heated through. Test with a thermometer. The temperature in the thickest part of the thigh should be at least 165°. Remove the hen from the pan. It should have a glaze to the top. Remove all toothpicks and twine. Slice in half and serve. Strain the basting liquid. If not thick enough, reduce further on the stove. Pour the jus on top of the hen.

Left Bank's Chocolate Fondant

6 ounces chopped bittersweet
    chocolate
1 cup unsalted butter, cut into
    cubes, plus 2 tablespoons at
    room temperature

8 eggs
1 cup granulated sugar
½ cup all-purpose flour
½ cup unsweetened cocoa
    powder

1. Melt chocolate and 1 cup butter in small saucepan over low heat, stirring till smooth. Pour into large bowl.
2. In another large bowl, whip eggs and sugar together. Fold in flour.
3. Fold egg mixture into chocolate mixture. Refrigerate 2 hours.
4. Brush bottoms and sides of eight 4-ounce ramekins with 2 tablespoons butter. Dust with cocoa powder. Spoon chilled batter into ramekins.
5. Place ramekins on sheet pan and bake at 400° till firm to touch and just beginning to pull away from sides of ramekins, about 12 to 14 minutes. Cool 3 to 5 minutes if serving immediately. If serving later, or if you want to unmold before serving, cool to room temperature. To reheat, place on sheet pan and heat in 400° oven for 3 to 5 minutes.

> **Serves 8**
>
> A signature dessert of the Left Bank, from chef/ owner Roland Passot. "When your fork cuts into the cake and the warm, molten, truffle-like chocolate oozes out, it is irresistible! And it is even more heavenly served with vanilla or coffee ice cream."

Bakers' Breeches

In 1569, France passed a law that few bakers would stand for today. They were forbidden to wear regular pants other than on Sunday. The result? They were easily identified in their bakers' garb, thus forcing them to continue slaving away in the kitchen. But the strictness did not stop there. Bakers, who were highly prized at this period in France, were not allowed to gather in groups or bear arms, such as a sword. Though, they were, of course, allowed to handle kitchen knives.

Chapter 23

Belgium:
More Than Just Chocolate

304 : Cucumber Salad with Mint

305 : Beer-Braised Chicken with Endives

306 : Belgian Endives in Mornay Sauce

307 : Cream of Brussels Sprout Soup

308 : Cream of Belgian Endive Soup

309 : Flemish-Style Red Cabbage

310 : Braised Squab with Caramelized Onions

311 : Glazed Turnips with Cinnamon

311 : Simple Fruit Compote

312 : Buttermilk Soup with Apples

313 : Mussels in Wine

314 : Stoemp with Caramelized Shallots

315 : Prune Tart

316 : Flemish Yeast Dough

317 : Belgian Waffles

318 : Bread Pudding with Belgian Beer

Cucumber Salad with Mint

Serves 6

Make sure to drain the cucumber slices well, or the salad will be watery. Feel free to jazz up the appearance of this simple dish by shaping the radishes into "radish flowers."

1 long European cucumber
1 teaspoon kosher salt, or as needed
2 Belgian endives
3 radishes
½ cup plain yogurt
1 tablespoon Dijon mustard

1 tablespoon freshly squeezed lemon juice
1 teaspoon granulated sugar
2 tablespoons chopped fresh mint leaves
Salt and pepper, to taste
Mint sprigs, for garnish

1. Peel the cucumber, remove the seeds, and cut in 1-inch slices. Place the cucumber slices in a colander and sprinkle with the salt. Let the cucumber drain for 15 minutes. Pat dry with paper towels.
2. Remove the stem from each endive, cut in half, and cut into strips. Thinly slice the radishes.
3. In a small mixing bowl, whisk together the yogurt, mustard, lemon juice, and sugar. Stir in the mint leaves. Season with salt and pepper, as desired.
4. To serve, lay out the cucumber slices on the outer edges of a plate. Working inward, lay out the sliced endive and then the radishes. Spoon the dressing into the middle. Top the dressing with fresh mint sprigs and serve.

Location, Location, Location

Considering its neighbors—France, Luxembourg, Germany, and Holland—it is easy to see why Belgium has had a myriad of culinary influences over the years. Belgium often boasts that its food is cooked with French refinement, while served with German-style generous portions. Due to its location, by the Middle Ages Belgium was at the center of the northern European spice trade. Everything from ginger to cinnamon, nutmeg, saffron, and peppercorns were used to season dishes. Today's Belgian cuisine still has its roots in medieval cookery. Spices, mustard, vinegar, and beer continue to be widely used in both savory and sweet recipes.

Beer-Braised Chicken with Endives

6 endives
4 chicken thighs
12 ounces beer, preferably
    Belgian, divided
1 tablespoon lemon juice
⅛ teaspoon garlic salt
Up to 2 tablespoons butter,
    if needed

⅓ cup heavy cream
¼ teaspoon freshly grated
    nutmeg
Salt and pepper, to taste
8 fresh parsley or mint sprigs,
    as desired

> **Serves 4**
>
> Need something more elegant for a special occasion? Replace the chicken thighs with a whole chicken, braise the endives separately, and serve the two together.

1. Remove the core from the endives, cut in half lengthwise, and cut into thin slices. Rinse the chicken thighs and pat dry with paper towels. Place the thighs in a resealable plastic bag. Add 6 ounces of the beer (use 2 bags if necessary). Marinate the chicken in the refrigerator for 1 hour. Discard the beer marinade.

2. Heat a frying pan on medium heat. Add the chicken thighs and sauté until cooked through (about 15 minutes), turning over halfway through cooking. Remove and drain on paper towels. Do not clean the pan.

3. Add a few tablespoons of the beer to the pan and deglaze, using a slotted spoon to stir up any browned bits. Add the endives to the pan. Sprinkle with the lemon juice and the garlic salt. Sauté the endives over medium-low heat until tender (about 30 minutes), taking care they do not burn and adding butter if necessary.

4. Add the chicken back into the pan. Add the remaining beer (about 5 ounces). Reduce the heat to low and simmer, covered, for 10 more minutes. Add the cream. Stir in the nutmeg. Simmer for 5 more minutes. Taste and season with salt or pepper if desired. Garnish with parsley or mint sprigs before serving.

Belgian Endives in Mornay Sauce

8 Belgian endives
2 teaspoons freshly squeezed lemon juice
1 tablespoon white wine vinegar
2½ tablespoons butter
2 tablespoons all-purpose flour
¼ cup whole milk
¼ cup light cream
¼ teaspoon (or to taste) ground nutmeg
Salt, to taste
Freshly ground black pepper, to taste
½ cup shredded Gruyère cheese

1. Core from the endives and cut in half lengthwise. Half-fill a medium saucepan with the lemon juice, white wine vinegar, and water as needed. Fit the steamer in the saucepan. Make sure the liquid is not touching the bottom of the steamer. Bring the liquid to a boil. Add the endives, cover and steam until tender (about 20 minutes).
2. Melt the butter in a small saucepan over low heat. Make a roux by adding the flour and cooking on low heat for 3 minutes, continually stirring. Whisk in the milk and cream and bring to a boil, whisking continually until thickened. Stir in the nutmeg, salt, and pepper, and ¼ cup of the shredded Gruyère cheese. Stir until the cheese has melted.
3. To serve, lay the endives out in a serving dish and pour the Mornay sauce over. Sprinkle with the remaining ¼ cup of Gruyère cheese.

Making a Roux

Using a roux, a combination of cooked flour and fat, is an easy way to thicken sauces. Simply combine equal parts butter and flour, and cook over low heat until the roux has the desired color, whisking constantly. (Using 2 tablespoons of butter and flour, after 2 minutes you'll have a white roux, and in approximately 4 minutes you'll have a golden or blond roux.) But be patient and take your time cooking it. Using higher heat to get the roux done faster may cause it to lose its thickening ability.

Cream of Brussels Sprout Soup

½ pound (about 2 cups)
   Brussels sprouts
2 tablespoons butter
2 large shallots, chopped
3 cups chicken broth
¾ cup whole milk

¼ cup heavy cream
¼ teaspoon nutmeg, or to taste
Salt and pepper, to taste
Pinch of cayenne pepper,
   optional

> **Serves 6**
>
> Finish off this simple but elegant soup by topping with a Brussels sprout garnish made by blanching 6 Brussels sprout halves and plunging in ice water to stop the cooking process.

1. Trim the tough outer layer from the Brussels sprouts. Bring a large pot of salted water to a boil. Add the Brussels sprouts and boil, uncovered, until they are tender (about 15 minutes). Remove the sprouts, drain thoroughly, and cut in half. Reserve 1 cup of the boiling liquid.
2. Cut the drained Brussels sprouts in half and purée in the food processor.
3. In a medium saucepan, melt the butter over low heat. Add the shallots and sauté until tender. Add the chicken broth, milk, reserved boiling water, and the puréed Brussels sprouts. Bring to a boil, stirring. Reduce the heat and simmer, uncovered, for about 10 minutes.
4. Remove the soup from the heat. Add the cream. Stir in the nutmeg, salt and pepper, and the cayenne pepper if using. Serve hot.

A Surprising Fact

Belgium has the highest per capita number of restaurants earning Michelin stars and it is one of the few places around the globe where McDonald's loses money. What could be better proof that fresh ingredients and fine cuisine are a cultural must in Belgium?

Cream of Belgian Endive Soup

Serves 4

Having a dinner party and planning to serve an appetizer along with the soup? Reserve a few endive leaves to serve as an eye-catching receptacle for the appetizers.

3 Belgian endives
2 large carrots
1 large potato, peeled and
    diced
½ white onion, diced
½ stalk celery
3½ cups chicken broth
2 tablespoons butter

½ cup heavy cream
1 tablespoon fresh chopped
    basil, or to taste
1 teaspoon bacon bits, optional
Salt and pepper, to taste

1. Wash all the vegetables. Remove the core from the endives, cut in half lengthwise, and cut into thin slices. Peel and dice the carrots, potato, and onion. String the celery and finely chop.

2. Bring a large pot of salted water to a boil. Add the vegetables and boil until they are very tender, or even a bit mushy. Remove the vegetables from the pot and drain thoroughly. Purée the vegetables in a food processor.

3. In a medium saucepan, bring the chicken broth and the puréed vegetables to a boil. Add the butter. Reduce the heat and simmer, uncovered, for about 10 minutes. Remove the soup from the heat. Add the cream. Stir in the fresh basil, bacon bits if using, and season with the salt and pepper. Serve hot or cold.

The Belgian Endive

Accidentally discovered by a Belgian farmer, Jan Lammers, in 1830, the Belgian endive is a staple of Belgian cuisine. Upon returning from war, Lammers discovered that a stored chicory plant, which he'd previously grown and used for coffee, had sprouted white leaves. This bitter taste appealed to his palette. Thirty years later witloof, or endive, finally became a successful crop. In 1872 it hit Paris, and became so popular it was called "white gold." It is almost always served hot in Belgium, whereas in the States we usually eat it raw, in salads. Another good fact to keep in mind: the fresher the endive is, the sweeter and less bitter the taste.

Flemish-Style Red Cabbage

1 red cabbage
2 tart apples, such as Baldwin
   or Jonathan
½ Spanish onion
2 slices bacon
1 tablespoon butter
6 tablespoons red wine vinegar

3 tablespoons packed brown
   sugar
Salt and pepper, to taste
3 to 4 fresh parsley sprigs,
   chopped

Serves 6–8

To keep from losing the cabbage's rich red color, instead of rinsing it, wipe it down with a wet cloth.

1. Remove the core from the red cabbage, cut into quarters, and shred. Peel the apples, remove the core, and thinly slice. Peel and finely chop the onion.

2. In a heavy frying pan, sauté the bacon until crisp. Remove, drain on paper towels, and chop. Do not drain the pan.

3. Add the chopped onion to the pan and cook over medium heat until the onion is soft and translucent. Push the onion to the sides of the pan. Add the butter, melt briefly, and add the apple slices. Cook the apple in the melted butter for 1 minute.

4. Add the shredded cabbage. Sauté for 1 minute. Stir in the red wine vinegar and the brown sugar. Cook, covered, over medium-low to medium heat until the cabbage is tender (about 20 minutes). Mix in the chopped bacon. Taste and season with salt and pepper, if desired. To serve, garnish with the fresh chopped parsley.

Braised Squab with Caramelized Onions

Serves 4

Don't have time to make your own chicken broth? Many specialty stores do the work for you, selling their own version of "homemade" chicken broth that tastes far superior to regular canned chicken broth.

3 slices smoked bacon

16 pearl onions, peeled

4 tablespoons unsalted butter, divided

2 teaspoons granulated sugar

4 squabs, 1 pound each

1 teaspoon salt

1 teaspoon pepper

½ cup dry red wine

½ cup homemade chicken broth

1 tablespoon finely chopped fresh parsley

1 tablespoon finely chopped fresh thyme

1. In a deep-sided frying pan, sauté the bacon until crisp. Remove, drain on paper towels, and chop. Clean out the pan.

2. Fill the pan with 1 inch of water. Add the pearl onions and bring the water to a boil. Cover and cook the onions over medium-low heat until tender and translucent (10 to 15 minutes). Use a slotted spoon to remove the onions. Drain the onions in a colander.

3. Melt 2 tablespoons unsalted butter in the frying pan. Stir in the sugar. Return the onions to the pan and cook over medium heat until they are sugar-glazed (5 to 7 minutes).

4. Rub the outside skin and the cavities of the squabs with salt and pepper. Melt the remaining 2 tablespoons of butter in the frying pan. Add the squabs and sauté over medium heat until browned all over. Remove the squabs from the skillet and set aside.

5. Pour the red wine and homemade chicken broth into the skillet and deglaze the pan over high heat, using a spoon to scrape up all the brown bits from the bottom of the pan. Add the caramelized onions and chopped bacon back into the pan with the squab. Stir in the chopped fresh parsley and thyme leaves. Cover and simmer over low heat until the squabs are tender (about 30 minutes). (The squab is cooked when its internal temperature reaches 150°.)

Glazed Turnips with Cinnamon

Serves 4–6

For extra flavor, add a pinch of paprika when sautéing the turnips.

1½ pounds turnips
2 tablespoons butter
1 teaspoon ground cinnamon

1 teaspoon granulated sugar
1 tablespoon Italian flat-leaf
  parsley, finely chopped

1. Peel the turnips and cut into 1-inch pieces. In a large frying pan place the turnips with enough salted water to cover. Bring the water to a boil. Reduce the heat to low and simmer the turnips, covered, until they are tender and can be easily pierced with a fork (about 10 minutes). Drain the turnips. Clean out the frying pan.
2. Melt the butter in the frying pan over medium-high heat. Add the turnips and toss with the cinnamon and sugar. Sauté until they turn golden brown (about 5–7 minutes). Stir in the parsley, and serve.

Simple Fruit Compote

Serves 4

Featuring various summer fruits, this simple light dessert makes the perfect finalé to a rich evening meal.

1 cup strawberries
1 cup blueberries
1 cup Bing cherries
2 tablespoons Ruby port or
  Madeira

2 tablespoons granulated sugar
1 tablespoon lemon juice
8 mint sprigs, for garnish

1. Wash and hull the strawberries. Rinse the blueberries and dry on paper towels. Pit the cherries and cut in half.
2. In a small bowl, combine the port, sugar, and lemon juice. Toss the fruit with the mixture. Chill, covered, in the refrigerator for 1 hour.
3. Spoon the fruit into individual dessert bowls. Garnish each dish with 2 mint sprigs.

Buttermilk Soup with Apples

⅓ cup uncooked oatmeal
6 cups buttermilk, divided
½ teaspoon salt
2 good cooking apples, such as
    Golden Delicious

¼ teaspoon ground cinnamon
1 tablespoon granulated sugar
¼ cup molasses
¼ cup brown sugar

1. In a medium saucepan, bring the oatmeal and 3 cups buttermilk to a boil on medium-high heat. Stir in the salt. Reduce the heat and simmer, uncovered, stirring occasionally, until the oatmeal is cooked (about 20 minutes).
2. While the oatmeal is cooking, peel and core the apples. Cut the apples into thin slices.
3. Add the apple slices and the remaining 3 cups buttermilk to the soup. Bring to a boil. Reduce heat to low and simmer, uncovered, until the apples are tender (about 15 minutes). Stir in the cinnamon and sugar. Serve immediately, with the molasses and brown sugar in individual serving bowls on the side.

Frites on the Run

If you're in Belgium and in a rush, odds are you will grab a tiny cone filled with fresh frites (or, as we know them, French fries). These tasty treats are served with several condiments that may seem odd to our palette: mayonnaise, béarnaise, and even curry dipping sauce. Many argue that while beer is Belgium's national drink, frites are their national food.

Mussels in Wine

Serves 4

When choosing mussels, look for ones with tightly closed shells. Make sure to clean the mussels thoroughly to prevent grit from settling at the bottom of the pan.

1½ pounds mussels
1 Belgian endive
½ stalk celery
1 tomato
4 shallots, chopped
2 cloves garlic, crushed
1 tablespoon olive oil
1 cup dry white wine

¼ cup low-sodium chicken broth
2 tablespoons light cream, optional
1 tablespoon chopped fresh parsley

1. Clean the mussels by scrubbing them with a stiff brush while holding them under cold running water. Debeard, but do not remove the shells.
2. Prepare the vegetables: Remove the stem from the Belgian endive, cut in half lengthwise, and thinly slice. String the celery and cut diagonally into 1-inch pieces. Cut the tomato into 6 wedges. Peel and chop the shallots. Smash, peel, and finely chop the garlic.
3. Heat the olive oil in a large frying pan over medium-high heat. Add the garlic and shallots and sauté for 2 to 3 minutes, until the shallots are golden.
4. Add the cleaned mussels and the wine. Cover and cook on high heat until the mussels have started to open (about 5 to 6 minutes).
5. Remove the mussels from the pan. Add the chicken broth, vegetables, and cream to the pan. Stir in the fresh parsley. Simmer, covered, for 10 to 15 minutes to give the flavors a chance to blend. To serve, place with the mussels in a large casserole dish.

Big on Mussels

Without direct ocean access, Belgium relies on its neighbor, Holland, for its mussels—a food Belgians eat often. Mussel preparation varies quite a lot; one night you may dine on mussels escargot made with parsley butter, and the next sit down to an enormous pot of mussels steamed in broth. Other dishes include mussels gratiné, with tomatoes and cheese, and cold-marinated mussels.

Stoemp with Caramelized Shallots

*4 large, baking potatoes,
    peeled and cubed
4 leeks
1 tablespoon salt
2 slices bacon
1 medium shallot, finely
    chopped*

*4 tablespoons butter
3 tablespoons light or heavy
    cream, as desired
Salt and black pepper, to taste
¼ teaspoon nutmeg, or to taste
2 tablespoons finely minced
    fresh parsley*

1. Peel the potatoes and cut lengthwise into thin slices. Remove the outer leaves from the leeks and cut off the white stems. Fill a large saucepan with lightly salted water and add the potatoes, leeks, and 1 tablespoon salt. Bring to boil over high heat. Reduce the heat and cook the vegetables, uncovered, for 20 minutes, or until the potatoes are tender and easily pierced with a fork.
2. While the potatoes and the leeks are cooking, cook the bacon in a frying pan on medium heat until crispy. Remove and drain on paper towels. Do not clean out the pan. Add the finely chopped shallot and sauté on low heat, until the shallot softens and begin to brown. Remove from the pan.
3. Finely chop the boiled leeks into thin slices ⅛- to ¼-inch thick. Finely chop the bacon.
4. Mash the potatoes in a large mixing bowl. Mix in the butter and cream. Season with the salt, pepper, and nutmeg. Stir in the chopped leeks, bacon, and shallot. Add the fresh parsley. Serve immediately.

Prune Tart

½ cup heavy cream
1 tablespoon buttermilk
12 pitted prunes, halved
6 tablespoons cognac

¼ cup granulated sugar
2-inch cinnamon stick
Flemish Yeast Dough (page
316)

> **Serves 6–8**
>
> For added decadence, spread whipped cream or ice cream on top of the tart before serving.

1. The day before the tarts will be made, prepare the homemade crème fraîche: mix together the heavy cream and buttermilk and refrigerate, covered, for 24 hours.
2. On the day that the tart is to be made, in a medium bowl, combine the prunes with the cognac. Let sit for 30 minutes to soften.
3. Combine the cognac-soaked prunes, crème fraîche, sugar, and the cinnamon stick in a medium saucepan. Bring to a boil. Reduce the heat and simmer, covered, for 1 hour, stirring occasionally. Remove from the heat, discard the cinnamon stick, and cool.
4. Preheat the oven to 350°. Grease a 12-inch tart pan.
5. Turn the tart dough out onto a floured surface and roll out into a 12-inch circle approximately 1-inch thick. Carefully transfer the dough to the greased tart pan. Fold the overhanging dough over or trim as desired. For a better appearance, crimp the edges.
6. Purée the cooled prune mixture in a food processor. Spread evenly over the tart dough. Bake for 25 to 30 minutes, until the tart is browned. Cool and serve.

Flemish Yeast Dough

1 large egg
½ cup whole milk
1 package active dry yeast

¼ teaspoon salt
¼ cup granulated sugar
1½ cups all-purpose flour

1. Lightly beat the egg. In a small saucepan, gently heat the milk on low heat until it is warm but not hot (less than 120°). In a small bowl, pour the warmed milk over the yeast and let sit for 5 minutes to soften.
2. In a large mixing bowl, combine the salt, sugar, and flour. Use a wooden spoon to gradually stir the lightly beaten egg and the milk and yeast mixture into the flour. Adjust the proportion of wet and dry ingredients as needed to make a smooth dough: add 2 to 3 tablespoons flour if the dough is too wet, or a bit of water if it is too dry.
3. Turn the dough out onto a lightly floured surface and knead until smooth and elastic (about 5 minutes). Place the dough in a bowl, cover, and let rise in a warm spot for 1 hour. Use as called for in the recipe.

Belgian Chocolate

Belgium has long been a major producer of some of the world's finest chocolates. Godiva is undoubtedly a household name, and Neuhaus is another top brand, while Wittamer is considered the crème de la crème. Interestingly, Belgian praline is a general term for filled chocolates, but also refers to a mixture of milk chocolate and finely ground nuts or toffee. Nougatine is the same as praline, except larger pieces of nuts or toffee are used for crunchiness. True Belgian chocolates are made with the freshest cream, and last only a few days.

Belgian Waffles

1 cup milk
½ cup soda water, room
  temperature
1 package dry active yeast
2 eggs, separated

2 cups all-purpose flour
4 tablespoons granulated sugar
1 tablespoon cinnamon
1 teaspoon salt
½ stick unsalted butter, melted

Serves 4

Not sure what to do with leftover waffles? They freeze beautifully—just cool and place in resealable plastic bags. Reheat the waffles in the oven or microwave.

1. In a small saucepan, gently heat the milk and the soda until it is fairly warm (more than 115°). Pour the warmed liquid over the yeast and let sit for 5 minutes to soften.
2. While the yeast is softening, prepare the eggs: use an electric mixer to beat the egg whites until stiff. Beat the egg yolks with a whisk. Set aside.
3. In a large bowl, combine the flour, sugar, cinnamon, and salt. Make a "well" in the middle of the flour mixture. Pour the milk, melted butter, and the beaten egg yolks into the well. Stir into the dry ingredients. Gently fold in the egg white. Place the dough in a bowl, cover, and let rise in a warm spot for 1 hour.
4. To make the waffles, heat the waffle iron. Cook the waffles according to the instructions on your waffle iron. Make sure to cook the waffles until steam is no longer escaping and they are crispy. Serve with your favorite fruit jam, powdered sugar, or even melted chocolate.

German Syrup

To make delicious German syrup, combine 2 cups brown sugar, 1 cup water, and 1 cup light corn syrup in a pot and boil for 3 to 4 minutes. In a small bowl, beat together ½ cup crème fraîche and 1 egg. Slowly add the cream mixture to the hot syrup. It yields 3 cups.

Bread Pudding with Belgian Beer

2 ounces dried cherries
2½ cups beer
1 loaf French or Italian bread
2 cups light cream
4 eggs, separated

¾ cup brown sugar
1 cup raisins
1 teaspoon grated orange peel
2 tablespoons confectioners'
   sugar, or as needed

1. Preheat the oven to 350°. Grease a 6-cup baking dish or a deep-sided casserole dish.
2. In a medium saucepan, heat the dried cherries with ½ cup beer over high heat. Lower the heat and simmer, covered, until the cherries are softened (10 to 15 minutes). Drain the cherries, reserving the liquid.
3. Slice the loaf of French bread into 1-inch pieces and place in a large mixing bowl. Whisk in the cream, egg yolks, egg whites, and brown sugar. Add the remaining 2 cups beer, cherries, reserved liquid, raisins, and the grated orange peel.
4. Pour the mixture into the greased baking dish. Let the pudding stand for 15 minutes to allow the bread to soak up the custard.
5. Bake for 45 minutes. Test for doneness by inserting a knife in the middle (if the knife comes out clean, the pudding has set). If the pudding is not ready, bake for up to 15 minutes more, covering the top with aluminum foil to prevent overbrowning. Lightly dust with the confectioners' sugar before serving.

Belgian Beer

We all know Belgian beer is famous, but perhaps we do not know why. First of all, how many countries have beer as their national drink? It is true that more beer than wine is consumed in Belgium—a fact that must horrify the French. Many beers are made by small artisanal brewers whose family recipes and techniques go back generations. Beer also features widely in the country's cuisine, even showing up in the national dish, carbonnades flamandes, a Flemish beef stew. The custom of using spices to flavor dishes also applies to beer—which may be one reason the Belgians chose to feature the often fruity and spicy brews as an ingredient in local dishes.

Chapter 24

Germany:
Have Your Own
Octoberfest

320 : German Baked Apple French Toast
321 : Beer-Basted Sausage with Caramelized Onions and
German Mustard
322 : Cold Wine Soup
323 : Dark Bread Soup
324 : Westphalian Cabbage
325 : Fruit-Stuffed Pork Chops
326 : Herbed Potato Salad
327 : Buttered Fillet of Sole
328 : Elderberry Soup with "Dumplings" and Apples
329 : Holstein Duck
330 : Black Forest Cherry Cake
331 : Hazelnut Torte
332 : Swabian Stuffed Pockets (Maultaschen)
333 : German Cucumber Salad

German Baked Apple French Toast

4 tart apples, such as McIntosh
8 slices crusty French bread
½ cup butter, softened
¾ cup brown sugar
¼ cup liquid honey
½ teaspoon grated lemon peel

4 large eggs
1 cup whole milk
1 teaspoon vanilla extract
½ teaspoon ground cinnamon
¼ teaspoon ground nutmeg

1. Peel and core the apples. Cut each apple into 6 to 8 wedges. Cut the bread into 1-inch cubes.
2. In a small saucepan over medium heat, combine the softened butter, brown sugar, honey, and the grated lemon peel, stirring, until the sugar dissolves. In a small bowl, lightly beat the eggs, milk, and vanilla. Stir in the ground cinnamon and nutmeg.
3. Lay half the bread cubes on the bottom of a deep-sided casserole dish. Pour the brown sugar–syrup mixture over. Lay the sliced apples on top. Add the remaining half of the bread cubes. Pour the beaten egg mixture over. Cover and refrigerate overnight.
4. Preheat the oven to 325°. Bake uncovered for 50 to 60 minutes. Cool and serve.

Drinking Apple Wine

It may not be to everyone's taste, but there is no denying that apple wine (Appelwoi) is more than just a drink—it is a way of life. Made mostly in Frankfurt's Sachsenhausen district, apple wine is delivered in patterned blue-and-gray earthen pitchers, and poured into tall ribbed glasses. You will find the homemade brew at taverns and garden restaurants throughout the area, and finding such garden restaurants is half the fun—simply look for a jug surrounded by a fresh wreath, hanging on the restaurant's outdoor sign. That translates as "apple wine made and served here." Used in some dishes such as apple wine soup, the slightly bitter and refreshing drink is most often drunk on its own, with sparkling lemonade, or sparkling water.

Beer-Basted Sausage with Caramelized Onions and German Mustard

1 white onion
2 tablespoons unsalted butter
3 tablespoons German hot
*   mustard, such as Dusseldorf*

8 German sausages
½ cup dark beer, preferably
*   German*

1. Preheat grill on medium-high heat. Peel the onion, cut in half, and finely chop.
2. Fill a deep 12-inch frying pan with 1 inch of water. Add the chopped onion and cook on medium heat until caramelized (about 10 minutes). Remove the onions from the pan and drain.
3. Melt the butter in the frying pan. Stir in the mustard. Return the onions to the pan and cook over medium heat until they are glazed (5 to 7 minutes).
4. Grill the sausages on medium-high heat, basting frequently with the beer, until browned and cooked through (8 to 10 minutes on each side). Serve with the caramelized onions.

Serves 4–6

This hearty dish combines several ingredients typically associated with German cuisine, including sausage, beer, and hot mustard. Bratwurst, wieners, or knackwurst are all good choices for the sausage.

What Is Brotzeit?

Famous in Munich, but served all over the German countryside, brotzeit can be eaten anywhere, at any time—and is most often shared by friends outside. Served on a cutting board, brotzeit is a rustic and traditional medley of regional specialties. Think smoked ham, sausages, liverwurst, blood sausages, wurstsalat, and local cheeses. The beauty of the dish is that it dramatically changes from region to region. Everything on the board is made by hand, and has a very homey, or *hausmacher*, quality.

Cold Wine Soup

4 cups water
1 lemon, cut into wedges
¼ cup semolina
2 eggs, separated
8 tablespoons granulated sugar, divided

1 cup white wine
1 teaspoon lemon juice
1 teaspoon ground cinnamon

1. In a medium saucepan, bring 3 cups of the water and the lemon wedges to a boil. Simmer for 5 minutes, uncovered, and remove the lemon.
2. Bring the water back to a boil. Mix the semolina with the remaining 1 cup of water. Slowly pour the semolina and water mixture into the boiling water, stirring continuously. Let boil for 1 minute. Reduce the heat and simmer, uncovered, until the semolina is cooked (about 20 minutes). Stir regularly.
3. In a medium bowl, whisk together the egg yolks, 2 tablespoons sugar, and the white wine. Stir into the soup. Simmer for 5 more minutes, stirring occasionally. Cool the soup and pour into a glass punch serving bowl. Cover and chill in the refrigerator.
4. Just before serving, beat the egg whites until they form stiff peaks. (Make sure to use eggs that are at room temperature.) Beat in the lemon juice, and gradually beat in the remaining 6 tablespoons of sugar. Drop small amounts of the beaten egg white into the soup. Sprinkle the soup with the ground cinnamon and serve.

Dark Bread Soup

1 clove garlic, cut in half
1 loaf German dark rye bread
4 cups water
2 beef bouillon cubes
1 cup cream

½ teaspoon caraway seeds
1 tablespoon freshly chopped
chives
Salt and pepper, to taste
½ pound Mettwurst sausage

Serves 4

Traditionally, this popular German soup is made by simmering meat bones overnight to form a rich, flavorful broth. Beef bouillon cubes make a quick and easy substitute.

1. Rub the garlic clove over 3 slices of bread. Toast the bread in the oven or a toaster oven. Cut each slice into 8 equal pieces.
2. In a large saucepan, bring the water and the bouillon cubes to a boil. Add the cream and let boil briefly. Add the bread slices. Reduce heat and simmer, uncovered, for 5 minutes. Stir in the caraway seeds and the fresh chives. Simmer for 2 more minutes. Taste and season with salt and pepper if desired.
3. Place the remainder of the rye bread on a serving dish with the sliced Mettwurst sausage. Serve with the soup.

On German Cuisine

Many people think of German food as heavy, sausage-laden, potato-oriented fare. While that may be true, there is also a new revolution in German cuisine that reflects today's obsession with gourmet (and also lighter) cuisine. Germany has a myriad of fresh produce, wine, and particularly high-quality meats that impart complex and developed flavors. Germans are also masters of garnishing, from simple mustards, to rich hollandaise, to sauerkraut. With its roots as a rural country, the evolution of German cuisine reflected the needs of its people—mainly to sustain themselves during hard physical labor. Thus, many of the dishes are quite hardy. But today a new army of chefs, armed with the latest in training, phenomenal regional products, and a vivd imagination, are redefining traditional favorites with fresh, epicurian interpretations.

Westphalian Cabbage

Serves 4

Serve with a good German smoked sausage, or as a side dish with Holstein Duck (page 329).

1 head red cabbage
2 large McIntosh apples
3 tablespoons butter
2 tablespoons minced shallots
2 teaspoons brown sugar
¾ cup beef broth

¼ cup red wine vinegar
2 tablespoons lemon juice
1 tablespoon caraway seeds
¼ teaspoon salt
2 tablespoons chopped fresh parsley

1. Wash the cabbage, remove the core, and shred. Peel the apples, remove the core, and cut into thin slices.
2. In a large saucepan or Dutch oven, melt the butter. Add the shallots and cook over medium heat until softened. Add the shredded cabbage and the sliced apples. Stir in the brown sugar. Sauté until the apple slices are browned (about 5 minutes).
3. Add the beef broth, red wine vinegar, and lemon juice. Bring to a boil. Stir in the caraway seeds and salt.
4. Reduce the heat to medium. Cook, uncovered, stirring occasionally, until the cabbage is tender and most of the liquid has been reduced. (about 30 minutes). Stir in the chopped parsley. Taste and season with salt and pepper if desired. Serve hot.

White Asparagus Season

From the end of April until June 24, much of Germany's sandy-soiled flat regions (e.g., south of Frankfurt, areas around Berlin, the lower Rhine region) feature the famed white asparagus. Unlike its green counterpart, white asparagus must be peeled all the way to the tip—but the extra step is worth it. Once boiled with a dash of salt, sugar, and 1 teaspoon of lemon juice for about 20 minutes, white asparagus is juicy, tender, and has a sweet earthiness that truly sets it apart. Germans are very proud of their white asparagus—their summer's white gold—and eat it as main dish. You will most often find it served with ham, potatoes, and homemade hollandaise.

Fruit-Stuffed Pork Chops

*4 pork chops, bone-in, about
    1½-inches thick*
¼ teaspoon salt
¼ teaspoon black pepper
*½ cup plus 2 tablespoons
    orange juice*
*½ cup prunes, pitted and
    quartered*
1 tablespoon brown sugar

½ cup chopped McIntosh apple
½ cup dried currants
*½ bunch fresh parsley, finely
    chopped*
*⅛ teaspoon ground cardamom,
    or to taste*
2 tablespoons butter
2 tablespoons water

Serves 4

Tart fruit like apples make a perfect foil for sweet pork. Feel free to substitute the currants with other dried fruit—such as cranberries or apricots—as desired.

1. Purchase pork chops already cut with a pocket, or slice open each pork chop yourself, cutting from the side and taking care not to go too near the edge. Season the outside of the pork chops with the salt and pepper.

2. In a medium saucepan, bring ½ cup of orange juice to a simmer. Add the prunes and simmer until softened (5 to 7 minutes). Remove the prunes with a slotted spoon. Stir the brown sugar into the orange juice. Add the chopped apple and simmer until tender. Stir in the dried currants, prunes, fresh parsley, and ground cardamom. Heat through. Remove the stuffing with a slotted spoon. Clean out the frying pan.

3. Stuff approximately ¼ cup of filling into the pouch of each pork chop. (Do not overfill.) Press down gently on the pork chop with a spatula to close.

4. Melt the butter in the pan. Brown the pork chops. Add the remaining 2 tablespoons of orange juice with the water. Simmer the pork chops, uncovered, over medium heat until the pork chops are tender (about 50 minutes). Serve hot.

Herbed Potato Salad

Serves 6

This recipe offsets the starch of the potatoes with the sharpness of red wine vinegar, flavored beautifully with bacon, shallots, and herbs.

2½ pounds small new or red potatoes

6 slices bacon

1 tablespoon olive oil

3 large shallots, peeled, finely minced

3 tablespoons extra-virgin olive oil

2½ tablespoons red wine vinegar

½ teaspoon granulated sugar

2 tablespoons chopped fresh dill

1 teaspoon mustard seed

Salt and pepper, to taste

1. Place the potatoes in a large saucepan with just enough salted water to cover. Bring the water to a boil. Reduce the heat and simmer, uncovered, until the potatoes are tender (about 20 minutes). Cool and cut into quarters.
2. While the potatoes are cooking, heat a large frying pan on medium-high and cook the bacon until crispy. Remove the bacon, drain on paper towels, and finely chop.
3. Clean out the pan and add 1 tablespoon olive oil. Add the shallots and sauté on medium-high heat until they are softened (3 to 4 minutes). In a small bowl, whisk together the extra-virgin olive oil, red wine vinegar, sugar, chopped fresh dill, and mustard seed until well blended.
4. Transfer the potatoes to a large bowl. Toss with the cooked shallot, bacon, and the salad dressing. Season with salt and pepper to taste. Serve warm.

Buttered Fillet of Sole

2 sole fillets

1 tablespoon freshly squeezed lemon juice

4½ tablespoons butter, divided

1 teaspoon dried dill

½ teaspoon German mustard

4 fresh parsley sprigs

1 lemon, cut into wedges

> **Serves 2**
>
> Serve this simple dish with good French bread and boiled or mashed potatoes.

1. Rinse the sole fillets and pat dry. Sprinkle the lemon juice over the fish and set aside.
2. In a frying pan over medium heat, melt 2 tablespoons of the butter. Add the fillets and sauté for 5 minutes, or until they are lightly browned and flake easily when tested with a fork. Turn each fillet over halfway through cooking.
3. Transfer the fillets to a hot platter. Add the remaining 2½ tablespoons butter to the pan. Stir in the dried dill and the mustard. As soon as the butter melts, pour it over the sole fillets. Serve, garnished with the parsley sprigs and lemon wedges.

Reading a German Wine Label

Producing about as much wine as the United States, Germany is a major force in the world of wine. Germany has thirteen wine-growing regions, 75 percent of which concentrate on white wines, most importantly Rieslings. To read a German wine label effectively, there are a few things you should know. The common classification is known as *qualitatswein bestimmter anbaugebiete*, or Q.b.A. for short. This refers to wines of good quality, destined for everyday consumption. A step up is the Q.m.P. (quality wine with distinction), most of which come from a specific wine-growing district. This category is divided into six subcategories, steadily increasing in natural sugar content and quality: Kabinetts, Spätleses, Ausleses, Beerenausleses, Eisweins, and Trockenbeerenausleses.

Elderberry Soup with "Dumplings" and Apples

8 cups elderberry juice

2½ teaspoons freshly squeezed lemon juice, divided

1 cup plus 1 teaspoon granulated sugar, divided

3 tart apples, chopped (unpeeled)

1 teaspoon ground cinnamon, divided

2 tablespoons Jamaican dark rum

2 egg whites

1. In a large saucepan, bring the elderberry juice, 2 teaspoons lemon juce, and 1 cup sugar to a boil. Add the chopped apples. Stir in ½ teaspoon ground cinnamon. Reduce the heat and simmer, uncovered, until the apples soften (4 to 5 minutes). Stir in the rum. Keep the soup warm on low heat while preparing the dumplings.
2. To make the dumplings: beat the egg whites until they form stiff peaks. Beat in ½ teaspoon lemon juice and 1 teaspoon sugar.
3. Remove the soup from the heat. Drop in large spoonfuls of the egg white mixture, turning lightly so that the dumplings absorb some of the liquid. If desired, sprinkle the remaining ½ teaspoon ground cinnamon on top of the dumplings. Serve immediately.

Holstein Duck

Serves 4–6

Before placing the duck in the oven, prick holes in several parts of the body, including underneath the wings. This allows the fat to drain during roasting.

1 duck (3–4 pounds)
½ teaspoon marjoram
¼ teaspoon salt
¼ teaspoon pepper
5 tart apples, such as McIntosh
1 sweet apple, such as Granny Smith
2 slices smoked ham

¼ stick unsalted butter
¼ cup minced shallots
2 tablespoons breadcrumbs
2 eggs
1½ cups sour cream
Italian flat-leaf parsley sprigs, for garnish

1. Preheat the oven to 375°.
2. Remove the liver and fat from the body cavity of the duck. Rinse the duck under hot running water and drain well. In a small dish, combine the marjoram and salt and pepper. Rub the spice mixture over the outside of the duck and sprinkle inside its body cavity.
3. Remove any connecting tissue from the duck liver and slice. Peel and core the apples and chop finely (keep the chopped Granny Smith separate). Dice the smoked ham.
4. Melt the unsalted butter in a frying pan over medium heat. Add the minced shallots and cook until softened. Add the duck liver, cook briefly, and add the ham and the chopped McIntosh apples. In a large bowl, combine the breadcrumbs with one of the eggs. Use your hands to mix the breadcrumbs with the duck liver, ham, apple and shallot mixture, and the other egg. If necessary, add a bit of water so that the stuffing is neither too dry nor too "mushy."
5. Fill the duck cavity with the stuffing. Place the duck on a rack in a shallow roasting pan. Cook the duck for 1½ hours, basting frequently with water. Drain off the fat and baste the duck with water again. Add the chopped Granny Smith apple to the roasting pan and cook for another 15 to 20 minutes, as needed. (The duck is cooked when the internal temperature of the fattest part of the thigh is 180°.)
6. Remove the duck and slice. Mix the roasted chopped apple with the sour cream. Slice the duck and garnish with the parsley sprigs. Serve with the sour cream–apple mixture.

Black Forest Cherry Cake

Serves 8

There are numerous versions of this popular cake that originated in Germany's Black Forest region. Feel free to beat 1 or 2 tablespoons of kirsch brandy liqueur into the whipped cream filling if desired.

1 cup all-purpose flour, sifted
1 cup granulated sugar
¼ teaspoon salt
¼ cup cocoa powder
3 eggs
1½ teaspoons vanilla extract, divided

1¼ cups sour cherry juice, divided
2 tablespoons granulated sugar
1½ cups whipping cream
¼ cup confectioners' sugar
2 cups canned sour cherries
1 ounce semisweet chocolate

1. Preheat the oven to 350°. Grease two 8-inch cake pans.
2. To make the cake, sift together the flour, sugar, salt and cocoa powder. Beat the eggs and 1 teaspoon vanilla extract until light and fluffy. Carefully fold the flour into the beaten egg. Pour the cake batter into the greased pans. Bake for 30 minutes, or until a toothpick inserted in the middle comes out clean. Cool the cakes completely.
3. To make the syrup, in a small saucepan bring 1 cup of the sour cherry juice and the granulated sugar to a boil. Cook, stirring, until the sugar dissolves.
4. To make the filling, beat the whipping cream until stiff peaks form. Beat in ½ teaspoon vanilla extract, the confectioners' sugar, and the remaining ¼ cup of sour cherry juice.
5. To assemble the cake, turn the cakes out onto 2 cake plates. Spread ½ of the syrup mixture over each cake. Let sit for 5 minutes, then spread ⅓ of the whipped cream filling over 1 cake. Add ½ cup of the cherries. Place the other cake on top. Spread the remaining ⅔ of the filling over the top and sides of the cake. Place the cherries on the top of the cake and the sides.
6. Grate the chocolate and sprinkle on top of the cake. Chill until ready to serve.

Hazelnut Torte

Serves 8

Guests are certain to be impressed by this delicious dessert. For an added touch, sprinkle a bit of confectioners' sugar or grated chocolate over the whipped cream topping.

8 large eggs, separated
1½ cups granulated sugar
1 teaspoon vanilla extract
1 cup finely ground hazelnuts

4 ounces semisweet chocolate, grated
¼ cup kirsch brandy liqueur
2 cups whipped cream

1. Preheat the oven to 350°. Grease two 9-inch springform pans and line the bottom with wax or parchment paper.
2. Beat the egg yolks until smooth and set aside. In a separate bowl, beat the egg whites until they form stiff peaks and are very light (about 5 minutes). Gradually add the sugar during beating. Beat in the vanilla extract.
3. Fold the egg white mixture into the yolks. Use a rubber spatula to carefully fold the chopped hazelnuts into the mixture. Fold in the grated chocolate.
4. Pour the batter into the cake pans, dividing it evenly between them. Bake for 35 to 40 minutes, until the cake is browned and springs back from the sides of the pan. Remove the cakes from the oven and cool on a wire rack.
5. Finish the torte by lightly brushing 2 tablespoons of the kirsch over the top of each cake. Place one of the cakes on top of the other. Spread the whipped cream on top and chill until ready to serve.

How to Grind Hazelnuts

First, blanch the hazelnuts by boiling them for 5 minutes. When they are cool enough to handle, remove the skins. To grind, place about ¼ cup at a time in a blender, or chop as finely as you can with a sharp knife.

Swabian Stuffed Pockets (Maultaschen)

Serves 4

The German version of ravioli, Maultaschen are traditionally served with a simple salad.

2¾ cups all-purpose flour

6 eggs, divided

¼ teaspoon salt

Water, as needed

⅓ cup breadcrumbs, or as needed

2 slices prosciutto, thinly sliced

¼ pound fresh sausage meat

½ pound ground pork

½ cup cooked spinach

¼ cup chopped fresh parsley

½ teaspoon grated nutmeg

Salt and black pepper, to taste

1. To make the dough, place the flour in a large bowl. Make a "well" in the middle and add 4 eggs and ¼ teaspoon salt. Combine the egg with the flour to form a dough, adjusting the level of flour and water as necessary: if the dough is too wet, add a bit more flour. If too dry, add 1 tablespoon of water at a time as needed. Keep kneading for at least 5 minutes, until the dough is smooth and elastic. Cover the dough and let rest for 30 minutes.

2. To make the filling, in a small bowl combine the breadcrumbs with 1 tablespoon water to soften. In a large bowl, combine the softened breadcrumbs, prosciutto, sausage, ground pork, spinach, parsley, the nutmeg, and the remaining 2 eggs, using your hands to mix everything together. Add a bit of water or milk if the filling is too dry. Season with salt and pepper as desired.

3. To make the ravioli, knead the rested dough for a few minutes more. Turn onto a floured surface and divide in half. Roll both halves out very thinly (⅛-inch if possible). Lay out one of the halves and use a pastry cutter to cut into 4-inch squares. Stack the squares, cover with a damp towel to keep from drying, and repeat with the other half.

4. To fill the ravioli, place a heaping teaspoon of filling in the middle of a square. Moisten all the edges of the square with water. Lay another square on top and press down to seal. Continue with the remainder of the ravioli.

5. To cook, bring a large saucepan of salted water to a boil. Cook the ravioli in the boiling water until they float to the top (7 to 10 minutes).

continues >>

Take care not to overcrowd the saucepan. Serve hot with tomato sauce or melted butter.

A German Ravioli

Maultaschen is a Swabian stuffed noodle with an amusing history. Swabia is a region and language in southern Germany, and long ago once included what is now modern Switzerland and Alsace. Swabians liked to eat meat, and they did not want to give it up for Lent. So in order to get around this challenging situation, they resorted to camouflage. They ground the meat, mixed it with spinach and onions, wrapped it in a thin pasta dough, and added melted cheese as a final cloak. This, they thought, would hide their secret ingredient from God. It is still served today, though in some restaurants you may find a modern "open-faced" interpretation.

German Cucumber Salad

2 medium cucumbers
1 red onion
3 tomatoes
½ cup sour cream
1 tablespoon German mustard
2 tablespoons granulated sugar

1 tablespoon red wine vinegar
2 tablespoons minced fresh dill
⅛ teaspoon salt, or to taste
⅛ teaspoon pepper, or to taste
4 sprigs fresh parsley, to
   garnish

Serves 4

For maximum flavor, chill the salad for at least 1 hour to give the flavors a chance to blend.

1. Peel the cucumbers and thinly slice. Peel and thinly slice the red onion. Cut each tomato into 4 to 6 wedges. Combine the vegetables in a salad bowl.
2. To make the dressing, combine the sour cream, German mustard, sugar, red wine vinegar, fresh dill, and salt and pepper in a small bowl. Pour the dressing over the prepared vegetables and chill. Garnish with the fresh parsley sprigs before serving.

Chapter 25

Greece:
Gourmet Island Hopping

336 : Roasted Potatoes with Garlic, Lemon, and Oregano

337 : Squid in Wine

338 : Pan-Fried Fish with Rosemary

339 : Lemon and Egg Soup

340 : Braised Octopus with Onions

341 : Tzatziki (Cucumber, Garlic, and Yogurt Dip)

341 : Feta and Mint Dip

342 : Moussaka

343 : Galaktoboureko (Greek-Style Pie)

344 : Roasted Leg of Lamb with Lemon-Garlic Potatoes

345 : Greek-Style Rabbit Stew

346 : Baklava

Roasted Potatoes with Garlic, Lemon, and Oregano

Serves 4–6

This dish is a specialty on the Greek island of Naxos, where it is frequently served with roast chicken or leg of lamb.

12 small red potatoes
4 tablespoons freshly squeezed lemon juice (2 lemons)
½ teaspoon garlic salt
1 tablespoon dried oregano
1 teaspoon salt
Freshly ground black pepper, to taste

¼ cup olive oil
1½ tablespoons chopped fresh oregano
4–6 fresh parsley sprigs

1. Preheat the oven to 425°.
2. Cut the unpeeled potatoes into quarters. In a medium bowl, toss the potatoes with the lemon juice, garlic salt, oregano, salt, and freshly ground black pepper.
3. Pour the olive oil into a shallow 9 × 13 inch baking pan. Use a paper towel or cloth to wipe the olive oil across the pan so that the pan is evenly coated. Spread out the potatoes on the pan.
4. Bake the potatoes until they are browned and pierce easily with a fork (about 30 minutes). Turn the potatoes 2 or 3 times during cooking. Garnish with the fresh oregano and parsley sprigs and serve.

The Greek Diet of Longevity

Greeks used to relate stories about the men and women of Crete who lived past the age of 100, thanks to a diet of little meat and that was rich in olive oil, greens, and grains. Strangely enough, those stories have now been proven true—this diet does increase lifespan. Although a large percentage of Greeks are still heavy smokers and the country doesn't enjoy one of the highest standards of living in Europe, the inhabitants of Greece have one of the world's highest life expectancies.

Squid in Wine

1 whole small squid, 1½
   pounds
¼ cup olive oil
2 cloves garlic, minced
1 cup dry red wine
2 tablespoons balsamic vinegar

¼ cup water
1 chopped green onion
2 tablespoons chopped fresh
   parsley
2 (3-inch) cinnamon sticks

Serves 4

Shellfish play a prominent role in Greek cuisine. In this dish, balsamic vinegar and red wine bring out squid's natural sweet flavor.

1. To clean the squid, pull out the entrails (body contents) and cut off the tentacles, making sure to remove the beak in the center of the tentacles. Discard the ink sac and the head. Lay the squid flat and carefully scrape off the dark outer skin. Rinse the squid body and the tentacles under cold running water. Pat dry with paper towels. Cut the tentacles in half lengthwise. Cut the main body into rings.

2. Heat the olive oil in a deep-sided frying pan. Add the minced garlic and squid pieces. Cook over medium heat, until the squid is lightly browned (about 5 minutes). Remove the squid from the pan and drain on paper towels.

3. Deglaze the pan by bringing ¼ cup of the red wine to a boil, using a spatula to scrape up the browned bits. Add the squid back into the pan. Add the remaining ¾ cup of red wine and balsamic vinegar. Add the ¼ cup water, or as much water as is needed to cover the squid. Stir in the chopped green onion and fresh parsley. Add the cinnamon sticks.

4. Bring to a boil, then reduce the heat and simmer, uncovered, until the squid is tender (about 60 minutes). Stir the squid occasionally, and add more water or wine if necessary to cover. Serve warm (remove the cinnamon sticks before serving).

Pan-Fried Fish with Rosemary

4 red snapper, fillets
¼ teaspoon salt, or as needed
5 tablespoons flour, divided
2 teaspoons dried rosemary
2 teaspoons dried thyme

5 tablespoons olive oil, divided
2 cloves garlic, minced
⅓ cup balsamic vinegar
1 lemon, cut into wedges
6 to 8 rosemary sprigs

1. Rinse the fish under cold running water, and pat dry with paper towels. Rub the salt over the fish. Set aside.
2. Combine ¼ cup flour, dried rosemary, and dried thyme on a piece of parchment or wax paper.
3. In a 12-inch frying pan, heat ¼ cup of the olive oil over medium-high heat. Cover the fillets with the seasoned flour mixture, pressing to coat. Lay the fish in the frying pan and cook until golden brown and crispy (2 to 3 minutes on each side). Remove the fish from the pan. Place on a serving dish and keep warm.
4. Add the remaining 1 tablespoon oil in the pan. Add the minced garlic and sauté on medium-heat until the garlic is lightly browned. Turn the heat up to medium-high and add the remaining 1 tablespoon of flour and the balsamic vinegar, stirring continuously to thicken. Pour the sauce over the fish and garnish with the lemon wedges and rosemary sprigs. Serve hot.

Macaroni—a Greek Pasta?

Making pasta was an ancient way of preserving grain. Though most of the words related to pasta are Italian, there is one—macaroni—that has its roots in Greece. It likely originated from the tradition known as the Feast of the Makarion (the Blessed) in Ancient Greece—festivals dedicated to the honoring of dead souls. It was (and still is in many places today in Greece) a tradition where, on that particular day, they cook grain and mainly pasta, since the seeds from the grain (Demeter and Persephone) symbolize death (sowing) and resurrection (sprouting).

Lemon and Egg Soup

¾ cup white or brown rice
6 cups chicken stock
6 tablespoons freshly squeezed
  lemon juice, divided
3 large eggs

2 teaspoons dried oregano
Salt and freshly ground black
  pepper, to taste
Lemon slices as desired, for
  garnish

> **Serves 6**
>
> The Greek version of chicken soup is made with egg for extra protein. Feel free to use your favorite type of rice, including long-grained or short-grained white rice.

1. Rinse the rice if desired. Bring the chicken stock to a boil in a large saucepan. Add the rice and 4 tablespoons lemon juice. Return the soup to boiling, reduce the heat, and simmer, uncovered until the rice is tender (10 to 15 minutes). Remove 1½ cups of the soup and set aside.

2. In a large bowl, use an electric mixer to beat the eggs until they are fluffy. Beat in the remaining 2 tablespoons of lemon juice. Whisk in the reserved 1½ cups of soup.

3. Pour the egg and soup mixture back into the saucepan, whisking continuously to thicken. Cook for 5 more minutes to give the flavors a chance to blend. Stir in the dried oregano. Taste and season with salt and pepper if desired. Serve hot with lemon wedges.

The Greek Leaf

Phyllo, which literally translates as "leaf" in Greek, is made of finely rolled and stretched sheets of dough. Practically see-through, these paper-thin sheets are stacked, rolled, wrapped, and then frozen. Phyllo dough is available at most supermarkets and at Greek and Middle Eastern specialty food stores (making your own is tricky). Because the dough is already rolled and precut, phyllo is relatively easy to work with.

Braised Octopus with Onions

4 sun-dried tomatoes (not oil-packed)
½ cup dry red wine
2 pounds octopus, cleaned
2 tablespoons olive oil
6 shallots, finely chopped
2 cloves garlic, finely chopped

2 tablespoons red wine vinegar
2 tablespoons chopped fresh basil
1 bay leaf
Salt and freshly ground black pepper, to taste

1. Reconstitute the sun-dried tomatoes by placing in a bowl with the red wine and enough water to cover. Soak in the wine and water mixture until softened (25 to 30 minutes). Pat dry with paper towels and cut into 1-inch slices. Reserve the soaking liquid.

2. Place the cleaned octopus body and tentacles in a saucepan. Do not add water. Cook, covered, over low heat, until the octopus is tender and easily pierced with a fork (about 20 minutes). Remove from the saucepan. Cut the octopus into 1-inch pieces. Cut off the suckers if desired. Reserve the cooking liquid.

3. Clean out the saucepan, and add the olive oil. Add the shallots, chopped garlic, and the sun-dried tomatoes. Sauté over medium to medium-high heat until the shallots have softened and the garlic starts to brown.

4. Add the octopus back into the pan, with the reserved tomato soaking liquid, reserved liquid from cooking the octopus, and the red wine vinegar. Bring to a boil. Stir in the basil, bay leaf, and salt and pepper to taste. Cook, covered, over low heat until the sauce has thickened and the octopus is tender (40 to 50 minutes). Remove the bay leaf before serving.

Tzatziki (Cucumber, Garlic, and Yogurt Dip)

1 English cucumber
½ teaspoon salt
2 cups Greek yogurt
4 cloves garlic, finely chopped
5 teaspoons virgin olive oil

2 teaspoons red wine vinegar
2 tablespoons chopped fresh
    sweet herbs (dill or mint)
Freshly ground black pepper, to
    taste

1. Peel and grate the cucumber. Drain the liquid from the cucumbers by placing them in a colander and sprinkling the salt over. Place a small plate on top of the cucumbers to help push out the liquid, and let drain for 1 hour.
2. Combine the yogurt, grated cucumber, chopped garlic, olive oil, red wine vinegar, and the chopped fresh herbs in a medium bowl. Season with the black pepper. Cover and chill until ready to serve.

> **Serves 4–6**
>
> Thick and creamy Greek yogurt has a higher percentage of milk-fat than other types of yogurt. It can be bought in specialty stores, or check your local supermarket for the brand Total Greek Style Yogurt, which comes from Greece.

Feta and Mint Dip

4 ounces feta cheese, crumbled
¾ cup plain yogurt
¾ cup sour cream
1 green onion, diced
1 tablespoon freshly chopped
    mint

Juice of 1 freshly squeezed
    lemon
⅛ teaspoon salt, or to taste
¼ teaspoon freshly ground
    black pepper, to taste
Mint leaves for garnish

In a food processor, purée all the ingredients except for the mint leaves until you have a smooth, creamy dip. Cover and refrigerate for at least 1 hour to give the flavors a chance to blend. Garnish with the fresh mint leaves before serving.

> **Serves 6–8**
>
> Serve this light, refreshing dip with crudités or toasted slices of Greek pita bread.

Moussaka

Serves 3–4

Ground beef makes a convenient substitute for lamb in this variation on classic Greek moussaka. Be sure to use truncheon-shaped western eggplant, and not the thinner Japanese eggplant.

2 medium eggplants
Salt, as needed
5 tablespoons olive oil, divided
1 medium white onion, finely
   chopped
1 pound lean ground beef
2 large cloves garlic, minced
¾ cup canned tomatoes
¼ cup dry white wine
1 teaspoon dried oregano
Freshly ground black pepper, to
   taste

1 tablespoon chopped fresh
   parsley
3 tablespoons butter
2½ tablespoons all-purpose
   flour
1 cup half-and-half
1 egg, lightly beaten
½ cup grated Parmesan or
   Gruyère cheese

1. Preheat the oven to 350°. Grease a 9 × 9-inch baking dish.
2. Peel the eggplants and cut into slices between ¼- and ½-inch thick. Degorge the eggplant slices by placing them in a colander and sprinkling with salt. Let the eggplant slices sit for at least 1 hour to release their liquid. Remove from the colander, lay on paper towels, and press down to remove the liquid.
3. Heat 3 tablespoons of olive oil in a frying pan. Add the eggplant slices and sauté over medium heat until they are browned. Remove and drain on paper towels. Clean out the frying pan.
4. Add 2 tablespoons olive oil to the frying pan. Add the onions and cook over medium heat until they are soft and translucent. Add the ground beef, using a spatula to break it up. Cook over medium heat until the beef is browned. Drain the fat from the frying pan. Add the garlic, tomatoes, and the white wine. Stir in the oregano and salt and pepper to taste. Reduce heat and simmer, uncovered, for 20 minutes, stirring occasionally. Stir in the fresh parsley.
5. While the meat is simmering, prepare the white sauce: melt the butter in a small saucepan over low heat. Add the flour, stirring continuously until the flour is mixed in with the butter (2 to 3 minutes). Slowly add the half-and-half. Continue stirring over medium heat until the

continues >>

sauce is thick and bubbly. Remove from the heat and stir in the lightly beaten egg.

6. To cook, add the eggplant and meat sauce to the dish in layers: lay out half the eggplant slices in the bottom of the baking dish and spread half of the meat sauce mixture on top of the eggplant. Repeat with the remaining half of the eggplant and meat sauce. Spread the béchamel sauce over top. Sprinkle with the grated cheese. Bake until the moussaka is heated through (about 45 minutes). Cut into squares to serve.

Galaktoboureko (Greek-Style Pie)

4 large eggs
1 tablespoon lemon juice
1¾ cups granulated sugar,
   divided

6 cups whole milk
1½ cups semolina flour
12 sheets phyllo dough, thawed
⅔ cup unsalted butter, melted

Serves 6

Finish off this delicious Greek dessert by topping with a simple sugar and water syrup, made by boiling 1¾ cups water and 1 cup granulated sugar, stirring to dissolve the sugar.

1. Preheat the oven to 350°. Grease a 9 × 13-inch pan.
2. In a large bowl, beat the eggs until fluffy, beating in the lemon juice and ¼ cup of sugar. In a large saucepan, heat the milk on medium-low heat until it is at a near boil, taking care not to burn or scorch. Remove the saucepan from the heat.
3. In a medium bowl, combine the semolina flour and the remaining sugar. Whisk the flour and sugar mixture into the warm milk. Gently stir in the beaten eggs.
4. Lay 6 of the phyllo sheets in the bottom of the pan. Brush with half of the melted butter. Carefully spread the egg custard mixture over the phyllo sheets, using a rubber spatula to make sure it is spread out evenly. Lay the other 6 phyllo sheets on top and brush with the remaining melted butter. Make horizontal cuts in the top layer of the phyllo, taking care not to cut through into the custard. Bake until the custard is firm and the topping is golden brown (45 to 50 minutes). Cool before serving.

Roasted Leg of Lamb with Lemon-Garlic Potatoes

¾ cup olive oil, divided

3 teaspoons minced garlic, divided

2½ tablespoons dried oregano, divided

4 teaspoons dried thyme, divided

2 sprigs chopped fresh rosemary

6–7 pound leg of lamb, bone in

3 pounds Yukon gold potatoes

Juice from 3 freshly squeezed lemons (6 tablespoons)

¾ teaspoon salt, or to taste

1. In a cup or small bowl, combine ¼ olive oil, 2 teaspoons minced garlic, 1½ tablespoons dried oregano, 1 teaspoon dried thyme, and rosemary, Rub the marinade over the lamb. Place the lamb in a large, deep container or shallow roasting pan. Cover and refrigerate overnight.

2. Preheat the oven to 325°. Remove the lamb from the pan and discard the marinade. Clean out the pan if this is the pan that will be used for roasting.

3. Wash the potatoes and cut into quarters. (Do not peel.) Place the potatoes in a large roasting pan and toss with ½ cup olive oil, lemon juice, 1 tablespoon oregano, 1 tablespoon thyme, 1 teaspoon minced garlic, and the salt. Place the lamb over the potatoes.

4. Roast the lamb, allowing 20 minutes per pound, until it reaches the desired level of doneness. Check for doneness by inserting a meat thermometer in the thickest part of the lamb: for medium-rare, the internal temperature should be 140°; it should be 170° for well-done. Baste the lamb with the juices and turn the potatoes occasionally during cooking.

5. To serve, remove the lamb from the oven and let stand for 10 minutes before carving. Check the potatoes: if they are not tender, continue cooking while the lamb is standing. Serve the lamb with the roasted potatoes.

Greek-Style Rabbit Stew

Serves 4

Sweet blood oranges and cinnamon combine to give this stew a unique fruity flavor.

3½ pound rabbit, cut into 6 serving pieces
½ cup all-purpose flour, or as needed
1 medium yellow onion, finely chopped
2 blood oranges or other sweet orange

¼ cup olive oil
1¼ cups dry red wine
1 bay leaf
10 juniper berries
1 (3-inch) cinnamon stick
Salt and black pepper, as needed

1. Rinse the rabbit pieces under cold running water and pat dry with paper towels. Dredge each piece in the flour. Peel and chop the yellow onion. Peel the orange and cut into 6 to 8 segments.

2. In a heavy saucepan, heat the olive oil. Add the rabbit and sauté over high heat until browned all over. Remove the rabbit from the pan. Add the chopped onion to the pan and cook over medium heat until the onion is soft and translucent.

3. Drain any excess oil out of the pan. Add ½ of the orange segments and ¼ cup wine. Simmer for 2 to 3 minutes. Add ¾ cup of the wine and bring to a boil. Add the bay leaf, juniper berries, and the cinnamon stick. Add the rabbit back into the pan. Cover and simmer for 30 minutes, turning the rabbit occasionally. Add the remaining ¼ cup of wine and simmer for 15 more minutes, or until the rabbit is tender and cooked through. Remove the bay leaf and the cinnamon stick. Taste and season with salt and pepper if desired. Serve on a warm platter garnished with the remaining orange wedges.

Baklava

Serves 6–8

Although Baklava is associated with Greek cuisine, it is found in many Middle and Near Eastern countries. Feel free to use any combination of chopped nuts.

2 cups warm water
1 cup granulated sugar
2 tablespoons honey
1 tablespoon rose water
4 sticks unsalted butter
2 cups walnuts, coarsely chopped
1 cup almonds, coarsely chopped

1 cup pecans, coarsely chopped
½ cup packed brown sugar
1 teaspoon ground cinnamon
½ teaspoon ground cloves
1 pound (24 sheets) phyllo dough, thawed

1. Preheat the oven to 350°. Grease a 9 × 13-inch baking pan.
2. To prepare the sugar syrup, bring the water, sugar, and honey to a boil, stirring to dissolve the honey and sugar. Add the rose water. Simmer for 1 minute longer; cool and refrigerate until needed.
3. In a medium saucepan, melt the unsalted butter over low heat. Keep warm. In a medium bowl, toss the coarsely chopped nuts with the brown sugar, cinnamon, and cloves.
4. Lay 12 of the phyllo dough sheets at the bottom of the baking pan. Spread a portion of the sweetened nut mixture over. Lay 1 phyllo sheet over the nut mixture. Use a pastry brush to brush the phyllo sheet with the melted butter. Spread more of the nut mixture on top. Continue layering in this way, alternating between a nut mixture and 1 phyllo sheet brushed with butter, until the filling is used up. Lay any remaining phyllo sheets on top. Brush with any remaining melted butter.
5. Use a sharp knife to cut through the first few layers of the baklava, cutting into triangle or diamond shapes as desired. Bake until the baklava is golden brown and cooked through (about 1 hour). Pour the syrup on top. Let sit for a minute to let the syrup sink through and serve.

Chapter 26

Italy:
Eating the Sun

348 Milk-Fed Veal Cutlet with Parmesan and Truffle Crust

349 Penne with Scallops, Bacon, and Chili Pepper

350 La Pasta d'Angelica

351 Marinated Olives

352 Pan-Roasted Swordfish with Plum Tomatoes

353 Braised Veal Shanks with Porcini Mushrooms

354 Pasta alla Puttanesca (Pasta with Harlot's Sauce)

355 Chicken in Wine

356 Sweet-and-Sour Eggplant Stew

357 Classic Risotto

357 Tiramisu

358 Panna Cotta

359 Bliss's Gnocchi

360 Bliss's Fresh Plum Tomato and Basil Sauce

Milk-Fed Veal Cutlet with Parmesan and Truffle Crust

Serves 1

Swiss-born Chef Marco Mazzei has made Danieli's, at St. Regis Beijing, one of the best Italian restaurants in town. If you can't find black truffles, use button mushrooms instead.

2 tablespoons olive oil
10½-ounce veal chop, with bone
Salt and pepper, to taste
½ red bell pepper, trimmed and cut in triangles
1 celery stalk, trimmed and cut in 1-inch pieces
½ red onion, peeled and cut lengthwise in wedges
1 tablespoon sun-dried tomatoes
½ cup butter
½ cup breadcrumbs
½ cup grated Parmesan cheese
¼ cup sliced black truffles
2 tablespoons dry white wine
3 tablespoons chicken stock
Dash dried rosemary
Fresh rosemary sprig

1. Preheat the oven to 375°. Heat the olive oil in a cast-iron skillet. Season the veal chop with salt and pepper, and pan-fry the chop for approximately 3 to 5 minutes on each side.
2. Transfer the veal chop to a roasting pan along with the bell pepper, celery, red onion, and sun-dried tomatoes. Roast for 7 to 8 minutes.
3. Transfer the veal chop to a plate and tent with foil to keep warm. Add the butter to the vegetables in the pan and bake until the vegetables are tender and lightly caramelized. Season with a pinch of salt, then transfer the vegetables to a plate and keep warm. Increase oven temperature to 400°.
4. In a small bowl, combine the breadcrumbs and Parmesan. Place the sliced truffles on the meat and cover with the bread mixture. Drizzle with a little olive oil and bake for a few minutes in the oven until golden brown.
5. Pour the white wine and chicken stock into the roasting pan and heat on medium-high on the stovetop. Use a wooden spoon to scrape up the leftover meat bits from the bottom of the pan (this is called deglazing). Flavor with a touch of rosemary and season with salt and pepper to taste. Place the roasted vegetables on a serving plate, top with the veal chop, and surround with sauce. Decorate with fresh rosemary and serve.

Penne with Scallops, Bacon, and Chili Pepper

1 strip bacon
¼ cup extra-virgin olive oil
1 garlic clove, peeled and
    crushed
⅛ pound fresh scallops
Salt and freshly ground black
    pepper, to taste

4 ounces penne pasta
Cherry tomatoes, cut into
    quarters
Arugula leaves or fresh spinach
    cut into strips
Dry or fresh chili, to taste

> **Serves 1**
>
> Here, Chef Marco Mazzei combines classical Venetian food items. "The dish is so well received," he says, "because local citizens in Beijing have a passion for seafood and pasta."

1. Cut the bacon into strips and fry gently over medium-high heat for several minutes until all the fat is rendered. Set aside the bacon and drain and discard the fat from the pan.
2. Add the olive oil to the frying pan and heat on low. Add the garlic and sauté, stirring continuously, for about 1 minute (make sure not to burn the garlic, otherwise it will be bitter). Add the scallops and sauté gently until opaque in the center, about 2 to 3 minutes. Season with salt and pepper, and transfer to a plate to keep warm.
3. Bring a pot of salted water to a boil, and cook the pasta until al dente. Drain, and add the penne to the frying pan.
4. Add the bacon, scallops, cherry tomatoes, and arugula leaves, and toss gently. Season to taste with chili and serve very hot.

Italy's Role in Gourmet Cuisine

When considering the roots of gourmet French cuisine, there is a marriage that must be credited—that between Catherine de Medici and Henry d'Orleans, who became Henry II, king of France. Catherine de Medici, niece of Laurence de Medici, duke of Urbino, had a reputation of being a gourmet and fond of her homemade Florentine cuisine. When she moved to France, her cooks and ingredients came with her, including artichokes, beans, peas, spinach, and olive oil. These ingredients appeared on the French cooking scene and helped define it.

La Pasta d'Angelica

Serves 3–4

For extra flavor, add several large kalamata olives with the pine nuts and other seasonings.

12 ounces angel hair pasta or
   spaghetti
½ white onion
2 garlic cloves
2 large tomatoes
¼ cup pine nuts
3 tablespoons olive oil

¼ cup red wine vinegar
½ cup golden raisins
¼ cup chopped basil
⅛ teaspoon ground cumin,
   or to taste
Salt and freshly ground black
   pepper, to taste

1. Fill a large saucepan with just enough salted water to cover the pasta. Bring to a boil. Add the pasta and cook, uncovered, until al dente (10 to 15 minutes). Drain the pasta thoroughly.
2. Peel and chop the onion. Smash, peel, and chop the garlic. Chop the tomatoes, reserving 2 tablespoons of the juice.
3. Heat a large frying pan over medium heat. Add the pine nuts and sauté, shaking the pan occasionally, until they are browned (about 2 minutes). Remove and set aside. Wipe the pan dry.
4. Heat the olive oil in the frying pan. Add the onion and cook over medium heat until the onion is soft and translucent. Stir in the garlic, chopped tomatoes, reserved tomato juice, and the red wine vinegar. Reduce heat and simmer, uncovered, until the tomatoes have softened (about 5 minutes).
5. Stir in toasted pine nuts, raisins, chopped basil, and the ground cumin. Heat through. Taste and season with salt and freshly ground pepper as desired. Add the pasta, tossing well to combine with the sauce. Serve hot.

Marinated Olives

1 pound large kalamata or oil-cured black olives
3 large cloves garlic, thinly sliced
¼ teaspoon cayenne pepper
1 tablespoon dried oregano
1 teaspoon dried rosemary
2 tablespoons red wine vinegar
1 teaspoon lemon juice
⅓ cup extra-virgin olive oil, or as needed

In a large bowl, combine the olives with the sliced garlic, cayenne pepper, dried oregano, dried rosemary, red wine vinegar, and lemon juice. Toss with ¼ cup of the olive oil. Add as much of the remaining oil as needed to lightly coat the olives. Cover and refrigerate for at least 1 hour before using, to give the flavors a chance to blend.

The Italian Olive

Olives are grown all over Italy, and each part of the country has its own way of dressing them. They are often served with aperitifs, along with salted almonds, and, in the home, olives are almost always offered with a glass of wine before a meal.

Pan-Roasted Swordfish with Plum Tomatoes

Serves 4

This swordfish dish can be on the table in less than 30 minutes. Feel free to use the same recipe to prepare fresh tuna.

4 large plum tomatoes
4 (5- to 6-ounce) skinless
   swordfish steaks
2 tablespoons capers
2 cloves garlic
4 tablespoons olive oil, divided
¼ cup balsamic vinegar
½ cup chopped fresh basil
1 tablespoon dried oregano

1 tablespoon granulated sugar
2 tablespoons fresh-squeezed
   lemon juice
Salt and freshly ground black
   pepper, to taste
Italian flat-leaf parsley,
   to garnish
1 lemon, cut into wedges,
   to garnish

1. In a medium saucepan, add enough water to cover the tomatoes. Heat to boiling and blanch the tomatoes briefly until the skins loosen (about 1 minute). Use a slotted spoon to remove the tomatoes from the boiling water. Drain thoroughly, peel the skin, and cut into thin slices. Cut each swordfish steak into 3 to 4 pieces on the diagonal. Rinse the capers. Peel and mince the garlic.

2. In a large frying pan, heat 2 tablespoons olive oil over medium heat. Add the garlic and cook until lightly browned. Add the tomatoes, capers, and the balsamic vinegar. Heat through; then stir in the basil, oregano, sugar, and lemon juice. Add the salt and pepper. Cook slowly over medium-low heat until the balsamic vinegar is reduced by half.

3. Brush 2 tablespoons olive oil over the swordfish pieces. Add to the pan. Cook over high heat until the fish is golden brown on the outside and cooked through (about 3 to 5 minutes). Transfer to a serving platter. Garnish with the parsley and lemon wedges. Serve immediately.

Braised Veal Shanks with Porcini Mushrooms

1 ounce dried porcini
   mushrooms
¾ cup all-purpose flour
½ stick unsalted butter
4 veal shank cuts, 1½ pounds
   total
½ cup dry white wine
   (preferably Italian)

1 small white onion, finely
   chopped
2 carrots, chopped
2 tablespoons tomato sauce
2 cups beef broth
Gremolata Seasoning (see
   sidebar below)

> **Serves 4**
>
> Delicate porcini mushrooms add an earthy flavor to the braised veal. Serve with Classic Risotto (page 357) for a complete meal.

1. Reconstitute the porcini mushrooms by soaking in water for 20 minutes. (Make sure the mushrooms are completely covered.) Remove the mushrooms, drain thoroughly, and chop.
2. Spread out the flour on a piece of wax or parchment paper. Dredge the veal in the flour. Melt the unsalted butter in a large frying pan. Add the veal and sear over high heat, until browned on both sides. Remove the veal to a large shallow baking dish.
3. Deglaze the pan by heating ¼ cup of the dry white wine on medium-high heat, using a spatula to scrape up any browned bits. Reduce the heat to medium, and add the chopped onion, carrots, and the porcini mushrooms. Stir in the tomato sauce. Heat through, and add the remaining ¼ cup of wine and the beef broth.
4. Return the veal to the pan. Reduce the heat and simmer the veal and sauce, covered, for about 1½ hours, until the meat is tender and cooked through. (The meat should be so tender that it is almost falling off the bone.) Add more beef broth or water if necessary.
5. While the veal is cooking, prepare the Gremolada seasoning. To serve the veal, place the shanks on a platter, spoon the sauce over them, and sprinkle with the seasoning.

Gremolata Seasoning

To make the seasoning, combine 3 minced cloves garlic, finely grated zest of 2 lemons, 2 rosemary sprigs, and 2 tablespoons chopped fresh Italian parsley.

Pasta alla Puttanesca (Pasta with Harlot's Sauce)

6 Roma tomatoes

10 Italian or Greek oil-cured olives

1 tablespoon capers

4 ounces canned anchovies

2 cloves garlic

1 pound spaghetti, or other long pasta

1 stick unsalted butter

1 tablespoon fresh chopped oregano

2 teaspoons fresh basil

½ teaspoon red pepper flakes

4 sprigs Italian flat parsley, to garnish

1. Wash the tomatoes and chop (do not peel or remove the seeds). Remove the pits from the olives and cut in half. Rinse the capers. Drain the oil from the anchovies and separate. Smash, peel, and mince the garlic.
2. Fill a large saucepan with just enough salted water to cover the pasta. Bring to a boil. Add the pasta and cook, uncovered, until al dente (10 to 15 minutes). Drain the pasta thoroughly.
3. Melt the unsalted butter in a frying pan. Add the garlic. Cook over low heat for 1 minute, then add the anchovies. Continue cooking over low heat, gently mashing the anchovies and mixing with the garlic. Add the tomatoes, olives, capers, oregano, basil, and the red pepper flakes. Turn the heat up to medium-low, and cook until the tomatoes have softened. If the sauce is too dry, add 1 tablespoon water or tomato paste.
4. To serve, combine the sauce with the cooked pasta. Garnish with the parsley.

A Bit About Basil

In Greek basil means "regal herb." Maybe that's why it takes center stage in the Mediterranean kitchen. Italians use basil almost as much as Americans use salt—it's essential to a wide variety of dishes. Deeply fragrant and posessesing a brilliant green color, basil is also exceptional to use as a granish. A simple basil flower can dress up a plate of pasta, especially when it is placed against a rich red sauce. In Italy there are two major varieties of basil: the Genovese type, perfect for pesto sauce, and the minty Neapolitan variety, best for drying. When using fresh basil, you should not chop or slice it with a knife—the leaves will blacken and lose their flavor. Instead, tear the leaves with your fingers.

Chicken in Wine

4 chicken breasts, boneless,
    skinless
¼ cup tomato juice
¼ cup red wine vinegar
3 tablespoons olive oil, divided
2 cloves garlic, crushed
2 tablespoons chopped fresh
    oregano, divided

1 white onion
1 red bell pepper
1 orange bell pepper
2 tomatoes
1 tablespoon freshly chopped
    basil
Salt and pepper, to taste

> **Serves 4**
>
> The marinade does double duty as a sauce in this easy-to-make chicken dish.

1. Rinse the chicken breasts and pat dry with paper towels. Place the chicken breasts in a shallow 9 × 13-inch baking dish. Add the tomato juice, red wine vinegar, 2 tablespoons olive oil, crushed garlic, and 1 tablespoon chopped oregano. Cover and marinate the chicken in the refrigerator for 2 hours.

2. Peel and finely chop the white onion. Cut the bell peppers in half, remove the seeds, and cut into thin strips. Peel the tomatoes, deseed, and cut into 6 wedges.

3. Remove the chicken from the baking dish. Reserve the marinade and place in a small saucepan. Let the marinade boil for 5 minutes. Turn the heat down to low and keep the marinade warm.

4. In a frying pan, heat 1 tablespoon olive oil over medium-high heat. Add the chicken breast halves and cook until the chicken is cooked through and the juices run clear when pierced with a knife. Remove the chicken from the frying pan and drain on paper towels.

5. Add the onion and garlic to the frying pan and cook until the onion is softened. Add the tomato wedges, pressing down on them with a wooden spoon to release their juices. Add the bell peppers. Add the reserved marinade. Return the chicken breasts to the pan, and stir in the chopped basil. Heat through. Taste and season with salt and pepper if desired. Serve over pasta.

Sweet-and-Sour Eggplant Stew

2 eggplant
1 large white onion
2 cloves garlic
1 ripe tomato
2 tablespoons capers
5 anchovy fillets

¾ cup olive oil, or as needed
2 cups fresh tomato sauce
½ cup red wine vinegar
½ cup granulated sugar
3 tablespoons chopped fresh
   basil

1. Peel and slice the eggplant. Degorge the eggplant by placing slices in a colander and sprinkling with salt. Let the eggplant slices sit for at least 1 hour. Remove from the colander, lay on paper towels, and press down to remove the liquid.

2. Peel and finely chop the onion and garlic. Peel and deseed the tomato, and cut into thin slices. Rinse the capers. Drain and separate the anchovies.

3. In a large frying pan, heat ½ inch of olive oil on medium heat. Add the degorged eggplant. Brown briefly, then cover and simmer on low heat until the eggplant is softened (about 10 minutes). Remove from the pan and clean out the pan.

4. Heat 6 tablespoons of the olive oil over medium heat. Add the chopped onion and garlic. Cook over medium heat for a few minutes, then turn the heat down to low and add the anchovies. Continue cooking on low heat, mashing the anchovies with the back of a spatula and mixing with the softened onion and garlic. Add the tomato and capers, gently pressing down on the back of the tomato to release its juices. Stir in the tomato sauce, red wine vinegar, and sugar.

5. Add the eggplant back into the pan. Turn the heat down to low and cook, stirring occasionally, for 5 more minutes. Sprinkle the fresh basil on top and serve.

Classic Risotto

2 tablespoons olive oil
1 small white onion, minced
½ cup short-grained rice,
preferably arborio
4 cups chicken stock

1 tablespoon butter
½ cup Parmigiano-Reggiano
cheese, coarsely grated
1 tablespoon freshly chopped
basil

1. Heat the olive oil in a medium saucepan. Add the minced onion, and sauté over medium heat until it is soft and translucent. Add the rice, and sauté for 1 to 2 minutes until the grains are shiny and opaque.
2. Stir in ¼ cup of the chicken stock. Continue slowly adding the broth, ¼ cup at a time, and stirring until it is absorbed. The texture of the rice should be rich and creamy.
3. Remove the saucepan from the heat and stir in the butter, Parmigiano-Reggiano cheese, and the chopped basil. Serve immediately.

Tiramisu

4 eggs, separated
¼ cup confectioners' sugar
½ teaspoon vanilla extract
1 pound mascarpone
2 tablespoons Marsala wine
½ cup strong, fresh brewed
espresso coffee

2 tablespoons coffee liqueur,
such as Kahlúa
24 ladyfingers
2 tablespoons powdered hot
chocolate

1. Beat the egg whites until they begin to form peaks but are not dry. Beat in the confectioners' sugar.
2. Beat the egg yolks until light and fluffy. Beat in the vanilla extract. Vigorously whisk the mascarpone cheese and Marsala wine into the egg yolks. Carefully fold the egg yolks into the egg white mixture.
3. In a small bowl, combine the espresso with the coffee liqueur. Dip the ladyfingers into the espresso. Line a deep 8 × 10-inch serving dish with the dipped ladyfingers. Carefully spread the mascarpone mixture over top. Cover and chill for at least 2 hours. Dust with the powdered chocolate just before serving.

Panna Cotta

Serves 6–8

The Italian version of vanilla ice cream, panna cotta tastes delicious served with fresh fruit in season. Using a vanilla bean instead of vanilla extract gives this dish extra flavor.

¼ cup warm water
1 envelope unflavored gelatin,
   such as Knox
1 vanilla bean

2¼ cups whipping cream or
   heavy cream
⅓ cup granulated sugar

1. Pour the warm water into a small bowl. Pour the gelatin over the water and let it stand for 5 minutes to soften. Cut the vanilla bean in half and remove the seeds.
2. In a medium saucepan, heat the whipping cream, vanilla bean and seeds, and the sugar over medium-low heat, stirring continuously to dissolve the sugar. Do not let the cream boil. Continue cooking for 2 to 3 minutes. Remove the vanilla bean.
3. Remove the saucepan from the stove element and stir in the softened gelatin. Continue stirring until the gelatin is completely dissolved. Pour the mixture into a bowl and set the bowl inside a larger bowl of ice water. Cool for 15 minutes, stirring continuously. Pour the liquid into 4-ounce ramekins or custard cups and refrigerate overnight.

An Eating Style Is Born

It was during the Renaissance that the first menus and rules for courses were printed. Table manners started to improve, albeit very slowly. The Italians were the educators of Europe and the famous *Galateo* by Monsignor della Casa was quickly translated and distributed abroad. The main innovation? The use of individual cutlery for various courses.

Bliss's Gnocchi

4 large Yukon gold potatoes
1 teaspoon kosher salt
1 cup all-purpose flour, sifted

1 egg, lightly beaten
1 teaspoon olive oil

Serves 8–10

Francesco Martorella, owner and chef of Bliss, located in Philadelphia, Pennsylvania, learned this recipe from his mother. Serve this with their Fresh Plum Tomato and Basil Sauce (page 360).

1. Place the potatoes in a large saucepan. Add enough cold water to cover and sprinkle in the salt. Bring to a boil over medium-high heat. Cook until tender, approximately 30 minutes. Drain, peel the potatoes, and set aside to dry slightly.
2. Mash the potatoes in a food mill or potato ricer and transfer to a large bowl. Add the flour, egg, and oil, and mix well with a rubber spatula to form smooth dough. Turn the dough onto a lightly floured work surface and roll into half-inch-thick tubes. Using a sharp knife, cut the tubes vertically to form the gnocchi, and set aside.
3. Bring a large saucepan filled with salted water to a boil, add the gnocchi, and cook until they rise to the top. Strain, and toss with the olive oil. Serve with tomato sauce.

The Origin of Pizza

In about 1522, tomatoes were brought back to Europe from the New World. They were originally thought to be poisonous. Later the poorer people of Naples added the fruits to their yeast dough and created the first simple pizza. They usually had only flour, olive oil, lard, cheese, and herbs with which to feed their families. All of Italy proclaimed the Neapolitan pies to be the best. At that time, the Tavern of the Cerriglio was a hangout for the Spanish soldiers of the Viceroy, and it is said that the people flocked there to feast on the specialty of the house—pizza.

Bliss's Fresh Plum Tomato and Basil Sauce

24 ripe plum tomatoes
6 ounces extra-virgin olive oil
6 cloves garlic
1 Thai chili or other hot pepper
* of your choice*

¼ cup fresh basil leaves,
* chopped*
Salt and freshly ground black
* pepper, to taste*

1. Bring 4 quarts water to a boil. Score the end of each tomato in a criss-cross motion, just deep enough to cut the skin. Blanch the tomatoes in the boiling water for 20 to 30 seconds to loosen the skin. Shock the tomatoes in ice water. Peel off the skin and slice the tomatoes in half. Remove and discard the seeds, and dice the tomatoes.

2. In a medium-sized pot, heat the olive oil on medium. Add the garlic and hot pepper, and cook for 1 minute. Add the basil and cook for 1 more minute. Add the tomatoes and season with salt and pepper. Reduce heat to medium-low and cook for 10 to 12 minutes. Serve over pasta.

Tournento Rossini

Gioacchino Rossini, the famed Italian composer of the opera *The Barber of Seville*, was born in Italy in 1792 and died in Paris in 1868. The musical genius also loved fine foods, including truffles and goose liver (foie gras). His famous creation was the "Tournento Rossini," a slice of beef fillet covered with a thin layer of lard. When cooked it is placed on fried or baked bread, with a slice of goose liver on top, and garnished with finely chopped truffles.

Chapter 27

Spain:
Dining after 10 P.M.

362 : Pan-Fried Flounder with Toasted Almonds
363 : Pork Chops with Prunes
364 : Radicchio Salad
364 : Gourmet Tuna Sandwich Spread
365 : Spanish Frittata
366 : Poached Shrimp and Avocado Appetizer
367 : Baked Plantains with Calvados
368 : Squid Ink Risotto
369 : Rabbit in Wine
370 : Chorizo in Wine
371 : Spinach with Raisins and Pine Nuts
372 : Marinated Salmon with Roasted Red Peppers
373 : Squid in Sherry
374 : Broiled Oysters on the Half Shell
375 : Braised Beef in Barolo
376 : Bacaco Español

Pan-Fried Flounder with Toasted Almonds

Serves 4

Toasted almonds lend flavor to this simple dish. Be sure to turn the almonds frequently during toasting so that they don't burn.

2 zucchini

2 tomatoes

6 shallots

2 cloves garlic

4 large, fresh flounder fillets, skinned

½ teaspoon salt, or as needed

½ teaspoon black pepper, or as needed

6 tablespoons olive oil, divided

1 tablespoon white wine vinegar

2 teaspoons fresh rosemary

¼ cup whole blanched almonds

¼ teaspoon paprika

2 lemons, cut into wedges

8 rosemary sprigs, to garnish

1. Peel the zucchini and cut into 1½-inch slices. Peel the tomatoes, remove the seeds, and cut into wedges. Peel and chop the shallots and garlic.
2. Season the flounder fillets with the salt and pepper. Lay the flounder out in a 9 × 13-inch shallow baking dish. In a small bowl, combine ¼ cup olive oil, white wine vinegar, fresh rosemary, and the chopped garlic. Pour the marinade over. Cover and marinate the fish in the refrigerator for 2 hours.
3. Twenty minutes before the fish has finished marinating, begin preparing the toasted almonds. Heat the oven to 325°. Spread the almonds on a baking sheet and bake, stirring occasionally, until they are golden brown (about 15 minutes). Remove from the oven.
4. Heat the remaining 2 tablespoons olive oil in a frying pan. Add the shallots and cook until softened. Stir in the paprika. Add the tomatoes, pressing down gently with the back of a spoon to release their juices. Add the zucchini. Cook briefly, then push to the side of the pan. Add the flounder. Cook the fillets until they turn golden brown (about 5–10 minutes). Turn over and cook the other side. Sprinkle the flounder with the toasted nuts and garnish with the lemon wedges and rosemary sprigs.

Pork Chops with Prunes

4 pork loin chops
¼ teaspoon black pepper
⅛ teaspoon paprika, or to taste
¾ pound unpitted prunes
1 tablespoon olive oil

½ cup dry red wine, divided
½ cup apple juice or cider
2-inch cinnamon stick
2 teaspoons brown sugar
¼ cup sour cream

1. Season the pork chops with the black pepper and paprika. Cut each of the prunes in half with a knife and remove the pit.
2. Heat the olive oil over medium-high heat. Add the pork chops and cook until browned, turning over once during cooking. Remove the pork chops. Deglaze the pan with ¼ cup of red wine, bringing the wine to a boil and use a spatula to stir up any browned bits at the bottom of the pan.
3. Add the prunes, the remaining red wine, the apple juice, and the cinnamon stick. Stir in the brown sugar. Add the pork back into the pan. Reduce the heat and simmer, covered, until the pork chops are tender (about 30 minutes). Remove the pork chops and the cinnamon stick from the pan.
4. Add the sour cream into the pan. Bring the prune and sour cream mixture to a boil, stirring to thicken. Pour the sauce over the pork chops and serve immediately.

La Sauce Mahonnaise

Though mayonnaise was invented in Spain, the inventor was actually French. In the early eighteenth century, Louis XIV sent his favorite general, the Duc de Richelieu, to Menorca to deal with some pesky Englishmen who were holed up in the fort near the Mahon harbor. During the long siege, the duke's cook had trouble keeping his master (accustomed to lavish Versailles banquets) happy with his dinners. He figured an interesting sauce might do the trick, but all he could find on the island were eggs and olive oil. He started beating, and soon produced what was christened on the spot as "la sauce mahonnaise."

Radicchio Salad

Serves 6–8

Spanish Cabrales cheese makes an interesting contrast to the slightly bitter taste of radicchio lettuce and endives in this recipe. Feel free to substitute Roquefort or Danish blue cheese if Cabrales is unavailable.

2 heads radicchio
2 endives
¼ cup pine nuts
2 tablespoons balsamic vinegar
2 tablespoons extra-virgin olive
    oil

1 teaspoon sugar
1 teaspoon Dijon mustard
8 ounces Cabrales cheese

1. Wash the radicchio lettuce, pat dry, and tear into bite-sized pieces. Remove the stem from each endive, cut in half, and cut into strips. Chop the pine nuts into thin slivers.
2. In a small bowl, whisk the balsamic vinegar, olive oil, sugar, and Dijon mustard.
3. In a large salad bowl, combine the radicchio and endives and crumble the Cabrales cheese over top. Drizzle with the vinaigrette. Sprinkle the pine nuts over and serve immediately.

Gourmet Tuna Sandwich Spread

Serves 6

Use this spicy spread on crusty French or Italian bread, or on a soft tortilla wrap. For best results, use tuna that is packed in olive oil.

8 capers
2 kalamata olives, pitted
2 (6-ounce) cans tuna
2 tablespoons Dijon mustard
¾ cup mayonnaise
¼ cup extra virgin olive oil
½ teaspoon ground cumin

1 teaspoon cayenne pepper, or
    to taste
1 tablespoon chopped pimiento
2 teaspoons chopped fresh
    parsley
1 teaspoon granulated sugar,
    optional

1. Rinse the capers and cut in half. Finely chop the olives.
2. In a medium bowl, combine the capers, chopped olives, tuna, Dijon mustard, mayonnaise, olive oil, ground cumin, cayenne pepper, pimiento, and fresh parsley. Taste and add the sugar if desired. Chill until ready to use.

Spanish Frittata

1 tablespoon capers
½ red bell pepper
½ green bell pepper
4 russet potatoes
1 medium Spanish onion
2 cloves garlic
1 tomato
6 medium eggs
⅛ teaspoon cayenne pepper, or
    to taste

¼ cup olive oil, divided
¼ teaspoon salt
¼ teaspoon freshly ground
    black pepper
¼ cup water
½ cup grated Parmesan cheese
2 tablespoons chopped fresh
    parsley

> **Serves 4**
>
> Made with potato, the Spanish version of an Italian frittata is called a tortilla in Spain. Serve it warm or at room temperature for breakfast or at brunch.

1. Rinse the capers and cut in half. Cut the red and green bell peppers into thin strips. Peel the potatoes and cut into thin slices. Peel and chop the onion and garlic. Peel the tomato, cut into 6 slices, and remove the seeds. In a small bowl, lightly beat the eggs. Stir in the cayenne pepper.

2. Heat 2 tablespoons of the oil in a 10-inch frying pan over medium heat. Add the onion, garlic, sliced potato, and the bell peppers. Sprinkle the salt and pepper over. Add the water. Reduce the heat and simmer, covered, until the potatoes are tender when pierced with a fork (10 to 15 minutes). Remove the vegetables from the pan and clean out the pan.

3. In a large bowl, combine the vegetables with the beaten egg. Heat 1 tablespoon olive oil in the frying pan on low-medium heat, making sure that all the pan is covered with the oil. Pour the egg mixture into the pan.

4. When the top of the frittata is firm but still moist, cover the frying pan with a plate. Turn the frying pan over so that the frittata falls on the plate. Clean out the pan and heat the remaining 1 tablespoon olive oil. Carefully slide the frittata back into the pan, so that the bottom is now on top. Sprinkle the cheese, capers and chopped parsley on top. To serve, cut the frittata into wedges.

Poached Shrimp and Avocado Appetizer

3 large ripe avocados
¼ red onion
2 cloves garlic
2 tablespoons capers
6 kalamata black olives, pitted
1½ pounds shrimp, shelled and deveined
7 cups water
1 teaspoon salt

1 bay leaf
2 tablespoons white wine vinegar
2 tablespoons freshly squeezed lemon juice
Zest of 1 lemon
½ teaspoon cayenne powder, or to taste

1. Cut each avocado in half around the pit and remove the pit. Refrigerate the avocado halves until needed. Peel and finely chop the red onion and garlic cloves. Rinse the capers and chop in half. Finely chop the black olives.

2. Rinse the shrimp and pat dry with paper towels. In a large saucepan, bring 6 cups water to a boil, with the salt, chopped onion and garlic cloves, bay leaf, white wine vinegar, lemon juice, and the grated lemon zest. Cover and simmer for 10 minutes. Add the shrimp and simmer, partially covered, until the shrimp turn pink and are cooked through (about 5 minutes). Remove the shrimp from the saucepan and drain. Chill if not serving immediately.

3. Toss the shrimp with the cayenne pepper. Spoon approximately ¼ tablespoon of the shrimp mixture onto each avocado half. Top with a few capers and about 1 teaspoon of the chopped olive. Serve immediately.

Dining on Tapas

Few small Spanish towns have proper restaurants—when people want to eat out, they order tapas. Tapas are the tasty tidbits you are served with drinks. When you want to have a meal, you simply take a table and order a *ración* of the various tapas. Usually a few *raciónes* plus a dish of salad and bread will sate a hungry couple. The custom in Spain is for everyone to eat from the same dishes, but if you ask for individual plates they'll be brought to you. Tapas bars are becoming increasingly popular in the States, especially as gathering spots for large groups of friends.

Baked Plantains with Calvados

6 cups lightly salted water
4 ripe plantains, unpeeled
2 tablespoons freshly squeezed lime juice
2 tablespoons brown sugar

3 tablespoons Calvados brandy
¼ cup balsamic vinegar
3 tablespoons chopped cilantro leaves

Serves 8

Make sure to use ripe yellow plantains. Immature green plantains have a bitter taste when cooked at high temperatures.

1. Preheat the oven to 350°. Grease a 9 × 13-inch glass baking dish.
2. In a large saucepan, bring the water to a boil. Add the plantains. Reduce the heat and simmer, covered, until the skin of the plantain is tender. Remove the plantains from the water and drain. Peel and cut the skin on the diagonal into 2-inch-thick slices.
3. Place the sliced plantain in the baking dish and sprinkle with the lime juice and brown sugar. Pour the Calvados and balsamic vinegar over. Cover the plantains with aluminum foil and bake until they are tender (about 1 hour). Turn the plantains over halfway through cooking. Garnish with the chopped cilantro before serving.

Not Quite a Banana

Plantains are extremely popular in Latin American countries as well as parts of Africa, Asia, and India. They are closely related to the banana, but are longer, have thicker skins, and are usually consumed cooked, not raw. While green, the plantain is considered a starch; later, when it is ripe and its skin turns to a brownish black, it is considered a fruit.

Squid Ink Risotto

Serves 2

Gourmet chefs have used the squid's black ink sac to add an exotic flavor and color to everything from pasta to ice cream.

1 small white onion
2 cloves garlic
1 red bell pepper
6 tablespoons olive oil, divided
1¼ pounds baby squid, cleaned
⅛ teaspoon salt
¼ teaspoon cayenne pepper, or
  to taste

1 cup short-grained rice,
  preferably arborio
3½ cups chicken broth, or as
  needed
1 squid ink sachet
3 tablespoons butter
¼ cup chopped flat-leaf parsley

1. Peel and finely chop the onion and garlic cloves. Cut the red bell pepper in half, remove the seeds, and dice.
2. Heat 4 tablespoons olive oil in a large frying pan. Add the onion and garlic and cook over medium heat until softened (5 to 7 minutes). Add the squid pieces and sprinkle with the salt and cayenne pepper. Cook over medium-high heat until browned (about 2 minutes). Add the red pepper and cook for 1 more minute.
3. Push the squid to the side of the pan. Heat 2 tablespoons olive oil over medium heat. Add the rice in batches, stirring until the grains are shiny and opaque. Add ¼ cup of the chicken stock and stir until it is absorbed. Add the ink from the squid sac and stir until absorbed. Continue slowly adding the broth, ¼ cup at a time, until it is entirely absorbed and the rice has a rich, creamy texture.
4. Remove the saucepan from the heat and stir in the butter and the chopped parsley. Serve immediately.

Harvesting Squid Ink

Squid ink can be expensive to buy. But you can avoid this cost if you harvest your own. To clean squid yourself, simply take the squid, grip the head in one hand, the body in the other, and pull them apart. The ink sac, which is thin and silvery, will be in the innards. Puncture the ink sac and squeeze the contents into a small bowl.

Rabbit in Wine

2½-pound rabbit, cut into
    8 pieces
2 teaspoons salt
2 teaspoons pepper
1 small white onion
2 cloves garlic
3 ripe tomatoes

4 carrots
3 tablespoons olive oil
½ teaspoon ground cinnamon
1 tablespoon chopped pimiento
¾ cup dry white wine
½ cup sherry vinegar

> **Serves 4**
>
> Serve this dish with boiled potatoes or over rice, with fresh herbs for garnish.

1. Bring a large pot of heavily salted water to boil. Add the prepared rabbit pieces. Turn the heat down and simmer the rabbit, covered for 1 hour to tenderize it. Remove the parboiled rabbit pieces from the pot and pat dry with paper towels. Season with the salt and pepper. Set aside.
2. Peel and finely chop the onion and garlic. Deseed the tomatoes and cut into thin slices. Peel the carrots and cut on the diagonal into thin slices.
3. In a large saucepan, heat the olive oil over medium heat. Add the onion and garlic. Cook until the onion is softened and translucent (5 to 7 minutes). Add the carrots. Brown for a minute, then add the tomatoes. Cook for another minute, pressing the back of the tomatoes gently with a spoon to release their juices. Stir in the ground cinnamon and the pimiento.
4. Add the wine and sherry vinegar to the pan. Bring to a boil, and add the rabbit pieces. Reduce the heat, cover, and simmer until the liquid has been reduced by half (20 to 30 minutes). Serve immediately.

Roasting a Chicken—Spanish Style

Try this next time you are craving comfort food, but want something new: take a (preferably free-range) chicken and rub it all over—inside and out—with sherry. Then stuff it with some chopped onion, herbs, and a small piece of chorizo sausage. Coat the bird with olive oil and as it cooks, baste it with the drippings. This gives it a wonderful orange color and a spicy kick. After the chicken is cooked, you can chop up the chorizo and add it to a stuffing.

Chorizo in Wine

Serves 4

Fruity red wine makes an interesting pairing with spicy chorizo sausage in this popular Spanish appetizer.

8 ounces chorizo sausage
2 cloves garlic
4 shallots
1 tablespoon olive oil
1 teaspoon paprika
⅓ cup dry red wine
1 bay leaf

2-inch cinnamon stick
1 tablespoon freshly squeezed
   lemon juice
¼ teaspoon ground nutmeg
½ loaf French or Italian bread,
   cut into cubes

1. Remove the chorizo sausage from its casing and cut on the diagonal into ¼-inch slices. Peel and chop the garlic cloves and shallots.
2. Heat the olive oil in a saucepan over medium heat. Add the chorizo and cook gently over medium heat until browned (about 2 minutes). Add the garlic and shallots. Stir in the paprika. Cook for 1 to 2 minutes more, until the chorizo is crisp.
3. Add the red wine and bring to a boil. Add the bay leaf and the cinnamon stick. Stir in the lemon juice and ground nutmeg. Reduce the heat and simmer, covered, until the wine has been absorbed (about 15 minutes). Remove the chorizo from the saucepan.
4. Cut the bread into squares. Fasten each slice of chorizo to a piece of bread with a toothpick. Serve immediately. Serve with the bread.

Pigging Out in Spain

Some say Spanish pork rivals prosciutto, but whichever you prefer, there is no denying that Spanish pork products are among the world's best. The Spanish do not eat large portions of pork, mostly because of their intense flavors—these products can be nibbled, rather than feasted upon. Some of the best known include air-dried serrano ham, found in most tapas bars and home kitchens, as well as the paper-thin Iberia ham made from native black-hooved, free-range pigs that eat only acorns. In terms of sausage, chorizo is the leader, while salchichon—a hard, garlicky sausage similar to salami—is also very popular.

Middle Eastern Stuffed Grape Leaves

Yields 40–45 leaves

1 bottle grape leaves
½ white onion, finely chopped
1 clove garlic
½ cup uncooked long-grain rice
¼ cup pine nuts
¼ cup currants

¼ cup finely chopped parsley
3 tablespoons tomato sauce
3 tablespoons olive oil
¼ cup water, or as needed
Lettuce leaves
2 lemons, cut into wedges

Traditionally, these appetizers are served with plain yogurt as a dipping sauce. Other options include tahini (Middle Eastern sesame paste) or lemon wedges.

1. Fill a medium saucepan with hot water. Place the grape leaves in the water and use a wooden spoon to separate the leaves. Remove the leaves from the pan and drain thoroughly. Peel the onion and finely chop. Smash, peel, and mince the garlic.
2. Toast the pine nuts by heating them in a large frying pan, shaking continuously, until the nuts are browned. Cool and coarsely chop.
3. In a large bowl, combine the chopped pine nuts, rice, currants, chopped onion, garlic, chopped parsley, tomato sauce, and olive oil. Add a bit more olive oil if the mixture is too dry.
4. To stuff the grape leaves, lay out a grape leaf with the shiny side down. Place 1 tablespoon of the mixture in the leaf and roll it up. Continue with the remainder of the leaves.
5. Steam the grape leaves in a frying pan or steamer lined with lettuce leaves on the bottom. Sprinkle the leaves with water and steam, covered, until the leaves are tender (about 45 minutes). Garnish with lemon wedges.

Armenian Nutmeg Cake

Serves 6

The Armenian version of a pound cake, nutmeg cake is both sweet and spicy.

2 cups all-purpose flour
½ cup firmly packed brown
   sugar
2 teaspoons baking powder
1 teaspoon salt
½ teaspoon baking soda
1 teaspoon ground nutmeg
2 sticks unsalted butter
   (8-ounces) plus 1
   tablespoon butter

1 cup granulated sugar
2 large eggs, lightly beaten
½ cup milk
1 teaspoon vanilla extract
½ cup chopped walnuts
2 tablespoons confectioners'
   sugar

1. Preheat the oven to 325°. Heavily grease an 8-inch square baking pan.
2. In a large bowl, combine the flour with the brown sugar, baking powder, salt, baking soda, and nutmeg. Add the butter, mixing it in with your hands until the mixture resembles fine breadcrumbs. (Press half the mixture into the prepared pan.)
3. Beat the butter with 1 cup granulated sugar until the mixture is creamy. Beat in the eggs and the milk. Beat in the vanilla extract.
4. Carefully fold the dry ingredients into the egg mixture. Stir in the walnuts. Pour the mixture into the pan. Bake for about 1 hour, or until a toothpick inserted in the middle of the cake comes out clean. Cool on a wire rack for 15 minutes. Sprinkle with confectioners' sugar before serving.

Spinach with Raisins and Pine Nuts

3 tablespoons golden raisins
¼ cup apple cider
¾ pound fresh spinach leaves
¾ cup canned chickpeas
2 tablespoons pine nuts
1½ tablespoons olive oil
2 tablespoons chopped red
    onion

2 cloves garlic, finely chopped
¼ teaspoon salt
¼ teaspoon granulated sugar
⅛ teaspoon paprika, or to taste
¼ cup chopped cilantro leaves

> **Serves 6**
>
> This recipe will even win over those who don't care for spinach. For best results, use tender young spinach leaves.

1. Plump up the raisins by placing them in a small bowl and covering with the cider. Let the raisins sit in the cider for 30 minutes. Drain.
2. Remove the spinach stems. Wash and drain the leaves, and tear into shreds. Rinse the chickpeas and drain in a colander.
3. Toast the pine nuts by heating them in a large frying pan, shaking continuously, until the nuts are browned (about 3 minutes). Remove from the pan and cool.
4. Heat the olive oil in the frying pan over medium heat. Add the onion and garlic and cook over medium heat until the onion is softened and the garlic is browned (5 to 7 minutes). Add the spinach leaves. Sprinkle the leaves with the salt and sugar. Add 2 tablespoons water, cover the pan, and cook until the spinach leaves turn bright green and wilt (about 2 minutes).
5. Add the chickpeas and the softened raisins. Stir in the paprika, chopped cilantro, and pine nuts. Heat through and serve hot.

Olive Oil

You may be surprised to learn that Spain is the world's largest producer of olive oil and olives. Olive oil is used in all manner of cooking, from deep-frying fish, to sautéing vegetables, to drizzling over salads, or whisking into baked goods and desserts—even ice cream! The oils range dramtically in color and flavor, from green to golden, and they have subtle distinguishing flavors.

Marinated Salmon with Roasted Red Peppers

4 salmon fillets, 8-ounces each
½ cup olive oil
2 tablespoons sherry vinegar
1 tablespoon chopped fresh
   rosemary
½ teaspoon salt, or as needed
½ teaspoon black pepper, or as
   needed

3 large red bell peppers
1 tablespoon red wine vinegar
4 ounces Cabrales cheese
1 jar pitted kalamata olives,
   drained

1. Place the salmon in a shallow 9 × 13-inch glass baking dish. In a small bowl, whisk the olive oil, sherry vinegar, rosemary, salt, and pepper. Marinate the salmon in the refrigerator, covered, for at least 2 hours.

2. Heat the broiler. Wash the red bell peppers. Place the peppers on a broiling pan and brush with the red wine vinegar. Broil the peppers until the skins are blackened and blistered. Immediately remove the peppers from the broiler. Place each pepper in a sealed plastic bag. Wait 15 minutes, then remove the pepper from the bag and peel off the skins. Cut the peppers into thin strips, removing the stems and seeds as you do so.

3. Remove the salmon steaks from the baking dish, reserving the marinade. Place the steaks in the broiler. Broil until the salmon is golden brown (6 to 7 minutes). While broiling, brush the salmon frequently with the marinade.

4. Sprinkle the Cabrales cheese over the roasted red pepper strips. Serve the salmon steaks with the roasted red pepper and the olives.

Squid in Sherry

½ red onion
1 clove garlic
1 pound cleaned squid
4 cups water
4 tablespoons olive oil

⅓ cup sherry vinegar
¼ teaspoon paprika, or to taste
2 tablespoons fresh chopped
     parsley

Serves 4
Strong sherry vinegar makes a frequent appearance in Spanish dishes. If unavailable, white wine vinegar can be used as a substitute.

1. Peel and finely chop the onion and garlic clove. Slice the squid cross-wise into thin rings that are no more than ¼-inch thick.

2. In a large saucepan, bring 4 cups water to a boil. Add the squid and cook, uncovered, in the boiling water for 30 seconds. Remove the squid rings and drain on paper towels. Reserve the boiling liquid.

3. In a large frying pan, heat the olive oil over medium heat. Add the red onion and garlic and cook until softened (5 to 7 minutes).

4. Remove the frying pan from the heat and add the sherry vinegar and water. Stir in the paprika.

5. Return the frying pan to the stove element and turn the heat up to high. Add the boiled squid pieces. Cook, covered, over high heat, until the sherry vinegar has been completely absorbed. Stir in the chopped fresh parsley. Serve immediately.

The Moorish Influence—Nuts and Spices

Spanish cuisine is rooted in the common use of five main ingredients: pork, olive oil, garlic, paprika, and saffron. With influences from both Italy and Provence, there is another player that helps define the distinct quality of Spanish cooking, setting it apart from its Mediterranean neighbors: the Moors. Having ruled Spain for almost 800 years, the Moors contributed an array of nuts and spices to Spanish cooking—including almonds, walnuts, saffron, cinnamon, nutmeg, and sesame—used in both savory and sweet dishes. But there are differences. For example, Spanish cooking uses a significant amount of pork, ham, and sausage, which are forbidden in the Muslim diet.

Broiled Oysters on the Half Shell

24 live oysters
¾ cup coarse breadcrumbs
1 small clove garlic, finely chopped
3 tablespoons lemon juice

3 tablespoons olive oil
¾ teaspoon paprika, or to taste
¼ teaspoon ground cumin
¼ cup freshly chopped parsley
4 lemons, cut into wedges

1. Scrub the outside of the oyster shells to remove any dirt or grit. To open the oysters, carefully insert a knife into the back hinge of the oyster between the top and bottom shell. Move back and forth with the knife, cutting the muscle, until you are able to open the shells. Remove the top shell, being careful not to drain off the oyster juice.
2. Preheat the broiler to medium.
3. In a blender or food processor, combine the breadcrumbs, chopped garlic, lemon juice, olive oil, paprika, and ground cumin, and process until the mixture has a crumb-like consistency (about 15 seconds).
4. Spread 1½ teaspoons of the breadcrumb mixture on top of the oysters. Place the oysters on the broiler and broil until the crumbs turn golden brown and the oysters are just cooked (2 to 3 minutes). Lightly garnish each broiled oyster with the chopped parsley and serve with the lemon wedges.

Chocolate Hits Spain, Then Travels Through Europe

Introduced into Spain in 1519 as a beverage, the term *chocolate* originally referred to a drink similar to today's hot chocolate. The Spanish conquistador Hernando Cortés brought the elixer back to Spain after returning from his Mexican expedition, where he was given a taste by the Aztec king Montezuma II. Gradually spreading from Spain throughout Europe, the chocolate drink gained popularity. In 1528 Cortez brought chocolate back from Mexico to the royal court of King Charles V, and monks, hidden away in Spanish monasteries, processed the cocoa beans, keeping chocolate a secret for nearly 100 years.

Braised Beef in Barolo

4 carrots
½ red onion
2 stalks celery
1 clove garlic
2½-pound beef chuck roast
4½ cups Barolo wine
2 slices bacon, chopped
2 teaspoons olive oil, if needed
2 tablespoons tomato paste

2 teaspoons freshly chopped
   thyme
1 tablespoon freshly chopped
   rosemary
Salt and freshly ground black
   pepper, to taste
1 cup beef broth
2 whole cloves
3-inch cinnamon stick

Serves 4

Made from Nebbiolo grapes, Barolo is often called the "King of Italian Wines." Here it lends flavor to a simple beef and vegetable dish.

1. Peel and chop the carrots and onion. String the celery and cut into thin pieces on the diagonal. Cut the garlic clove in half and rub over the beef. Place the beef in a casserole dish and pour 1 cup of the Barolo over. Cover the beef and marinate overnight in the refrigerator.
2. Remove the meat from the refrigerator, reserving the marinade. In a small saucepan, bring the marinade to a boil, and boil for 5 minutes.
3. In a large saucepan or Dutch oven, add the chopped bacon. Cook over medium heat until crispy. Remove the bacon from the pan, but do not clean out the pan.
4. Add the marinated beef to the saucepan and brown on medium-high heat, adding up to 2 teaspoons olive oil if necessary. Remove the beef from the pan. Add the onion, carrots, and celery. Brown briefly, then stir in the tomato paste. Cook for 1 minute, then stir in the thyme, rosemary, salt, and pepper.
5. Add the beef and bacon back into the pan with the marinade and beef broth. Add the cloves and the cinnamon stick. Cook, covered, over medium-low heat until the beef is tender (about 2½ hours). To serve, remove the beef from the pan and cut into thin slices.

Bacaco Español

Serves 4

Make sure to check the codfish and remove any small bones before cooking.

2 large sweet potatoes
1-pound cod fillet
½ red onion
2 cloves garlic
3 ripe tomatoes

3 tablespoons olive oil
⅛ teaspoon cayenne pepper
¼ teaspoon salt
1 tablespoon sherry vinegar

1. Peel the sweet potatoes and cut into chunks. In a large saucepan, add the sweet potatoes with enough salted water to cover them and bring to a boil. Reduce the heat to low, cover, and let simmer until the potatoes are tender when pierced with a fork (about 20 minutes). Remove the potatoes from the saucepan and drain. Cut into large chunks to serve.

2. Chop the codfish into bite-sized chunks. Peel and finely chop the onion and garlic. Peel the tomatoes, remove the seeds, and cut into wedges.

3. Heat the olive oil in a large frying pan over medium heat. Add the onion and garlic, and cook until softened and the onion is translucent (5 to 7 minutes). Add the tomatoes. Cook for 1 minute, pressing gently on the tomatoes with the back of a spatula to release their juices. Stir in the cayenne pepper and salt.

4. Add the cod pieces and the sherry vinegar. Turn the heat down to low. Cook, stirring occasionally, until the cod is opaque (about 15 minutes). Serve immediately with the sweet potatoes.

Saffron

Coming from the *Crocus sativus* flower, saffron is actually the three stigmas from each blossom. Delicate, orange-yellow filaments, they must be plucked by hand. Spain is the leading producer of saffron, or what they call "Spanish gold," in the world. They use this exotic spice in plenty of stews, sauces, and even in the broth for rice. Most importantly, it's the famous seasoner of paella and bacalao vizcaina, both famed Spanish dishes. Why is saffron so expensive? It takes 225,000 stigmas to yield just 1 pound of saffron. When buying saffron, be careful not to get cheated—many sell look-alikes that are actually dried marigold and safflower petals, which offer almost no color or flavor.

Chapter 28

Scandinavia:
Straight from the Sea

378 : Grilled Whitefish

378 : Gravlax

379 : Crispy Salad of Vendace Roe

380 : Horn of Plenty Mushroom Soup

381 : Blueberry Soufflé

381 : Cloudberry Parfait

382 : Norwegian Salmon Salad

383 : Bergen Fish Soup

384 : Vodka-Marinated Sirloin

385 : Lemony Baked Parsnips with Salmon Roe

385 : Cloudberry Cream Dessert

386 : Danish Apple Soup

387 : Danish Stuffed Cabbage

388 : Rich Cream Sauce

389 : Danish Rum Raisin Muffins

390 : Danish Christmas Goose with Apples and Prunes

391 : Finnish Sauerkraut Soup

392 : Swedish Apricot and Prune Pork Loin

393 : Swedish Apple Cake

394 : Vanilla Sour Cream Sauce

394 : Lingonberry Sherbet for Adults

395 : Crayfish Quiche

396 : Swedish Potato Dumplings

Grilled Whitefish

Serves 2
(as an appetizer)

The secret to preparing whitefish is not to overcook it. Sear the fish on the skin side only, just long enough to make the skin crispy.

6-ounce fresh whitefish fillet, skin on
⅓ cup orange juice
1 tablespoon sea salt
¼ teaspoon white pepper
1 teaspoon granulated sugar
1 tablespoon fresh dill
1 tablespoon olive oil

1. Remove all the bones from the fillet, and cut into 4 equal pieces.
2. In a small bowl, whisk the orange juice, sea salt, white pepper, sugar, and fresh dill. Place the whitefish pieces in a shallow glass baking dish and pour the marinade over. Cover and marinate in the refrigerator for 1 hour.
3. Remove the fish from the refrigerator and discard the marinade. In a heavy frying pan, heat the oil over medium heat. Add the fish pieces, skin-side down. Cook briefly, searing the fish on the skin side only. Serve the whitefish appetizer with Crispy Salad of Vendace Roe (page 103).

Gravlax

Serves 8–10

This tastes delicious served on Norwegian rye bread, with mustard for spreading.

2 salmon fillets, about 1½ pounds each
2 tablespoons capers
6 tablespoons granulated sugar
6 tablespoons salt

1. Rinse the salmon fillets and pat dry with paper towels. Check over the fillets for any small bones and remove them with tweezers. Rinse the capers and cut in half.
2. In a small bowl, combine the sugar and salt. Lay the salmon so that the fleshy side is on the bottom. Season the top half of the fillets with the sugar and salt mixture, using your fingers to rub it in. Wrap each of the fillets in aluminum foil and place in a resealable plastic bag. Seal the bag, place the fillets in the refrigerator and leave for 2 days.
3. To serve, unwrap the aluminum foil and drain off any excess water. Cut the fillets into thin pieces. Sprinkle the capers over top.

Crispy Salad of Vendace Roe

2 tablespoons mayonnaise
2 tablespoons sour cream
1 tablespoon olive oil
2 tablespoons red wine vinegar
½ teaspoon sugar
¼ teaspoon salt, or to taste
⅛ teaspoon freshly ground
   black pepper

2 cups mixed salad greens
2 tablespoons finely chopped
   red onion
1 slice dark Finn Crisp bread
2 ounces vendace roe

**Serves 2
(as an appetizer)**

If you cannot find vendace roe, you can substitute another caviar. Toasted rye bread can be used instead of the Finnish dark bread.

1. In a medium bowl, combine the mayonnaise, sour cream, olive oil, red wine vinegar, sugar, salt, and pepper.
2. Wash the mixed salad greens and drain thoroughly. Shred the leaves. Combine the salad greens with the chopped red onion. Toss the salad with the mayonnaise dressing mixture. Crush the bread and mix into the salad. Spread the roe over top. Serve immediately.

Finland's Answer to Caviar

King of all Finnish roes, vendace roe is often compared to caviar. Roe is commonly eaten with toast, rye, or white bread. A Russian specialty, blinis are also often served with roe. At Restaurant Lasipalatsi, there are blini theme weeks every January and February, when a variety of blinis are served with different garnishes, vendace roe being the most popular blini garnish.

Horn of Plenty Mushroom Soup

Serves 2 (as an appetizer)

The nutty flavor of these delicate mushrooms makes them a popular addition to soups and stews. Here they are enjoyed alone as an appetizer.

6 ounces horn of plenty
  mushrooms
1 parsnip
1 carrot
1 clove garlic
3 tablespoons butter
½ cup chicken stock

½ cup dry white wine
1 cup light cream
¼ teaspoon nutmeg
1 teaspoon chopped fresh
  thyme
Salt and black pepper, to taste

1. Wipe the mushrooms with a damp cloth and chop. Peel and dice the parsnip and carrot. Peel and mince the garlic.
2. Melt the butter over medium heat in a medium-sized saucepan. Add the garlic and cook until browned. Add the carrot, parsnip, and ½ of the mushrooms.
3. Add the chicken stock, white wine, and cream to the pan. Bring to a boil. Stir in the nutmeg and the thyme. Reduce the heat to low and simmer gently, covered, until the vegetables are tender (30 to 35 minutes).
4. In a blender or food processor, purée the soup. Taste and season with salt and pepper if desired.
5. In the saucepan, heat 1 tablespoon butter over medium heat. Sauté the remainder of the chopped mushrooms until they are softened. Sprinkle over the soup and serve.

Trumpet of Death

In Finland's forests you can find many mushrooms—so much so that each year they name a "mushroom of the year." In 2004 it was the horn of plenty mushroom, also known as the "trumpet of death." Despite its off-putting name, it is a true delicacy. A kind of chanterelle, the horn of plenty is actually black and hollow, but chanterelles are a fine substitute.

Blueberry Soufflé

Serves 4

1 cup blueberries
1 tablespoon lemon juice
4 eggs, separated
¼ teaspoon cream of tartar

6 tablespoons granulated sugar,
  divided
2½ ounces fromage blanc
8 fresh mint leaves, for garnish

Made from whole milk,
fromage blanc has a
texture similar to cream
cheese. If unavailable,
yogurt made from
whole milk can be used
as a substitute.

1. Preheat the oven to 375°. Prepare 4 individual soufflé molds.
2. Rinse the blueberries and drain. In a food processor or blender, purée the blueberries with the lemon juice.
3. Use a blender to beat the egg whites until they begin to stiffen. Beat in the cream of tartar. Beat in 4 tablespoons sugar.
4. Stir the fromage blanc into the blueberries. Carefully fold the blueberry mixture into the egg whites. Spoon the mixture into the soufflé dishes. Bake the soufflés until they are golden and firm (about 15 minutes). Dust with the remaining 2 tablespoons of sugar. Garnish each dish with 2 fresh mint leaves.

Cloudberry Parfait

Serves 2–4

4 cups cloudberries
¼ cup granulated sugar

2 cups heavy (whipping) cream
1 teaspoon almond extract

This is a great dessert to
serve when you're in a
hurry. Feel free to substitute cloudberries with
fresh raspberries if needed.

1. In a small saucepan, combine the cloudberries with the sugar.
2. In a medium bowl, use an electric mixer to beat the whipping cream into stiff peaks. Beat in the almond extract.
3. Set out 4 tall parfait glasses. Spoon ¼ cup of the whipping cream into a glass. Add ¼ cup of the berries on top. Add another layer of whipping cream and berries. Continue with the remainder of the whipping cream and berries. Chill briefly and serve.

Norwegian Salmon Salad

Serves 4

Not only is Norwegian salmon famous for its rich taste and texture, it is high in heart-healthy omega-3 fatty acids.

1 carrot
2 plum tomatoes
2 Seville oranges
½ fennel bulb
3 tablespoons extra-virgin olive
   oil

3 tablespoons red wine vinegar
2 tablespoons orange juice
¼ teaspoon red pepper flakes
8 ounces Norwegian salmon,
2 tablespoons chopped fresh
   dill leaves

1. Wash the vegetables. Peel and grate the carrot. Dice the tomatoes. Peel and cut the white pith from the oranges. Cut the oranges into sections, reserving 2 tablespoons of the juice. Thinly slice the fennel bulb.
2. In a small bowl, whisk together the olive oil, red wine vinegar, orange juice, and red pepper flakes.
3. Cut the salmon into chunks. Arrange the salmon in a salad bowl with the tomatoes, oranges, fennel, and grated carrot. Drizzle the dressing over top. Refrigerate until ready to serve. Garnish with the fresh dill before serving.

Hearty Fare

Fermented fish (*rakfisk*), sour milk cheese (*gammelost*), and cured leg of mutton (*fenålår*) probably do not sound particularly gourmet. Norway had no history of aristocratic and bourgeois classes to help raise the culinary bar, as did France. Norway's cuisine was rooted in using the country's bounty of fresh ingredients such as cod, mutton, and cabbage. What makes some of today's Norwegian cuisine "gourmet" is the adoption of foreign, usually French, culinary practices, used to highlight their native culinary resources.

Bergen Fish Soup

Serves 10

To make your own fish stock for this dish, boil 3 pounds of fish heads and bones with 8 cups of water. Add a few vegetables such as carrots and potato, and seasonings, and simmer until the stock is flavorful. Strain through a metal sieve and use in the recipe.

2 carrots
1 large celeriac
1 parsnip
½ yellow onion
1 large red potato
¾ pound halibut fillets
¾ pound cod fillets
2 tablespoons freshly squeezed lemon juice

1 tablespoon butter
8 cups fish stock
½ teaspoon sea salt, or to taste
½ teaspoon black pepper, or to taste
½ cup heavy (whipping) cream
½ cup sour cream
2 tablespoons chopped fresh parsley

1. Peel the carrots, celeriac, and parsnip, and cut into thin matchsticks. Peel and chop the onion and potato. Rinse the fillets, pat dry, and season with the lemon juice. Cut the fillets into chunks.

2. In a large saucepan, add the butter and heat over medium heat. Add the chopped onion and cook until it is soft and translucent. Add the fish stock. Bring to a boil. Add the carrots, parsnip, potato, and celeriac. Stir in the sea salt and black pepper. Reduce the heat to low and cook for 5 minutes. Add the fish and cook for another 10 minutes, or until the vegetables are tender and the fish is cooked through.

3. In a small bowl, whisk together the heavy cream and the sour cream. Remove the soup from the stove element. Whisk the cream mixture into the soup. Stir in the chopped parsley. Serve immediately.

Vodka-Marinated Sirloin

½ cup vodka
2 tablespoons olive oil
1 teaspoon crushed black
   peppercorns
1 teaspoon dried thyme
1 teaspoon mustard seed

1 tablespoon finely chopped
   fresh parsley
2 cloves garlic, crushed
3 pound boneless sirloin roast
   or beef tenderloin roast
6 parsley sprigs

1. In a large resealable bag, combine the vodka, olive oil, crushed peppercorns, dried thyme, mustard seed, chopped parsley, and the crushed garlic. Add the roast. Place in the refrigerator and marinate, covered, for at least 8 hours or overnight. Turn the bag occasionally to make sure the roast is completely coated in the marinade.
2. Preheat the oven to 425°. Remove the meat from the bag, and reserve the marinade.
3. In a small saucepan, bring the marinade to a boil over medium-high heat. Reduce the heat to medium and let the marinade boil for 5 minutes. Remove from the heat.
4. Place the roast on a rack in the roasting pan. Insert a meat thermometer into the thickest section of the roast. Roast until the internal temperature of the roast reaches at least 140° (about 1 hour). Brush the roast frequently with the marinade during cooking. Transfer the cooked roast to a cutting board and let stand for 5 minutes before cutting. Serve immediately, garnished with the parsley sprigs.

A Cure for Meat

With such dramatically long winters, Norway's food often did not last. Cows could only go out to pasture for a few short months, and the people relied heavily on cured meats to get them through these winters. Thus began a long tradition of curing, smoking, salting, and pickling. In the old days the healthiest and freshest meats were reserved for the wealthy, while the poor made due with fatty cuts of mutton. Different methods were used to infuse flavor into the low-quality meat, most notably cabbage and whole peppercorns, which today makes up the national dish—farikal.

Lemony Baked Parsnips with Salmon Roe

4 parsnips
¼ cup unsalted butter, melted
4 tablespoons lemon juice

1 tablespoon ground cumin
2 teaspoons ground turmeric
½ cup salmon roe

1. Preheat the oven to 350°. Grease a shallow glass baking dish.
2. Wash the parsnips, peel and cut in half. Cut each half lengthwise, so that you have 4 pieces.
3. Place the parsnips in the baking dish. Brush with the melted butter. Sprinkle with the lemon juice, ground cumin, and the turmeric. Cover with foil and bake until the parsnips are tender (about 30 minutes). To serve, spoon a heaping tablespoon of the salmon roe over each parsnip slice.

> **Serves 6 (as an appetizer)**
>
> Sometimes called red caviar, salmon roe has a flavor similar to beluga caviar but without the hefty price tag. Feel free to substitute other root vegetables, such as carrots or turnips, for the parsnips in this recipe.

Cloudberry Cream Dessert

1 cup fresh cloudberries
3 tablespoons granulated sugar,
*   or as needed*
1½ cups whipping cream

1 teaspoon pure vanilla extract
1 teaspoon freshly squeezed
*   lime juice*

1. Toss the cloudberries with the sugar. If desired, add up to 1 more table-spoon sugar so that they are sweet, but still a bit tart.
2. In a medium bowl, beat the whipping cream with an electric mixer until it forms stiff peaks. Beat in the vanilla extract.
3. Dish ¾ cup of the whipping cream into a dessert bowl. Top with ¼ cup of the cloudberries. Sprinkle with a few drops of lime juice. Repeat with the remainder of the whipping cream and berries.

> **Serves 4**
>
> Similar to raspberries in appearance, cloudberries grow only in Arctic regions such as Scandinavia, Alaska, and northern Canada. If cloudberries are not available, substitute fresh raspberries.

Danish Apple Soup

2 large McIntosh apples
4 shallots
4 tablespoons butter
2 tablespoons brown sugar
1 teaspoon curry powder
1 cup dry white wine
3 cups plus 2 tablespoons
   water, divided

2 whole cloves
1 teaspoon grated orange peel
3-inch cinnamon stick
2 teaspoons cornstarch
½ cup light cream
Fresh mint leaves, as garnish

1. Peel the apples, remove the core, and chop. Peel and chop the shallots. In a large saucepan, heat the butter over medium heat. Add the shallots. Cook for 2 to 3 minutes, then add the apples and brown sugar. Cook, stirring occasionally, until the apples are tender (about 5 minutes). Stir in the curry powder.
2. Add the wine and 3 cups water and bring to a boil. Add the cloves, grated orange peel, and cinnamon stick. Turn down the heat and simmer, uncovered, for 10 minutes. Remove the cinnamon stick.
3. In a small saucepan, dissolve the cornstarch in 2 tablespoons water. Add the cream. Bring to a boil, stirring to thicken. Remove the soup from the heat and allow to cool. Use a blender or food processor to purée the soup until it is smooth. Chill the puréed soup for at least 2 hours before serving.

Sitting Down to a Smorgasbord

Though smorgasbords vary from country to country, even from region to region, you will generally find a few items in common: lobster, smoked or dill-cured salmon, smoked trout, prawns, shrimps, pickled or cured herring, smoked eel, roast beef, veal, pork, smoked reindeer meat, reindeer tongue, ham, liver pastes, tomatoes, onion rings, eggs, pickled cucumber, gherkins, beet root, and many preserves such as cranberry or red whortleberry. Cheeses include local varieties of Danish blue, sweet goat cheese, and (be warned—this one is powerful) the exceedingly strong Norwegian gamalost.

Danish Stuffed Cabbage

Serves 6

The entire cabbage, and not just the leaves, is stuffed in this Danish dish. For an added touch, sprinkle grated Jarslberg cheese over the cream sauce.

1 large head green cabbage
1 pound lean hamburger
½ yellow onion, finely chopped
1 egg, lightly beaten
1½ cups tomato sauce
1 cup crushed breadcrumbs

3 tablespoons white vinegar
1 tablespoon granulated sugar
¼ teaspoon ground nutmeg
1 recipe Rich Cream Sauce
  (page 388)

1. Preheat the oven to 350°. Grease a shallow 9 × 13-inch glass baking dish.
2. Core the cabbage. Remove the outer leaves, reserving a few. Use a knife to carefully hollow out the cabbage, leaving a shell ½ to 1 inch thick. In a large saucepan, add enough salted water to cover the cabbage. Heat to boiling. Add the cabbage. Turn off the heat and let the cabbage stand in the boiling salted water for 15 minutes. Remove and drain.
3. In a medium bowl, combine the hamburger, chopped onion, egg, tomato sauce, breadcrumbs, vinegar, sugar, and nutmeg. Carefully fill the shell of the cabbage with the hamburger mixture. Lay the reserved leaves over the top and bottom holes and secure with toothpicks.
4. Fill an ovenproof saucepan with 4 cups of water. Stand the cabbage in the pot. Cover and bake the cabbage for 1 hour, or until the filling is cooked through.
5. When the cabbage has nearly finished baking, prepare the cream sauce. To serve, cut the cabbage into wedges and pour the sauce over.

Rich Cream Sauce

Yields 2 cups

This flavorful sauce makes the perfect topping for Danish Stuffed Cabbage (page 387).

2 yellow onions
6 whole cloves
4 tablespoons butter
3 tablespoons all-purpose flour
2 cups light cream

¼ teaspoon celery salt, or to taste
¼ teaspoon grated nutmeg
Salt and pepper, to taste

1. Peel the onions. Stud each onion with 3 cloves, stuffing each clove in different parts of the onion.
2. In a medium saucepan, melt the butter over low heat. Make a roux by adding the flour, whisking continuously, until the flour is fully incorporated into the butter (2 to 3 minutes). Slowly add the cream and bring to a boil. Remove from the heat and add the studded onions. Stir in the celery salt.
3. Cook over low heat until the sauce has thickened (about 20 minutes). Remove the onions. Sprinkle the nutmeg over top. Season with salt and pepper if desired. Use as called for in a recipe.

Three Main Types of Finnish Cuisine

Finnish cuisine can be divided into three main categories. Starting in the north, you will find Lappish cuisine that includes such "wilderness" dishes as reindeer, salmon, trout, arctic berries, mushrooms, and willow grouse. Cooking styles and methods tend to be simple, and food is often prepared on an open fire. But Finnish cuisine is also a product of historical influences. Two centuries ago, Finland was part of Sweden, then the Russian Empire. Thus, many dishes on the west coast have strong Swedish influences, while in the east in places like Carelia you will taste Russian influences.

Danish Rum Raisin Muffins

Yields 18

For an extra touch, add a dollop of whipped cream to the muffins before serving.

1 cup raisins
1¼ cups dark rum
1½ cups all-purpose flour
1½ teaspoons baking powder
½ teaspoon baking soda
½ cup granulated sugar
¼ cup brown sugar

¼ teaspoon salt
¼ teaspoon ground nutmeg
⅛ teaspoon ground allspice
1 stick unsalted butter
2 eggs
¾ teaspoon vanilla extract
1 cup sour cream

1. Soak the raisins in the rum for 2 hours. Drain the raisins. Reserve 2 tablespoons of the rum.
2. Preheat the oven to 375°. Grease a muffin pan.
3. In a large bowl, combine the flour, baking powder, baking soda, granulated sugar, brown sugar, salt, nutmeg, and allspice. Cut in the butter and mix with your hands so that it forms coarse crumbs.
4. Lightly beat the eggs. Stir in the vanilla extract and the sour cream. Make a well in the middle of the flour and add the sour cream mixture. Stir the sour cream mixture into the flour to form a lumpy batter similar to pancake batter (do not overmix the batter). Stir in the raisins and up to 2 tablespoons rum as desired.
5. Spoon the mixture into the muffin tins, filling them approximately ¾ full. Bake until the muffins are browned and a toothpick inserted in the middle comes out clean (20 to 25 minutes). Cool on a wire rack before serving.

Danish Christmas Goose with Apples and Prunes

Serves 8–10

For an authentic Danish Christmas meal, serve this goose dish at your holiday table. The cooking time for goose is 20 to 25 minutes per pound, so adjust the cooking time according to the size of your bird.

1 pound prunes
3 cups dry white wine
3 tart red apples

1 yellow onion
8- to 10-pound young goose
1 lemon, cut in half

1. Soak the prunes overnight in the wine to soften.
2. Preheat the oven to 350°.
3. Drain and chop the prunes. Peel the apple, remove the core, and cut into thin slices. Peel the onion and cut into quarters.
4. Remove the giblets and neck from inside the goose. Rinse the goose under cold running water, and pat dry with paper towels. Rub the outer skin of the goose with the lemon. Lightly stuff the inside of the goose with the sliced apples, chopped prunes, and onion. Place the goose, breast-side up, on a large roasting pan. Prick the skin in several places to drain off the fat. Use string to tie the legs and and tail of the goose together. Use skewers to close the stuffing cavity. Insert a meat thermometer into the thickest part of the thigh.
5. Roast the stuffed goose for 2½ hours. Cover the goose with aluminum foil, and roast for another 30 minutes, or until the internal temperature reaches 180°. Let the goose stand for 10 minutes before carving. Remove the stuffing and serve on the side.

Finnish Sauerkraut Soup

1 pound stewing beef
¼ cup smoked ham
½ white onion
2 carrots
2 tablespoons vegetable oil
8 cups beef broth

3½ cups sauerkraut
½ teaspoon caraway seeds
1 tablespoon brown sugar
½ teaspoon paprika
Salt and pepper, to taste
¼ cup sour cream

1. Cut the beef into thin cubes. Dice the smoked ham slices. Peel and chop the onion. Peel and dice the carrots.

2. In a frying pan, heat the oil over medium heat. Add the onion and cook until soft and translucent (5 to 7 minutes). Add the beef and cook until browned. Cook the beef in 2 batches if necessary.

3. In a large saucepan, heat 4 cups of the beef broth to a boil. Add the sauerkraut. Cook, uncovered, for 20 minutes, or until the sauerkraut is tender.

4. Add the onion, browned beef, diced ham, and carrots. Add the remaining 4 cups of broth. Heat to boiling. Stir in the caraway seeds, brown sugar, and paprika. Reduce the heat and simmer, uncovered, for 30 minutes. Taste and season with salt and pepper, if desired. Remove from the heat and stir in the sour cream. Serve immediately.

'Tis the Season

With such starkly defined seasons, the Finnish put tremendous value on seasonal dishes. In early spring, when the lakes and seas are still covered with ice, the specialty is "turbot," eaten with its roe and liver. As Finland enters warmer seasons, new potatoes appear, and are eaten boiled with butter, dill, and marinated herring. June 21 marks the start of crayfish season, when crayfish parties are all the rage. Boiled in salty water with lots of dill, the crayfish are then eaten cold with toast, butter, and chopped fresh dill. Wild mushrooms and berry season starts in June, with chanterelles and blueberries. When the first snow arrives, the Finnish focus on root vegetables, and everything they gathered—now stored in their freezers—during summer and autumn.

Swedish Apricot and Prune Pork Loin

Serves 6–8

Apricot and pork make a great combination. If desired, feel free to thicken the sauce by adding a "cornstarch slurry" made by dissolving 1 tablespoon cornstarch in 2 tablespoons of water.

3½ cups water, divided
¼ teaspoon ground allspice
20 dried apricots, pitted
3-pound pork loin, visible fat removed
1 teaspoon salt
¼ teaspoon freshly ground black pepper

1 teaspoon dried thyme
1 cup chicken broth
1 cup dry white wine
2 teaspoons brown sugar
1½ tablespoons orange marmalade

1. In a medium bowl, bring 2½ cups water to a boil over medium heat. Stir in the ground allspice. Add the dried apricots. Simmer uncovered, stirring occasionally, until the apricots have softened (about 5 minutes). Remove the apricots with a slotted spoon. Reserve the juice.
2. Preheat the oven to 325°.
3. With a sharp knife, make 10 slits across the pork loin. Rub the roast with salt, pepper, and dried thyme. Insert 1 cooked apricot in each slit.
4. Place the pork in a large roasting pan, with a meat thermometer inserted in the center. Place 1 cup water and the chicken broth in the bottom of the pan. Roast the pork for 1½ hours, or until the temperature on the meat thermometer reaches 155°. Remove the roast and let it stand for 15 minutes.
5. While the cooked roast is standing, prepare the sauce. Finely chop the remaining 10 apricots. In a small saucepan, bring the chopped apricots, wine, brown sugar, and orange marmalade to a boil. Reduce the heat and simmer until thickened (about 5 minutes). Purée in a blender or food processor until smooth. Reheat and serve with the pork.

Swedish Apple Cake

Serves 6–8

Homemade applesauce adds extra flavor to this simple apple cake recipe. It can also be served with vanilla ice cream instead of the sour cream sauce.

7 Granny Smith apples
2 cups water
2 teaspoons ground cinnamon, divided
½ teaspoon ground nutmeg
½ cup butter, softened

2 cups unseasoned dry bread-crumbs
¼ cup granulated sugar
Vanilla Sour Cream Sauce (page 394)

1. Peel the apples, remove the core, and chop. In a medium saucepan, bring the apples and water to a boil. Stir in 1 teaspoon cinnamon and the nutmeg. Reduce the heat to medium-low and simmer the apples, covered, until they are softened (about 25 minutes). Stir the mixture occasionally and add more water if it gets too dry. Remove and cool. Mash the apples into a sauce.
2. Preheat the oven to 350°. Grease the bottom of a 9-inch square cake pan.
3. In a medium saucepan, melt the butter over low heat. Stir in the bread-crumbs, sugar, and 1 teaspoon cinnamon.
4. Spread half the crumb mixture in the bottom of the pan, pressing down firmly into the pan. Add the applesauce. Top with the remaining crumb mixture.
5. Bake the cake for 30 minutes, or until browned. Let cool on a wire rack for 15 minutes. To serve, top with the sour cream sauce.

Glogg, Glogg, Glogg

A traditional drink of the Swedish and Finnish Advent season (the six weeks leading up to Christmas), glogg is made from red wine and is served in a glass containing a few almonds and raisins. Glogg's origins date back to the medieval days of mulled wine (wine heated with spices). But glogg tends to be much sweeter than its mulled counterpart, and generally has a higher alcohol content. A few key treats such as gingersnaps, gingerbread, and cinnamon rolls are served with glogg.

Vanilla Sour Cream Sauce

Yields about 2 cups

This simple sauce adds the crowning touch to Swedish Apple Cake (page 393) It also tastes delicious served over fresh fruit in season.

1½ cups sour cream
½ cup plain yogurt
2 tablespoons brown sugar
2 tablespoons granulated sugar

Juice from 2 lemons
1 tablespoon apple brandy liqueur, optional

In a small bowl, combine the sour cream, yogurt, sugars, and lemon juice. Add the liqueur if using. Chill until ready to use.

Lingonberry Sherbet for Adults

Serves 2–4

Don't have an ice cream maker? Purée the frozen berry mixture in the blender.

¾ cup lingonberries
2 tablespoons lemon juice
²⁄₃ cup water

½ cup granulated sugar
2 tablespoons vodka

1. Combine the berries, lemon juice, water, and sugar in a saucepan over medium-high heat. Bring to a boil and cook for 5 minutes, stirring continuously, until the mixture has thickened.
2. Strain the mixture through a mesh strainer into a bowl. Let cool. Stir the vodka into the berry mixture. Place the mixture in an ice cream maker and freeze according to the manufacturer's directions. Keep the sherbet frozen until ready to serve.

Crayfish Quiche

2 tablespoons butter
2 tablespoons minced shallots
2 tablespoons minced celery
1 cup peeled crayfish tails
¼ teaspoon salt, or to taste
⅛ teaspoon black pepper, or to
   taste
½ cup sliced plum tomatoes
3 large eggs
1 cup light cream

¼ teaspoon ground nutmeg
¼ teaspoon cayenne pepper
2 tablespoons chopped fresh
   dill
1 tablespoon Worcestershire
   sauce
1½ cups Jarlsberg cheese,
   grated
1 (9-inch) baked pie shell

Serves 6–8

For the crowning touch, serve the quiche with a dollop of Citrus Crème Fraîche (see sidebar on this page).

1. Preheat the oven to 350°.
2. Melt the butter in a pan over medium heat. Add the shallots and the celery, and sauté until tender. Stir in the crayfish tails, and the salt and pepper. Add the tomatoes and cook until the tomatoes are softened.
3. In a medium bowl, whisk the eggs with the cream, nutmeg, cayenne pepper, chopped dill, and the Worcestershire sauce.
4. Lay ¾ cup of the Jarlsberg cheese over the pie shell. Top with the cooked crayfish and tomato mixture. Pour the beaten egg over. Sprinkle the remaining ¾ cup cheese over top.
5. Bake until the quiche has set, and a toothpick inserted in the middle comes out clean (about 35 to 40 minutes).

Citrus Crème Fraîche

The crayfish quiche goes great with a dollop of this. To prepare homemade crème fraîche, combine ¼ cup heavy cream with 1½ teaspoons buttermilk and refrigerate for 24 hours. The day you want to make the quiche, simply add the juice from 1 orange and 1 lemon to the crème fraîche, along with 1 teaspoon dried chervil. Season with salt and pepper as desired.

Swedish Potato Dumplings

Yields 16–20 dumplings

Good filling choices for these dumplings include crisp cooked bacon, smoked ham, or caramelized pearl onions.

2 pounds russet potatoes
¼ cup butter or margarine
3 tablespoons milk

2 eggs, lightly beaten
¾ cup all-purpose flour
¼ teaspoon salt

1. Peel the potatoes and cut into quarters. Fill a large saucepan with enough salted water to cover the potatoes. Boil the potatoes until they are tender when pierced with a fork (about 20 minutes). Drain the potatoes.
2. In a large bowl, mash the potatoes with the butter and milk. Stir in the eggs, flour, and salt. Allow the mixture to cool.
3. Use your hands to form the dough into 16 to 20 balls. With your thumb, make an indentation in the top of each dumpling. Fill the hole with the filling mixture of your choice and pinch the hole closed. Press down lightly on each dumpling so that it has a flat surface.
4. Bring a large saucepan of lightly salted water to boil. Add the dumplings, a few at a time. Bring the water back to a near-boil, and cook the dumplings in the simmering water until they float to the surface (10 to 15 minutes). Serve immediately.

Swedish Sour Baltic Herring

Caught in the months of May and June, processors immerse the herring for 24 hours in brine, then remove its head and clean it. The next step is to stack the herring in barrels, leaving them in the sun for a day, jump-starting the fermentation process. Next the herring is placed in a cool storage room and fermented, and the aroma grows stronger. Gifted canners determine the precise point at which they are ready for canning. Swedes eat ripe sour Baltic herring with thin, hard bread and boiled potatoes. Sometimes they eat it with milk, though a more common accompanying beverage is beer or aquavit. Intrepid eaters devour the herring without pause, while others first rinse it in soda water.

Chapter 29

Great Britain:
It's Not Just
Fish and Chips

398	Twice-Baked Lobster Soufflé
399	Glazed Champagne and Oyster Sauce
400	Chicory and Orange Salad
400	Apple and Onion Purée
401	Braised Conway Mussels
402	Bread and Butter Pudding
403	Seared Scallops with Saffron Mash
403	Citrus and Shallot Dressing
404	Smoked Salmon Pancakes
405	Basic Cheese Soufflé

Twice-Baked Lobster Soufflé

Serves 6

This delicious signature dish of the West Arms Hotel, Llanarmon DC, North Wales, by Chef Grant Williams, combines the rich sweetness of lobster with the effervescence of champagne.

2 tablespoons butter
½ cup Parmesan, grated
2 tablespoons self-rising flour
½ cup whole milk
½ onion, peeled
1 bay leaf
2 peppercorns
2 egg yolks, lightly beaten

2 ounces lobster meat, cooked
1 tablespoon snipped fresh chives
3 egg whites
1 recipe Glazed Champagne and Oyster Sauce (page 399)

1. Brush 6 small ramekins with butter and sprinkle with a little of the Parmesan cheese.
2. Melt the butter in a saucepan over medium heat. Add the flour and whisk constantly to form a roux. In another saucepan, heat the milk on medium with the onion, bay leaf, and peppercorns. Strain the milk, discarding the solids, and add it to the roux. Stirring constantly, cook until the sauce thickens. Remove from heat and let cool slightly. Add the egg yolks, lobster, remaining Parmesan, and chives.
3. Preheat the oven to 320°.
4. Whisk the egg whites until stiff and carefully fold into the lobster mixture. Bake in a bain-marie for 15 to 20 minutes. Let cool, then remove from the ramekins and place on wax or parchment paper. (The soufflés can be kept in the refrigerator for up to 4 days.)
5. When you're ready to serve, put the soufflés back into a preheated oven for 10 minutes until well risen. Serve over the oyster sauce.

Lady Lobsters Only

Lobsters can grow all the way to 10 pounds but are best eaten when they are between 1 and 3 pounds. "When choosing a lobster," warns Chef Graham Tinsley of Castle Hotel, Conway, "always buy a female because their flesh has a more subtle flavor, whereas the male lobster has a dense, meatier flesh." There are two ways to identify female lobsters. First, the tail of the female is much broader and straighter than that of the male, which tapers slightly. Second, if the first two legs closest to the body are very spindly compared to the others, it is a female.

Glazed Champagne and Oyster Sauce

Serves 6

Serve this with the Twice-Baked Lobster Soufflé (page 398).

18 oysters
⅓ cup total small-diced
vegetables (such as carrot,
celery, leek, and shallots)
¾ cup champagne
1 cup fish stock
1¾ cups heavy cream (or
double cream, if available)
3 egg yolks
Salt and freshly ground pepper,
to taste

1. Open the oysters and reserve all the juices. Bring the oyster juice to the boil, plunge in the oysters for 30 seconds, then remove with a slotted spoon and keep warm.
2. Combine the oyster juice, vegetables, champagne, and fish stock in a pan and simmer over medium heat until reduced to a syrupy consistency. Add 1¼ cups of the cream and cook until thickened, about 2 or 3 minutes.
3. Whip the remaining cream, remove the sauce from the heat, and fold in the egg yolks and the whipped cream. Season with salt and pepper.
4. To serve the dish: Place 3 oysters on each plate, cover with the sauce, and place under a very hot grill until the sauce is golden brown. Put a soufflé in the center of each plate and serve immediately.

Rags to Riches for the Oyster

Once a staple food of the poor in England, oysters are now considered a luxury, or "gourmet," food. Oysters are best eaten raw, straight from the shell with just a squeeze of lemon or a touch of shallot vinegar. Oysters, like all shellfish, should be bought live, and their shells should be tightly closed. Traditionally, fresh oysters should be bought only during the months with an *r* in them.

Chicory and Orange Salad

Serves 4

Also known as corn salad, lamb's lettuce leaves add a nutty flavor to this salad recipe. For an added touch, garnish the salad with radish "roses" before serving.

1 head chicory
1 bunch lamb's lettuce
2 seedless oranges
2 tablesoons fresh red or pink
   currants
2 tablespoons freshly squeezed
   lemon juice

2 teaspoons olive oil
2 tablespoons Perrier or other
   mineral water
⅛ teaspoon fleur de sel (French
   sea salt)

1. Wash the chicory, drain thoroughly, and shred. If using fresh lamb's lettuce, carefully rinse it under running water and drain. (If using prepackaged lamb's lettuce, there is no need to clean it.) Peel the oranges and separate into segments. Rinse the currants and pat dry with paper towels.
2. Whisk together the lemon juice, olive oil, mineral water, and fleur de sel.
3. Combine all the salad ingredients. Drizzle the dressing over top. Serve immediately or refrigerate until ready to serve.

Apple and Onion Purée

Serves 4
(as an accompaniment to meat)

This simple combination blends two distinct types of sweetness and is delicious served alongside almost any meat.

2 green apples, peeled and
   diced

½ onion, peeled and diced
2 tablespoons olive oil

Combine the apples and onion. Sauté in pan with olive oil for 5 minutes. Transfer to a blender or food processor and purée until smooth.

The Hearty British Breakfast
Once upon a time the British used to sit down to a monster-sized breakfast including ham, deviled kidneys, bacon rolls, scrambled eggs, sausage, black pudding, pheasant, pie, hot toast, rolls, sweet butter, marmalades, jams, and fruit. In the twentieth century, war rations led to downsizing the hearty meal, and today it is modest by comparison, usually made up of cereal, eggs, and bacon, toast, marmalade, and tea or coffee.

Braised Conway Mussels

4½ pounds mussels
2 large shallots
1 clove garlic
½ cup dry white wine
1 cup heavy cream (or double
    cream, if available)

2 tablespoons chopped fresh
    parsley
Freshly ground black pepper, to
    taste

Serves 4

Chef Graham Tinsley says, "I never use any other mussels, and I'm sure if you have the chance to try them for yourself, you will agree they are the best." Discard any mussels that are damaged or that are fully open and don't close if you give them a squeeze.

1. Clean the mussels by removing all the barnacles and the beards from the outside of the shells in plenty of cold running water.
2. Peel and finely chop the shallots and garlic.
3. Heat a heavy-bottomed saucepan that has a tight-fitting lid. Add the mussels, shallots, garlic, and white wine to the pan, cover with the lid, and cook until the mussels open (this should take only 2 to 3 minutes). When the mussels are open, remove from the pan with a slotted spoon.
4. Simmer the cooking liquid over medium heat until it is reduced by half, then add the double cream. Bring the sauce to a boil and add the parsley.
5. Return the mussels to the pan with the sauce to reheat. Season with freshly ground black pepper and serve.

Le Moule Est Arrivé!

At one minute past midnight on the third Thursday of each November, over 1 million cases of Beaujolais Nouveau are shipped, and met with almost fanatical worldwide expectation. But in Conway, they have a variation on the theme: "Le moule est arrivé!" (The mussels have arrived!). Once upon a time collected for their pearls, today Conway mussels adorn plates, not earlobes.

Bread and Butter Pudding

Serves 4–6

To dress up this dish, add a touch of vanilla-scented whipped cream and a few sautéed apricots.

About 4 tablespoons butter
4 slices thick white bread
2 ounces sultanas
2¼ cups whole milk
2¼ cups heavy cream (or double cream, if available)

1 vanilla pod, split
8 eggs
½ cup caster (or "superfine") sugar
¼ cup apricot jam
6 fresh apricots, sautéed in butter

1. Preheat the oven to 300°.
2. Butter the bread, cut off the crusts, and cut each slice into 4 triangles. Sprinkle the bottom of an earthenware dish with the sultanas and arrange the bread over the top.
3. In a saucepan over medium heat, combine the milk, cream, and vanilla pod. In a bowl, whisk together the eggs and the sugar. When the milk mixture comes to a boil, pour over the egg mixture, whisking to form a custard. Pour over the bread and place the dish in a bain-marie. Bake for 45 to 50 minutes, until the custard feels firm.
4. Heat the apricot jam in a saucepan with a little water and brush over the surface of the pudding. Garnish each with a sautéed apricot and serve at room temperature.

The Origin of Eggnog

Eggnog is an English creation, descending from a hot British drink called posset, made of eggs, milk, and wine or ale. The second half of its name ("nog") is a British word for strong ale, made from eggs beaten with sugar, milk or cream, and some kind of spirit. Eggnog has made its way into kitchens across the world: in the American South, for example, it is served with bourbon, not ale. People in New Orleans also drink plenty of eggnog, and during the holidays it is served alongside syllabub (an equally rich, but less potent mixture, made with milk, sugar, and wine).

Seared Scallops with Saffron Mash

12 diver scallops
Pinch saffron
1¼ cups mashed potatoes
Pinch salt

1¼ cups Citrus and Shallot
Dressing
1 teaspoon chervil

> **Serves 4**
>
> This is a favorite recipe of Chef Glen Watson of London's restaurant Brasserie Roux, at the Sofitel St. James.

1. Prepare a grill to medium-high heat. Grill the scallops for 1½ minutes on each side.
2. Line a strainer with cheesecloth and add the saffron and enough water to moisten; then drain the water through. Add the saffron to the mashed potatoes. Heat up the mash, if necessary, and place 3 small mounds on each serving plate. Place a cooked scallop on each mound of mash.
3. Warm the dressing and spoon it down the sides of each plate. Sprinkle with chervil. Serve immediately.

Citrus and Shallot Dressing

1¼ cups finely chopped shallots
¼ cup olive oil, divided
¾ cup fresh-squeezed lemon
    juice
½ cup fresh-squeezed lime juice
1 teaspoon caster sugar

1 teaspoon chopped fresh dill
1 teaspoon chopped fresh flat-
    leaf parsley
Salt and pepper, to taste
1 cup diced plum tomato

> **Serves 4**
>
> This light dressing bursts with citrus flavor from lime and lemon juice. Serve over Seared Scallops with Saffron Mash.

1. Sauté the shallots quickly in 1 tablespoon of the oil over medium heat until just softened.
2. Add the lemon and lime juice, sugar, chopped herbs, salt, and pepper. Add the rest of the oil. Remove from heat and let cool.
3. Add the tomatoes and mix well.

Smoked Salmon Pancakes

Serves 6

Britain is famous for its smoked fish dishes. The next time you're preparing poached or scrambled eggs, try serving them with smoked fish instead of sausage or bacon.

6 ounces smoked salmon
4 boiling potatoes
6 tablespoons butter, divided
⅔ cup light cream, divided
¼ teaspoon salt

½ teaspoon ground nutmeg
2 tablespoons chopped fresh
  dill
2 large eggs, lightly beaten
½ teaspoon black pepper

1. Finely chop the smoked salmon. Wash and peel the potatoes, and cut into chunks. Fill a large saucepan with enough salted water to cover the potatoes. Bring to a boil. Cook the potatoes in the boiling water until they are tender and can easily be pierced with a fork. Drain.
2. Place the potatoes in a bowl and add ¼ cup butter. Mash, using a fork or a potato masher. Add in 2 tablespoons of the cream as you are mashing, and stir in the salt and nutmeg.
3. Stir in the remainder of the cream, the fresh dill, the beaten egg, and the pepper. In a food processor, process the smoked salmon with the mashed potato mixture until smooth. Process in batches if necessary.
4. Heat 2 tablespoons margarine in a frying pan over medium heat. Drop a heaping tablespoon of the mashed potato and smoked salmon mixture into the frying pan. Cook until golden brown, turning over once. Continue with the remainder of the pancakes. Serve hot.

Fish and Chips

Fish and chips were born in the nineteenth century, served in working-class districts as a cheap meal easily consumed after a hard day's work. The fish was cooked in shallow pans and usually just eaten plain and cold. The evolution continued, with some shops soon serving baked potatoes in addition to fish, before chips took center stage. There is a rivalry in London about who first served them: was it Malin's in the East End in 1868, or John Lees's wooden hut in Mossley, Manchester, in 1863? The real answer may never be known. Today fish and chips dishes are even offered in upscale gourmet restaurants, though the recipes are usually adapted, using expensive fish and a choice of sauces.

Basic Cheese Soufflé

Serves 4

Feel free to experiment with this basic soufflé recipe by adding tomatoes or other garden vegetables and fresh herbs as desired.

¼ cup unsalted butter
¼ cup all-purpose flour
⅛ teaspoon salt
⅛ teaspoon black pepper

1 cup cold whole milk
4 large eggs, separated
4 ounces Jarlsberg cheese,
    grated

1. Preheat the oven to 350°. Grease a soufflé dish.
2. To prepare the soufflé base, melt the butter over medium heat in a heavy saucepan. Make a roux by adding the flour, salt, and pepper and stirring continuously for 2 to 3 minutes, until the flour is incorporated. Gradually whisk in the milk, stirring continuously until the mixture thickens. Remove from the heat and whisk in the egg yolks. Stir in the cheese.
3. Beat the egg whites until stiff peaks form. Carefully fold the egg whites into the base mixture.
4. Pour the soufflé mixture into the dish. Bake until soufflé turns a light golden brown and a toothpick inserted in the middle comes out clean. Serve immediately.

Medieval Game

Not chess, checkers, or backgammon. Think partridge, quail, and turtledoves. In medieval days, game featured prominently in the diet, especially during winter. Stuffings were created to both flavor the game and make the dishes last longer. Typically stuffings were very rich and could include a multitude of ingredients: saffron, oysters, prunes, cinnamon, oranges and lemons, cloves, etc., mixed together with bread and some sort of fat (bacon was common). The birds were often served with fruit sauces, much like today's use of currants, blackberries, and cranberries in many gourmet sauces.

Chapter 30

Central and South America: Carnivalé in Your Own Home

408 : Brazilian Hot Cocoa
408 : Brazilian Bananas with Rum
409 : Bahian-Style Shrimp Stew
410 : Mined Pork
411 : Paulista Shrimp Cake
412 : Veal and Vegetable Stew

Brazilian Hot Cocoa

Seves 4

Instant cocoa mix can't compare to this rich drink, which gets its flavor from real chocolate and strong coffee.

4 ounces bittersweet chocolate
4 ounces semisweet chocolate
1¾ cups boiling water
3 cups whole milk

1 cup coffee cream
½ cup strongly brewed coffee
1 cup granulated sugar

1. Break the chocolate into pieces. In a medium saucepan, bring the water to a boil. Add the chocolate and melt in the boiling water, stirring continuously. Remove the melted chocolate from the heat and cool.
2. In a large saucepan, heat the milk and coffee cream until nearly boiling. Add the hot coffee and sugar, stirring continuously to dissolve the sugar. Stir in the melted chocolate. Serve hot.

Brazilian Bananas with Rum

Serves 4–6

For best results, use underripe bananas in this recipe. Ripe bananas may fall apart during baking or become "mushy."

1 tablespoon butter
¼ cup firmly packed brown
   sugar
¼ cup granulated sugar
⅓ cup fresh lemon juice

2 tablespoons pineapple juice
2 tablespoons white rum
4 medium-sized underripe
   bananas
2 tablespoons toasted coconut

1. Preheat the oven to 400°. Grease a shallow glass 9 × 13-inch baking dish.
2. In a medium bowl, cream the butter with the brown sugar. Stir in the white sugar, lemon juice, pineapple juice, and rum.
3. Peel the bananas and slice in half lengthwise. Lay the bananas in the baking dish, flat-side down. Spread the sugar and juice mixture over. Bake for about 15 minutes, until the bananas are tender but still slightly firm. Baste the bananas with the sugar mixture once or twice during cooking. Cool. Sprinkle with the toasted coconut before serving.

Bahian-Style Shrimp Stew

Serves 4

A type of palm oil, dende oil's orange color and nutty flavor make it a staple ingredient in Brazilian cooking. Substitute palm oil if dende oil is unavailable.

¾ pound frozen cooked
    tiger shrimp, shelled and
    deveined
1 small white onion
2 cloves garlic
2 tablespoons olive oil
2 tablespoons tomato paste
1 tablespoon freshly squeezed
    lemon juice

½ teaspoon granulated sugar
¾ cup thin coconut milk
½ cup thick coconut milk
3 tablespoons dende oil
½ teaspoon salt
Freshly ground black pepper, to
    taste
1 tablespoon chopped fresh
    cilantro leaves

1. Rinse the frozen shrimp under warm running water until thawed. Pat dry on paper towels. Peel and finely chop the onion and garlic.

2. In a large frying pan, heat the olive oil. Add the chopped onion and garlic. Cook over medium heat until the onion is soft and translucent (5 to 7 minutes). Stir in the tomato paste, lemon juice, and sugar. Cook briefly, then add the coconut milk and dende oil. Bring to a boil. Add the chopped shrimp, salt, and pepper. Stir in the cilantro leaves. Cook over medium heat for 5 more minutes. Serve hot.

Thin Coconut Milk?

For the coconut milk called for in the recipe, buy canned and spoon off the top layer for the thick coconut milk and pour out the liquid underneath for the thin coconut milk. Canned coconut milk naturally separates.

Mined Pork

Serves 6

Can't find Portuguese chourico sausage? Use Mexican chorizo sausage instead. In either case, be sure to remove the sausage from its casing before adding it to the pan.

½ pound smoked chourico sausage

2 large tomatoes

1 malagueta pepper (bird chilies)

1 white onion

1 tablespoon olive oil

2 pounds boneless pork, finely chopped

2 tablespoons lemon juice

1 tablespoon white vinegar

Salt and freshly ground black pepper, to taste

3 hard-boiled eggs, finely chopped

2 tablespoons minced fresh parsley

1. Remove the chourico sausage from its casing and cut into ¼-inch slices. Blanch the tomatoes, remove the peels, and cut each tomato into thin slices. Cut the malagueta pepper in half, remove the seeds, and mince. Peel and finely chop the onion.

2. Heat the olive oil in a heavy frying pan on medium heat. Add the pork and cook, stirring frequently, until it is browned. Remove the pork from the pan, but do not clean out the pan.

3. Add the chopped onion and cook until the onion is soft and translucent (5 to 7 minutes). Add the tomatoes, and cook over medium-low heat, gently squeezing the tomatoes with the back of a rubber spatula so that they release their juices. Add the malagueta pepper, lemon juice, and white vinegar. Stir in the salt and pepper.

4. Add the pork back into the pan and add just enough water to cover. Simmer, uncovered, over low heat until the pork is tender and the water has been absorbed. Remove the mixture from the pan, place in a large bowl, and toss with the chopped egg. Sprinkle with the fresh parsley. Season with added salt and pepper if desired. Serve immediately.

Paulista Shrimp Cake

2 pounds medium fresh shrimp,
   peeled and deveined
2 tablespoons lemon juice
1 small white onion
1 garlic clove
1 (14-ounce) can palm hearts
1 red bell pepper
1 green onion
2 hard-boiled eggs
1 teaspoon salt
1 cup water

½ teaspoon cornstarch
4 teaspoons tapioca starch
½ cup olive oil, divided
1¼ cups canned tomatoes
Salt and pepper
1 cup green peas
½ cup finely chopped black
   olives
2 tablespoons chopped fresh
   parsley

> **Serves 6**
>
> A featured dish in the state of São Paulo in Brazil, this is a favorite of Ambassador Rubens Barbosa, whose mother cooked it frequently when he was growing up.

1. Rinse the shrimp under warm running water. Pat dry with paper towels. Place the drained shrimp in a bowl and toss with the lemon juice. Peel and finely chop the onion. Smash, peel, and mince the garlic. Rinse the canned palm hearts and drain in a colander. Cut the red bell pepper in half, remove the seeds, and finely chop. Rinse the green onion and dice. Peel and mash the hard-boiled eggs.

2. Dissolve the salt in the water. Add the cornstarch and the tapioca starch to the water, stirring to dissolve. Let stand for 1 hour.

3. Heat 2 tablespoons olive oil in a frying pan. Cook the onion and garlic over medium heat until the onion is softened (about 5 minutes). Add the shrimp and the chopped pepper. Stir in the canned tomatoes, and the salt and pepper. Bring to a boil. Reduce the heat to low, and stir in the green peas, palm hearts, green onion, olives, and the parsley. Remove the frying pan from the heat. Give the starch and water mixture a quick re-stir and mix it in thoroughly.

4. Place the shrimp mixture in a large bowl. Stir in the hard-boiled egg pieces. Take a heaping tablespoon of the mixture, and flatten between the palms of your hands to form a thin cake. Continue with the remainder of the shrimp mixture.

5. Heat the remaining olive oil in a frying pan. Cook the shrimp cakes over medium heat, until they are golden brown (about 6 minutes). Turn the cakes over once during cooking.

Veal and Vegetable Stew

2 medium white onions
3 cloves garlic, mashed
2 carrots
3 sweet potatoes
1 small acorn squash
2 tablespoons olive oil, divided
2 pounds veal, cubed
2 cups beef broth, or as needed

1 (14-ounce) can crushed
   tomatoes, with juice
½ teaspoon salt
¼ teaspoon black pepper
½ teaspoon dried parsley
½ cup water, or as needed
1 cup canned apricots or
   peaches

1. Peel and chop the white onions. Smash, peel, and chop the garlic cloves. Wash and peel the carrots and cut into matchsticks. Peel and chop the potatoes and the acorn squash.
2. In a large saucepan or Dutch oven, heat 1 tablespoon olive oil. Add half the veal and cook over medium-high heat until browned. Remove from the pan. Brown the remainder of the veal and remove from the pan. Do not clean out the pan.
3. Heat 1 tablespoon olive oil. Add the carrots. Cook over medium heat for 5 minutes, then add the onion and garlic. Cook over medium heat for 5 more minutes, until the carrots are browned and the onion is softened. Deglaze the pan by adding ½ cup beef broth and bringing to a boil, using a spatula to stir up any browned bits from the bottom of the saucepan.
4. Add the tomatoes and remaining 1½ cups beef broth. Bring to a boil. Stir in the salt, pepper, and dried parsley. Add the veal, chopped potatoes, and squash. Reduce heat to low and simmer, covered, until the veal is cooked and the vegetables are tender (about 45 minutes), adding water as necessary. Add the canned apricots. Heat through and serve hot.

Tasting Ecuador

When in Ecuador, try to sample the following dishes: caldo or sopa (soups, available as a breakfast item in markets); lechón (roasted suckling pig); llapin-gachos (potato and cheese pancake, often served with small bits of meat); locro, soup (with potatoes, corn, and avocado); parrilla (mixed meat bar-bequed Argentine style).

Chapter 31

India:
Spicing Up Your Life

414 Aloo Tikki (Indian Potato Cakes)

414 Fresh Mango Chutney

415 Lamb Curry with Banana Raita

416 Yogurt Sauce

417 Chilled Cucumber Soup

418 Quail with Curry

419 Lobster Korma

420 Rose-Flavored Yogurt Lassi

421 Akhni Stock

422 Curried Lamb Kebabs

423 Shrimp in Coconut Milk

424 Salmon in Saffron-Flavored Curry

425 Split Lentil Dumplings

426 Gooseberry Chutney

427 Mango Cheesecake

Aloo Tikki (Indian Potato Cakes)

**Serves 10
(as an appetizer)**

This recipe is from Chef Rajesh Kattaria of the Ritz-Carlton, Dearborn, MI. Aloo Tikki is the dish that inspired him to become a chef. Serve with Fresh Mango Chutney (below).

2 pounds Idaho potato, peeled
2 ounces channa dahl (Indian
 lentils) or chickpeas
Salt, to taste
Red chili powder, to taste
1 egg yolk

2 teaspoons finely chopped
 ginger
2 cloves garlic, finely chopped
¼ cup finely chopped cilantro
3 tablespoons olive oil

1. Boil the potatoes until tender. Drain and let cool. Mash the potatoes.
2. Boil the lentils until softened (about 30 minutes). Let cool.
3. Add the cooled lentils, salt, red chili powder, egg yolk, ginger, garlic, and the cilantro to the mashed potatoes. Combine the lentil and mashed potato mixtures and form into patties.
4. Heat the olive oil over medium-high heat. Pan-fry the patties until golden brown on both sides.

Fresh Mango Chutney

Yields approximately 1 cup

Let the chutney marinate in the refrigerator for 1 or 2 hours before serving.

1 medium-sized slightly
 underripe mango
1 fresh jalapeño, sliced into thin
 rings

1 tablespoon finely chopped
 fresh cilantro
1 teaspoon salt
⅛ teaspoon ground cayenne
 pepper

Cut the flesh of the mango away from the large seed inside. Cut the mango into paper-thin slices. Place in a bowl. Add the jalapeño, cilantro, salt, and cayenne, and toss gently.

Lamb Curry with Banana Raita

4 cups plain yogurt, divided
3½ tablespoons garam masala
1 tablespoon lemon juice
3 tablespoons chopped fresh
    parsley
2 pounds lamb shoulder, cubed
3 large bananas
2 tablespoons tahini (sesame
    paste)
1 teaspoon ground cardamom
¼ teaspoon chili paste, or to
    taste

¼ cup chopped coriander
    (cilantro) leaves
2 tablespoons olive oil
2 onions, finely chopped
2 medium cloves garlic, finely
    chopped
2 jalapeño chili peppers,
    deseeded and chopped
1 cup water, or as needed

Serves 6–8

Sweet banana raita makes
the perfect side dish for
spicy lamb curry.

1. In a shallow glass 9 × 13-inch baking dish, combine 3 cups yogurt, the garam masala spice mixture, lemon juice, and fresh parsley. Add the lamb cubes, turning to make sure all the cubes are coated in the marinade. Cover and refrigerate for 2 hours.
2. To make the Banana Raita, peel the bananas and cut into 4 to 5 pieces. In a food processor, process the chopped banana until smooth. Stir in 1 cup yogurt, tahini, ground cardamom, chili paste, and chopped cilantro. Process again until smooth. Chill the raita while preparing the lamb curry.
3. In a heavy frying pan or Dutch oven, heat the olive oil over medium heat. Add the onion and garlic and cook until the onion is softened. Add the chili peppers and cook until the skin begins to blister and brown.
4. Add the lamb to the pan with the yogurt marinade. Reduce heat and simmer, covered, until the lamb is tender and cooked through (about 2 hours). Add water as is necessary during cooking. Serve the curry over rice, with the banana raita.

Yogurt Sauce

Yields approximately 1½ cups

Feel free to use this sauce with beef or chicken, or as a substitute for margarine in a pita bread sandwich.

1 cup plain yogurt
½ cup sour cream
1 tablespoon lemon juice
⅛ teaspoon ground cumin
1 tablespoon chopped fresh
   mint

¼ teaspoon chili paste, or as
   desired
4 mint sprigs, as garnish

In a medium bowl, combine the yogurt, sour cream, lemon juice, ground cumin, chopped mint, and chili paste. Cover and chill for at least 1 hour to give the flavors a chance to blend. Serve chilled, with the mint sprigs as garnish.

Yogurt

Yogurt, though popular for years in Europe, Eastern Europe, the Middle East, and Western Asia, only recently became popular in the United States. We can credit its rise in popularity to the immigration of people from other countries to the United States. Many cultures have their own varieties.

Chilled Cucumber Soup

1 large cucumber, peeled and
    grated
1 small garlic clove, crushed
2 cups plain yogurt
2 cups water

Table salt, to taste
1 tablespoon vegetable oil
¼ teaspoon cumin seeds
1 teaspoon finely chopped fresh
    mint for garnish

Serves 6

In the sweltering heat of summer, this soup has a wonderful cooling effect.

1. Place the cucumber in a bowl and chill for about 30 minutes. Pour off the cucumber juice that collects in the bowl. Press down on the cucumber to get out as much juice as possible.
2. Combine the cucumber and garlic; then stir in the yogurt and water. Combine thoroughly. Add salt to taste. Set aside.
3. Heat the oil in a small skillet on medium. Add the cumin seeds and sauté for about 1 minute or until the seeds start to crackle and you can smell the aroma. Remove from heat.
4. Stir the cumin into the yogurt soup. Cover and refrigerate for 2 hours.
5. When ready to serve, pour equal portions into 6 shallow bowls and garnish with the mint.

Vegetarianism in India

While many Indians are vegetarian—having been influenced by Buddha (founder of Buddhism) and Mahavir (founder of Jainism)—there are still those who do consume meat. The so-called lower strata of society—namely, the scheduled castes, the scheduled tribes, and the backward castes—fall into this category. Many of them practice the Beast's Day Out, a "selective vegetarianism"; people opt not to eat meat on certain days of the week (e.g., no fish on Mondays). One major factor contributing to the rise of vegetarianism in India was that kings such as Ashoka discouraged the killing of animals.

Quail with Curry

Serves 4

Garam masala rub provides most of the heat in this spicy curry dish. For best results, make sure to get a good garam masala from an international or specialty market, or make your own.

1 tablespoon garam masala
   spice mixture
½ cup plain yogurt
4 whole quail, deboned
1 white onion
2 cloves garlic
2 tomatoes
4 tablespoons ghee (clarified
   butter), divided

3-inch cinnamon stick
1 tablespoon chickpea flour
   (besan)
2 tablespoons water
2 tablespoons garam masala
   curry paste
¼ cup thick coconut milk
½ teaspoon turmeric

1. In a small bowl, combine the garam masala spice mixture with the yogurt. Clean the quail. Use a knife to make several diagonal cuts in the skin. Rub the spiced yogurt over the quail. Cover and marinate, overnight, in the refrigerator.

2. Preheat the oven to 325°. Peel and chop the onion and garlic. Peel the tomatoes, remove the seeds, and thinly slice. Remove the quail from the refrigerator and place on a large baking sheet (do not clean off the yogurt). Bake until the quail are cooked through (about 1 hour).

3. While the quail is baking, prepare the remainder of the vegetables. In a frying pan, heat 2 tablespoons ghee over medium heat. Add the onion and garlic and cook until soft and translucent (5 to 7 minutes). Add the tomatoes, pressing down gently with a spatula to release their juices. Add the cinnamon stick. Reduce the heat to low and cook gently, stirring occasionally, for 10 minutes. Remove the cinnamon stick.

4. In a small bowl, whisk the chickpea flour into the water. Set aside. In a small saucepan, heat 2 tablespoons ghee over medium-high heat. Stir in the garam masala curry paste. Heat briefly, and then add the chickpea flour and water mixture, stirring quickly to thicken. Slowly whisk in the coconut milk. Stir in the turmeric. Remove from the heat.

5. To serve, place the quail on a large platter, surrounded by the vegetables. Pour the sauce over the quail.

Lobster Korma

2 live lobsters, about 1½
    pounds each
1 teaspoon saffron strands
1 cup evaporated milk, plus 2
    tablespoons
3 tablespoons ghee (clarified
    butter)
1 ice-cube container garlic
    purée, thawed (see below)

1 tablespoon minced ginger
4 ice-cube containers onion
    purée, thawed (see below)
1 teaspoon turmeric
1 teaspoon garam masala spice
    mixture
⅓ cup plain yogurt
¼ cup chopped fresh coriander
    (cilantro) leaves

> **Serves 4**
>
> Enhance the exotic appearance of this dish by reserving the lobster shells and using them as a "bowl" in which to serve the korma.

1. In a large saucepan, bring at least 8 cups salted water to a boil. Add 1 of the lobsters to the boiling water. Bring the water back to a boil. Reduce the heat and simmer, covered, until the lobster shell turns red and the meat is cooked (about 10 to 12 minutes for a 1½-pound lobster). Use tongs to remove the lobster. Drain the lobster in a colander. Repeat with the other lobster. Remove the cooked lobster meat from the shell, and chop into bite-sized chunks.

2. Place the saffron strands in a small bowl and add 2 tablespoons evaporated milk. Soften for 5 minutes. Remove the saffron strands. Discard the milk.

3. To make the korma mixture, heat the ghee in a large frying pan. Add the garlic purée, ginger, and the onion purée. Cook over medium heat until the onion is softened. Stir in the turmeric and the garam masala spice mixture. Add the yogurt. Heat to boiling, then add the chopped lobster meat. Stir in the saffron strands and chopped cilantro leaves. Heat through. Serve immediately.

Garlic and Onion Purée

For the garlic purée, take 30 peeled garlic cloves and purée in a blender or food processor, adding no water. Scrape the garlic purée out of the container, divide evenly among 10 ice-cube molds, and freeze. For the onion purée, peel 10 medium-sized Spanish onions. Coarsely chop the onions and place them in boiling water for 3 minutes. Drain, and then purée in a blender or food processor until very fine in texture. Scrape out of the container, divide evenly among 10 ice-cube molds, and freeze.

Rose-Flavored Yogurt Lassi

Serves 4

If you cannot find rose water, substitute your favorite syrup. *Lassi* has a short shelf life and is best served fresh.

4 cups plain yogurt
2 tablespoons sugar
1½ tablespoons rose water

½ cup water
5–6 ice cubes
Rose petals, for garnish

1. Line a sieve with several layers of cheesecloth. Place the yogurt in the sieve and suspend over a bowl.
2. Let any liquid drain into the bowl, then discard the liquid. Tie the ends of the cheesecloth to form a pouch. Weigh it down using a few cans in a plastic bag as weight. Let it sit for about 2 hours to allow any remaining liquid to drain out. Remove the cheesecloth.
3. In a blender, combine the yogurt, sugar, rose water, water, and ice cubes; blend well. Add more water if you like a thinner consistency. Serve garnished with rose petals.

Rose Water
Rose water is made, as the name suggests, from roses. Cotton balls doused in chilled rose water make wonderful facial cleansers.

Akhni Stock

8 cups water
2 Spanish onions, chopped
4 ounces garlic purée
  (page 419)
2 teaspoons minced ginger
10 whole green cardamom
  pods

2 bay leaves
4 whole cloves
¼ cup chopped cilantro
1 teaspoon salt
1 tablespoon unsalted butter
2 (3-inch) cinnamon sticks

Yields 6 cups

Follow the directions in "Garlic and Onion Purée" (page 143) to make the garlic purée for this recipe. For a more authentic touch, replace the butter with ghee (clarified butter) if desired.

1. Bring the water to a boil over medium heat. Add chopped onion, puréed garlic, ginger, cardamom pods, bay leaves, cloves, chopped cilantro, salt, clarified butter, and the cinnamon sticks. Reduce heat and simmer, covered, for 30 minutes.

2. Remove the bay leaves and the cinnamon sticks, and strain the soup through a mesh strainer. Refrigerate or freeze until ready to use as called for in a recipe.

The Art of Drinking in India

Brewing and drinking of various liquors was developed as an art in ancient India. Karnataka is the homeland to a variety of indigenous alcohol and liquors including ones brewed from rice, ragi (sweet barley), palm, and ichala (wild palm), as well as milder ones made with grapes, mangoes, jackfruit, coconut, and dates flavored with flower essences. Sculptures and Kavyas depict drunkards and drinking scenes, suggesting that drinking provided occasional amusement and relief, though abstinence from alcohol was respected and widely practiced.

Curried Lamb Kebabs

Serves 2–4

Zucchini, tomatoes, and fresh mushrooms would all be good choices to cook with the lamb. Thinly cut the vegetables and thread onto the skewers with the lamb, alternating between a meat and a vegetable.

1 papaya
1¼ cups plain yogurt, divided
1½ pounds lamb, cut into 1½-inch cubes
4 cloves garlic
2 tablespoons lemon juice, divided

1 teaspoon cayenne pepper
1 teaspoon ground coriander
1 teaspoon ground cumin
6 cardamom pods, crushed
¼ cup olive oil

1. Peel the papaya and cut into thin slices. In a food processor, purée the papaya with 1 cup yogurt until smooth. Place the lamb cubes in a shallow 9 × 13-inch baking dish. Coat the lamb with the yogurt and papaya mixture. Cover and marinate in the refrigerator overnight.
2. Smash, peel, and mince the garlic. In a blender or food processor, purée the minced garlic with 1 tablespoon lemon juice to form a paste.
3. Preheat the grill.
4. In a large bowl, combine the garlic paste, cayenne pepper, coriander, ground cumin, and crushed cardamom, olive oil, and the remaining 1 tablespoon lemon juice and ¼ cup yogurt. Remove the marinated lamb from the refrigerator and coat with the mixture.
5. Thread the marinated lamb onto skewers. Grill on medium heat until the lamb reaches the desired level of doneness (about 10 minutes for medium rare). Serve immediately.

Not So Hot

Indian dishes use spices most often in an aromatic and subtle way—not necessarily to make a dish hot. Indians consider the ways elements in a recipe interact, and will commonly use cooling as well as warming spices, bland spices together with pungent spices, and sweet spices alongside hot spices. Spices are also used as a simple and effective way to add color and healthful properties.

Shrimp in Coconut Milk

Serves 4

A nice variation is to fry the shrimp first. It adds a nice crispness. Serve with steamed white rice.

1 bay leaf
1 teaspoon cumin seeds
1 (1-inch) cinnamon stick
2 cloves
4 black peppercorns
1-inch piece fresh gingerroot, peeled and sliced
4 garlic cloves
Water, as needed

3 tablespoons vegetable oil
1 large red onion, minced
½ teaspoon turmeric powder
1 pound shrimp, peeled and deveined
1 (14-ounce) can light coconut milk
Table salt, to taste

1. In a spice grinder, roughly grind the bay leaf, cumin seeds, cinnamon stick, cloves, peppercorns, ginger, and garlic. Add 1 tablespoon of water if needed.
2. In a medium-sized skillet, heat the vegetable oil. Add the ground spice mixture and sauté for about 1 minute. Add the onions and sauté for 7 to 8 minutes or until the onions are well browned.
3. Add the turmeric and mix well. Add the shrimp and sauté for about 2 to 3 minutes, until no longer pink.
4. Add the coconut milk and salt. Simmer for 10 minutes or until the gravy starts to thicken. Remove from heat and serve hot.

Consummate Hosts

If you travel throughout India, you soon realize that they are the consummate hosts. In Sanskrit literature, three famous words, *Atithi Devo Bhava* ("the guest is truly your god") suggest how Indians feel about hospitality. Indians believe they are honored to share their meal, and even the poorest are anxious to share what they have. An Indian host is typically very proud and would be horrified if a guest were to leave hungry or unhappy. Thus when invited to someone's home in India, it is best to happily agree—and be sure to leave plenty of room to eat.

Salmon in Saffron-Flavored Curry

Serves 4

"The king of the sea marries the queen of spices" is the best way to describe this dish. Serve with naan bread.

4 tablespoons vegetable oil
1 large onion, finely chopped
1 teaspoon ginger-garlic paste
   (see sidebar below)
½ teaspoon red chili powder
¼ teaspoon turmeric powder
2 teaspoons coriander powder

Table salt, to taste
1 pound salmon, boned and
   cubed
½ cup plain yogurt, whipped
8 tablespoons whole milk
1 teaspoon saffron threads

1. In a large, nonstick skillet, heat the vegetable oil. Add the onions and sauté for 3 to 4 minutes or until transparent. Add the ginger-garlic paste and sauté for 1 minute.
2. Add the red chili powder, turmeric, coriander, and salt; mix well. Add the salmon and sauté for 3 to 4 minutes. Add the yogurt and lower the heat. Simmer until the salmon has cooked through.
3. Warm the milk over low heat until it is warm to the touch (but not hot).
4. In a dry skillet, dry roast the saffron threads over low heat until fragrant, about 1 minute. Remove from heat. Combine the warm milk and saffron threads, and add to the salmon and mix well. Cook for 1 minute. Serve hot.

Ginger-Garlic Paste

To make the ginger-garlic paste, in a food processor, combine the following: 2 serrano green chilies (stems removed), ½ cup fresh gingerroot (peeled), ½ cup garlic cloves (peeled), and 1 tablespoon cold water. Purée to form a smooth paste. Add no more than 1 tablespoon of water to help form a smooth consistency. Store the paste in an airtight jar in the refrigerator. It will keep for up to two weeks.

Split Lentil Dumplings

1 cup skinned and split black
gram (also called white
lentils), rinsed
½ teaspoon fenugreek seeds
4 cups hot water

1-inch piece fresh gingerroot,
peeled and coarsely chopped
2 serrano green chilies
Table salt, to taste
Vegetable oil for deep-frying

> **Serves 4**
>
> These delightful dump-lings can be served as cocktail appetizers.

1. Soak the gram and fenugreek seeds together in the hot water for about 2 hours. Drain.
2. In a food processor, combine the soaked gram, ginger, chilies, and salt. Process to a smooth batter. Add up to 2 tablespoons of water if needed. Transfer to a bowl.
3. Heat the vegetable oil in a deep pan or a deep fryer to 375°. Place a few tablespoons of the mixture, one at a time, into the oil. Make sure you do not overcrowd the pan. Deep-fry the balls until golden brown all over, about 2 to 3 minutes. Remove with a slotted spoon and drain on a paper towel. Let the oil return to temperature between batches. Continue until all the mixture is used. Serve hot.

The Requisite Condiments

You will almost always find a selection of fresh chutneys, dried fruit chutneys, and hot pickles as an accompaniment to an Indian meal. Aimed at heightening and balancing flavors, condiments can make an enormous impact on the taste of a dish. Working on several levels, these items often taste simultaneously sweet, pungent, hot, and sour. Some of the leading chutneys are cilantro, mint, and coconut, while pickle favorites (which are preserved in oil, not vinegar) include lime, mango, and eggplant.

Gooseberry Chutney

3 tablespoons vegetable oil
2 teaspoons minced ginger
1 clove garlic, minced
2 tablespoons finely chopped onion
1¼ cups cider vinegar
1½ cups granulated sugar

4 cups fresh green gooseberries
¼ cup balsamic vinegar
½ teaspoon ground cinnamon
⅛ teaspoon cayenne pepper, or to taste
¼ teaspoon salt

1. In a heavy-bottomed saucepan, heat the oil. Stir in the minced ginger and garlic. Add the chopped onion. Cook over medium heat until the onion is soft and translucent (5 to 7 minutes).

2. Add the cider vinegar and sugar and bring to a boil, stirring to dissolve the sugar. Add the gooseberries, balsamic vinegar, ground cinnamon, cayenne pepper, and salt. Bring back to a boil, stirring continually. Reduce the heat and let the chutney simmer, uncovered, until the gooseberries are softened and the mixture has thickened (about 30 minutes). Cool. Serve immediately, or cover and refrigerate to give the flavors a chance to blend. (The chutney will keep for up to a week.)

Regional Distinctions

There are strong distinctions between regional Indian dishes. In the north and the west, Kashmiri and Mughlai cuisines show strong Central Asian influences. To the east, the Bengali and Assamese resemble the cuisines of East Asia. All coastal kitchens make use of fish and coconuts, while desert cuisines of Rajasthan and Gujarat use an immense variety of dahls and achars (preserves) to substitute for the relative lack of fresh vegetables. All along the northern plain, a variety of flours are used to make chapatis and other breads.

Mango Cheesecake

¼ cup water
1 envelope unflavored gelatin
2 cups Indian cheese (paneer), crumbled
1 cup ricotta cheese
4 tablespoons sweetened mango pulp

2 tablespoons sweetened condensed milk
1 cup heavy cream, whipped
1 (15-ounce) can Alphonso mango slices, drained, or fresh mango slices, coarsely chopped

1. Heat the water on low in a small pan, sprinkle the gelatin on top, and heat until the gelatin completely dissolves. Set aside.
2. In a bowl, combine the Indian cheese, ricotta cheese, mango pulp, and condensed milk. Mix well and make sure that there are no lumps. A handheld blender works well for this.
3. Slowly add the gelatin to the cheese mixture; mix well.
4. Fold in the whipped cream, and pour into a lightly buttered 6-cup mold. Chill until firm, about 2 hours.
5. When ready to serve, invert the mold onto a serving platter and top the cheesecake with the Alphonso mango.

Royal Kitchens

It was in large part thanks to Indian royalty, the rajahs, that Indian cuisine reached for culinary heights. Rulers encouraged their personal chefs to create elaborate feasts and unique dishes. Chefs vied with one another to succeed in creating the most exotic dishes, pushing the envelope when it came to innovative combinations and ornate presentation. The result? Centuries of patronage to the art of cooking, and a large repertoire of delicious recipes.

Chapter 32

Thailand:
Land of Lemongrass, Coconut, and Curry

430 : Tamarind Sauce

430 : Chili Prawns with Tomato Sauce

431 : Jungle Curry Paste

432 : Chicken in Coconut Milk

433 : Green Mango and Shrimp Salad

434 : Stir-Fried Asparagus, Oyster Mushrooms, and Shrimp in Garlic Sauce

435 : Crab Spring Rolls

436 : Hot and Sour Prawn Soup

437 : Bananas in Coconut Milk

438 : Tom Ka Kai

439 : Pumpkin Curry Soup

440 : Bangkok-Style Roasted Pork Tenderloin

441 : Sweet and Savory Grilled Coconut-Rice Hotcakes

442 : Lemongrass Chicken Skewers

443 : Sambal Bunchies (Green Beans)

444 : Pad Thai

445 : Fire Noodles

446 : Spicy Scallops

447 : Thai Beef with Rice Noodles

448 : Crispy Crepes with Fresh Fruits

Tamarind Sauce

Serves 4

This sauce is used to complement many different Thai dishes.

½ cup fish sauce
7 tablespoons tamarind juice

½ cup palm sugar
1 teaspoon red chili oil

Mix together all the ingredients in a pan over medium heat. Cook until the sugar melts, stirring throughout. Remove from heat when slightly caramelized.

Chili Prawns with Tomato Sauce

Serves 4

Tropika Restaurant, in Vancouver, British Columbia, serves Malaysian, Indonesian, and Thai cuisine that appeals to the large number of immigrants living in the city. This recipe comes from Tropika.

1 tablespoon vegetable oil
½ teaspoon minced garlic
1 green onion, cut into 2-inch-long pieces
1 large tomato, cut into 8 pieces
1 pound tiger prawns, peeled, deveined, and cleaned

½ teaspoon chili sauce
1 tablespoon tomato sauce
½ teaspoon salt
2 teaspoons granulated sugar
1 tablespoon coconut milk
1 egg, beaten well

Preheat a wok on high, then add the oil and swirl it around to coat the pan. Add the garlic, green onion, and tomato. Stir-fry for 1 minute. Add the prawns, chili sauce, tomato sauce, salt, and sugar. Stir-fry until the prawns turn golden yellow. Add the coconut milk and egg, reduce heat to medium-low, and keep stirring until the egg is cooked. Serve.

Jungle Curry Paste

2 tablespoons vegetable oil

12 serrano chilies, seeded and
   chopped

6–8 Thai bird chilies, seeded
   and chopped

1 tablespoon shrimp paste

1 stalk lemongrass, tough
   outer leaves removed
   and discarded, inner core
   minced

1 (3-inch) piece ginger, peeled
   and chopped

4 shallots, chopped

1 cup chopped basil

½ cup chopped mint

¼ cup chopped chives

¼ cup chopped arugula

> **Yields approximately
> 2 cups**
>
> This curry has the look of a pesto. In fact, you can use it in a similar manner, tossing a tablespoon or so to taste with hot pasta.

1. In a medium-sized sauté pan, heat the oil on medium. Add the chilies, shrimp paste, lemongrass, ginger, and shallots, and sauté until the shallots begin to turn translucent and the mixture is very fragrant.
2. Transfer the mixture to a food processor and process until smooth, adding 1 or 2 tablespoons of water to help with the grinding.
3. Add the remaining ingredients and more water if necessary and continue to process until coarsely blended.

Arugula

Arugula is a specialty green with a peppery, somewhat bitter taste. Although we Westerners associate it with Italian cuisine, it was originally cultivated in western Asia. If you can't find it (check in the herb section), you can substitute spinach in this recipe, although with a slightly less flavorful result.

Chicken in Coconut Milk

Serves 2

This is a classic Thai recipe, offered by Banyan Tree Phuket, bordered by the golden sands of the Andaman Sea. This is an excellent dish to pair with rice. Serrano chilies are extremely hot—feel free to substitute a milder chili pepper if desired.

3 cups coconut milk

2 sticks lemongrass

1 small red serrano chili, crushed

2 tablespoons chopped galangal root

1 knob turmeric root

3 kaffir lime leaves

½-pound skinless, boneless chicken breast, thinly sliced

2 tablespoons fresh-squeezed lemon juice

2 tablespoons fish sauce

3 shiitake mushrooms

1 tablespoon chopped green onion

1 tablespoon chili oil

1 tablespoon cilantro leaves

In a pan over low heat, warm the coconut milk with the lemongrass, chili, galangal, turmeric, and lime leaves for about 2 to 3 minutes, until fragrant. Add the chicken, increase heat to medium-low, and simmer, uncovered, until the chicken is cooked through. Add the lemon juice and fish sauce. Add the mushrooms and cook until just tender. Remove the galangal root. Serve in bowls, garnished with the green onion, chili oil, and cilantro leaves.

What Is Galangal?

Galangal is a root that you can find in many Asian specialty markets. Galangal gives a distinctive, lightly acid taste to dishes, and often galangal slices are added to various curries and soups. Some people even crush the bulb, boil it in water, and eat it to cure upset stomachs.

Green Mango and Shrimp Salad

Serves 4

This original creation by Chef Sean Beaton of Rendezvous Restaurant and Winery in Belize is rooted in Asian culture. You can substitute chayote for the green mango, and jicama for the green papaya.

20 medium shrimp, deveined and butterflied

3 green mangoes

1 carrot, peeled

2 tablespoons fish sauce

2 tablespoons fresh-squeezed lime juice

½ teaspoon granulated sugar

1 clove garlic, finely chopped

½ green onion, chopped

Chopped fresh cilantro, to taste

½ cup coconut cream

Dry shrimp powder

Unsalted roasted peanuts, crushed

1. Bring a large saucepan with water to a near boil. Add the shrimp. Poach the shrimp in the just simmering water until they turn pink. Be careful not to overcook. Drain the poached shrimp on paper towels.
2. Finely julienne the mango and carrot, and mix together in a large bowl.
3. In another large bowl, mix together the fish sauce, lime juice, sugar, and garlic until the sugar dissolves. Add the green onion, cilantro, and poached shrimp. Add the coconut cream and stir to mix.
4. Pour the shrimp mixture over the mango and carrot, and toss to mix. Garnish each serving with shrimp powder and crushed peanuts.

Eating Habits in Thailand

Thai people do not use knives and forks, but rather forks and spoons, holding the fork in their left hand to help get the food onto the spoon, held in the right hand. They then eat directly from the spoon. Most Western cultures eat with the fork because they have to cut their food, whereas in Thai food everything is usually precut. But beware: Stuffing your mouth is considered impolite, and you should avoid scraping the utensils against your plate. The Thai people also do not scoop portions onto their plates—instead, they share from a common dish, placed at the center of the table, taking only enough for a bite or two at a time.

Stir-Fried Asparagus, Oyster Mushrooms, and Shrimp in Garlic Sauce

8 ounces oyster mushrooms
¾ pound fresh medium-sized
    shrimp
¾ pound asparagus
2 cloves garlic
3 tablespoons vegetable oil
2 teaspoons oyster sauce

2 tablespoons fish sauce
½ teaspoon brown sugar
1 tablespoon chopped fresh
    cilantro leaves
¼ teaspoon chili paste with
    garlic

1. Wipe the oyster mushrooms clean with a damp cloth. Cut in half if the caps are very large. Rinse the shrimp in warm water and pat dry with paper towels. Remove the shells from the shrimp, but leave the tails intact. Wash the asparagus and drain thoroughly. Remove the tough ends and cut on the diagonal into 1-inch pieces. Smash, peel, and finely chop the garlic.

2. Heat a wok over high heat. Add the oil, swirling so that the entire surface is coated. When the oil is hot, add the garlic and stir-fry until fragrant (about 30 seconds). Add the shrimp and stir-fry until it turns pink. Add the asparagus pieces. Stir-fry for 1 minute, then add the mushrooms.

3. Stir in the oyster sauce, fish sauce, and brown sugar. Heat through and stir in the cilantro leaves, and chili paste if using. Serve hot.

Crab Spring Rolls

Yields 15 rolls

The key to keeping the fat to a minimum when deep-frying is using clean, hot cooking oil and immediately transferring the rolls to paper towels to absorb excess oil.

1 pound crabmeat, picked over to remove any shells, and shredded
1 tablespoon mayonnaise
¼–½ teaspoon grated lime peel
15 spring roll or egg roll wrappers
2 egg yolks, lightly beaten
Canola oil for deep frying
15 small, tender Boston lettuce leaves
Mint leaves
Parsley leaves

1. In a small bowl, mix the crabmeat with the mayonnaise and lime peel.
2. Place 1 tablespoon of the crabmeat mixture in the center of 1 spring roll wrapper. Fold a pointed end of the wrapper over the crabmeat, then fold the opposite point over the top of the folded point. Brush a bit of the egg yolk over the top of the exposed wrapper, then fold the bottom point over the crabmeat and roll to form a tight packet; set aside. Repeat with the remaining crabmeat and wrappers.
3. Heat the oil to 365° in a skillet or deep fryer. Deep-fry the rolls 3 to 4 at a time for 2 minutes or so, until they are a golden brown; drain on paper towels.
4. To serve, wrap each spring roll in a wrapper with a single piece of lettuce, and a sprinkling of mint and parsley. Serve with your favorite dipping sauce.

Defining Thai Cuisine

Like the word *Thai* (which means "free"), Thai cooks are often flexible in their cooking, not bogged down by exact measurements. Thai food combines the best of several Eastern cuisines: the bite of Szechwan Chinese, the tropical flavor of Malaysian, the coconut creaminess of southern Indian, and the aromatic spices of Arabian food. Thai food is often made hot using chilies, and then toned down with the addition of locally grown roots and aromatic herbs.

Hot and Sour Prawn Soup

Serves 4

For extra flavor, crush the prawn shells with a mortar and pestle and add them to the broth. If using the shells, strain the soup before serving.

1 pound medium-sized fresh
    prawns, shelled and
    deveined
15-ounce can straw mushrooms
8-ounce can baby corn
4 hot Thai chilies (prig hang)
1 lemongrass stalk
4 kaffir lime leaves
4 cups water

1 cup chicken or fish stock
1 tablespoon freshly squeezed
    lemon juice
2 tablespoons freshly squeezed
    lime juice
1 tablespoon fish sauce
2 tablespoons soy sauce
1 teaspoon brown sugar
2 tablespoons chopped cilantro

1. Soak the prawns in warm salted water for 5 minutes, and pat dry with paper towels. Chop into small pieces. Rinse the mushrooms and baby corn under warm running water and drain. Thinly slice the mushrooms.
2. Cut the chili peppers in half, remove the seeds, and chop thinly. (Wear plastic gloves while working with the chilies and wash your hands afterward.) Bruise the lemongrass by pounding it with a mallet and thinly slice. Finely chop the kaffir leaves.
3. In a medium saucepan, bring the water, stock, and the lemongrass to a boil. Reduce heat and simmer, covered, for 15 minutes, until the water and stock is infused with the lemongrass flavor.
4. Add the kaffir leaves, chilies, lemon juice, lime juice, mushrooms, and baby corn. Simmer for 2 minutes, then stir in the fish sauce, soy sauce, and brown sugar. Add the prawns, heat through. Garnish with the chopped cilantro just before serving.

Bananas in Coconut Milk

6 medium bananas,
   not over-ripe
¾ cup thick coconut milk
¾ cup thin coconut milk

⅓ cup granulated sugar
¼ teaspoon ground cinnamon
3 tablespoons crushed peanuts

Serves 4–6

This is a simple version of a popular Thai treat. For added decadence, top with a dollop of "ice cream" made from coconut milk.

1. Peel the bananas and cut on the diagonal into 2-inch pieces.
2. In a medium saucepan, bring the coconut milk to a boil. Add the sugar, stirring to dissolve. Stir in the ground cinnamon.
3. Add the sliced banana. Reduce the heat and allow the bananas to simmer, uncovered, until the bananas are softened but not mushy (3 to 5 minutes, depending on the ripeness of the banana). To serve, spoon the heated bananas and coconut milk into dessert bowls. Sprinkle the crushed peanuts over top.

History of Thai Cuisine

Thai cuisine, known worldwide for its blend of aromatic herbs, fragrant spices, and colorful presentation, was born out of a centuries-old tradition. The cuisine of Thailand is, like many, the synthesis of styles from different races of people in the country. Thai food ranges from simple home cooking for the family, to the "Royal Cuisine," which, in the past, was prepared only in the inner court's palace and served solely to royal and aristocratic households and their guests.

Tom Ka Kai

Serves 4–6

This soup can be served as is or ladled over mounds of rice in individual serving bowls. It goes great with some cooked noodles thrown in.

2 cups chicken broth
1 teaspoon sliced kaffir lime leaves
1 (2-inch) piece lemongrass, bruised
1 (1-inch) piece ginger, sliced thinly
4 tablespoons fish sauce

2 tablespoons lime juice
1 boneless, skinless chicken breast, cut into bite-sized pieces
5 ounces coconut milk
2–4 Thai chilies (to taste), slightly crushed

1. In a medium-sized soup pot, heat the broth on medium. Add the lime leaves, lemongrass, ginger, fish sauce, and lime juice.
2. Bring the mixture to a boil, add the chicken and coconut milk, and bring to a boil again.
3. Reduce the heat, add the chilies, and cover; let simmer until the chicken is cooked through, about 3 to 5 minutes.
4. Remove the chilies and the lemongrass stalk with a slotted spoon before serving.

Quick Thai Favorites

Next time you scroll through a Thai menu, why not try a few of these: *tom yam koong* (lemon-flavored sour shrimp soup); *hor mok* (a seafood dish with a red curry custard base); *tom kha kai* (a mild spicy chicken soup with coconut milk); *tod man* (a savory deep-fried fish or prawn quenelles); *chor ladda* or *chor muang* (minced pork or prawn dumplings); *kang khieu wan kai* (thick green chicken curry); *kang masaman* (southern Thai beef and potatoes curry); *mee krob* (deep-fried rice vermicelli).

Pumpkin Curry Soup

1 pound kabocha squash
2 kaffir leaves
4 cups chicken or vegetable
   stock
1 cup unsweetened coconut
   milk
2 teaspoons freshly squeezed
   lime juice

2 tablespoons palm sugar
2 tablespoons chili paste, or to
   taste
Fresh Thai basil leaves, as
   garnish

Serves 4–6

Thai basil has a distinctive flavor similar to licorice or anise. Both Thai basil and kabocha squash can be found at Asian markets.

1. Cut the kabocha in half, remove the seed and stringy pith in the middle. Peel off the greenish skin and cut into 1½-inch chunks. Chop the kaffir leaves.
2. In a large saucepan, bring the chicken stock, coconut milk, kabocha, kaffir leaves, lime juice, and palm sugar to a boil. Reduce the heat to low and simmer, partially covered, until the kabocha is tender when pierced with a fork (about 20 minutes). Stir in the chili paste.
3. Purée the broth in a blender or food processor. Pour into soup bowls and garnish with the Thai basil.

What Is Curry?

Curry is an English word most probably derived from the South Indian word *kaikaari*. Kaikaari, or kaari, referred to vegetables cooked with spices and coconut. In India curry means gravy. In America many believe curry is an Indian spice, but curry powder is actually a blend of spices, mainly garam masala mixed with ground coriander and turmeric. There is a plant, however, that has leaves that are called curry leaves (*meetha neem* in Hindi) or kadhi leaves. They look like tiny lemon leaves and grow wild in most forest regions of India and are used as a seasoning.

Bangkok-Style Roasted Pork Tenderloin

Serves 4

This is a great dish to make when you're in a hurry. Serve with a salad, some vegetables, and rice, and you can still have the whole meal ready in less than 30 minutes.

1 teaspoon salt

¼ teaspoon ground ginger

¼ teaspoon ground cardamom

¼–½ teaspoon freshly ground black pepper

2 (1-pound) pork tenderloins, trimmed

Olive oil

½ cup chicken, pork, or vegetable stock, or water

1. Place rack on bottom third of the oven, then preheat the oven to 500°.
2. Combine the spices in a small bowl.
3. Rub each of the tenderloins with half of the spice mixture and a bit of olive oil. Place the tenderloins in a roasting pan and cook for 10 minutes.
4. Turn the tenderloins over and roast for 10 more minutes or until done to your liking.
5. Transfer the pork to a serving platter, cover with foil, and let rest.
6. Pour off any fat that has accumulated in the roasting pan. Place the pan on the stovetop over high heat and add the stock (or water). Bring to a boil, scraping the bottom of the pan to loosen any cooked-on bits. Season with salt and pepper to taste.
7. To serve, slice the tenderloins into thin slices. Pour a bit of the sauce over top, passing more separately at the table.

Sweet and Savory Grilled Coconut-Rice Hotcakes

3 (14-ounce) cans coconut milk
¼ cup, plus 2 tablespoons granulated sugar (keep separate)
2½ tablespoons tapioca starch or arrowroot flour
3 tablespoons uncooked short-grain white rice
⅓ cup finely shredded fresh coconut

2 cups rice flour
2 teaspoons sea salt
2–3 tablespoons peanut or corn oil

Optional filling ingredients:
¼ cup sliced green onions
¼ cup fresh corn kernels
2 tablespoons chopped fresh cilantro leaves

> **Serves 6**
>
> Executive Chef Sean O'Connell of Banyan Tree Phuket offers this wonderful recipe inspired by the restaurant's tropical location. If you can't find fresh coconut, substitute ¼ cup dried, unsweetened shredded coconut.

1. Do not shake the cans of coconut milk before opening. Spoon off the thickest cream from the top of the cans to yield 1¾ cups. Heat the coconut cream in a saucepan, just enough to smooth out the lumps. Add the ¼ cup sugar to the coconut cream and stir to dissolve. Let cool, and mix in 2 tablespoons of the tapioca starch. Stir until smooth. Set aside.

2. Pour the remaining coconut milk from the cans into a large bowl and stir until smooth. (Heat it if necessary to melt the coagulated parts, and let cool.) Grind the uncooked white rice in a clean coffee grinder as finely as possible. Do the same with the shredded coconut. Add the ground rice and coconut, the rice flour, salt, and remaining 2 tablespoons sugar to the bowl with the thin coconut milk. Stir and mix until well blended and smooth. (This is the main rice batter.)

3. Heat a well-seasoned pancake griddle on the stove. When the griddle is hot, lightly brush the surface with the oil. Wait a few seconds before spooning the rice batter onto the griddle. The batter should sizzle when it hits the hot metal.

4. Immediately add a dab of the sweet coconut-cream mixture over the top to fill the indentations, and sprinkle the center of each hotcake with a little of one of the optional toppings, or leave plain. Cover with a round lid and cook for a few minutes, until the hotcakes are firm and crispy brown on the bottom. Remove gently with a spoon and place on a cooling rack. Regrease the griddle before making the next batch. Because rice flour tends to settle, stir the batter well each time before pouring it onto the griddle. Serve warm.

Lemongrass Chicken Skewers

Serves 4

These chicken skewers are based on a recipe from award-winning chef Jean-Georges Vongerichten, whose French-inspired Thai cuisine has won praise the world over. Vongerichten has a line of tasty sauces and marinades that is available in stores.

5 stalks lemongrass, trimmed
12 large cubes chicken breast
    meat, a little over 1 ounce
    each
Black pepper
2 tablespoons vegetable oil,
    divided

Pinch of dried red pepper flakes
Juice of 1 lime
2 teaspoons fish sauce
Pinch of sugar
Sea salt to taste

1. Remove 2 inches from the thick end of each stalk of lemongrass; set aside. Bruise 4 of the lemongrass stalks with the back of a knife. Remove the tough outer layer of the fifth stalk, exposing the tender core; mince.
2. Skewer 3 cubes of chicken on each lemongrass stalk. Sprinkle the skewers with the minced lemongrass and black pepper, and drizzle with 1 tablespoon of oil. Cover with plastic wrap and refrigerate for 12 to 24 hours.
3. Chop all of the reserved lemongrass stalk ends. Place in a small saucepan and cover with water. Bring to a boil, cover, and let reduce until approximately 2 tablespoons of liquid are left; strain. Return the liquid to the saucepan and further reduce to 1 tablespoon.
4. Combine the lemongrass liquid with the red pepper flakes, lime juice, fish sauce, sugar, and remaining tablespoon of oil; set aside.
5. Prepare a grill to high heat. Grill the chicken skewers for approximately 2 to 3 minutes per side, or until done to your liking.
6. To serve, spoon a little of the lemongrass sauce over the top of each skewer and sprinkle with sea salt.

Sambal Bunchies (Green Beans)

½ pound green beans, washed
  and cut into 3-inch-long
  pieces
1 jalapeño chili pepper
¼ lemongrass stalk

2 cloves garlic
½ teaspoon palm or brown
  sugar
1 teaspoon shrimp paste.
1 cup vegetable oil

1. Wash the green beans, drain, and cut into 2-inch-long pieces. Cut the jalapeño in half, remove the seeds, and finely chop. Finely chop the lemongrass stalk. Smash, peel, and finely chop the garlic.

2. In a food processor, purée the chopped chili pepper, garlic, and the lemongrass pieces. Add the palm sugar and shrimp paste and process again. The sauce should have a paste-like consistency.

3. Heat the wok over high heat. Add 1 cup of oil. When the oil is hot, add the green beans. Let the beans cook in the hot oil for 1 minute, then remove with a slotted spoon. Remove all but 2 teaspoons oil from the wok.

4. Turn the heat down to medium-high and add the shrimp paste mixture. Stir for 30 seconds. Add the green beans back into the pan. Mix with the sauce and serve hot.

Herbs and Spice and Everything Nice

Twenty-seven main herbs and spices form the foundation of Thai cooking. There are several basils, including horapa, ga-prow, and manglug, and more than ten types of chilies. Other favorites include garlic, mint, sesame (usually as oil), mace (the outer shell of nutmeg), nutmeg, lemongrass, bay leaves, cloves, cardamon, cinnamon, cumin, ginger, galangal (a fragrant root similar to ginger), gra-shai (a type of ginger added to fish curries), turmeric, kaffir lime, mandarin oranges, and jasmine (used as a scent in drinking water, tea, and desserts).

Pad Thai

Serves 4

Tart tamarind water can be purchased at Asian markets. If unavailable, substitute 3 tablespoons lemon juice mixed with 1 tablespoon tomato sauce.

½ pound dried rice stick noodles (rice vermicelli)

½ pound firm tofu

2 large eggs

⅛ teaspoon salt

2 green onions

1 cup mung bean sprouts

¼ cup vegetable or peanut oil

2 cloves garlic, chopped

1 teaspoon minced ginger

½ pound small shrimp

¼ cup tamarind water

2 tablespoons fish sauce or soy sauce

3 tablespoons fresh-squeezed lime juice

2 teaspoons granulated sugar

2 teaspoons brown sugar

¼ cup warm water

⅓ cup ground unsalted roasted peanuts

2 limes or lemons, cut into wedges

1. Soak the rice vermicelli in warm water for 20 minutes, or until the noodles are softened and slippery. Drain thoroughly. Place the tofu on a plate lined with paper towels, and cover with a book or plate to squeeze out the water. Drain the water from the plate and change the paper towels as needed. Cut the drained tofu into 1-inch cubes.
2. In a small bowl, lightly beat the eggs with the salt. Wash the green onions and cut into 1-inch pieces. Rinse and drain the mung bean sprouts.
3. Heat the wok. Add the oil and heat over medium-high heat until very hot. Add the garlic and ginger and stir-fry for 30 seconds until aromatic. Add the shrimp and stir-fry until they turn pink. Stir-fry for 1 minute, then add the tamarind water, fish sauce, lime juice, and sugars, stirring the entire time.
4. Push the ingredients up to the sides of the wok. Add the beaten eggs into the middle of the pan, and quickly scramble. Add the noodles, mung bean sprouts, and green onion, stirring the entire time. Add as much of the warm water as needed.
5. Sprinkle the crushed peanuts over top. Garnish with the lime or lemon wedges.

Fire Noodles

Serves 4–6

If you bite into a chili that is just too hot to handle, try sucking on a spoonful of sugar or sucking on a hard candy.

15–20 (or to taste) Thai bird chilies, stemmed and seeded

5–10 (or to taste) cloves garlic

1 pound presliced fresh rice noodles (available at Asian grocery stores and on the Internet)

2 tablespoons vegetable oil

2 whole, boneless, skinless chicken breasts, cut into bite-sized pieces

2 tablespoons fish sauce

2 tablespoons sweet black soy sauce

1 tablespoon oyster sauce

1 teaspoon white pepper

1½ tablespoons sugar

1 (8-ounce) can bamboo shoots, drained

1½ cups loose-packed basil and/or mint

1. Place the chilies and garlic cloves in a food processor and process until thoroughly mashed together; set aside.
2. Bring a kettle of water to a boil. Place the noodles in a large colander and pour the hot water over them. Carefully unfold and separate the noodles; set aside.
3. Heat the oil in a wok or large skillet over medium-high heat. When it is quite hot, carefully add the reserved chili-garlic mixture and stir-fry for 15 seconds to release the aromas.
4. Raise the heat to high, add the chicken, and stir-fry until it begins to lose its color, about 30 seconds.
5. Stir in the fish sauce, soy sauce, oyster sauce, white pepper, and sugar.
6. Add the noodles and continue to stir-fry for 30 seconds, tossing them with the other ingredients.
7. Add the bamboo shoots and cook for another minute.
8. Turn off the heat and add the basil.

Spicy Scallops

Serves 4

These scallops are simple to make but are sure to impress even your fussiest guests. They are also tasty over pasta as a main course. Make sure to use the freshest scallops you can find.

1 teaspoon vegetable oil
1 clove garlic, minced
1 jalapeño, seeded and minced
1 (½-inch) piece ginger, peeled and minced

⅛ teaspoon ground coriander
2 tablespoons soy sauce
2 tablespoons water
8 large scallops, cleaned

1. In a pan large enough to hold all of the scallops, heat the oil over medium heat. Add the garlic, jalapeño, and ginger, and stir-fry for about 1 minute.
2. Add the coriander, soy sauce, and water, stirring to combine; simmer for 2 to 3 minutes. Strain the liquid through a fine-mesh sieve. Allow the pan to cool slightly.
3. Add the scallops to the pan and spoon the reserved liquid over the top of them. Return the pan to the stove, increasing the heat to medium-high. Cover the pan and let the scallops steam for about 2 to 3 minutes, or until done to your liking. Serve immediately.

Thai Beef with Rice Noodles

Serves 2–4

You can use a bag of organic baby spinach leaves for the greens in this recipe to make it easier—they are prewashed and small enough that you can skip the process of cutting them into strips.

¾ pound sirloin, trimmed of all fat, rinsed, and patted dry
½ pound dried rice noodles
¼ cup soy sauce
2 tablespoons fish sauce
2 tablespoons dark brown sugar
Freshly ground black pepper
5 tablespoons vegetable oil, divided
2 tablespoons minced garlic
1 pound greens (such as spinach or bok choy), cleaned and cut into ½-inch strips
2 eggs, beaten
Crushed dried red pepper flakes to taste
Rice vinegar to taste

1. Slice the meat into 2-inch-long, ½-inch-wide strips.
2. Cover the noodles with warm water for 5 minutes, then drain.
3. In a small bowl, combine the soy sauce, fish sauce, brown sugar, and black pepper; set aside.
4. Heat a wok or heavy skillet over high heat. Add approximately 2 tablespoons of the vegetable oil. When the oil is hot, but not smoking, add the garlic. After stirring for 5 seconds, add the greens and stir-fry for approximately 2 minutes; set aside.
5. Add 2 more tablespoons of oil to the wok. Add the beef and stir-fry until browned on all sides, about 2 minutes; set aside.
6. Heat 1 tablespoon of oil in the wok and add the noodles. Toss until warmed through, approximately 2 minutes; set aside.
7. Heat the oil remaining in the wok. Add the eggs and cook, without stirring until they are set, about 30 seconds. Break up the eggs slightly and stir in the reserved noodles, beef, and greens, and the red pepper flakes. Stir the reserved soy mixture, then add it to the wok. Toss to coat and heat through. Serve immediately with rice vinegar to sprinkle over the top.

Crispy Crepes with Fresh Fruits

1 package frozen puff pastry sheets, thawed according to package instructions
2 tablespoons confectioners' sugar, divided
2 cups raspberries, blueberries, or other fresh fruit, the best 12 berries reserved for garnish
1 cup heavy cream
¼ cup shredded, unsweetened coconut
1 tablespoon unflavored rum or coconut-flavored rum

1. Preheat the oven to 400°.
2. Place the puff pastry sheet on a work surface and cut into 12 equal-sized pieces. Place the pastry pieces on a baking sheet.
3. Bake the pastry approximately 10 minutes. Remove from the oven and use a sifter to shake a bit of the confectioners' sugar over the puff pastry. Return to the oven and continue baking for approximately 5 minutes or until golden. Place the puff pastry on a wire rack and let cool to room temperature.
4. Place the berries in a food processor and briefly process to form a rough purée.
5. Whip the cream with the remaining confectioners' sugar until thick, but not stiff. Stir in the coconut and the rum.
6. To serve, place 1 piece of puff pastry in the middle of each serving plate, spoon some cream over the pastry, and then top with some purée. Place another pastry on top, garnish with some of the remaining berries, any leftover juice from the purée, and a sprinkle of confectioners' sugar.

Chapter 33

China:
New Food for
the New Year

450 Watermelon with Beef and Tangerine Herb

451 Steamed Tilapia with Mushrooms and
Black Bean Sauce

451 Steamed Prawns with Crushed Garlic

452 Tomato Egg-Flower Soup

453 Snail in Black Bean and Orange Peel Sauce

454 Lemon Chicken

455 Pork and Crab Lumpia

456 Stuffed Red Peppers

456 Achara

457 Sesame Chicken

458 Lobster Cantonese

459 Asparagus with Pork

460 Straits Sea Bass

461 Pork and Ginger Pot Stickers

462 Tommy Toy's Minced Squab Imperial

463 Wok-Seared Beef Medallions with Asparagus Tips

464 Tommy Toy's Four Seasons Fried Rice

465 Honey Walnut Shrimp

466 Mango Chicken

467 Ham with Asian Pear

468 Dry Ginger Beef

469 Savory Shanghai Noodles

Watermelon with Beef and Tangerine Herb

Serves 2

Joseph Poon, chef/owner of Asian Fusion Restaurant in Philadelphia, leads diners on a journey of taste and flavor that includes all the regions of China.

Marinade:

½ tablespoon light soy sauce

3 tablespoons port wine or red wine

¼ cup water

2 teaspoons sesame oil

1 teaspoon cornstarch

Watermelon beef:

½ pound lean sirloin tip beef, sliced

1 tablespoon soybean oil

1 teaspoon minced garlic

1 teaspoon minced ginger

1 cup seeded and sliced watermelon

1 tangerine peel, soaked in sherry

½ cup snow peas

¼ red bell pepper, cubed

¼ yellow bell pepper, cubed

¼ red onion, cubed

Stir–fry sauce:

½ cup water or veal stock

½ teaspoon oyster sauce

½ teaspoon light soy sauce

1 teaspoon granulated sugar

3 tablespoons port wine or red wine

1 tablespoon hoisin sauce

½ teaspoon cornstarch, dissolved in 1 tablespoon water

Garnish:

4 drops sesame oil

Watermelon wedges

1. Mix together all the marinade ingredients and add the beef. Marinate for at least 30 minutes at room temperature. Sauté the beef in a nonstick pan over medium-high heat until brown on all sides. Set aside.

2. Heat the soybean oil on medium-high in a wok or large sauté pan. Add the garlic, ginger, watermelon, and tangerine, and sauté for 30 seconds. Add all the peas, bell peppers, and onions, stirring constantly to sweat the onions and peppers.

3. Mix together all the stir-fry sauce ingredients except the cornstarch and add it to the wok, stirring to mix. Bring to a boil. Pour in the dissolved cornstarch to thicken the sauce, add the beef, and mix thoroughly.

4. Spoon onto serving plates and top each with a couple drops of sesame oil. Garnish with triangular wedge of watermelon, if desired.

Steamed Tilapia with Mushrooms and Black Bean Sauce

*8 to 12 ounces fresh tilapia,
cleaned*
1 pinch salt
*2–3 Chinese mushrooms,
shredded*
1 tablespoon minced ginger

*1 tablespoon canned black
beans, drained*
½ cup diced green onions
1 teaspoon hot chili oil
*¼ cup light soy sauce, or as
needed*

Place the fish in a metal steamer over a saucepan filled with boiling water. Sprinkle the salt, mushrooms, ginger, black beans, and green onions on the top of the fish. Steam for 10 to 15 minutes (depending on the size), until the flesh flakes easily when tested with a fork. Drizzle the hot chili oil over top. Serve with light soy sauce for dipping.

> **Serves 2**
>
> Another recipe by Chef Joseph Poon. He suggests "steaming the tilapia a bit longer if it is on the larger size." Perch can be used instead in this recipe if tilapia is unavailable.

Steamed Prawns with Crushed Garlic

½ pound prawns
5 garlic cloves, crushed
½ teaspoon salt

½ teaspoon chicken bouillon
*½ cup, plus 2 tablespoons
vegetable oil*

1. Cut open the top ¼ inch of each prawn and remove the intestine. Rinse clean and set aside.
2. Crush the garlic cloves and place in a heat-resistant bowl. Stir in the salt and chicken bouillon. Bring the oil to a boil and pour it into the bowl of crushed garlic. Stir, and let cool. Spread the mixture on the open tops of the prawns.
3. Fill a steamer with water and bring to a boil. Place prawns on a deep plate and place in steamer and cover. Steam the prawns for 5 minutes. Serve.

> **Serves 6**
>
> This flavorful dish is a signature dish that is enjoyed in many of Hong Kong's finest restaurants.

Tomato Egg-Flower Soup

Serves 4

Beef and tomato are a natural combination. For a heartier soup, add ½ cup of ground beef or lean beef.

4 cups beef broth
2 medium tomatoes
⅛ teaspoon white pepper
¼ teaspoon salt
½ teaspoon sugar
1 teaspoon Chinese rice wine or
   dry sherry

1 tablespoon cornstarch
4 tablespoons water
1 egg white, lightly beaten
2 green onions, minced
A few drops of sesame oil

1. Bring the 4 cups of beef broth to a boil.
2. Bring a large pot of water to a boil. Blanch the tomatoes briefly in the boiling water. (This will make it easier to remove the peel.) Peel the tomatoes and cut each into 6 equal pieces.
3. When the beef broth comes to a boil, add the white pepper, salt, sugar, rice wine, and tomatoes. Bring the broth back to boiling.
4. Mix the cornstarch and water, and pour it into the soup, stirring to thicken. Turn off the heat.
5. Pour the egg white into the soup and quickly stir in a clockwise direction to form thin shreds.
6. Add the green onions and a few drops of sesame oil. Give the soup a final stir.

Cholesterol Concerns

Using egg whites instead of eggs in the Egg Drop Soup–type recipes helps reduce the amount of cholesterol. Another option is to forgo the egg altogether—heartier soups taste fine without it.

Snail in Black Bean and Orange Peel Sauce

Serves 2

In this recipe, Chef Poon creates a unique Asian-style version of the classic French dish, escargots.

Several large lettuce or cabbage leaves

1–1½ pounds fresh snails

1 tablespoon vegetable oil

1 teaspoon chopped fresh garlic

1 teaspoon chopped fresh ginger

½ cup mix of diced red, yellow, and green bell peppers

¼ cup diced white onion

1 tablespoon fermented black beans

1 tablespoon lemon zest

1 tablespoon dried orange peel, softened in water

½ cup Chardonnay

1 cup chicken broth

1 tablespoon oyster sauce

1 teaspoon mushroom soy sauce

1 teaspoon light soy sauce

1 tablespoon granulated sugar

2 tablespoons cornstarch dissolved in 4 tablespoons water

1 teaspoon sesame oil

1. Line a bamboo steaming basket with lettuce or cabbage leaves. Place the snails on the leaves and place the basket in a wok half-filled with boiling water. Steam the snails until cooked through (8 to 10 minutes) and place on a serving plate.

2. Heat the oil in a frying pan on high heat. When the oil is hot, add the garlic and ginger and stir-fry until fragrant (about 30 seconds). Add the bell peppers, onion, and black beans. Stir-fry for several minutes, until the peppers and onion are tender. Stir in all the remaining ingredients except the sesame oil and cook for several minutes on high heat. Add the sesame oil at the last minute (otherwise it will lose its favor). Pour the sauce over the top of the cooked snails.

Lemon Chicken

Serves 4

Fresh lemon makes the perfect garnish for this delicately flavored dish. Serve with basmati or jasmine steamed scented rice.

1 pound skinless, boneless chicken breasts, cut into 1-inch cubes

4 tablespoons soy sauce, divided

2 tablespoons cornstarch, divided

1 red bell pepper

1 green bell pepper

1 bunch green onions

6 tablespoons water, divided

1 tablespoon granulated sugar

2 tablespoons freshly squeezed lemon juice

¾ teaspoon lemon peel, grated

4 tablespoons vegetable oil, divided

1 slice ginger, unpeeled

1. Place the chicken cubes in a medium bowl. Add 2 tablespoons of the soy sauce and 1 tablespoon cornstarch, using your fingers to mix in the cornstarch. Cover and marinate in the refrigerator for 30 minutes. Remove the stems and seeds from the bell peppers and cut into cubes. Chop the green onion on the diagonal into 1-inch pieces.

2. Meanwhile, combine the remaining 2 tablespoons soy sauce, ¼ cup water, sugar, lemon juice, and grated lemon peel. Set aside. Mix the remaining 1 tablespoon of cornstarch in 2 tablespoons of water to make a cornstarch "slurry." Set aside.

3. Heat 2 tablespoons oil in a preheated wok over high heat. Add the chicken cubes into the pan. Brown briefly; then stir-fry until the chicken turns white and is nearly cooked through. Remove and drain on paper towels.

4. Heat the remaining oil in the wok over high heat. When the oil is hot, add the ginger. Stir-fry for 30 seconds until fragrant. Add the cubed green pepper. Stir-fry for 1 minute, and add the red pepper cubes.

5. Push the peppers up to the side. Add the sauce into the middle of the wok. Add the cornstarch slurry to the sauce, stirring quickly to thicken. Add the chicken back into the pan. Stir in the green onions. Stir to lightly glaze the chicken and peppers with the lemony sauce. Serve immediately, removing the ginger before serving.

Pork and Crab Lumpia

2 to 3 tablespoons crabmeat,
  as needed
¼ pound ground pork
1 egg, lightly beaten
1 tablespoon minced green
  onions
1 tablespoon minced water
  chestnuts

1 teaspoon fresh minced ginger
Salt and pepper, to taste
Pinch granulated sugar
8 spring roll wrappers
Vegetable oil, as needed

Serves 4

This recipe from Executive Chef Michael Viloria of Vancouver, British Columbia, is considered a wonderful accompaniment to an elaborate Filipino feast. Serve with Achara (page 456).

1. In a medium-sized bowl, mix together the crabmeat, pork, and egg. In a small bowl, mix together the scallions, water chestnut, and ginger, and add to the crabmeat mixture. Add the salt, pepper, and sugar, and mix thoroughly.
2. Place a wrapper on a flat surface diagonally. Place ⅛ of the mixture onto the wrapper. Shape the mixture into a tube shape and roll the sides of the spring roll wrapper in toward the center. Fold the bottom of the wrapper over the top of the filling and roll it away from you into the shape of a cylinder (instructions on how to roll the spring rolls should be on the package of the wrappers). Repeat with the remaining wrappers and filling.
3. Fill a pot ⅓ of the way with vegetable oil and heat on medium. Deep-fry the lumpias until golden brown (you may have to turn them occasionally so they cook evenly). Serve.

Stuffed Red Peppers

Serves 1

The Chinese version of miso, brown bean sauce is made with soybeans and spicy seasonings such as chili and garlic.

1 red bell pepper
1 cup ground pork
1 tablespoon brown bean sauce
2 tablespoons soy sauce, divided

½ teaspoon sugar
1 teaspoon Chinese rice wine or dry sherry
1 green onion, minced
1 clove garlic, chopped

1. Preheat the oven to 300°F.
2. Wash the red pepper; cut off the top and set it aside. Remove the seeds.
3. In a medium-sized bowl, use your hands to mix the ground pork with the brown bean sauce, 1 tablespoon soy sauce, sugar, and rice wine. Add the green onion and chopped garlic.
4. Stuff the red pepper with the ground pork mixture. Add 1 tablespoon soy sauce on top and replace the lid. Place in a heatproof dish in the oven, and bake until the pork is cooked through, about 45–55 minutes.

Achara

Serves 3–4 (as a sauce)

Inspired by a classic Filippino dish, this sweet and tangy treat tastes great served over rice or noodles.

1 habanero chili pepper
1 green papaya
½ large carrot
2-inch piece daikon radish

3 tablespoons granulated sugar
⅓ cup cider or Asian rice vinegar
1 teaspoon salt

1. Deseed the red chili pepper. Peel the papaya and the carrot. Thinly slice the papaya, carrot, daikon radish, and the chili pepper lengthwise to resemble matchsticks.
2. Whisk together the sugar, rice vinegar, and salt. Add to the papaya mixture and refrigerate, covered, for 1 hour to give the flavors a chance to blend. Use within a few days.

Sesame Chicken

10 chicken thighs
3 tablespoons light soy sauce
2 tablespoons Chinese rice wine or dry sherry
1 teaspoon grated ginger
1 green onion, chopped

2 tablespoons cornstarch
4 tablespoons white sesame seeds
6 cups peanut oil for deep-frying

1. Cut the chicken thighs in half across the thigh bone, and place in a shallow dish. In a small bowl, mix together the soy sauce, rice wine, grated ginger, green onion, and cornstarch. Cover and marinate the chicken thighs in the refrigerator for 1 hour, turning over once to make sure all the chicken is evenly coated in the marinade.
2. While the chicken is marinating, toast the sesame seeds. Spread the seeds out in a frying pan and cook on medium heat, shaking the pan continuously, until the seeds are browned. Remove the toasted seeds from the pan and cool.
3. In a large pot, bring the peanut oil to 375°. Carefully slide ¼ of the marinated chicken pieces into the hot oil and deep-fry until golden brown. Remove the chicken from the wok with a slotted spoon and drain on paper towels. Continue deep-frying the remainder of the chicken.
4. Sprinkle the toasted sesame seeds over the chicken and serve hot.

Why Chopsticks, Not Knives, at the Table?

You probably expect to receive a pair of chopsticks when you sit down to a meal in a Chinese restaurant. In fact, the Chinese were using chopsticks long before Europeans were lifting forks and spoons to their mouths. The knife was invented earlier—but as a weapon, not a cooking utensil. It turns out chopsticks were advocated by the famed Chinese philosopher Confucius. His reason? That as an advancing society, instruments used for killing should be banned from the dining table. Thus knives were not permitted, and that is why Chinese food is always chopped into bite-size pieces before it reaches the table.

Lobster Cantonese

1 teaspoon fermented black
    beans
1 clove garlic, minced
¾ cup chicken broth
2 tablespoons Chinese rice
    wine or dry sherry, divided
1 tablespoon soy sauce
2 tablespoons oil for stir-frying
¼ pound ground pork

3 slices ginger, minced
1 green onion, thinly sliced
1 tablespoon cornstarch mixed
    with 4 tablespoons water
2 lobster tails, cut into ½-inch
    pieces
1 teaspoon sugar
1 egg, lightly beaten

1. Soak the beans in warm water and rinse. Mash, chop finely, and mix with the garlic clove.
2. Combine the chicken broth, 1 tablespoon rice wine, and soy sauce. Set aside.
3. Add oil to a preheated wok or skillet. When oil is hot, add the garlic and black bean mixture. Stir-fry briefly until aromatic. Add the pork and stir-fry for several minutes, until cooked through.
4. Push the ingredients up to the side of the wok. Add the ginger and green onion in the middle. Stir-fry briefly. Add the sauce and bring to a boil. Give the cornstarch-and-water mixture a quick stir and add, stirring quickly to thicken.
5. Add the lobster, the sugar, and 1 tablespoon rice wine. Stir-fry for about 2 minutes, then stream in the egg. Mix together and serve.

Preparing Fermented Black Beans
Soak the beans until they are softened. Mash the beans by flattening them under the blade of a knife or cleaver, and then mince or chop as called for in the recipe.

Asparagus with Pork

¼ pound lean ground pork

1 tablespoon light soy sauce

2 teaspoons sesame oil

1 green onion, washed and
    diced

1 teaspoon cornstarch

¼ cup low-sodium chicken
    broth

1 tablespoon oyster sauce

1 tablespoon dark soy sauce

1 teaspoon granulated sugar

3 ounces fresh shiitake
    mushrooms

½ white onion

4 cups water

1 pound fresh asparagus,
    trimmed

2 tablespoons vegetable oil

> **Serves 4**
>
> To enhance the savory flavor of this dish, use vegetarian oyster sauce, made with mushrooms instead of boiled oysters.

1. In a small bowl, combine the ground pork with the soy sauce, sesame oil, diced green onion, and cornstarch, making sure to add the cornstarch last. Marinate the pork for 15 minutes.

2. Combine the chicken broth, oyster sauce, dark soy sauce, and sugar in a small bowl. Set aside. Wipe the mushrooms clean with a damp cloth and cut into thick slices. Peel and finely chop the white onion.

3. Heat the water to boiling. Add the asparagus and blanch for 1 minute, or until the asparagus turns bright green and is tender but still firm. Plunge into a bowl filled with cold water. Remove and drain thoroughly. Lay the asparagus spears on a large serving platter and keep warm.

4. Heat the oil in a preheated wok or large skillet over medium-high heat. Add the marinated ground pork, using chopsticks or a spatula to separate the individual pork bits. Stir-fry for approximately 1 minute, until the pork changes color and is nearly cooked.

5. Push the ground pork up to the side of the wok or skillet. Add the onion, and stir-fry for 1 minute. Add the mushrooms and stir-fry for 2 more minutes. Turn the heat to high and add the chicken broth mixture to the middle of the pan. Mix everything together. To serve, pour the pork and mushroom mixture over the asparagus.

Straits Sea Bass

Serves 6

Christopher Yeo, owner and executive chef of Straits Restaurants, is among the first restaurateurs to bring authentic Singaporean cuisine to the San Francisco Bay Area. Wolfberry is available at Asian markets.

6 (6-ounce) sea bass fillets, 1-inch thick
1 red bell pepper, julienned
1 yellow bell pepper, julienned
1 green bell pepper, julienned
12 shiitake mushrooms, julienned
2-inch piece ginger, julienned
6 teaspoons dried longan (or litchi)

3 teaspoons wolfberry
6 teaspoons sesame oil
1¼ cups Chinese rice wine or dry sherry
5 tablespoons fish sauce
1 tablespoon granulated sugar
Salt and white pepper, to taste

Preheat the oven to 400°. Place the sea bass in an ovenproof baking dish. Cover evenly with the bell peppers, mushrooms, ginger, longan, and wolfberry. Mix together the sesame oil, wine, fish sauce, and sugar. Pour the sauce into the baking dish and sprinkle with salt and pepper. Cover pan with foil and bake for 15 to 20 minutes, until the fish is just cooked through. It should flake easily when tested with a fork.

Garlic and Ginger: Two Chinese Staples

What do garlic and ginger have in common? One is their prominence in Chinese cuisine, but they are also known for their curative properties. Vitamins A, C, and D can be found in garlic, and ginger is rich with vitamin C. Both offer extreme flavors, and complement each other beautifully, despite their differences. When storing peeled ginger be sure to put the unused portion in a covered jar, filling it up with vodka to preserve it. You can also store peeled ginger in a paper bag in the refrigerator for about 1 month.

Pork and Ginger Pot Stickers

6 tablespoons vegetable oil,
   divided
½ cup finely diced white onion
1 pound ground pork or ground
   beef
½ cup finely diced garlic chives
   (also called Chinese chives)
   or regular chives

1 teaspoon finely diced ginger
1 teaspoon oyster sauce
24 pot sticker wrappers
1 egg yolk, lightly beaten with a
   few drops of water

Yields 24 pot stickers

Pot stickers are an Asian tradition. This recipe is from Chef Kiong Banh of Twenty Manning in Philadelphia, who learned this from his grandmother.

1. Preheat a sauté pan on high, then add 2 tablespoons of the oil. Sauté the onion for 1 minute. Remove from heat and let cool.
2. In medium-sized mixing bowl, combine the ground pork, garlic chives, ginger, and oyster sauce. Mix well.
3. Lay out 1 wrapper and brush the egg around the edges. Place 1 teaspoon of the pork mixture in the center of the wrapper. Fold into a half-moon shape. Repeat with the remaining wrappers and filling.
4. In a 4-quart pot bring 2 quarts of water to a boil. Blanch the pot stickers for about 1 minute, until they rise to the surface of the water. Remove with a slotted spoon and let stand until dry.
5. Preheat a sauté pan over medium heat and add the remaining oil. Pan–sear the pot stickers until golden brown. Serve.

Tommy Toy's Minced Squab Imperial

Serves 4

In addition to being delicious, part of the fun is eating the Minced Squab Imperial: just pick it up like a taco and dive in. Take a page out of Tommy Toy's book, and provide your guests with lemon-scented hot towels, to clean their hands.

3 teaspoons peanut oil
1 teaspoon chopped fresh ginger
1 teaspoon chopped green onions (white part only)
2 fillets of squab, skin removed, deboned, and diced
3 black mushrooms, soaked in water for 30 minutes and thinly sliced
1 ounce bamboo shoots, diced

1 teaspoon rice wine
1½ teaspoons cornstarch
3 teaspoons chicken broth
1 tablespoon oyster sauce
2 teaspoons soy sauce
½ teaspoon granulated sugar
¼ teaspoon salt
Dash sesame seed oil
1 head crispy lettuce
4 dashes seafood (or hoisin) sauce

1. Preheat a wok, then add the peanut oil and heat on high. When the oil is hot, add the ginger and green onions, and sauté for about 1 minute. Add the squab, mushrooms, and bamboo shoots, and cook for about 1 minute.
2. Add all of the remaining ingredients except the lettuce and seafood/hoisin sauce, and stir-fry for about 2 minutes. Remove from heat.
3. Pull off the 4 largest and freshest leaves from the head (do not cut the lettuce). Spoon equal amounts of the squab mixture into each leaf and add a dash of seafood sauce on top of each serving.

Wok-Seared Beef Medallions with Asparagus Tips

*18-ounce filet mignon or eye
    fillet, cut into 4 medallions*
¼ cup balsamic vinegar
*3 tablespoons light soy sauce,
    divided*
1 tablespoon olive oil
2 cloves garlic, crushed
1 green onion, chopped

1 pound asparagus tips
1 tablespoon Asian rice vinegar
½ teaspoon granulated sugar
A few drops sesame oil
2 tablespoons vegetable oil
1 clove garlic, finely chopped
Cilantro sprigs, for garnish

Serves 4

Plunging the blanched asparagus tips into ice water helps them keep their bright green color and firm texture. They make an interesting contrast in flavor and texture to the beef medallions.

1. Marinate the filet medallions overnight in the balsamic vinegar, 1 tablespoon light soy sauce, olive oil, crushed garlic, and green onion. Discard the marinade after using.

2. Prepare a bowl with ice-cold water. Fill a large saucepan with enough salted water to cover the asparagus tips and bring to a boil. Blanch the asparagus tips in the water until they turn bright green and are tender (about 2 minutes). Plunge the asparagus briefly into the ice-cold water to stop the cooking process. Remove immediately and drain in a colander.

3. In a small bowl, whisk together the remaining 2 tablespoons light soy sauce, rice vinegar, sugar, and sesame oil. Set the vinaigrette aside.

4. Heat a wok and add 2 tablespoons vegetable oil (not olive oil). When the oil is hot, add the chopped garlic. Stir-fry for 30 seconds. Add the marinated beef medallions. Lay flat for a minute, then fry, stirring occasionally, until the beef is cooked according to your preference.

5. To serve, lay the blanched asparagus on a serving dish. Drizzle with the vinaigrette. Surround with the beef medallions. Garnish with the cilantro.

Tommy Toy's Four Seasons Fried Rice

Serves 6

Another of Tommy Toy's recipes, this is a very simple recipe, perfect for a casual but tasty meal.

2 large eggs

2 teaspoons, plus 1 tablespoon vegetable oil

⅛ pound barbecue pork, minced

⅛ pound minced sirloin or flank steak

⅛ pound chicken, minced

⅛ pound bay shrimp, minced

3 cups cooked long-grain white rice

1 tablespoon soy sauce

¼ teaspoon salt

¼ teaspoon ground white pepper

1. Lightly beat the eggs. Preheat a wok or skillet over medium-high heat until hot but not smoking. Add the 2 teaspoons oil and the beaten eggs. Cook for 1 to 2 minutes, tilting the pan so that the egg covers the surface as thinly as possible, to make a pancake. Allow the egg to cool, then julienne the egg pancake.
2. Add the remaining oil to the wok. Sauté the pork, beef, chicken, and bay shrimp for 1 to 2 minutes. Add the rice to the wok and stir-fry for 2 to 3 minutes, breaking up the rice to separate the grains. Add the eggs, soy sauce, salt, and pepper, and stir-fry until well combined. Transfer to plate and serve.

Soy Sauce—More to It Than You Might Think

The making of soy sauce, known in Chinese as *jiang you*, is a complex process. It begins with cleaning dried soybeans, then soaking them until soft. They are then steamed, mixed with yeast culture and wheat flour, and incubated for 3 to 5 weeks. They are then fermented with a brine solution for 6 to 24 months, and set out to dry in the sun for 100 days. A "soy master" oversees the entire process. Something to think about the next time you reach for a bottle at a restaurant.

Honey Walnut Shrimp

½ cup chopped walnut pieces
¼ cup sugar
½ pound shrimp
3 cups oil for deep-frying
1 egg, lightly beaten
4 tablespoons cornstarch

1½ tablespoons honey
3 tablespoons mayonnaise
3¾ teaspoons freshly squeezed
   lemon juice
3 tablespoons coconut milk

1. Earlier in the day, boil the walnut pieces for 5 minutes. Drain well. Spread the sugar on a piece of wax paper. Roll the walnut pieces in the sugar and allow to dry.
2. Peel and devein the shrimp. Wash and pat dry with paper towels.
3. Heat oil to 375°F. While waiting for oil to heat, mix the egg with the cornstarch to form a batter. Dip the shrimp in the egg batter. Deep-fry the shrimp until they turn golden brown. Remove from the wok with a slotted spoon and drain on paper towels. Cool.
4. Combine the honey, mayonnaise, lemon juice, and coconut milk. Mix in with the shrimp. Serve on a platter with the sugared walnuts arranged around the shrimp.

Mango Chicken

Serves 4

Turmeric is a distant relative of ginger. In this recipe it gives the chicken a nice yellow color.

4 boneless, skinless chicken breasts
1 egg white
1 tablespoon Chinese rice wine or dry sherry
¼ teaspoon salt
2 teaspoons cornstarch
2 tablespoons rice vinegar
2 tablespoons plus 1 teaspoon brown sugar
1 can mango slices with reserved juice
1 cup oil for frying
1 tablespoon minced ginger
1 teaspoon curry paste
½ teaspoon turmeric

1. Cut the chicken into cubes. Mix in the egg white, rice wine, salt, and cornstarch. Marinate the chicken for 30 minutes.
2. In a small saucepan, bring the rice vinegar, brown sugar, and ¾ cup of reserved mango juice to a boil. Keep warm on low heat.
3. Add 1 cup oil to a preheated wok or skillet. When the oil is hot, velvet the chicken by cooking very briefly in the hot oil, until it changes color and is nearly cooked through (about 30 seconds). Use tongs or cooking chopsticks to separate the individual pieces of chicken while it is cooking.
4. Remove all but 2 tablespoons oil from the wok. (Wipe out the wok with a paper towel if necessary.) When oil is hot, add the ginger, curry paste, and turmeric. Stir-fry for about 1 minute until aromatic. Add the chicken and mix with the curry paste.
5. Add the sauce and bring to a boil. Stir in the mango slices. Mix all the ingredients and serve hot.

Ham with Asian Pear

Serves 4–6

Although China's Yunnan hams are famous throughout Europe, they are hard to find in the West. Smithfield hams are a good substitute.

1½ pounds ham, thinly sliced
2 teaspoons sesame oil
2 teaspoons cornstarch
2 tablespoons soy sauce
2 tablespoons dark soy sauce

2 tablespoons honey
1 green onion
2 tablespoons oil for frying
2 Asian pears, sliced

1. Marinate the ham for 30 minutes in the sesame oil and cornstarch.
2. Combine the soy sauce, dark soy sauce, and honey. Set aside. Cut the green onion into 1-inch slices on the diagonal.
3. Add 2 tablespoons oil to a preheated wok or skillet. When oil is hot, add the sliced ham and brown briefly. Remove and drain on paper towels.
4. Prepare the wok for steaming. Place the sliced ham on a heatproof dish on a bamboo steamer. Brush ½ the sauce over. Cover and steam, adding more boiling water as necessary.
5. After 25 minutes, drain the ham juices, combine with the remaining half of the sauce, and bring to a boil in a small saucepan. Arrange the pear slices with the ham. Steam the ham for another 5 minutes, or until it is cooked. Pour the cooked sauce over the ham before serving. Garnish with the green onion.

Yin and Yang

Chinese culture is influenced by the philosophy of "yin" and "yang." So it should come as no surprise that Chinese food is also dominated by these two principles. Literally, yin and yang mean the dark and sunny side of a hill. And though most people interpret the terms as meaning opposing forces, they really are complementary. The Chinese believe in a perfect balance between these forces in the environment, and also in food. Any Chinese dish emphasizes the balance between several elements: taste, color, and texture. Certain foods are also thought to have yin or "cooling" properties, while others have "warm," or yang, properties. Even cooking methods are divided. Boiling, steaming, and poaching are all "yin," whereas roasting, deep-frying, and stir-frying are considered "yang."

Dry Ginger Beef

Serves 2

For an added touch, top with a few slices of preserved red ginger before serving.

1 tablespoon soy sauce
½ teaspoon Chinese rice wine
  or dry sherry
¼ teaspoon sugar
¼ teaspoon baking soda
½ pound flank steak, shredded
½ red bell pepper
2 tablespoons dark soy sauce

1 tablespoon plus 1 teaspoon
  oyster sauce
1½ teaspoons sugar
½ cup water
4–5 tablespoons oil for frying
2 slices ginger, minced
½ cup mushrooms, sliced

1. Add the soy sauce, rice wine, sugar, and baking soda to the beef. Marinate the beef for 30 minutes.
2. Wash the red pepper, remove the seeds, and cut into thin slices.
3. Combine the dark soy sauce, oyster sauce, sugar, and water and set aside.
4. Add 3 tablespoons oil to a preheated wok or skillet. When oil is hot, add the beef. Lay flat and fry for 2 minutes, then turn over and fry for another 2 minutes. Stir-fry the beef until it turns a dark brown (this will take about 8 minutes). Remove from the wok and drain on paper towels.
5. Add 1–2 tablespoons oil to the wok. When oil is hot, add the ginger and stir-fry briefly until aromatic. Add the mushrooms and red pepper and stir-fry until tender. Add the sauce to the middle of the wok and bring to a boil. Add the beef. Mix everything through and serve hot.

Preserving Foods—A Chinese Tradition

For centuries the Chinese have been employing a clever trick to draw out the shelf life of their foods: preserving. There are many methods of preserving food, from smoking, to salting, sugaring, pickling, drying, soaking in soy sauces, etc. Not only did this enable them to whip up foods quickly, but it also ensured that during hard times they would have a constant supply of nourishment. What began as a means of preserving life (both the foods' and the Chinese peoples') is now a means of flavoring.

Savory Shanghai Noodles

Serves 2–4

Frying the shrimp briefly in 1 cup of hot oil gives it a soft, velvety texture.

½ pound (8 ounces) fresh cooked shrimp, tails and vein removed

½ teaspoon sugar

½ teaspoon cornstarch

1 bunch spinach

¾ cup chicken broth

¼ cup water

2 tablespoons plus 2 teaspoons oyster sauce

1 teaspoon Chinese rice wine or dry sherry

1¼ cups oil for frying

1 garlic clove, finely chopped

2 slices ginger, finely chopped

½ pound fresh Shanghai noodles

½ teaspoon sesame oil

1. Rinse the shrimp in warm water and pat dry. Marinate the shrimp in the sugar and cornstarch for 15 minutes.

2. Wash the spinach and drain thoroughly. Mix together the chicken broth, water, oyster sauce, and rice wine, and set aside.

3. Add 1 cup oil to a preheated wok or skillet. When oil is hot, add the shrimp and fry briefly for 1 minute (if using raw shrimp, fry longer until the shrimp turn pink and firm up around the edges). Remove the shrimp from the wok with a slotted spoon and drain on paper towels.

4. Remove all but 2 tablespoons oil from the wok. Add the spinach and fry until it changes color. Add seasonings such as salt or soy sauce, if desired. Remove from the wok and set aside.

5. Add the garlic and ginger and stir-fry briefly until aromatic. Add the noodles. Stir-fry and toss with the sesame oil. Make a well in the middle of the wok and add the sauce. Bring to a boil. Add the spinach and the shrimp back into the wok. Mix everything through and serve hot.

Chapter 34

Japan:
Japanese Without the Chopsticks

472   Edamame Soup à la Chef Nobu

472   Scallops Broiled in Sake

473   Eggplant Miso Soup

474   Roasted Tomato Vinaigrette

474   Daikon Salad with Cucumber

475   Butterfly Shrimp Tempura

476   California Rolls

477   Marinated Teriyaki Salmon

478   Green Tea Crepes

479   Oyster Mushroom and Jasmine Tea Rice

480   Dashi Soup Stock

480   Sweet Simmered Squash

Edamame Soup à la Chef Nobu

1 medium-sized yellow onion, peeled and minced
1 tablespoon unsalted butter
3 cups chicken stock

½ teaspoon sea salt
Peeled edamame (soybeans)
2-inch piece ginger, minced

1. Sauté the onion in the butter until translucent. Add the chicken broth and bring to a boil. Add the salt and simmer for 1 hour. Add the edamame and cook at medium temperature for 10 minutes.
2. Let cool to room temperature, purée in a blender, and refrigerate overnight.
3. Garnish with the minced ginger and serve.

Add a Swirl of Elegance

Chef Nobu garnishes his edamame soup with a spiral of ginger crème fraîche and tiny pearls of tonburi, or Japanese "caviar," which is not caviar at all, but seeds. The soup is often featured on the chef's 8-course omakase menu, paired with a chilled sake.

Scallops Broiled in Sake

2 tablespoons vegetable oil
¾ pound sea scallops, shelled and cleaned
3 tablespoons Japanese soy sauce

2 tablespoons sake
¼ teaspoon Asian sesame oil
Fresh cilantro sprigs

Heat the oil in a frying pan or wok. Sauté the scallops just until they turn color. Stir in the soy sauce and sake. Cook for 1 to 2 more minutes, and add the sesame oil. Garnish with the cilantro. Serve immediately.

Eggplant Miso Soup

½ pound firm tofu
2 carrots
2 eggplants, preferably Asian
2 green onions

5 cups water
1 package dashi soup stock
2 tablespoons miso paste
¼ teaspoon Asian sesame oil

Serves 6

For best results, use firm tofu in this recipe, as it will hold its shape in the hot broth. Instant dashi soup stock is available in most supermarkets, or you can use the recipe on page 480.

1. Thirty minutes ahead of time, drain the tofu: place the tofu on a plate lined with paper towels. Place a book or plate on top of the tofu to squeeze out the water. Drain the plate and change the paper towels as needed. Cut the drained tofu into ½-inch cubes.

2. Wash the vegetables. Peel and julienne the carrots and eggplants. Chop the green onions.

3. In a large saucepan, bring 4½ cups water to a boil. Stir in the dashi soup stock. Add the vegetables and return to a boil. Reduce the heat and simmer, uncovered, until the vegetables are tender but not mushy (7 to 8 minutes).

4. In a small bowl, mix the miso with ½ cup water to form a paste. Remove the saucepan from the heat. Stir in the miso. Season the soup with a few drops of sesame oil and serve immediately.

Savory Hot Pots

One popular Japanese cuisine is savory hot pots known as *nabemono*. A simmering pot of broth is placed on a burner in the center of the table with plates of various raw meats and vegetables, which diners poach and serve up themselves. Two varieties are *shabu shabu*, named for the swishing motion made by the chopsticks of the diners as they cook the various ingredients of their individual portions at the table, and *nabe*, a hearty meat and vegetable stew that is a treasured treat for sumo wrestlers.

Roasted Tomato Vinaigrette

**Serves 8–10
(as a topping)**

The roasted tomatoes are rich in flavor and are a perfect ingredient for a unique vinaigrette.

4 cups Roma tomatoes
2 red bell peppers
1 tablespoon chopped garlic
1 cup olive oil

3 tablespoons red wine vinegar
Salt and freshly ground black
    pepper, to taste

1. Preheat the oven to 350°.
2. Cut the tomatoes in half and dice the bell peppers. In a bowl, coat the vegetables with the garlic and 2 tablespoons of the oil. Place on a baking sheet and bake for 10 minutes.
3. Transfer the tomatoes and bell peppers to a blender and purée until very smooth. Add the vinegar and oil and blend lightly. Season with salt and pepper.

Daikon Salad with Cucumber

Serves 6

For an added touch, serve with fresh fruit in season, such as apricots or plums.

½ large daikon radish
1 carrot
1 English cucumber
½ teaspoon salt
4 tablespoons rice vinegar
2 tablespoons mirin

2 teaspoons Japanese soy
    sauce
1½ tablespoons granulated
    sugar
2 tablespoons white sesame
    seeds

1. Peel the daikon radish and grate. Peel and grate the carrot. Peel the cucumber and cut into thin slices. Sprinkle the cucumber slices with the salt and drain for 15 minutes. Pat dry with paper towels.
2. In a small bowl, whisk the rice vinegar, mirin, Japanese soy sauce, and granulated sugar.
3. In a small serving dish, arrange the cucumber slices and the grated daikon and carrots. Drizzle the vinegar dressing over top. Sprinkle with the sesame seeds and serve.

Butterfly Shrimp Tempura

Serves 2–4

The Japanese version of deep-frying, tempura is easy to make. In addition to sliced lemon, serve the tempura with soy sauce, cayenne pepper, or salt and black pepper for dipping.

4 cups vegetable oil
12 large shrimp
1 egg
¾ cup ice-cold water

1 cup all-purpose flour
2 tablespoons fresh cilantro
    leaves, as garnish
3 lemons, sliced

1. Heat the oil to 350° in a deep-fat fryer, large heavy saucepan, wok, or electric fondue pot.
2. Rinse the shrimp under warm running water and pat dry with paper towels. Remove the main shell from the shrimp, but leave on the tails. To butterfly the shrimp, cut a deep slit along the back of shrimp. (Be careful not to cut right through the shrimp.) Press out the flesh on either side of the cut to form the butterfly "wings."
3. In a small bowl, stir the egg into the ice water. Stir in the flour to form a thick, lumpy batter, being careful not to overmix (the batter should resemble a pancake batter).
4. Dip the shrimp into the batter and deep-fry in the heated oil. Fry the shrimp until the batter is golden brown and crispy. Use a slotted spoon to remove the shrimp. Drain on paper towels. To serve, place the tempura on a plate and garnish with the fresh cilantro leaves and lemon slices.

To the Table

Does Japanese cuisine seems full of obscure and unknown foods? If so, you can take heart in knowing that its most important ingredient is very familiar. The answer is found in the Japanese expression for "Let's have a meal" (*Gohan ni shimasho*). *Gohan* means cooked rice, so the phrase literally is "Let's eat cooked rice."

California Rolls

Yields 4 rolls (32 pieces)

Sushi fans will love
California rolls, which are
simply sushi rolled inside
out, so that the seaweed is
on the inside.

1½ cups short or medium-grain
   rice
Water, as needed
6 tablespoons rice vinegar
2 tablespoons granulated sugar
1 teaspoon salt
2 avocados
2 tablespoons lemon juice

1 cucumber
½ pound imitation crab
4 teaspoons mayonnaise,
   preferably Japanese
4 nori (seaweed) sheets
¼ cup toasted sesame seeds
Pickled ginger, wasabi, and soy
   sauce for dipping

1. Rinse the rice 2 or 3 times, until the water runs clear. In a medium saucepan, add the rice and just enough water to cover. Bring the water and rice mixture to a boil. Turn the heat down to low and simmer, covered, until the rice is cooked through and has absorbed most of the liquid (about 20 minutes). Remove the rice from the heat and let it stand, still covered, for 15 to 20 minutes.

2. While the rice is standing, heat the rice vinegar, sugar, and salt in a small saucepan over low heat, stirring to dissolve the sugar. Sprinkle the mixture over the cooked rice, and slowly work it into the rice, taking care not to mash the grains. (Use a rice paddle if you have one.)

3. Peel the avocadoes, cut in half, and remove the pit in the middle. Cut into 1½-inch strips. Toss the strips with the lemon juice. Peel the cucumber, cut in half, and remove the seeds. Cut the cucumber into thin strips ⅛-inch long. In a small bowl, mix the crabmeat with the mayonnaise in a small bowl.

4. To make the rolls, cover a bamboo sushi rolling mat with a piece of plastic wrap. Lay 1 nori sheet on the mat, shiny-side down. Spread ¾ cup of the sushi rice over the nori, pressing it down firmly. Sprinkle with 1 tablespoon of the toasted sesame seeds. Lay another sheet of plastic wrap on top. Carefully turn the nori over. Remove the plastic sheet that was on the bottom.

5. Lay ¼ of the avocado and cucumber strips on the nori. Spread 1 teaspoon of the crabmeat and mayonnaise mixture over. Carefully roll up the nori into a cylinder, moving the bamboo sheet forward as you do so. Repeat with the remainder of the nori.

continues >>

6. Cut each nori roll into bite-sized pieces. Serve with the wasabi, pickled ginger, and soy sauce for dipping.

America's Favorite Japanese Food

The word *sushi* is thought to be derived from an ancient term meaning "acid" or "tart." In the 1800s, sushi was a kind of fast food, sold from small booths scattered around the city. Others claim the term came on the scene when snacks were sold during the intermission at kabuki theater. But the true origin is much older, and probably originated in China. Fish was salted and placed between layers of rice, then covered with a heavy stone as a way to preserve it for use up to several years later. Over time, using rice to preserve fish disappeared due to food shortages. Today fish and rice are reunited in what is surely America's favorite Japanese food.

Marinated Teriyaki Salmon

¼ cup olive oil	1 teaspoon grated ginger
¼ cup Japanese soy sauce	1 clove garlic, minced
2 tablespoons mirin (Japanese rice wine)	1 green onion, chopped
1 teaspoon brown sugar	4 salmon steaks, 6 to 7 ounces, skinned

Serves 4

A liqueur made from rice, mirin is the secret ingredient that gives Japanese teriyaki sauce its rich, mellow flavor. Mirin is available in the international cuisine section of many supermarkets.

1. In a medium bowl, combine the olive oil, soy sauce, mirin, brown sugar, ginger, garlic, and green onion. Place the salmon steaks in a shallow 9 × 13-inch baking dish. Pour the marinade over the steaks. Cover the salmon and marinate in the refrigerator for 2 hours.
2. Remove the salmon from the refrigerator. Reserve the marinade.
3. Heat the broiler. Place the marinated salmon fillets, skin-side down, on a greased rack in the broiler. Broil the salmon steaks until opaque throughout (10 to 12 minutes). Brush the steaks frequently with the reserved marinade during cooking.

Green Tea Crepes

Serves 6

Make sure to keep the pan at a medium temperature when cooking the crepes— if the pan is too hot, the batter won't spread out to cover the pan.

1¼ cups silken tofu
¾ cup all-purpose flour
1 teaspoon matcha green tea powder
½ cup granulated sugar
2 cups whole milk

1 teaspoon salt
½ teaspoon almond extract
4 tablespoons melted unsalted butter, divided
3 cups green tea ice cream

1. Mash the silken tofu and purée in the blender. Add the flour, green tea powder, sugar, milk, salt, almond extract, and 2 tablespoons of the unmelted butter to the puréed tofu. Mix at medium speed for 1 to 2 minutes, until a smooth batter is formed.

2. Heat a crepe pan or 8-inch frying pan over medium heat (when you spatter a bit of water in the pan and it sizzles, it is ready). Lightly brush the pan with about 1 teaspoon of the remaining melted butter to prevent sticking. Pour 4 tablespoons of the crepe batter into the pan. Immediately begin tilting and rotating the pan so that the batter spreads out evenly to cover the entire pan. Check for doneness by carefully lifting one side with your fingers—when the crepe is golden brown underneath, turn it over and cook the side until golden brown. Stack the crepes on top of one another, with a piece of wax or parchment paper between each one. Continue until all the crepes are cooked. Let the crepes cool.

3. To serve, spread ⅓ to ½ cup green tea ice cream over each crepe, as needed. Roll up the crepes, brushing with any leftover melted butter. Serve immediately.

Dainty Desserts

Japanese desserts tend to be quite small and are often made with tiny sweetened red beans called *adzuki*. Another typical dessert is fruits in gelatin, as well as the famed green tea ice cream. Depending on the season, fresh fruits are also common, and often marinated with grated ginger and mirin.

Oyster Mushroom and Jasmine Tea Rice

1 cup Asian scented rice
1¼ cups water
2 teaspoons jasmine tea leaves
½ pound fresh oyster
    mushrooms
2 green onions
1 tablespoon vegetable oil

2 tablespoons Japanese soy
    sauce
A few drops Asian sesame oil,
    or as desired
1 tablespoon white sesame
    seeds

> **Serves 4**
>
> Use scented jasmine or basmatic rice in this dish. For an added touch, enhance the nutty flavor of the sesame seeds by toasting them before adding to the cooked rice and mushrooms.

1. Rinse the rice, using your hands, until the water runs clear, without any milkiness. Drain and set aside.

2. In a medium saucepan, bring the water to a boil. Remove from the heat. Place the leaves in a teapot and pour the water over. Let the tea steep for 5 minutes, then strain to remove the leaves.

3. In a large saucepan, combine the rice with the jasmine tea. Let it sit for 1 hour or longer (overnight if possible). To cook, bring the water and rice mixture to a boil. Turn the heat down to low and simmer, covered, until the rice is cooked through and has absorbed most of the liquid (about 20 minutes). Remove the rice from the heat and let it stand, still covered, for 15 to 20 minutes.

4. While the rice is cooking, prepare the vegetables. Wipe the oyster mushrooms clean with a damp cloth. Cut off the stems and cut the tops into ½-inch pieces. Chop the green onions.

5. In a large frying pan, heat the oil on medium-high heat. Add the green onions, cook briefly, then add the oyster mushrooms. Stir in the soy sauce. Cook, stirring, until the mushrooms have softened. Stir in the sesame oil.

6. Use a fork or chopsticks to fluff up the cooked rice. To serve, combine the jasmine tea rice with the sautéed mushrooms. Garnish with the sesame seeds.

Dashi Soup Stock

Yields 4 cups

The secret ingredient that gives dashi soup stock its savory flavor is konbu kelp, which contains the same chemical that is used to make monosodium glutamate (MSG) seasoning.

1 (6-inch) piece high-quality konbu (kelp)
4½ cups water

3 tablespoons dried bonito flakes (hana-katsuo)

1. Clean the konbu by wiping it dry with a damp cloth. (Don't wash the konbu under running water, as this removes the flavor.) In a medium saucepan, place the konbu in the water. Soak for 2 hours.
2. Bring the water to a boil. When the water is boiling, stir in the dried bonito flakes. Remove the saucepan from the heat. Let stand for 5 minutes, then remove the dried konbu and strain out the bonito flakes. Use the broth as called for in the recipe. (Refrigerated, it will last for 2 to 3 days.)

Sweet Simmered Squash

Serves 4

The Dashi Soup Stock lends a savory flavor to this vegetable dish.

1 small acorn squash (kabocha)
1½ cups Dashi Soup Stock
3 tablespoons Japanese soy sauce

2 tablespoons sake
4 tablespoons granulated sugar

1. Use a strong knife to cut the acorn squash in half. Remove the seeds from the middle, and cut the squash into 2-inch slices.
2. In a heavy-sided frying pan, heat the Dashi Soup Stock on medium-high heat. Stir in the soy sauce, sake, and sugar. Reduce the heat to medium. Simmer briefly, then add the sliced squash. Simmer, covered, until the squash is tender and the liquid has been nearly absorbed (15 to 20 minutes). Cool and serve immediately.

Chapter 35

The Middle East:
At the Root of It All

482 : Savory Crispy Wheat Cake
483 : Lamb and Artichoke with "Terbiye"
484 : Vine Leaf Envelopes with Raisins
485 : Blintzes
486 : Jewish Honey Cake
487 : Potato Pancakes (Latkes)
488 : Rhubarb Khoresh
489 : Chicken in Pomegranate Sauce
490 : Cold Yogurt and Cucumber Soup
490 : Turkish Delight
491 : Chicken with Mushrooms
492 : Afghani Lamb with Spinach
493 : Lebanese Rice Pudding
494 : Turkish Lamb Casserole Cooked in Paper
495 : Middle Eastern Stuffed Grape Leaves
496 : Armenian Nutmeg Cake
497 : Palace-Style Rose Milk Pudding

Savory Crispy Wheat Cake

Serves 4

Another creation by Executive Chef Erdem Dönmez, this dish uses hulled wheat, as do many Turkish recipes, in both savory and sweet dishes.

1 cup hulled wheat
3 cups chicken broth
1 bunch basil, chopped
2 cloves garlic, sliced
1 medium onion, chopped
3 tablespoons olive oil

¼ cup grated Parmesan cheese
3 tablespoons softened butter, plus extra as needed for frying
Salt, to taste

1. Soak the wheat in cold water overnight. Cook, covered, over low heat in a medium-sized pot with the broth for about 20 minutes.
2. In a pan over medium heat, sauté the basil, garlic, and onion in the olive oil. Add to the cooked wheat, along with the Parmesan, butter, and salt. Mix well.
3. Transfer the mixture to a rectangular pan large enough to spread the mixture into a layer 1 inch thick. Let cool. When ready to serve, cut into squares and fry in butter until crisp on each side. Serve hot.

Crusading Kitchens

Ever wonder what the crusaders, when they weren't busy plundering and pillaging, stopped to eat? Record has it that the crusaders fell in love with the Arabic cooking style of continuously hanging a large cauldron over a low-burning fire, and every day adding what was available to the pot. These cauldrons were a constant fixture in the crusader camps, delivering thick soups, stews, and dumplings to hungry warriors.

Lamb and Artichoke with "Terbiye"

Serves 4

This recipe comes from Vedat Basaran, chef and manager of the Feriye Restaurant in Istanbul. Terbiye is a thickener made of lemon and eggs, usually with an addition of yogurt and a little bit of flour.

Juice of 2 lemons
8 small artichokes, trimmed
    and cleaned
1 pound lamb, cut in kebab-size
    pieces
Butter, as needed
20 shallots
Salt and white pepper, to taste
Fresh dill

Terbiye:
½ tablespoon all-purpose flour
3 tablespoons plain yogurt
2 egg yolks
Juice of 1 lemon

1. Fill a pot with water and add the juice from the 2 lemons. Put the artichokes in the water and set aside (this keeps the artichokes from turning black before you are ready to cook them).

2. Bring another pot of water to boil and boil the lamb for 2 to 3 minutes. Drain and set the meat aside. Heat the butter in the pot and sauté the shallots on medium until browned. Add the meat pieces and sauté for about 1 minute. Add enough water to the pan to cover the meat and cook for about 30 to 40 minutes over medium heat, covered.

3. Add the cleaned artichokes to the pot and cook until the artichokes are tender, about 15 minutes. Meanwhile, mix together all the terbiye ingredients thoroughly.

4. When the artichokes and the meat are tender, take 3 to 4 spoonfuls of the broth and add it to the terbiye mixture (so the mixture will not curdle when it is added to the pot). Add the diluted terbiye slowly to the pot, mixing constantly with a wooden spoon. Add the salt and pepper. Warm over low heat for another minute. Serve garnished with fresh dill.

Vine Leaf Envelopes with Raisins

6 ounces goat cheese
1 tablespoon fresh thyme or
  mint leaves
1 tablespoon chopped fresh
  basil
2 tablespoons heavy cream
  (optional)
4 large vine leaves

Olive oil, as needed
3 tablespoons chopped walnuts
2 tablespoons white sultana
  raisins
1 teaspoon granulated sugar
  (optional)
Lettuce leaves, to serve

1. Mix together the goat cheese, fresh thyme, basil, and cream, if using. Shape into 4 balls, and flatten a bit. Roll up the balls in the vine leaves (you can fold the leaves around the filling like envelopes if it is easier).
2. Sauté the envelopes in a little olive oil, taking care not to brown them too much. Remove the envelopes from the pan, and sauté the walnuts for about 1 minute; remove, set aside, and then sauté the raisins just to give them a shine, about 1 minute. If desired, add the granulated sugar and caramelize the raisins (this will give them a slightly different texture).
3. Serve the envelopes or the rolls over the lettuce leaves with the walnuts and raisins sprinkled over them.

In Persian Culture, You Are What You Eat

Iranians have long considered food and drink the foundation of both physical and mental health. For example, it was thought that consuming red meat and fats led to evil thoughts, and made one selfish. Consuming a healthy diet of fruits, vegetables, fish, fowl, mixed petals, and blossoms had the opposite effect—your soul would be generous and good. The records on classical Persian cooking are scarce, and most of the techniques have been passed down from generation to generation through the women—the ones who typically do all the cooking.

Blintzes

1 cup ricotta or farmer's cheese
8 ounces cream cheese
1 egg, lightly beaten
¼ teaspoon ground cinnamon
1 teaspoon vanilla extract
3 tablespoons granulated sugar
1 stick unsalted butter

3 large eggs, not beaten
1 cup all-purpose flour
1⅓ cups milk
1 teaspoon salt
¼ cup confectioners' sugar, or as needed

1. In a medium bowl, combine the ricotta cheese, cream cheese, lightly beaten egg, ground cinnamon, vanilla extract, and sugar. Refrigerate until needed.

2. Melt the butter in a small saucepan on low heat. To make the crepe batter: combine the eggs, flour, milk, salt, and 2 tablespoons of the melted butter in a blender and mix at medium speed for 1 to 2 minutes, until a smooth batter is formed. (The batter should be thinner and smoother than pancake batter.) Pour into a large bowl, cover, and refrigerate for 1 hour.

3. Heat a crepe pan or 5- to 6-inch frying pan over medium heat. Lightly brush the pan with about 1 teaspoon of the melted butter to prevent sticking. Pour just enough batter into the pan to make a thin crepe (about 3 tablespoons). Immediately begin tilting and rotating the pan so that the batter spreads out evenly to cover the entire pan. Cook until the crepe is lightly browned on top, and just beginning to pull away from the edges of the pan. Carefully lift the crepe from the pan. Stack the crepes on a warm plate. Continue until all the crepes are cooked.

4. To make the blintz, place 1 level tablespoon of the cream cheese filling mixture on the edge of the crepe and roll it up. Continue with the remainder of the crepes. Dust with the confectioners' sugar. Serve immediately.

Jewish Honey Cake

Serves 6

Traditionally served during the Jewish New Year season, sweet honey cake symbolizes the wishes for a good year ahead.

3 large eggs
1¼ cups granulated sugar
4 teaspoons vegetable oil
3 cups sifted all-purpose flour
¾ teaspoon salt
2 teaspoons baking powder
1 teaspoon baking soda
1 teaspoon ground cinnamon

⅛ teaspoon ground cloves
¼ teaspoon ground ginger
1 cup honey
1¼ cups brewed coffee
½ cup chopped walnuts
2 teaspoons grated orange rind
3 tablespoons confectioners' sugar, or as needed

1. Preheat the oven to 350°. Grease a 10-cup bundt pan.
2. In a small bowl, beat the eggs until fluffy. Beat in the sugar and oil.
3. Sift together the flour, salt, baking powder, baking soda, cinnamon, cloves, and ginger. Make a well in the center of the bowl, and add in the beaten egg, honey, and the coffee. Stir in the walnuts and the grated orange rind.
4. Pour the batter into the bundt pan and bake for 60 minutes or until the cake is done and a toothpick comes out clean when inserted in the center. Cool on a cake rack before removing from the pan. Dust with the confectioners' sugar and serve.

Influences on Israeli Cooking

When traveling and eating in Israel, you will notice plenty of other Middle Eastern influences. From Iran came the tradition of cooking meat with fruits and lentils. Lebanon inspired a method of cooking fish with cayenne pepper, paprika, cinnamon, and other spices. And Jordanian lamb and beef kebabs are also very common. Other dishes you might find include Syrian or Kurdish *kubbeh*—lamb and cracked wheat paste served in fried patties stuffed with meat, onion, and pine nuts—and Egyptian *sfeeha*—small pastry shells filled with spiced ground lamb, pine nuts, and yogurt.

Potato Pancakes (Latkes)

Serves 4–6

For a more "gourmet" touch, replace the yogurt and sour cream topping with whipped cream infused with an apple liqueur.

1 egg, lightly beaten
⅛ teaspoon salt, or to taste
¼ teaspoon black pepper, or to taste
4 russet or purple potatoes
½ red onion
2 tablespoons all-purpose flour

⅓ cup vegetable oil, or as needed
2 tablespoons freshly chopped chives
½ cup sour cream
½ cup natural yogurt

1. In a small bowl, lightly beat the egg, stirring in the salt and pepper. Peel and grate the potatoes, squeezing out any excess liquid. Peel and finely chop the onion.
2. In a medium-sized bowl, mix the potatoes and onion with the lightly beaten egg and the flour.
3. In a heavy-bottomed frying pan, heat the oil over medium heat. Carefully add 2 to 3 tablespoons of the potato mixture. Use a spatula to gently press the mixture down into the shape of a small pattie. Brown briefly, then turn and brown the other side. Remove and drain on paper towels.
4. Stir 1 tablespoon of the chives into the sour cream, and the remaining tablespoon into the yogurt. Serve the yogurt and sour cream with the potato latkes.

The Yiddish Kitchen

The dishes that define Yiddish cuisine came out of Central and Eastern Europe. Having evolved in the *shtetls* (the small towns and villages once inhabited by Jews, before the Holocaust), these are the foods considered by most Americans and Europeans to be typically "Jewish." Among them are *gefilte fish* (fish balls made of finely minced carp, pike, or a mixture of both, served in their own jelly and often with horseradish), *kishke* (a peppery blend of bread crumbs, chicken fat, and onions prepared sausagelike in beef casings), and *knaidlach* (egg and matzo meal–based dumplings). Other popular offerings include *kreplach* (dumplings filled with ground meat or cheese and boiled or fried) and *latkes* (fried potato pancakes), often served with applesauce.

Rhubarb Khoresh

2 small yellow onions
4 tablespoons vegetable oil, divided
1 pound boneless lamb shoulder, cubed
1 teaspoon ground cinnamon
¼ teaspoon ground turmeric
1 teaspoon salt

¼ teaspoon freshly ground black pepper
2 tablespoons tomato paste
2 cups water, or as needed
2 teaspoons lemon juice
½ pound fresh or frozen rhubarb
6 mint sprigs, for garnish

1. Peel and thinly slice the onions. In a large saucepan or Dutch oven, heat 2 tablespoons of the vegetable oil. Add the cubed lamb and brown over medium heat. Remove the lamb, but do not clean out the pan. Heat 1 more tablespoon of oil in the pan and add the chopped onion. Cook the onion over medium heat until it is soft and translucent (about 5 minutes).

2. Stir in the ground cinnamon, turmeric, salt and pepper, and the tomato paste. Cook for 1 minute, stirring then add the lamb back into the pan with the water and lemon juice. Make sure there is enough water to cover the lamb.

3. Simmer the stew, covered, for 45 minutes. Add the rhubarb to the pan, Continue cooking, covered, until the meat is tender (50 to 60 minutes). If necessary, add 1 to 2 more tablespoons of water. Serve the khoresh hot and garnished with the mint sprigs.

The History of Couscous

The North African nations of Morocco, Algeria, and Tunisia had a major influence on Israeli cuisine, especially when it came to couscous. A stew based on hard wheat semolina, couscous was born in the desert by wandering Berber tribesmen, about 4,000 years ago. Couscous is served in a variety of styles, but is typically topped with simple meats and a variety of vegetables. Algerian versions almost always include tomatoes; Moroccan couscous uses saffron; and Tunisian couscous is highly spiced.

Chicken in Pomegranate Sauce

3 pomegranates, to make 1¼
    cups juice
2 cups coarsely chopped
    walnuts
4 tablespoons olive oil, divided
1 pound chicken pieces,
    boneless, skinless
1 large red onion, peeled and
    finely chopped
2 garlic cloves, crushed

2 tablespoons tomato paste
1 cup water
½ teaspoon turmeric
1 teaspoon ground cinnamon
1 tablespoon granulated sugar
Salt to taste
Freshly ground black pepper,
    to taste

Serves 4

To increase the sourness,
add 1 or 2 tablespoons
pomegranate juice to
the sauce, reducing the
amount of water as
needed. To increase the
sweetness, add
extra sugar.

1. Wash the pomegranates, pat dry, and cut in half. Squeeze out the pomegranate juice, either by hand or with a juicer. Strain the juice through a mesh sieve. Reserve 1¼ cups.

2. Coarsely chop the walnuts, and then grind to a paste in the food processor. Mix in the freshly squeezed pomegranate juice. Process until you have a thick liquid.

3. In a large saucepan, heat the olive oil. Add the chicken pieces and cook over medium heat until browned. Remove the chicken pieces and drain on paper towels.

4. In a separate saucepan, heat 2 tablespoons oil. Add the chopped onion and garlic. Cook over medium heat until the onion is softened. Turn the heat down to low and stir in the tomato paste. Stir for a minute, and then slowly add the pomegranate/walnut mixture and the water. Stir in the turmeric, ground cinnamon, sugar, salt, and black pepper.

5. Add the browned chicken to the pomegranate sauce mixture. Simmer, covered, until the chicken is tender and cooked through (about 35 minutes). Serve hot over steamed rice.

Cold Yogurt and Cucumber Soup

Serves 4

This is a perfect soup to serve on hot summer days. Feel free to add a few ice cubes before serving.

1 English cucumber
1 small red onion
3 cups plain yogurt
1 cup light cream
2 tablespoons lemon juice
2 tablespoons finely chopped fresh mint

1 tablespoon finely chopped fresh dill
¼ cup chopped walnuts
1 teaspoon salt
Freshly ground black pepper, to taste

1. Peel the cucumber, cut lengthwise and remove the seeds, and finely chop. Peel and finely chop the red onion.
2. In a large bowl, combine all the ingredients. Refrigerate, covered, for at least 3 hours before serving to chill the soup and give the flavors a chance to blend.

Turkish Delight

Serves 6–8

For an authentic touch, serve this exotic Middle Eastern treat with strong coffee.

1 cup water
1 cup granulated sugar
¾ cup corn syrup
½ teaspoon cream of tartar

1 tablespoon lemon juice
1 teaspoon grated lemon rind
¼ teaspoon rose water
½ cup raw shelled pistachios

1. In a heavy saucepan, bring the water to a boil. Add the sugar and the corn syrup, stirring to dissolve the sugar. Stir in the cream of tartar. Reduce the heat and simmer, uncovered, until the mixture has the texture of a softened ball instead of a liquid. Stir in the lemon juice, grated lemon rind, and the rose water. Cook for 5 more minutes, stirring.
2. Pour the mixture into an 8 × 8-inch greased pan. Stir in the pistachios. Cool, stirring occasionally. Cut into squares and serve.

Chicken with Mushrooms

8 ounces button mushrooms
4 chicken breasts, boneless,
    skinless
⅓ cup all-purpose flour
½ teaspoon turmeric
1 teaspoon salt
Pinch of black pepper
¼ cup olive oil, divided

2 cloves garlic
½ red onion
2 tablespoons tomato paste
2 teaspoons granulated sugar
1 tablespoon lemon juice
1 cup dry white wine

Serves 4

The combination of chicken and mushrooms is found in many ethnic cuisines. Here it is enlivened with a sweet and sour sauce made with tomato paste, lemon juice, and sugar.

1. Wipe the mushrooms clean with a damp cloth and cut into thin slices. Rinse the chicken breasts and pat dry with paper towels.

2. In a small bowl, combine the flour with the turmeric, salt, and pepper. In a frying pan, heat 2 tablespoons olive oil over medium heat. Coat the chicken breasts in the seasoned flour mixture and add to the pan. Cook the chicken over medium heat until the chicken is cooked through and the juices run clear when pricked with a fork. Remove the chicken from the pan.

3. Add the garlic cloves and red onion to the pan. Cook over medium heat until the garlic is browned and the onion is soft and translucent (5 to 7 minutes). Add the tomato paste, sugar, and lemon juice. Cook for a minute, stirring, and add the wine. Bring to a boil, then turn down the heat and add the mushrooms. Cook for 5 more minutes.

4. Add the chicken and heat through. Serve hot.

Afghani Lamb with Spinach

Serves 4

Serve this dish over a classic Middle Eastern rice pilaf, made with wild rice, dried fruit, and toasted pine nuts.

⅓ cup olive oil

2 pounds lamb stew meat, cubed

2 small white onions

2 cloves garlic

1 cup crushed tomatoes with juice

2 teaspoons ground turmeric

6 cardamom pods

½ teaspoon ground coriander

1 teaspoon cayenne pepper

¼ teaspoon ground cinnamon

3 cups beef broth

10 spinach leaves, washed and torn

1 cup water, or as needed

½ cup pine nuts

Cold Yogurt and Cucumber Soup (page 490)

1. Heat 1 tablespoon olive oil in a heavy frying pan or Dutch oven. Add the cubed lamb and sear over medium-high heat. Remove the lamb from the pan.

2. Add 1 tablespoon olive oil to the pan. Add the chopped onion and garlic. Cook over medium heat until the onion is nearly softened (4 to 5 minutes). Add the garlic and cook for 1 more minute. Add the canned tomatoes, and the turmeric, cardamom, coriander, cayenne pepper, and cinnamon. Cook for a minute, stirring, then add the beef broth. Add the lamb back into the pan. Turn down the heat and simmer, covered, until the lamb is tender (about 1 hour). Add the spinach leaves and simmer for 5 more minutes, adding as much of the water as necessary to keep the stew from drying out.

3. Garnish the stew with the pine nuts and serve with the Cold Cucumber and Yogurt Soup.

Toasting Pine Nuts

Toasted pine nuts make a delicious garnish for this dish. To toast, place the nuts in a large skillet and shake continuously over medium heat until the nuts turn a light brown.

Lebanese Rice Pudding

Serves 8

In Lebanon, this rice is traditionally served to celebrate the birth of a child. Authentic rice pudding is made with "pounded rice"—rice that is ground with a mortar and pestle until it has a powder-like consistency.

1 cup jasmine or Basmati short-grained rice
1½ cups cold water, divided
½ cup golden raisins
5 cups whole milk

½ cup granulated sugar
2 teaspoons ground cinnamon
½ teaspoon caraway seeds
1 tablespoon shelled pistachios

1. Rinse the rice until the water runs clear and there is no milkiness. Soak the rice in 1 cup of water for 30 minutes to soften. Drain out most of the water, leaving about 1 tablespoon. In a small bowl, soak the raisins in ½ cup water to soften. Drain.

2. In a medium saucepan, heat the milk to a near boil. Add the sugar and the soaked rice. Bring to a boil, stirring constantly to thicken. Stir in the ground cinnamon, caraway seeds, and the pistachios. Reduce heat and simmer, covered, until the pudding has a thick texture similar to porridge.

3. To serve, pour the pudding into bowls and garnish with the raisins. Sprinkle extra pistachios on top if desired.

Turkish Lamb Casserole Cooked in Paper

Serves 6

This is a fun and elegant way to present a basic lamb casserole dish. Feel free to dress up the packages by wrapping them in aluminum foil instead of wax paper, with a spring of parsley or thyme for the "bow."

1 yellow onion
2 new potatoes
2 carrots
4 tablespoons olive oil
2 pounds lamb, cubed
1 tablespoon tomato sauce
1 teaspoon dried thyme

½ teaspoon dried parsley
½ teaspoon granulated sugar
3 tablespoons red wine vinegar
½ cup grated strong cheddar cheese
¼ cup chopped fresh cilantro

1. Preheat the oven to 375°. Grease two 9 × 13-inch baking sheets. Peel and finely chop the onion. Peel and thinly slice the potatoes and carrots.
2. In a heavy frying pan, heat 1 tablespoon olive oil. Add the cubed lamb and cook over medium-high heat until browned. Remove the lamb and clean out the pan.
3. Heat 3 tablespoons olive oil in the pan. Add the chopped onion and cook over medium heat until softened (5 to 7 minutes). Add the sliced potatoes, carrots, and the tomato sauce. Stir in the dried thyme, parsley, and sugar. Add the red wine vinegar. Sauté the potatoes and carrots over medium heat until browned (about 10 minutes). Add the lamb back into the pan and stir everything together.
4. Cut a large sheet of wax paper into six 12-inch squares. Spoon a heaping portion of the stew in the center section of each square. Sprinkle with the cheddar cheese and chopped cilantro. Wrap up each package. Bake for 20 minutes. Cool before serving. Serve in the wax paper.

Palace-Style Rose Milk Pudding

6 cups whole milk
1 small piece mastic
2 teaspoons granulated sugar
1 tablespoon rose water
1 teaspoon rice flour

2 pounds fresh strawberries,
sliced
1 tablespoon chopped fresh
mint

Serves 10

From Chef Aydyn Demir of Tugra, the Turkish fine-dining restaurant in Ciragan Palace Hotel Kempinski, Istanbul.

1. In a large saucepan, combine the milk, mastic, sugar, and rose water, and bring to a boil.
2. In a small bowl, mix the rice flour with little bit of cold water, then add the mixture to the boiling milk. Cook for 3 minutes. Pour into small, elegant serving glasses and cover with the strawberries and garnish with mint.

Mare's Milk in the Nomadic Diet

Milk and dairy products were an essential part of the nomadic diet, and it was mare's milk—not sheep's or cow's—that was most highly prized. (Mare's milk has four times more vitamin C than cow's milk.) It was simmered in shallow pans and the cream, which rose to the surface, was consumed, while the remaining milk was dried in the sun and stored as powder. Milk and thick cream were the basic elements of a nomad's breakfast. Mare's milk was also fermented to make a strong alcoholic beverage known as *kimiz*, which is still widely consumed among the Turkish people of Central Asia.

Chapter 36

Africa: A Food Safari

500 : Slow-Roasted Balsamic Tomato Soup

500 : Preserved Lemons

501 : African Squash and Yams

502 : Orange Salad with Orange Flower Water

503 : Moambé Stew

504 : Greens with Peanuts

505 : Tagine-Style Beef Stew with Lemons

506 : Egyptian Fava Beans (Fool Medames)

507 : Lamb Kebabs

508 : Cucumber Salad with Fresh Mint

509 : Moroccan Stuffed Chicken

510 : Almond Paste

Slow-Roasted Balsamic Tomato Soup

12 tomatoes, cut into wedges
6 cloves garlic, crushed
1 large onion, crushed
3 sprigs thyme
⅓ cup balsamic vinegar

Salt and crushed black pepper, to taste
½ cup olive oil
4 cups strong vegetable stock

1. Preheat the oven to 350°.
2. Mix together all the ingredients except the vegetable stock and place in a roasting tray. Slow-roast for approximately 30 minutes in the oven until slightly browned. Remove from the oven and place in a pot with the vegetable stock. Simmer on medium heat for 35 minutes. Adjust seasoning to taste, and purée the mixture in a food processor or blender. Serve with chopped fresh basil, if desired.

Preserved Lemons

12 lemons

¾ cup sea salt, or as needed

1. Cut a thin strip off both ends of a lemon. Stand up the lemon and cut through the middle, almost to the bottom, taking care not to cut right through the lemon. Spread the two cut halves of the lemon apart and add up to 1 tablespoon salt on the flesh. Close up the lemon. Continue with the remainder of the lemons.
2. Place 1 tablespoon salt on the bottom of a sterilized glass jar. Pack in the lemons. Cover tightly. Leave the preserved lemons for at least 1 week, shaking the jar occasionally to distribute the lemon juice. Remove from the jar and store in a sealed container in the refrigerator. (The lemons will last for 2 to 3 months.) Use as called for in a recipe.

African Squash and Yams

1 medium onion

2 medium sweet potatoes
   (yams)

1 butternut squash

2 tablespoons vegetable oil

¾ cup thin coconut milk

¼ cup thick coconut milk

1 teaspoon brown sugar

½ teaspoon grated lemon rind

½ teaspoon salt

¼ teaspoon ground cloves

Serves 6

Starchy foods such as yam make a frequent appearance in African cooking. This recipe blends two starches with the delicate flavor of coconut milk.

1. Peel and chop the onion. Peel the sweet potatoes and cut into 1-inch chunks. Peel and remove the seeds from the butternut squash. Cut into 1-inch chunks.

2. In a large frying pan, heat the vegetable oil. Add the onion and cook over medium heat until soft and translucent (5 to 7 minutes). Add the sweet potatoes and the butternut squash. Cook for 1 minute, then add the thin and thick coconut milk. Stir in the brown sugar, grated lemon rind, salt, and the ground cloves. Reduce heat to low and simmer, covered, for 30 minutes, or until the vegetables are tender. Serve immediately.

A Basic Native African Meal

Africa is a continent, and thus its cuisine cannot be summarized in a few lines or a chapter of a cookbook. But there are some basic tenants of the African table, and some general cooking principles. For starters, starch is a major focal point of the African meal, with a stew of meat and/or vegetables cooked to go with it. Common main root vegetables include yams and cassava, and other typical ingredients are steamed greens, spices, and peanuts (called "groundnuts" in Africa), which can be a simple garnish or the main ingredient, as in peanut soup.

Orange Salad with Orange Flower Water

Serves 6

Particularly prominent in Egyptian cooking, orange flower water is made from distilled orange blossoms. It is relatively easy to find, and usually comes in a beautiful, deep blue bottle.

½ cup unblanched almonds
6 ripe, juicy oranges
½ teaspoon granulated sugar
¼ teaspoon ground cinnamon
10 pitted dates, sliced
  lengthwise

2 teaspoons orange flower
  water
4 fresh mint sprigs, for garnish

1. In a small saucepan, add the almonds and cold water. Bring to a boil. Boil for 1 minute, then remove the almonds and place in a bowl filled with cold water. Remove the skin by holding the almond between your thumb and forefinger and pressing until the skin slips off. Continue with the remainder of the almonds. Chop the blanched almonds into thin slivers.

2. Peel the oranges, removing all the pith, and slice. Toss the sliced oranges with the sugar and ground cinnamon. Place the oranges in a serving bowl. Add the sliced dates and the blanched almonds. Sprinkle the orange flower water over top. Cover and chill for 1 hour. Garnish with the fresh mint leaves just before serving.

A Lean Bird with a Mean Kick

Ostrich, a bird with a very powerful kick (just ask anyone who has gotten in the way), is a fabulous meat to eat. Many entrepreneurs tried their hand at running ostrich farms and selling the meat, but it never became the craze many thought it would in America. Fortunately, you can find the meat at many specialty stores.

Moambé Stew

2 yellow onions
1 garlic clove, crushed
2 large tomatoes
½ pound fresh spinach leaves
1 jalapeño chili pepper
2 pounds stewing beef, cut into
    bite-sized pieces
⅓ cup freshly squeezed
    grapefruit juice

2 tablespoons peanut oil
1½ cups water
½ teaspoon salt
¼ teaspoon ground cumin
¼ teaspoon cayenne pepper
1 cup smooth peanut butter

Serves 6

Traditionally, this African stew dish would be served with palm oil instead of peanut oil, and palm butter in place of the peanut butter.

1. Chop the yellow onion and smash the garlic clove. Blanch the tomatoes briefly in boiling water. Drain, peel off the skins, and chop. Wash the spinach leaves, drain, and tear into shreds. Cut the chili pepper in half, remove the seeds, and chop thinly. (Wear plastic gloves while working with the chilies and wash your hands afterward.) Crush the garlic.

2. In a shallow 9 × 13-inch glass baking dish, combine the stewing beef, grapefruit juice, garlic, and chili. Cover and marinate in the refrigerator for 1 hour, turning occasionally.

3. In a large saucepan, heat the peanut oil over medium heat. Add the beef and cook over medium to medium-high heat until browned (about 5 minutes). Cook the meat in 2 batches if necessary. Remove the meat from the pan but don't clean out the pan.

4. Add the onions and 3 tablespoons water. Cook over medium heat until the onion is soft and translucent. Add the tomatoes and 1½ cups water. Stir in the salt, ground cumin, and cayenne pepper. Heat to boiling. Add the stewing beef. Reduce the heat and simmer, covered, for 15 minutes. Stir in the peanut butter and spinach leaves. Simmer for 45 minutes more, or until the beef is cooked. Add more water if necessary to prevent the stew from drying out. Serve hot.

Greens with Peanuts

Serves 4–6

Many Congo dishes feature cassava leaves that come from the cassava plant (also called the yucca plant). Feel free to replace the spinach leaves in this recipe with cassava leaves if they are available.

1 cup unsalted peanuts, without skins
¼ teaspoon salt
2 pounds spinach leaves
1 jalapeño chili pepper
½ white onion

1 red bell pepper
1 tablespoon peanut oil or palm oil
2 cups water
2 cups chickpeas
1 teaspoon granulated sugar

1. Heat oven to 350°. Spread the peanuts out in a 9 × 13-inch baking sheet. Roast for 15 minutes, or until the peanuts are browned. Cool. Use a blender or food processor to crush the cooled peanuts with the salt. Process 2 or 3 times until the peanuts have a crumb-like texture.

2. Wash the spinach leaves and pat dry with paper towels. Tear into shreds. Cut the chili pepper in half, remove the seeds, and chop thinly. (Wear plastic gloves while working with the chilies and wash your hands afterward.) Peel and chop the onion. Cut the red bell pepper in half, remove the seeds, and cut into strips.

3. In a large saucepan or deep-sided frying pan, heat the peanut oil. Add the onion and cook over medium heat until it is softened (5 to 7 minutes). Add the chili pepper and the red bell pepper and cook briefly, until the skin of the chili begins to blister. Add 1¼ cups water and bring to a boil. Stir in the crushed peanuts and the spinach.

4. Reduce the heat and simmer, covered, until the spinach is wilted and tender. Add the chickpeas. Stir in the sugar. Heat through and serve hot.

Making Your Own Peanut Paste

To make your own homemade peanut paste, first shell the peanuts, then roast in a large skillet on the stove, stirring often. Remove the skins and place the peanuts in a saucepan. Add enough water to partially cover them and bring to a slow boil, stirring often. Reduce heat. Mash the peanuts into a paste with a potato-masher.

Tagine-Style Beef Stew with Lemons

2 pounds stewing beef, cut into chunks
Salt and pepper, to taste
2 cloves garlic
1 red onion
1 (14-ounce) can plum tomatoes
1 tablespoon palm or peanut oil
2 cups water
2 cups beef broth

1½ teaspoons ground cumin
½ teaspoon cayenne pepper, or to taste
2 teaspoons turmeric
1 (3-inch) cinnamon stick
1 cup golden raisins
½ cup chopped cilantro leaves
2 Preserved Lemons, cut into slices (page 500)

Serves 4 to 6

A North African specialty, tagine is a spicy stew traditionally served in a clay cooking pot. Serve the tagine over couscous or boiled rice.

1. Season the stewing beef with salt and pepper. Crush the garlic cloves. Peel and chop the red onion. Cut the plum tomatoes into quarters, but reserve the juice from the can.

2. In a large saucepan or Dutch oven, heat the oil. Add the beef and cook over medium-high heat until browned. Remove the beef from the pan, but do not clean out the pan.

3. Add the chopped onion and garlic. Add 1 tablespoon water and cook the onion over medium heat until soft and translucent. Add the beef broth and 1 cup water. Bring to a boil, then stir in the ground cumin, cayenne pepper, and turmeric. Add the cinnamon stick.

4. Add the beef back into the pan. Turn down the heat, cover, and simmer. After the stew has been simmering for 1 hour, add the raisins, plum tomatoes, and chopped cilantro. Simmer, covered, for 30 more minutes, adding the remaining 1 cup of water as needed. Taste and add salt and pepper, as desired. Serve hot, garnished with Preserved Lemons.

Egyptian Fava Beans (Fool Medames)

Serves 6–8

A member of the pea family, fava beans are a popular ingredient in Egyptian dishes. Feel free to use lima or pinto beans as a substitute if they are unavailable.

4 cups fresh fava beans,
    unshelled
2 Preserved Lemons (page 224)
1 small white onion, chopped
2 cloves garlic
2 ripe tomatoes
¼ cup olive oil

1 teaspoon ground cumin
1 teaspoon ground coriander
½ teaspoon turmeric
2 tablespoons chopped cilantro
    leaves
Salt and freshly ground black
    pepper, to taste

1. Shell the fava beans by cutting a slit down the side of each bean and removing the tough outer pod. Rinse the Preserved Lemons and pat dry with paper towels. Remove the pulp and chop finely. Peel and finely chop the onion and garlic. Wash and dice the tomatoes.
2. Heat the olive oil in a large saucepan over medium heat. Add the onion and garlic. Cook over medium heat until the onion is soft and translucent. Add the fava beans and tomatoes. Stir in the ground cumin, ground coriander, turmeric, and the chopped cilantro.
3. Cook until the beans have softened but are not mushy (3 to 5 minutes in total). To serve, toss the bean mixture with the chopped lemons. Season with salt and pepper as desired.

Lamb Kebabs

2 pounds boneless leg of lamb
1½ cups plain yogurt
2 cloves garlic, crushed
2 slices ginger, minced
Juice from 2 freshly squeezed
    lemons

½ teaspoon ground cinnamon
¼ teaspoon mild curry powder
½ teaspoon salt
½ teaspoon freshly ground
    black pepper

> **Serves 6**
>
> Marinating the lamb in yogurt helps to tenderize it. When grilling the lamb, be careful not to cook it too long or it will toughen.

1. Cut the lamb into 1½-inch cubes, and place in a 9 × 13-inch shallow glass baking dish. In a large bowl, combine the yogurt, garlic, ginger, lemon juice, ground cinnamon, curry powder, and the salt and pepper. Spoon the yogurt marinade over the lamb cubes. Marinate the lamb, covered, in the refrigerator for 4 hours, stirring occasionally.
2. Preheat the grill. Thread the marinated lamb kebabs onto skewers. (Reserve the yogurt marinade.) Cook over medium heat, turning, until the meat is cooked according to your preference (8 minutes for medium-rare). Baste the lamb frequently with reserved marinade while grilling. Serve hot.

On Alcohol in Africa

Outside of Muslim Africa you can find many types of alcoholic beverages. Most famous are the wine regions of South Africa, which produce exceptional whites and reds. South Africa also produces an unusual beverage—a tangerine-based liqueur called Van der Hum. And the famed Kenyan beer Tusker is exported for those who want to try it without a transatlantic flight. But most famous is the Ethiopian honey wine, Tej, invented centuries ago (bees, it turns out, are the earliest domesticated creature). Wine made from their honey somewhat resembles mead made in Old England.

Cucumber Salad with Fresh Mint

Serves 6

Although they are more commonly associated with Middle Eastern cuisine, chickpeas are also found in North African dishes. If you can't find chickpeas at the supermarket, try looking for them under their other name, garbanzo beans.

2 tablespoons pine nuts
2 cucumbers
1 tablespoon virgin olive oil
3 tablespoons balsamic vinegar
1 teaspoon granulated sugar
½ teaspoon marjoram

1¼ cups chickpeas
1 can mandarin orange
    segments
2 tablespoons freshly chopped
    mint

1. Chop the pine nuts into thin slivers. Peel and grate the cucumbers. Drain the liquid from the cucumbers by placing them in a sieve and sprinkling the salt over. Place a small plate on top of the cucumbers to help push out the liquid, and let drain for 1 hour. Toss the drained cucumber slices with the olive oil, balsamic vinegar, sugar, and marjoram.
2. Place the chickpeas in a serving bowl. Add the mandarin orange segments and arrange the seasoned cucumber slices and slivered pine nuts on top. Sprinkle with the freshly chopped mint.

African Cooking Terms

Efo. Gombo. Foofoo. These may sound like the babblings of a small child, but in fact they are African cooking terms. Here are a few of the more unusual-sounding terms used in Africa: *efo* (a multipurpose name for greens, including mustard, collards, chard, and turnip), *elubo* (yam flour), *foofoo* (mashed yam, or yam, corn, and plantain pudding), *gombo* (the West African word for okra).

Moroccan Stuffed Chicken

Serves 4

Always make sure to tuck the wing tips under the body when roasting a chicken.

½ cup toasted almonds
½ cup golden raisins
½ cup plus 2 tablespoons
   orange juice
4 tablespoons butter
1½ cups water
10 saffron threads

1 cup couscous
1 tablespoon liquid honey
½ teaspoon ground cinnamon
¼ teaspoon ground ginger
¼ teaspoon cayenne pepper
1 teaspoon salt
3½-pound roasting chicken

1. To make the couscous stuffing: chop the toasted almonds into slivers. Plump up the raisins by placing them in a small bowl with the orange juice. Let the raisins sit in the juice for 30 minutes. Drain.
2. In a medium saucepan, melt the butter. Add the water and saffron threads and bring to a boil. Stir in the coucous. Stir briefly and remove from the heat. Let the couscous stand for 15 minutes.
3. Stir the toasted almonds, raisins, honey, ground cinnamon, ground ginger, and cayenne pepper into the couscous. Use your hands to make sure the ingredients are thoroughly mixed together.
4. Preheat the oven to 425°. Clean the chicken cavity, rinse, and pat dry with paper towels. Rub salt over the outside skin. Spoon the couscous stuffing into the cavity of the chicken, and pack loosely. Use poultry skewers to close the cavity opening. Tie the legs together with string. Place the chicken on a rack in a roasting pan. Roast uncovered, basting frequently with the chicken juices, for 1 to 1¼ hours. (The chicken is done when the temperature in the thickest part of the thigh reaches 175°.)

Almond Paste

Almond paste makes
an appearance in many
Moroccan dessert recipes;
it can also be
enjoyed spread on freshly
baked bread.

*1½ cups blanched whole
   almonds*

½ cup walnut oil
¼ cup liquid honey

1. Toast the almonds by heating them in a frying pan over medium heat, shaking the pan continuously, until they turn golden. Cool and chop finely.
2. Process the almonds in the food processor until they have formed a fine paste. Stir in the walnut oil and process again. Stir in the liquid honey.

Ethiopian Bread

Ethiopian bread is known as *injera*. Made from *teff*, the smallest form of millet, it is ground into flour, then made into a thin fermented batter. It is poured onto a griddle in a large spiral, where it blends into a large, 24-inch circular flatbread. Cooked in minutes, the spongy bread acts as the plate for the dish and replaces a spoon.

Chapter 37

USA: The Melting Pot

512   BLT: Buster Crab, Lettuce, and Tomato Sandwich

513   Young Garlic Soup with Crème Fraîche and
Spring Pea Shoots

514   Tomato Marmalade

514   Sweet Corn and Cipollini Onion Soup

515   Red Velvet Cake

516   Snapper with Jumbo Lump Crabmeat

517   Bourbon Molasses Glacé

517   Buttery Mashed Potatoes

518   Pecan-Crusted Chicken

519   Lollypop Veal Chop

520   Roasted Butternut Squash Soup

521   Jumbo Lump Crab Cakes

522   Corn-Pickled Okra Relish

522   Spicy Remoulade

523   Roasted Tomato, Zucchini, and Goat Cheese Tarts

524   Elegant Cream of Celery Soup

525   Shiitake Mushroom Soup

525   Cranberry Salad

BLT: Buster Crab, Lettuce, and Tomato Sandwich

1 buster crab, cleaned
Salt and pepper, to taste
¼ cup cornmeal
¼ cup seasoned flour
¼ cup canola oil
¼ cup grape tomatoes, peeled
1 dash 25-year-old balsamic
*   vinegar*

1 teaspoon extra-virgin olive oil
1 pinch minced chives
Salt and pepper, to taste
1 slice brioche, well-toasted
2 teaspoons aioli
1 pinch micro greens or any
*   sproutlike lettuce*

1. Season the crab with salt and pepper. Combine the cornmeal and seasoned flour, and toss the crab in the mixture to coat.
2. In a sauté pan, heat the canola oil over medium heat. Place the coated crab in the oil and cook for 1 minute on each side. Remove from pan and allow to drain on paper towels.
3. Toss the tomatoes with the vinegar, olive oil, chives, and salt and pepper. On serving plate, place the tomatoes on top of the brioche. Place the crab on top of the tomatoes, and top with a dollop of aioli and the micro greens.

What's in a Salad?

A staple of the American diet, salads have been around since ancient times. The 1930s saw the invention of Jell-O, as well as the Cobb (invented at the Brown Derby Restaurant in 1937). In the latter half of the twentieth century, salad enjoyed one of its most significant revolutions, when hippies embraced natural and organic ingredients including nuts and berries, alfalfa sprouts, and sunflower seeds. Today there is almost no limit to what you might find in a salad: chefs choose from a plethora of organic mixed greens, edible flowers, and unique dressings, which keep this simple dish a constantly evolving treat.

Young Garlic Soup with Crème Fraîche and Spring Pea Shoots

1 tablespoon extra-virgin olive
   oil
½ pound fresh young garlic
   bulbs, roughly chopped
1 small yellow onion, small
   diced
1 stalk celery, small diced
1 pound Yukon gold potatoes,
   peeled and diced
2 quarts chicken or vegetable
   stock

¼ teaspoon cayenne pepper
1 cup heavy whipping cream
1 sprig fresh thyme, leaves
   picked from stem
Salt and freshly ground white
   pepper, to taste
¼ cup crème fraîche (or sour
   cream or plain yogurt)
¼ pound pea shoots

> **Serves 8**
>
> Another recipe from Chef John Besh of Restaurant August in New Orleans. It can be served hot or chilled. If you can't find pea shoots, substitute watercress for the garnish.

1. Heat the olive oil in a 2-gallon pot over medium heat. Add the garlic, onion, and celery, and cook for 5 minutes.
2. Add the potatoes, stock, and whipping cream to pot. Bring to a boil, lower heat, and simmer for 20 minutes. Add the thyme, cayenne, salt, and white pepper.
3. Purée the soup in a blender, then strain through a fine-mesh sieve. Adjust seasonings to taste. Pour into soup bowls or cups and garnish each with a spoonful of the crème fraîche and pea shoots.

Garlic and Crème Fraîche Are Trés Francais

"I love early spring garlic," muses Chef John Besh of Louisiana's Restaurant August. "It has not yet formed each individual toe, and may look more like a small onion bulb than a head of garlic." Garlic and crème fraîche are featured prominently in the traditional French culinary style. Chef Besh, who trained extensively in Provence, likes to emphasize the historic culinary bond between France and New Orleans, using these ingredients in many signature recipes.

Tomato Marmalade

Serves 8 (as a spread)

Chef Besh's Tomato Marmalade is a wonderful gourmet solution to having a surplus of the fruit on hand at summer's end. Serve spoonfuls alongside grilled beef at dinner, or use as a spread on your favorite sandwich.

½ teaspoon cumin seeds
10 peppercorns
1 cup granulated sugar
1½ cups red wine vinegar

10 tomatoes, peeled, seeded, and diced
2–4 jalapeños, seeded and finely diced

1. Tie the cumin seeds and peppercorns together in a cheesecloth sack.
2. In a saucepan over medium heat, cook the sugar and vinegar to a syrup consistency.
3. Add the tomatoes, jalapeños, and cheesecloth sack to the saucepan. Cook slowly over low heat until the mixture reaches desired thickness. Use immediately, or pour into sterilized jars to save.

Sweet Corn and Cipollini Onion Soup

Serves 8

Another of Chef Scott Johnson's favorite dishes, this combines the sweetness of corn with the sweetness of cipollini onions.

3 cups whole sweet corn kernels
2 cups diced cipollini onion
1 cup diced potatoes
2 teaspoons olive oil

1 teaspoon dried thyme
1 bay leaf
3 cups chicken broth
Salt and pepper, to taste

1. In a soup pot over medium heat, cook the corn, onion, and potatoes in the oil. Sauté for 5 to 10 minutes. Add the thyme, bay leaf, chicken broth, salt, and pepper. Simmer for 30 to 40 minutes.
2. Transfer to a blender or food processor and purée until smooth. Adjust seasoning to taste, and serve.

Red Velvet Cake

3 cups all-purpose flour, divided
1 teaspoon salt
1½ teaspoons baking soda
3 tablespoons cocoa powder
2¼ cups granulated sugar, divided

1 cup unsalted butter, divided
2 large eggs
1½ teaspoons vanilla extract, divided
2 cups buttermilk, divided
4 tablespoons red food coloring

1. Preheat the oven to 350°. Grease 2 round 9-inch cake pans.
2. In a large bowl, combine the 2½ cups flour, salt, baking soda, and cocoa powder. In a separate bowl, use an electric mixer to cream 1¼ cups sugar and ½ cup unsalted butter. Beat in the eggs and 1 teaspoon vanilla extract. Gradually add in 1 cup buttermilk.
3. Make a well in the middle of the flour and add in the liquid ingredients. Combine with the flour, taking care not to overmix the batter. Stir in the red food coloring. Pour the batter into the prepared cake pans. Bake for 30 minutes, or until the cake springs back when a toothpick is inserted in the middle. Cool for 15 minutes and turn the cakes out of their pans.
4. To make the icing, whisk together ½ cup flour and 1 cup buttermilk. Bring to a boil. Reduce the heat to medium, and continue whisking until the mixture thickens. Remove from the heat and cool.
5. Cream together ½ cup unsalted butter and 1 cup sugar. Beat in ½ teaspoon vanilla extract. Gradually beat in the cooled milk mixture until it is light and fluffy. Spread the icing over the cake and serve.

Snapper with Jumbo Lump Crabmeat

Serves 4

This recipe, by Chef Matthew Murphy of Victor's Grill at the Ritz-Carlton, New Orleans, combines the richness of snapper and crab, finished with a warm Bacon Dressing.

¾ pound red snapper fillet

¼ cup olive oil, plus extra for brushing

Salt and freshly ground black pepper, to taste

1 lemon

3 ounces jumbo lump crabmeat

2 tablespoons Chardonnay

2 tablespoons butter

1 small zucchini, cut on a bias

1 red bell pepper, sliced thickly

1 tablespoon cane vinegar

2 tablespoons Bacon Dressing (see sidebar on this page)

½ cup baby spinach

1. Brush the snapper with a little olive oil and season with salt and pepper. Squeeze the lemon over it. Cook the snapper in a medium-sized sauté pan over medium heat, turning once, until fish is cooked through and opaque. Add the crabmeat and chardonnay. When warm, add the butter and stir to melt. Remove from heat.

2. Toss the vegetables with the olive oil, salt and pepper, and the cane vinegar. Grill until cooked through. Place a medium-sized metal bowl on the grill and add the Bacon Dressing and baby spinach and toss. Add the grilled vegetables and toss to mix. Serve alongside the fish.

Bacon Dressing

To make the Bacon Dressing, combine ¼ pound cooked, chopped bacon (together with the fat), ¼ cup balsamic vinegar, ¾ cup shallot stock, and 1 teaspoon of honey.

Bourbon Molasses Glacé

2 cups bourbon
1 cup light corn syrup

½ cup molasses

Reduce the bourbon by ⅓ in a deep pot (because you will be releasing the alcohol, be careful not to expose it to an open flame). Add the corn syrup and molasses, and cook for 5 minutes.

> **Serves 4**
>
> This is a delicious sauce that goes with many meat dishes. It is especially good with the Pecan-Crusted Chicken (page 518).

Buttery Mashed Potatoes

2 pounds medium Yukon gold
*   potatoes*
1 pound European-style butter
*   (such as Plugra brand) or*
*   regular unsalted butter, at*
*   room temperature*

½ cup plus 1 tablespoon heavy
*   cream*
Salt and freshly ground white
*   pepper, to taste*

1. Place the potatoes (skin on) in a pot and cover with cold water. Bring to a simmer and cook for about 20 minutes, until tender and easily pierced with a fork. Drain and peel away the skin.
2. Using a potato ricer, mash the potatoes and butter together. Fold in the cream and salt and pepper. Your mashed potatoes should be fluffy and light. At this point you may add different flavors, such as olive oil, pesto, white truffle, etc.

> **Serves 4**
>
> Chef Matthew Murphy of the Ritz–Carlton in New Orleans uses only Yukon for mashed potatoes because "they have an excellent amount of starch, and have a perfect texture to be mashed."

Pecan-Crusted Chicken

Serves 4

Serve this with Bourbon Molasses Glacé (page 517).

2 tomatoes, halved
3 cloves garlic, chopped
Salt and freshly ground black
    pepper, to taste
2 eggs
2 cups whole milk
2½ cups pecan halves
3 cups all-purpose flour
4 (7-ounce) skinless, boneless
    chicken breasts

½ cup clarified butter
4 teaspoons extra-virgin olive
    oil
¼ pound onion, diced
1 pound baby spinach
1 tablespoon unsalted butter
1 tablespoon creole spices
1 recipe Buttery Mashed
    Potatoes (page 517)

1. Preheat the oven to 180°. Sprinkle the tomato halves with a little of the chopped garlic, salt, and pepper. Place on a baking tray and bake for about 20 minutes. Remove from oven and let cool. These can be reheated when assembling the dish.

2. While the tomatoes are cooking, make an egg wash by beating together the eggs and milk. Set aside. In a food processor, chop 2 cups of the pecans and 2 cups of the flour together until the pecans are fine and well mixed with the flour. Season the chicken breasts with salt and pepper. Dredge each breast in the remaining 1 cup flour, then dip into the egg wash, and then coat in the pecan flour. Make sure the chicken breasts are completely coated.

3. After the tomatoes have been removed from the oven, increase oven temperature to 375°. In a large cast-iron skillet over medium to high heat, warm the clarified butter. Add the chicken breasts and cook until they are a nice golden color on bottom. Turn the breasts over, and transfer the pan to the oven. Bake for about 8 to 10 minutes, until golden brown on top.

4. While the chicken is cooking, warm the olive oil in a pan and add the onions, then the remaining garlic. (Adding the onions first helps the garlic to cook better.) Cook until onions begin to soften, then add the spinach. When it begins to wilt, remove from heat and season to taste.

continues >>

5. Melt butter in a skillet. Add the pecans and toss with the butter. Sprinkle in the creole seasoning, and toss to coat all the pecans evenly. Cook over medium heat, stirring frequently, for 2 to 3 minutes.

6. To serve, spoon the mashed potato in the center of serving plates and place the spinach to the side. Place the chicken breast on top of the spinach. Arrange the roasted tomatoes beside the chicken and drizzle the sauce around. Spoon the pecans on top of the mashed potatoes.

Balsamic Vinaigrette—A Classic

Whisk together ½ cup balsamic vinegar, 3 tablespoons Dijon mustard, 3 tablespoons honey, 2 finely minced garlic cloves, 2 finely minced small shallots, a bit of salt, and freshly ground pepper to taste. Then very gradually whisk in 1 cup of extra-virgin olive oil (yields 1²/₃ cups).

Lollypop Veal Chop

4 (12-ounce) veal chops
Olive oil, as needed
Course salt and freshly ground
    black pepper, to taste
8 cloves garlic

½ bottle Cabernet wine
1 cup Chambord
1 cup fresh raspberries
1 cup granulated sugar

Serves 4

This dish comes from Chef Paul O'Connor of Alchemy Restaurant at CopperWynd Resort and Club in Fountain Hills, Arizona. Have your butcher tie and French trim each chop to resemble a lollypop.

1. Rub the veal chops with olive oil and salt and pepper. Let marinate in the refrigerator while preparing the sauce.

2. Combine all the remaining ingredients in a saucepan. Cook over medium heat until the mixture is a syrup consistency, about 2 hours. Remove from heat and let cool. Strain the syrup through a fine-mesh sieve, holding the candied garlic cloves to the side. Set aside the syrup and garlic.

3. Grill the veal chops over medium heat to desired doneness, basting with the raspberry syrup. Serve the chops with the remaining sauce and garnish with the candied garlic cloves.

Roasted Butternut Squash Soup

Serves 4

This hearty and flavorful soup is very low in fat and is a favorite of Washington, DC's 2004 Chef of the Year, Jeff Tunks of the restaurant DC Coast.

1 large butternut squash
¼ cup olive oil
1 small yellow onion, thinly sliced
1 clove garlic, chopped
1 quart chicken stock

1 bay leaf
1 sprig fresh thyme
Salt, to taste
1 smoked chicken breast, diced
1 tablespoon minced fresh chives

1. Preheat the oven to 350°. Split the squash in half lengthwise and remove the seeds. Place cut-side down in ½ inch of water in a baking dish. Roast until tender, about 30 to 45 minutes. Remove from oven and remove the skin.
2. In a large soup pot, heat the olive oil on medium. Add the sliced onion and sauté until tender. Add the garlic and sauté for 1 minute (do not brown). Add the roasted squash, the chicken stock, bay leaf, and thyme, and simmer for 20 minutes.
3. Remove and discard the bay leaf and thyme stem, and purée the soup until smooth. Season with salt.
4. Place a quarter of the diced chicken and the minced chives in the center of each soup plate. Ladle 1 cup of the hot soup around the chicken. Serve immediately.

Cooking in Early American Kitchens

Early colonial housewives didn't have it easy. Their day typically began at 4 A.M., at which time they fetched wood, built a fire, milked the cows, and gathered eggs. Most of their day focused on the main meal—dinner, served in the afternoon. Working until sunset, many American housewives during this period perished from major kitchen accidents caused by their aprons or dresses catching on fire. This was because they cooked in large fireplaces, which held boiling pots. Later "cranes" were introduced, which helped hoist large pots over the fire, but preparing the meals was still dangerous business.

Jumbo Lump Crab Cakes

1 pound jumbo lump crabmeat
1 egg
Juice of ½ lemon
1 tablespoon mayonnaise
1 tablespoon minced fresh
 chives
Pinch cayenne pepper

Salt, to taste
¼–½ cup fresh brioche crumbs
6 tablespoons olive oil
Corn-Pickled Okra Relish
 (page 522)
Spicy Remoulade (page 522)

Serves 5 (as an appetizer)

This is among the most popular dishes served by Jeff Tunks at his restaurant, DC Coast, in Washington, DC.

1. Preheat the oven to 350°.
2. Gently remove the shells from the crabmeat, being careful not to break up the lumps.
3. In a large mixing bowl, combine the egg, lemon juice, mayonnaise, chives, cayenne, and salt. Gently fold in the crabmeat. Add the brioche crumbs sparingly to lightly bind the meat. Form into 5 cakes.
4. Sauté the crab cakes in olive oil until golden brown. Transfer to a baking sheet and bake for 10 minutes. On individual plates, mound a generous spoonful of okra relish, top with a crab cake, then top with the remoulade.

The Revival of Comfort Food

It's hard to say exactly what defines an "American" meal, at least these days. But not so long ago the following might have been considered typical American family dishes: mashed potatoes, pot roast, fried chicken, chili, roast chicken, pork chops and gravy, sloppy joes, spaghetti, meat loaf, and beef stew. "Comfort foods," as many of these are now known, are actually making a gourmet comeback. Restaurants such as Jones in Philadelphia elevate comfort food to the level of upscale dining. Favorites include creamed corn, turkey dinner (served year-round), and homemade apple pie. But this is not exactly how Mom used to make it—it's even better.

Corn-Pickled Okra Relish

Serves 5 (as a garnish)

Serve with Jumbo Lump
Crab Cakes (page 245).

2 ears fresh white corn, husks on
½ small red onion, minced
1 clove garlic, minced
12 pickled okra, sliced
1 tomato, diced

¼ cup olive oil
2 tablespoons red wine vinegar
Salt and freshly ground black
    pepper, to taste
1 tablespoon chopped cilantro

1. Preheat the oven to 350° or prepare outdoor grill.
2. Roast or grill the corn in the husk for 20 to 25 minutes. Let cool. Remove the husk and cut the kernels off the cob. Combine the corn with the remaining relish ingredients.

Spicy Remoulade

Serves 5 (as a garnish)

Serve with Jumbo Lump
Crab Cakes.

4 tablespoons mayonnaise
1 teaspoon horseradish
1 teaspoon Creole mustard
½ teaspoon Tabasco
1 tablespoon chili sauce

Juice of ½ lemon
Salt and freshly ground black
    pepper, to taste
½ teaspoon Worcestershire
    sauce

Mix together all the ingredients until smooth. Serve atop crab cakes.

Roasted Tomato, Zucchini, and Goat Cheese Tarts

4 green zucchini, sliced
2 tablespoons olive oil
2 teaspoons chopped garlic
1 quart heavy cream
4 eggs
Salt and freshly ground black
    pepper, to taste
10 tomatoes, halved, deseeded,
    and juice drained off

2 tablespoons extra-virgin olive
    oil
Herbes de Provence
8 ounces goat cheese
¼ bunch basil
10 puff pastry shells

Serves 10

Award-winning Chef Frédéric Castan serves this savory appetizer at Sofitel Chicago Water Tower Hotel's stylish Café des Architectes. Serve with a salad of mixed baby winter greens tossed in a balsamic vinaigrette.

1. Sauté the zucchini in the olive oil. Add the garlic and then the cream. Let cook for 30 minutes and blend together. Add the eggs and season with salt and pepper.

2. Preheat the oven to 250°. Mix together the tomatoes, extra-virgin olive oil, herbes de Provence, and salt. Roast on a baking sheet in the oven for approximately 3 to 4 hours, until they are dry.

3. When the tomatoes are done, increase oven temperature to 350°. Mix the goat cheese with the basil. In each tart shell, place a layer of tomatoes on the bottom, add a layer of goat cheese, and cover with the zucchini mix. Place on a baking sheet and bake for 15 minutes.

Elegant Cream of Celery Soup

Serves 4

A mascarpone béchamel sauce lends extra richness and flavor to a basic creamed soup recipe. For an extra gourmet touch, garnish the soup with black truffle shavings just before serving.

4 stalks celery
½ sweet Vidalia onion
4 shallots
2 tablespoons olive oil
3 cups water
½ cup chicken broth
3 tablespoons butter

2½ tablespoons all-purpose flour
1 cup light cream
¼ teaspoon celery salt, to taste
⅛ teaspoon paprika, or to taste
2 tablespoons mascarpone

1. String the celery and cut on the diagonal into thin strips. Peel and finely chop the onion and shallots.
2. Heat the olive oil over medium heat. Sauté the celery, onion, and shallots until softened. Cook for 1 more minute, then remove the vegetables from the pan.
3. In a large saucepan, bring the water and chicken broth to a boil. Add the vegetables. Turn the heat down to low while preparing the béchamel sauce. (Do not cover the saucepan.)
4. In a small saucepan, melt the butter in a small saucepan over low heat. Add the flour, whisking continuously until the flour is mixed in with the butter (2 to 3 minutes). Slowly add the light cream. Continue whisking over medium heat until the sauce is thick and bubbly. Add the celery salt and paprika. Remove from the heat and slowly stir in the mascarpone, 1 tablespoon at a time.
5. Carefully pour the béchamel sauce into the celery soup. Turn up the heat and cook for 1 more minute to thicken. Serve immediately.

A Mild-Mannered Onion

Cipollini onions are very mild in flavor, and impart a certain sweetness. The cipollini onion comes from Italy and is harvested in the United States and sold at specialty and farmer's markets. It is a small heirloom onion, shaped like a saucer, and can be found fresh, with the green top still on, or dried like the common yellow onion.

Shiitake Mushroom Soup

¼ cup butter
½ cup diced yellow onion
½ cup chopped celery
1 pound shiitake mushrooms,
    washed
2 cups chicken stock

2 sprigs fresh thyme
1 sprig rosemary
1 cup cream
Salt and freshly ground black
    pepper, to taste

Serves 4

This is from Chef Scott Johnson of Canoe Bay. A Relais and Chateaux wilderness estate in Wisconsin, Canoe Bay is one of the most romantic hideaways in the Midwest.

1. In a large pot over medium heat, melt the butter. Add the onion, celery, and mushrooms. Cook until the onions are translucent. Reduce heat to low and add the chicken stock, thyme, and rosemary. Let cook until reduced by half.
2. Purée the soup in blender, then return it to the pot. Heat the cream in a saucepan until hot, then fold it into the soup. Season with salt and pepper, and serve.

Cranberry Salad

1 pound cooked wild rice
⅓ cups dried cranberries
½ cup walnuts, toasted
1 apple, diced
¼ cup maple syrup

2 tablespoons cider vinegar
½ cup olive oil
Salt and freshly ground black
    pepper, to taste

Serves 8

This is the perfect afternoon dish to enjoy outside on the deck, or as a refreshing part of a picnic lunch.

In a large bowl, mix together all the ingredients.

Chapter 38

Oh Canada:
Taste of the Provinces

528   Merrit Venison Carpaccio

529   Mountain Huckleberry Vinaigrette

530   Brine-Marinated Salmon

530   Horseradish Vodka Dip

531   Duck Confit in Phyllo with Caramelized Apples

532   Warm Dungeness Crab and Brie Melt

532   Pickled Okanagan Apples

533   Belgian Endive Salad with Maple Vinaigrette

533   Scallion Scones

534   Red Laver Sea Lettuce "Kimchi"

535   Ahi Tuna Tartar

536   Nasturtium-Wrapped Halibut with Lobster Ragout

537   Wild Boar and Orzo Salad

Merrit Venison Carpaccio

Serves 8

Executive Chef Wayne Martin, at the the Four Seasons in Vancouver, takes advantage of the availability of high-quality venison from a local farm in Merrit, British Columbia, for this recipe. Fleur de sel is a sea salt from Brittany, France.

8 baby carrots
4 baby gold beets
4 baby striped beets
16 fine green beans
4 stalks asparagus
1 small shallot, finely chopped
4 large leaves basil, chopped
1 ounce toasted pine nuts
Juice of 1 lemon
2 tablespoons (or more, as needed) extra-virgin olive oil

Fleur de sel or sea salt, to taste
Freshly ground black pepper, to taste
¾ pound center-cut venison tenderloin
1 cup Mountain Huckleberry Vinaigrette (page 529)
A few chervil leaves

1. Blanch all the vegetables separately until they are easily pierced with a knife. Transfer to a bowl filled with ice water to cool. Remove from the water and peel the carrots. Trim off the tops of the beets. Peel the beets and cut into quarters. Cut the beans in half. Cut the asparagus into 4 pieces each. Set aside.

2. Toss the shallot with the vegetables, along with the basil, pine nuts, lemon juice, 1 tablespoon of the olive oil, salt, and pepper.

3. Slice the venison into 8 equal pieces and place in between 2 pieces of cling film. Gently pound out the meat into as thin a sheet as possible. Brush the venison with the remaining extra-virgin olive oil, and season with salt and pepper.

4. To assemble, place the venison on serving plates and place the mixed vegetables on top. Drizzle the vinaigrette over everything and garnish with the chervil leaves.

Mountain Huckleberry Vinaigrette

¼ cup huckleberries
1 shallot, peeled and roughly
   chopped
2 teaspoons raspberry vinegar
2 tablespoons olive oil

1 teaspoon honey mustard
¼ cup water
Salt and freshly ground black
   pepper, to taste

Mix together all the ingredients and serve.

Serves 8

Serve this delicious dressing over Merrit Venison Carpaccio (page 528).

BC Farms Provide Unique Organic Choices

British Columbia is filled with specialty produce stores and farms such as the Glorious Garnish and Seasonal Salad Company, providing professional and home chefs with colorful, fresh organic produce. You can find nearly everything there: beets, green beans, carrots, and asparagus. The bright mustard-colored gold beets and red-and-white-striped variety add dramatic color to this dish. Red beets, which may be easier to find, are a suitable substitute. The huckleberries add a distinct West Coast touch and can also be found at many specialty produce markets in the Lower Mainland. Frozen or preserved huckleberries can be substituted, as can fresh or frozen local blackberries.

Brine-Marinated Salmon

6 cups water
1 tablespoon salt
2/3 cup brown sugar
1/2 cup honey
1/2 orange, sliced
1/2 lime, sliced

1/2 lemon, sliced
4 sprigs dill
1 (4-pound) fillet fresh Atlantic
    salmon or wild sockeye,
    dressed

1. Place all the ingredients except the salmon into a stockpot. Bring to a boil. Remove from heat immediately. Once the mixture is cool, submerge the salmon in it.
2. Marinate in the refrigerator for approximately 24 hours. Then cook the fillet as you prefer. One suggestion: smoke the fillets over a 250° wood fire for approximately 2 hours, until the fillets are firm to the touch. Peel off the skin and serve.

Horseradish Vodka Dip

5 tablespoons sour cream
1/3 teaspoon horseradish
2 tablespoons vodka
1 teaspoon honey

6 drops Tabasco
Salt and freshly ground white
    pepper, to taste

Mix together all the ingredients and refrigerate. Serve cold with salmon.

Salt Spring Island

Coined the "Organic Capital of Canada," Salt Spring Island (just off Vancouver Island) hosts a bevy of regional farmers, artisans, and organic specialists. The Salt Spring Island Farmers' Market is a must-see for those looking to taste the region's best organic produce. Locals sell vegetables, herbs, jellies, and baked goods all with ingredients from their farms, every Saturday from mid-April to mid-October, in the town of Ganges.

Duck Confit in Phyllo with Caramelized Apples

1 pound duck confit meat
⅓ cup minced shallots
5 leaves fresh basil, chopped
12 sheets frozen phyllo dough,
*   thawed in the refrigerator*

½ cup unsalted butter, melted
2 Golden Delicious apples
1 tablespoon olive oil

Serves 6 (as an appetizer)

This comes from Executive Chef Patrick Bourachot of the Fairmont Le Chateau Montebello in Quebec. Purchase 1¾ pounds whole duck confit leg at a gourmet shop or high-end butcher, to yield the 1 pound required.

1. Prepare the duck confit by removing the bones, skin, and fat. Shred the meat by pulling it apart with your fingers. Place the meat in a bowl, add the shallots and chopped basil, and mix well to combine. Set aside.
2. Preheat the oven to 350°. Line a baking sheet with parchment paper.
3. Place 1 sheet of the phyllo dough on a clean work surface and brush butter across the surface. Place a second sheet on top of the first and spread with butter. Repeat with a third and fourth phyllo sheet, but do not brush final layer with butter. Prepare 2 separate stacks of phyllo squares the same way.
4. Cut each square in half, for a total of a 6 rectangular phyllo sheet stacks. Spread ⅙ of the confit mixture along the short edge of 1 phyllo rectangle and roll up into a log about 1 inch thick. Place on the prepared baking sheet. Repeat with remaining confit mixture and phyllo rectangles to make six logs in total.
5. Brush the logs lightly with the remaining melted butter and bake until warm and golden, about 7 minutes.
6. Peel the apples and remove the cores, then cut each apple into 8 wedges. In a nonstick fry pan, heat the oil and fry the apples until lightly browned on each side, about 2 minutes per side. To serve, cut each baked confit "log" in half diagonally, and garnish with caramelized apple wedges.

Warm Dungeness Crab and Brie Melt

Serves 2

This is a new take on tuna melts from Executive Chef Michael Viloria of Delta Vancouver Suites. This version is served at Manhattan Restaurant in Vancouver.

4 ounces Dungeness crabmeat
2 tablespoons mayonnaise
1 teaspoon lemon juice
Pinch lemon zest
Pinch salt
Pinch pepper

2 Scallion Scones
(page 533)
2 ounces Brie cheese
Pickled Okanagan Apples

1. Preheat broiler. Mix together the crabmeat, mayonnaise, lemon juice and zest, salt, and pepper.
2. Split the scones in half and place on a baking tray. Place the crab mixture on both halves of the scone. Slice the Brie cheese and place on top of the crab mixture (it is best to slice the cheese when it is cold, directly from the refrigerator, because of its soft texture). Broil until the cheese melts. Serve with the pickled apples.

Pickled Okanagan Apples

Serves 2

These are delicious served with Scallion Scones (page 533) or Warm Dungeness Crab and Brie Melt.

1 Okanagan apple
2 tablespoons apple cider
  vinegar

1 teaspoon salt
2 teaspoons granulated sugar
Pinch white pepper

1. Peel and slice the apples thinly.
2. Mix together all the remaining ingredients in a bowl, add the apples, and let marinate for 5 minutes before serving.

Belgian Endive Salad with Maple Vinaigrette

7 tablespoons grape seed oil
7 tablespoons maple syrup
4 tablespoons cider vinegar
2 tablespoons whole-grain
    mustard
1 tablespoon Dijon mustard

Salt and freshly ground black
    pepper, to taste
12 slices baguette
12 slices Brie
6 Belgian endive leaves
1 tablespoon pecans

Serves 4

Jean-Paul Giroux of the restaurant Le Saint-Augustine in Quebec suggests also using this vinaigrette with smoked salmon or cooked ham.

1. Preheat broiler on medium heat. Combine the oil, maple syrup, vinegar, both mustards, and the salt and pepper. Mix the vinaigrette well and set aside.
2. Place the baguette slices on a baking sheet and top each with a slice of the Brie. Broil until the cheese has melted. Cut up into croutons.
3. Cut the endives into slivers. In a bowl, toss the endive with the pecans and the vinaigrette. Serve with the Brie croutons.

Scallion Scones

2 cups all-purpose flour
½ cup granulated sugar
1 tablespoon baking powder
½ teaspoon salt
1 scallion, minced

½ cup butter
1 egg
⅓ cup whole milk, plus a bit
    extra for brushing

Yields 12 scones

For an unusual accompaniment, try serving these scones with Pickled Okanagan Apples (page 532).

1. Preheat the oven to 425°.
2. Mix together flour, sugar, baking powder, salt, and scallion. Cut the butter into the flour mixture with a fork. Add the egg and milk, and mix to form the dough.
3. Sprinkle flour on a work surface and roll out the dough to a thickness of 1½ inches.
4. Cut the dough into rounds with a cookie cutter or the mouth of a drinking glass. Brush the surface of the dough with a little bit of milk. Bake for 15 minutes or until golden brown.

Red Laver Sea Lettuce "Kimchi"

Serves 10

From Executive Chef Jonathan Chovancek comes this Canadian version of the classic Korean condiment. If you cannot purchase fresh sea lettuce, it is available dried in most Japanese grocery stores.

1 pound white cabbage, cut
    into ½-inch squares
2 tablespoons kosher salt
4 ounces fresh Red Laver
    sea lettuce, washed and
    julienned
½ cup apple cider vinegar

¼ cup wild flower honey
2 cloves garlic, sliced thinly
3 teaspoons grated fresh ginger
2 teaspoons dried red pepper
    flakes
2 teaspoons fennel seeds,
    toasted

1. Spread the cabbage onto a baking sheet and cover evenly with 1 table-spoon of the kosher salt. Leave to dry and cure uncovered for 24 hours.
2. When the cabbage is cured, remove from the tray, discarding extra liquid. In a large, nonreactive bowl, mix the cabbage with the sea lettuce.
3. Place the vinegar, honey, remaining salt, garlic, ginger, red pepper flakes, and fennel seeds in a nonreactive saucepan and bring to a boil. Remove from heat and let cool completely.
4. Pour the cooled liquid over the cabbage mixture and place in a nonreactive, sealable container. Refrigerate for 2 weeks.
5. When ready to use, remove the cabbage mixture from the liquid with clean tongs. Do not rinse. Use as you would pickles. Keep refrigerated.

Some of British Columbia's Best Chefs Float

Imagine checking into a luxury resort floating in the middle of a fjord. Then imagine feasting on king crab claws, poached wild Pacific winter-spring salmon, and flourless dark chocolate hazelnut cake. Some of Canada's best chefs are chopping, blanching, and sautéing in world-class resorts such as King Pacific Lodge, a Clayoquot Wilderness Resort.

Ahi Tuna Tartar

½ pound fresh yellowfin tuna
    (ahi tuna)
1 tablespoon toasted pine nuts
¼ green apple, peeled and
    diced
½ teaspoon chopped fresh
    ginger
1 tablespoon chopped fresh
    parsley

¼ teaspoon fresh-squeezed
    lemon juice
1 teaspoon soy sauce
½ teaspoon Dijon mustard
1 teaspoon olive oil
½ teaspoon wasabi powder
Salt and cracked black pepper,
    to taste

> **Serves 3**
>
> Chef Sean Riley of Glowbal Grill and Satay Bar in Vancouver says, "Be sure to use only fresh sashimi-grade ahi tuna, and mix ingredients together just before serving. Also keep all items cool when preparing." Serve with crostinis and sliced avocado, if desired.

1. In a stainless steel bowl, mix together the tuna, pine nuts, green apples, ginger, parsley, and lemon juice. Chill in the refrigerator for at least three hours.
2. In a separate bowl, whisk together the soy sauce, mustard, olive oil, and wasabi. Mix with the tuna mixture.
3. Season to taste with salt and cracked black pepper. Serve cold.

Canada's Varied Cuisine

From tasty Alberta beef to Manitoba's vast agriculture, Canada is an enormous country with a myriad of provinces and styles of cuisine. The Northwest Territories offer total diversity—from dining in chic modern restaurants, to tasting foods that sustained the Inuit in cozy rustic cabins. New Brunswick is the place for seafood, with five-star restaurants as well as wharf-side fish and chip stands. And in Nova Scotia you are never more than a half-hour from the sea. Prince Edward Island diners enjoy a cross between the rugged, seafaring culture of the East Coast and the elegant Victorian era, and in Quebec you will discover something altogether different—French-style restaurants that rival Parisian bistros.

Nasturtium-Wrapped Halibut with Lobster Ragout

2 (1-pound) cooked lobsters
1 small peeled onion
3 stalks celery
1 teaspoon dried thyme
4 bay leaves
1 teaspoon peppercorns
3 sprigs parsley
1 large shallot, diced
½ red bell pepper, diced
2 tablespoons chopped fresh cilantro

1 tablespoon finely chopped garlic
¼ cup whipping cream
1 tablespoon cornstarch, mixed with 1 tablespoon water
Sea salt and cracked pepper, to taste
12 nasturtium leaves
4 (5-ounce) fillets fresh Atlantic halibut

1. Shuck the cooked lobsters, cut into bite-sized pieces, and set aside. Place the lobster bodies and shells in a stockpot and cover with water. Add the onion, celery, thyme, bay leaves, peppercorns, and parsley. Bring to a boil and simmer the lobster broth for 1 hour.
2. Sauté the shallot and bell pepper. Add 2 cups of the lobster broth, the cilantro, and garlic. Simmer for 5 minutes, then add the cream. Stir the cornstarch slurry into the pot and cook until thickened. Add the lobster meat and season with salt and pepper.
3. Preheat the oven to 400°.
4. Heat the nasturtium leaves in the microwave for 10 seconds to wilt. Place them topside down. Salt and pepper the halibut on both sides, then carefully wrap each portion with 3 wilted nasturtium leaves so the fillet is completely covered. Place in a baking dish and bake for 12 minutes.
5. Divide the lobster ragout among 4 large pasta bowls. Serve the nasturtium-covered halibut on top.

Wild Boar and Orzo Salad

Serves 4

Serve this with the Nasturtium-Wrapped Halibut with Lobster Ragout (page 532).

3 ounces wild boar bacon
1 large shallot, peeled and
    diced
½ red bell pepper, diced
3 baby yellow beets, peeled,
    blanched, and sliced

1 cup orzo pasta
2 cups chicken stock
Fresh-chopped thyme, rosemary,
    sage, and chives, to taste
Salt and pepper, to taste
¼ cup sour cream

1. Cut the wild boar bacon into small dice and sauté in a deep skillet over medium heat. Add the shallot, red bell pepper, beets, pasta, and chicken stock. Cook over medium heat for 8 to 10 minutes, until the pasta is al dente.
2. Add the chopped herbs, season with salt and pepper, and add the sour cream. Serve warm.

Okanagan Valley

Located in south-central British Columbia, the Thompson Okanagan is a long valley, dominated by Lake Okanagan, running seventy miles down the center of the valley. Over the past ten years the valley's wine industry has blossomed and now boasts over 60 boutique producers. A large number of the wineries are concentrated in the southern part of the valley, between Penticton and Oliver, and include Tinhorn Creek Vineyards, Burrowing Owl, Hawthorne Mountain, Blue Mountain, and Inniskillin Wineries. Meanwhile, a few of the larger producers are in the Kelowna area, including Mission Hill, Summerhill, Quail's Gate, Calona, and Cedar Creek. Visitors can sample local vintages and eat meals highlighting local produce in a series of boutique restaurants overlooking Lake Okanagan.

Chapter 39

Mexico:
Food for Any Fiesta

540   Tuna Ceviche

541   Broiled Sea Bass Fillet over Tomatillo Rice

542   Cold Avocado Soup, Atlixco Style

543   Five-Minute Recado

543   Fish Tacos

544   Cold Coconut Soup

545   Veal Medallions in Almond Stew

546   Roasted Vegetable Salad

547   Jicama with Lime

547   Ceviche de Pescado

548   Mole Poblano with Chicken

549   Plantains with Whipped Cream

550   Pasta with Chilies

551   Ancho Chili Fudge Pie

Tuna Ceviche

Serves 4

Erick Anguiano of
...kal del Mar serves
...o one of the best ceviche
...enus in Mexico. Here is a
recipe that no one who
visits can resist.

1 tablespoon olive oil
1 garlic clove, chopped
1¾ pounds tuna
2 tablespoons fresh-squeezed
    lime juice
1 tablespoon fresh-squeezed
    grapefruit juice
2 tablespoons dry red wine

½ white onion, diced
1 pound tomatoes, diced
1 tablespoon finely chopped
    fresh cilantro
Salt and freshly ground black
    pepper, to taste
½ red onion, sliced

1. Heat the olive oil in a sauté pan. Add the garlic and sauté for a few minutes, until aromatic and just slightly golden.
2. Cut the tuna into 4 squares, and mix with the lime and grapefruit juice in a glass bowl. Let marinate for 2 minutes. Add the red wine, white onion, tomato, cilantro, salt, and pepper. Mix well. Place the tuna mixture on serving plates and top with the garlic and its sautéing oil. Place sliced red onion on top, and serve.

Mexi-terranean?

The cuisine at Ikal del Mar has been described as "Mexi-terranean," an eclectic culinary mix combining the flavors of the Mediterranean and the vibrant tastes and colors of Mexico. Azul, the restaurant where these delectable ceviches are made, also offers Mayan-influenced dishes such as Mayan tortilla soup, and sea bass topped with a Mayan black bean sauce.

Broiled Sea Bass Fillet over Tomatillo Rice

Serves 4

This recipe, from Casa del Mar in Los Cabos, suggests sea bass, but you can use any fresh, firm fish such as snapper, grouper, or mahi-mahi.

¼ cup extra-virgin olive oil, plus extra for garnish
4 (7-ounce) sea bass fillets
2 teaspoons kosher salt
1 teaspoon fresh-cracked black pepper
1 pound green tomatillos

1 sweet Vidalia onion, peeled and quartered
2 cloves garlic, peeled
1 bunch fresh cilantro, leaves chopped, plus extra sprigs for garnish
4 cups cooked basmati rice

1. Drizzle the olive oil onto each fish fillet and season with kosher salt and pepper. Pan-fry for 4 minutes each side over medium heat.
2. Preheat broiler on high. Peel off and discard the husks from the tomatillos and rinse under cold, running water. Place the green tomatoes, onions, and garlic on a baking sheet and roast for 7 minutes. Chop the roasted ingredients and combine in a medium-sized bowl. Add the cilantro and season with salt and pepper. Add the cooked rice and mix to combine.
3. Place a scoop of tomatillo rice in the center of each serving plate. (Line the plates with a flat corn husk or a square of banana leaf, if desired.) Place the sea bass fillets over the rice. Garnish with fresh cilantro sprigs and drizzle extra-virgin olive oil around the rice and fish mounds.

From the Sea

Being able to use fresh fish from the Sea of Cortez or the Pacific Ocean is a unique advantage in Los Cabos. Combining them with Mexican ingredients such as tomatillos and fresh cilantro is a signature culinary experience at Casa del Mar, one of Mexico's finest resorts.

Cold Avocado Soup, Atlixco Style

Serves 8

recipe comes from Careyes Beach Resort, located in the state of Jalisco. Atlixco is one of the most important avocado-producing regions of Mexico.

For the broth:

5 quarts water

4 chicken legs with thighs

6 chicken wings

1 white onion, sliced

1 head garlic, unpeeled and halved

3 carrots

6 stalks celery

2 bay leaves

6 mint leaves

6 black peppercorns

Salt, to taste

For the soup:

½ cup butter

1 white onion, puréed

2 cloves garlic, puréed

½ leek, puréed

1 carrot, peeled and puréed

6 ripe California avocados, peeled

1 cup créme fraîche or heavy cream

1 cup plain yogurt, beaten

Salt, to taste

2 tablespoons fresh-squeezed lime juice

½ cup olive oil

¼ cup finely chopped white onion

2 tablespoons finely chopped cilantro

1. To prepare the broth, bring the water to a boil in a stockpot. Add all the remaining broth ingredients. Simmer over low heat until the mixture foams. Skim off the foam and simmer for 2 hours. Remove from heat and let cool for 1 hour. Strain through a fine-mesh sieve and discard the solids. Skim off fat, and refrigerate. If the broth separates, reheat slightly before using.

2. To prepare the soup, melt butter in a saucepan. Add the puréed onion, garlic, leek, and carrot along with 3 cups of the broth. Cook until thick, about 25 minutes. Remove from heat and let cool.

3. Meanwhile, blend the avocados with 6 cups of the broth (blend in batches, if necessary) in a blender or food processor. Strain through a fine-mesh sieve. Add the créme fraîche and yogurt. Stir in the vegetable mixture, and add salt to taste. Add the lime juice and olive oil. If the soup is too thick, add a little more broth. Chill in the freezer for 1 hour.

4. To serve, pour the cold avocado soup into soup bowls fitted in liners filled with crushed ice (if available). Garnish with the chopped onion and cilantro.

Five-Minute Recado

½ cup achiote paste
½ cup freshly squeezed lime juice
½ cup orange juice
2 tablespoons white vinegar
2 tablespoons tequila

1 teaspoon freshly ground cumin
¼ teaspoon Tabasco sauce, or to taste
½ teaspoon freshly ground black pepper
1 clove garlic, minced

In a food processor or blender, process all the ingredients until smooth. Cover and refrigerate overnight to give the flavors a chance to blend.

Recado Paste

Recado paste comes from the Yucatán, where it is often used with suckling pig. The pig is rubbed with the recado, wrapped in banana leaves, and then cooked in a stone-lined pit until the meat is so tender it falls off the bones. Grilling is a less traditional, but far easier, method.

Fish Tacos

4 fish fillets, such as cod
3 tablespoons lime juice
3 tablespoons olive oil
1 green onion, chopped
1 clove garlic, minced

2 teaspoons granulated sugar
1 tablespoon ancho paste
12 soft corn tortillas
2 cups Mexican salsa, various types

1. Rinse the fish fillets and pat dry. In a small bowl, whisk together the lime juice, olive oil, green onion, minced garlic, sugar, and ancho paste. Rub the mixture over the fish. Place the fillets in a large baking dish. Cover and marinate in the refrigerator for 2 hours.
2. Heat the grill. Remove the fish from the refrigerator. Discard the marinade. Grill the fish over medium heat until it is opaque and cooked through. Chop the fish.
3. Serve the fish with the warmed corn tortillas and at least 2 types of salsa.

Cold Coconut Soup

Serves 8

...uts are native to the
...astal state of Colima.
This soup, made at
El Tamarindo Golf Resort,
uses this abundant
ingredient to make a
delicious first course.

1 quart whole milk
2 cups finely shredded fresh
   coconut
2 cups fresh coconut water
2 cups canned coconut milk

½ cup granulated sugar
Salt, to taste
1½ cups heavy cream
Ground cinnamon, for garnish

1. Bring the whole milk to a boil in a medium-sized saucepan. Reduce to a simmer, and stir in the shredded coconut. Simmer for 20 minutes.
2. Remove from heat and blend in a blender or food processor. Return the mixture to the saucepan and add the coconut water and coconut milk. Season with sugar and salt. Add the cream, beating occasionally with a whisk. Cook over medium heat for 25 minutes or until the soup thickens slightly. If the soup is too thick, add a little more cream. Cool the soup on a bed of crushed ice and refrigerate.
3. To serve, pour the chilled soup into hollowed-out coconut shells. Sprinkle cinnamon on top.

Mexican Cheeses: The Whole Enchilada

You may not hear much about Mexican cheeses, but they exist, and are an intricate part of authentic Mexican cuisine. *Queso* means "cheese" in Spanish, and Hispanic cheeses can be grouped into three basic types: fresh cheeses (best known for being moist, crumbly, and prized for their ability to become soft when heated), melting cheeses (which resist separating when heated), and hard cheeses (usually a finely grated or crumbled dry cheese that finishes off a dish). Here are a few examples: (fresh) *queso blanco*, *queso cresco*, and *panela*; (melting) *queso asadero*, *Oaxaca*, *quesadilla*, and *Chihuahua*; (hard) *queso cotija*, and *queso enchilado*.

Veal Medallions in Almond Stew

6 tablespoons olive oil, divided

2-inch cinnamon stick

⅓ cup whole skinned almonds

2 tablespoons white sesame
    seeds

2 small cloves

2 peppercorns

2½ ounces semisweet yeast
    bread, torn into pieces

2 pinches dried oregano

2 pinches dried thyme

3½ cups chicken or veal broth

½ pound tomatoes, slightly
    charred and skinned

½ white pearl onion, grilled

2 cloves garlic, roasted and
    peeled

1 tablespoon whole capers,
    rinsed

10 pitted green olives

Pickled jalapeños, to taste

12 (2½-ounce) veal medallions

Salt and freshly ground black
    pepper, to taste

All-purpose flour, as needed

Corn tortillas, warmed

Serves 6

This recipe comes from
Chef Horacio Reyes of
Hotel Hacienda Los
Laureles in Oaxaca,
Mexico, who learned
this recipe from his
grandmother.

1. Heat 4 tablespoons of the olive oil in a skillet and fry the cinnamon, almonds, sesame seeds, cloves, peppercorns, yeast bread, oregano, and thyme until golden. Transfer the mixture to a blender. Add the broth, tomatoes, onion, and garlic, and blend well.

2. Heat the remaining 2 tablespoons olive oil in a pan. Add the blended ingredients and the capers, olives, and pickled jalapeños. Cook for 10 minutes over medium heat, scraping the bottom of the pan often to avoid sticking. (Add more broth if the mole gets too thick.) Continue cooking until the stew turns a bright orange color and is reduced.

3. In the meantime, preheat the oven to 350°. Season the veal with salt and pepper, and flour lightly. Sear in an ovenproof pan over medium-high heat on the stovetop for 1 to 2 minutes on each side. Transfer the pan to the oven and cook according to desired doneness, about 15 minutes for medium-rare.

4. To serve, place pieces of the cooked veal on warmed plates and cover with the stew. Serve with warm corn tortillas.

Roasted Vegetable Salad

Serves 4

...d vegetables lend a
...eet, smoky flavor to
...s simple salad dish. For
...est results, use fresh corn
right off the cob.

2 fresh cobs of corn
4 cloves garlic
2 red bell peppers
4 teaspoons olive oil
3 tablespoons lime juice
2 tablespoons orange juice

3 tablespoons virgin olive oil
¼ teaspoon ground cumin
½ teaspoon freshly ground
    black pepper
1 tablespoon chopped cilantro
1 tablespoon minced red onion

1. Preheat the broiler. Remove the silk from the corn cobs without removing the husks. Use string to tie the husks around the corn cobs. Cover in cold water and soak for 5 minutes. Peel the garlic.

2. Brush each bell pepper with 2 teaspoons olive oil. Lay the peppers on a broiling pan. Broil, turning frequently, until the skins are blackened and charred (about 20 minutes). Place each pepper in a sealed plastic bag for 15 minutes. Peel off the skins, and remove the stems and the seeds. Cut the peppers lengthwise into strips.

3. To roast the garlic, reduce the oven temperature to 400°. Place the garlic cloves on a baking sheet. Roast until softened (about 20 minutes). Remove and cool.

4. To roast the corn, reduce the oven temperature to 375°. Place the corn on a baking sheet and roast, turning frequently, until the husks are browned (about 20 minutes). Cool. Remove the husks. Remove the corn from the cob.

5. In a small bowl, whisk together the lime juice, orange juice, virgin olive oil, ground cumin, freshly ground black pepper, chopped cilantro, and the minced red onion. Drizzle over the roasted vegetables.

Jicama with Lime

2 red chili peppers
2 tablespoons sea salt

3 tablespoons freshly squeezed
   lime juice
2 pounds jicama

1. Cut the red chili peppers in half, remove the seeds, and finely chop. Toss with the sea salt and the lime juice. Purée in a blender or food processor until smooth. Refrigerate the sauce for 1 hour to give the flavors a chance to blend.
2. To serve, peel the jicama and cut into 1-inch slices. Arrange on a serving tray. To eat, dip the sliced jicama into the lime mixture.

Serves 6

Serve this spicy snack with margaritas on a warm afternoon.

Ceviche de Pescado

3 pounds fresh snapper fillets
3 cups fresh-squeezed lime
   juice (approx. 5–6 limes)
3 tablespoons kosher salt
1 cup diced white onion
½ cup diced radish
½ cup diced jalapeño

1 cup seeded and diced Roma
   tomato
2 avocados, sliced
Freshly ground black pepper,
   to taste
Lime slices, for garnish
½ cup chopped fresh cilantro,
   for garnish

Serves 6–8

Chef Alex Padilla of Consuelo Mexican Bistro provides this recipe, which was inspired by fishermen from different beaches in Mexico.

1. Check for bones and cut the fish into ¼-inch cubes. Combine lime juice with the fish cubes. Add of the kosher salt and marinate for at least 2 hours in the refrigerator.
2. Combine marinated fish, white onion, radish, and jalapeño. Spoon into a clear margarita glass. Top each with the tomato, avocado slices, and freshly ground black pepper to taste. Garnish with the lime slices and cilantro. Serve immediately with tostadas.

Mole Poblano with Chicken

Serves 4–6

For best results, use milder, sweeter chilies that complement the rich chocolate.

2 dried guajillo chilies
2 dried ancho chilies
¾ cup whole blanched
   almonds
¼ cup white sesame seeds
4 medium tomatoes
½ small red onion
1 clove garlic
1 cup chicken stock
¼ cup lightly packed seedless
   raisins
1 teaspoon ground cumin
½ teaspoon ground coriander

½ teaspoon ground cinnamon
¼ teaspoon chili powder, or to
   taste
2 tablespoons olive oil
3½-pound chicken, cut into 6
   serving pieces
2 ounces unsweetened
   chocolate, chopped
1 tablespoon chopped fresh
   Mexican oregano, optional

1. Cut the chilies in half, remove the seeds, and finely chop. Cover the chilies in hot water and let sit until softened (about 30 minutes). Toast the almonds and the sesame seeds by heating them in a frying pan over medium heat, shaking the pan continuously, until they turn golden. Cool and chop finely. Dice the tomatoes. Peel and mince the red onion and garlic.

2. In a blender or food processor, process the toasted nuts, softened chilies, chicken stock, raisins, minced garlic, ground cumin, ground coriander, ground cinnamon, and the chili powder until smooth.

3. Heat the olive oil in 12-inch heavy-bottomed skillet over medium-high heat. Add the chicken pieces and cook until lightly browned, cooking the chicken in 2 batches if necessary. Remove the chicken from the frying pan. Do not clean out the pan.

4. Pour the mole sauce into the frying pan. Cook for 1 minute, then add the unsweetened chocolate. Cook over low heat, uncovered, and stir frequently, until the chocolate melts. Be careful not to let the chocolate burn.

continues >>

5. Add the chicken back into the pan. Reduce the heat to low and simmer, covered, until the chicken is cooked through and the juices run clear when pierced with a knife (about 30 minutes). Baste the chicken frequently with the sauce during cooking. Sprinkle the mole with the fresh oregano and serve.

Mole

The word *mole* (pronounced MOH-lay) is from the Nahuatl word *molli*, meaning "concoction, or mixture." Red mole is from central Mexico in the Puebla and Oaxaca regions, also known as the Land of Seven Moles. Other mole colors include brown, black, green, and yellow. Generally, mole is a smooth sauce blended of onion, garlic, several varieties of chilies, ground seeds, and a small amount of chocolate. Not all moles contain chocolate.

Plantains with Whipped Cream

2 large, ripe plantains
½ cup heavy whipping cream
2 tablespoons orange juice

1 teaspoon pure Mexican
    vanilla extract
Mint sprigs, for garnish

Serves 2 to 4

Sweet whipping cream provides a nice counterbalance to starchy plantains. For a lighter version of this simple dessert, replace the whipped cream with plain yogurt flavored with a bit of freshly squeezed lime juice.

1. Fill a saucepan with enough salted water to cover the plantains and bring to a boil. Add the plantains and cook, uncovered, in the boiling water until they are tender (about 20 minutes). Remove from the water and cool. Peel the plantains and cut into thin slices.
2. Use an electric mixer to beat the whipping cream with the orange juice and the vanilla extract until it forms stiff peaks. Spoon the whipping cream over the plantain slices and serve. Garnish with the mint sprigs.

Pasta with Chilies

Serves 4

Mild, sweet guajillo chilies add a Mexican touch to Italian pasta in this fusion dish. Feel free to dress it up by sprinkling a bit of grated cheese on top and a sprig of fresh cilantro.

8 ounces linguine
2 guajillo chilies
4 shallots
2 large cloves garlic
2 ripe tomatoes
8 ounces Italian sausage

1 tablespoon butter
3 tablespoons finely chopped
   fresh basil leaves
Salt, to taste
Freshly ground black pepper, to
   taste

1. Fill a large saucepan with just enough salted water to cover the pasta. Bring to a boil. Add the pasta and cook, uncovered, until al dente (10 to 15 minutes). Drain thoroughly. Remove the seeds from the guajillo chilies and chop. Peel and finely chop the shallots and garlic. Peel the tomatoes, deseed, and slice.

2. Remove the Italian sausage from its casing. Cook the sausage in a frying pan over medium-high heat until thoroughly browned. Remove from the pan, but leave 2 tablespoons of drippings in the pan. Drain the sausage on paper towels.

3. Reduce the heat to medium and add the garlic and shallots. Sauté until the garlic is browned, and the shallots are softened. Melt the butter in the pan and add the chilies. Cook until the skin from the chilies begins to blister.

4. Add the tomatoes and cook until softened. Toss the cooked sauce with the linguine. Stir in the fresh basil. Season with salt and freshly ground black pepper as desired.

Working with Hot Chilies

Make sure to wear rubber gloves when handling dried or fresh chilies, and be very careful not to touch your eyes or face after touching them. Keeping chilies under running water while you work keeps the fumes from getting in your eyes. And wash your hands carefully with soap and water after handling either fresh or dried chilies.

Ancho Chili Fudge Pie

2 tablespoons light cream

3 ounces unsweetened
  chocolate

3 ounces semisweet chocolate

½ cup all-purpose flour

½ teaspoon salt

¼ cup granulated sugar

¾ packed cup brown sugar
  (or piloncillo)

2 large eggs

1 tablespoon Mexican vanilla
  extract

½ cup unsalted butter, melted

¼ cup chopped pecans

¼ cup chopped pistachios

2 tablespoons ancho paste

9-inch unbaked pastry shell

Serves 8

Made from poblano chilies, ancho chili paste makes an excellent addition to everything from soups and stir-fries to desserts. It is available in most specialty stores.

1. Preheat the oven to 350°.
2. Fill the bottom of a double boiler with water and place over medium heat. Combine the light cream and the chocolate in the top of the double boiler and melt. (If you don't have a double boiler, melt the chocolate in a metal bowl placed above a saucepan half-filled with barely simmering water.)
3. In a large bowl, combine the flour, salt, and the sugars. Lightly beat the eggs with the vanilla extract. Add the beaten egg and the melted butter to the flour. Stir in the melted chocolate, nuts, and the ancho paste. Spoon the mixture into the pastry shell. Bake until lightly browned (about 1 hour).

Ancho Chilies

The word *ancho* means "wide" in Spanish. It is the dried form of the poblano chili. When dried, it is very dark in color and has a deep, rich, sweet taste. The ancho is part of the "holy trinity" of chilies used to make traditional mole sauces.

Chapter 40

Bermuda
and the Caribbean:
Island Eats

554 Guava Mousse

555 Conch Chowder

556 Chicken and Soba Noodle Salad

556 Grilled Portobello Mushroom Caps

557 Balsamic Dressing

557 Seared Asian-Style Glazed Tuna

558 Asian Salad

559 Guava Fritters with Banana Syrup

560 Bermuda Fish Chowder

561 Bermuda Onion Soup

562 Jerk Marinade

563 Avocado, Crab, and Sour Cream Timbale

564 Risotto with Lobster and Parmesan

Guava Mousse

Serves 4

Guava fruit comes in many sizes—this recipe calls for the larger fruit that is approximately the same size as apples.

¼ cup warm water
1 package unflavored gelatin, such as Knox
5 large green guavas
¾ cup plus 2 tablespoons whole milk, divided

1 vanilla bean
1 cup light cream
½ cup granulated sugar
2 tablespoons confectioners' sugar, for garnish
8 mint sprigs, for garnish

1. Pour the warm water into a small bowl. Pour the gelatin over the water and let it stand for 5 minutes to soften.

2. Cut the guavas in half. Scoop out the flesh, removing the section containing the seeds. In a blender or food processor, purée the guava fruit with 2 tablespoons milk until smooth. Measure out 1 cup of puréed guava. Discard the remainder or use in another recipe.

3. Cut the vanilla bean in half lengthwise. Remove the seeds. In a medium-sized saucepan, bring ¾ cup milk, the light cream, vanilla bean, vanilla seeds, and granulated sugar to a near boil. Continue cooking for 2 to 3 minutes, stirring to dissolve the sugar. Remove the vanilla bean.

4. Remove the saucepan from the stove element and stir in the softened gelatin. Continue stirring until the gelatin is completely dissolved (about 5 minutes).

5. Combine the gelatin mixture with the puréed guava and process until smooth. Pour into four 6-ounce custard cups. Cover and chill in the refrigerator for 4 hours. To serve, dust with the confectioners' sugar and garnish with mint sprigs.

Conch Chowder

½ green bell pepper
½ red bell pepper
3 large red potatoes
1 white onion
4 cloves garlic
2 stalks celery
1 jalapeño chili pepper
4 tomatoes
1 pound conch, cleaned
⅓ cup lime juice
¼ cup tomato paste
3 tablespoons olive oil

¼ teaspoon cayenne pepper, or
    to taste
1 tablespoon chopped fresh
    parsley
4 cups water
¼ cup rum
1 bay leaf
Salt and freshly ground black
    pepper, to taste
2 tablespoons chopped fresh
    cilantro leaves

> **Serves 4–6**
>
> Conch chowder is the Bahamian version of Manhattan clam chowder, made with conch snails instead of clams and seasoned with tart lime juice.

1. Cut the bell peppers in half, remove the seeds, and cut into cubes. Peel and dice the potatoes. Peel and finely chop the onion and garlic. String the celery and cut on the diagonal into thin slices. Cut the jalapeño chili pepper in half, remove the seeds, and finely chop. Peel the tomatoes, deseed, and cut into thin slices.

2. Cut the conch into 1-inch pieces. Marinate the conch pieces in the lime juice and tomato paste for 1 hour.

3. In a large saucepan, heat the olive oil over medium heat. Add the onion, garlic, celery, bell peppers, and the chili pepper. Brown the vegetables. Add the tomatoes, pushing down gently with the back of a spoon to release their juices. Stir in the cayenne pepper and chopped parsley.

4. Add the water, conch pieces and the lime juice marinade, potatoes, rum, and the bay leaf. Bring to boil, then reduce the heat and simmer, uncovered, until the potatoes are tender when pierced with a fork (about 30 minutes). Taste and add salt and pepper if desired. Remove the bay leaf. Sprinkle with the fresh cilantro and serve hot.

Conch—More Than a Beautiful Shell

Conch is the second-most famous edible snail, the first being escargot from France. Conch meat is subtle and sweet, but it is extremely tough and must be pounded or marinated in lime juice to tenderize it before cooking.

Chicken and Soba Noodle Salad

Serves 3

This light chicken salad is one of the many delicious dishes served on Richard Branson's private Necker Island resort.

¼ pack soba noodles
3 tablespoons sesame oil
3 skinless, boneless chicken
 breasts, cut into strips
2 tablespoons Thai fish sauce

½ bunch chives, chopped
½ red onion, sliced
10 cherry tomatoes, cut in half
Juice of 1 lemon
1 dried red chili, finely chopped

1. In a pot of salted, boiling water, cook the soba noodles for 7 minutes. Drain the noodles and run cold water over them until cold. Add 2 tablespoons of the sesame oil to the noodles.
2. Cook the chicken in a pan with the remaining 1 tablespoon sesame oil. Remove from heat and let cool.
3. Mix together all the ingredients, and serve.

Grilled Portobello Mushroom Caps

Serves 4

Serve this dish with the Balsamic Dressing (page 557).

4 portobello mushrooms, stems
 removed
4 tablespoons olive oil
4 tablespoons balsamic vinegar
Salt and freshly ground black
 pepper, to taste

4 slices goat cheese
4 handfuls mixed salad leaves
4 tablespoons Balsamic
 Dressing (page 557)

1. Preheat the oven to 350°.
2. Put the mushrooms in a baking tray, topside down. Drizzle with the olive oil and balsamic vinegar, and season with the salt and pepper. Bake in the oven for about 6 minutes.
3. In the meantime, place the salad leaves in the middle of 4 serving plates, top each plate with a slice of goat cheese, and drizzle with the dressing. Place the cooked mushrooms on top of the salad.

Balsamic Dressing

2 tablespoons balsamic vinegar
6 tablespoons olive oil
1 teaspoon minced onion

1 teaspoon minced fresh thyme
Salt and freshly ground black
   pepper, to taste

Combine all the ingredients and mix well. Serve over greens.

Serves 4

A good balsamic dressing
is a must to have on hand.
It is ideal to use on almost
any combination of greens.

Seared Asian-Style Glazed Tuna

1 tuna fillet, about 9 inches long
   and 1 inch thick
¼ cup light soy sauce
1 teaspoon lime juice
1 clove garlic, minced

½ teaspoon brown sugar
2 tablespoons white sesame
   seeds
1 tablespoon olive oil
2 limes, cut into wedges

Serves 2

Serve this simple dish with
Asian Salad (page 282) for
a complete meal for two.

1. Place the tuna fillet in a shallow 9 × 13-inch glass baking dish. In a small bowl, whisk the soy sauce, lime juice, garlic, brown sugar, and sesame seeds. Pour the marinade over the tuna. Cover and marinate in the refrigerator for 2 hours.

2. Heat the oil in a frying pan on high heat. Sear the tuna for about 30 seconds on each side. Return the tuna to the refrigerator and chill. To serve, cut the chilled tuna into thin slices and garnish with the lime wedges.

Serve with Seared Asian-Style Glazed Tuna (page 557) for a complete Asian-style dinner for two.

Asian Salad

Serves 2

1 mango
1 mild green chili pepper
½ red bell pepper
½ yellow bell pepper
½ cucumber

2 tablespoons chopped red onion
½ cup shredded red cabbage
Easy Asian Salad Dressing (see sidebar on this page)

1. Peel and shred the mango. Cut the chili pepper in half, remove the seeds, and finely chop. Remove the seeds from the bell peppers and dice. Peel and slice the cucumber.
2. Combine all the ingredients and drizzle with the Asian Salad Dressing.

Easy Asian Salad Dressing

Mix together 2 tablespoons fish sauce, 2 tablespoons freshly squeezed lemon juice, 2 tablespoons virgin olive oil, 1 teaspoon palm sugar, a few drops sesame oil, and a pinch of ground cinnamon. Serve over the salad.

Guava Fritters with Banana Syrup

Serves 4

This recipe comes from Glowbal Grill and Satay Bar in Vancouver, British Colombia.

2 bananas, sliced
1 cup maple syrup
¾ cup cornstarch
3 cups plus 3 tablespoons all-
    purpose flour
2 teaspoons baking soda

Pinch salt
Sparkling water, as needed
Vegetable oil, as needed
2–3 guavas, peeled, seeded,
    and cut into wedges

1. Combine the bananas and syrup in a saucepan over low heat and warm gently for a few minutes. Remove from heat and let cool slightly. Process in a blender or food processor until smooth.
2. Mix together the cornstarch, 3 cups of the flour, the baking soda, and salt. Add sparkling water as needed to reach the consistency of a batter.
3. Heat enough oil to cover the guavas in a deep-fryer to a high temperature. Coat the guava wedges in the remaining 3 tablespoons of flour, then dip into the batter mix, and deep-fry until golden brown. Serve with the banana and maple syrup sauce.

No Fryer? No Problem.

As a fryer substitute, you can use a deep saucepan. Fill it with about 2 inches of quality vegetable oil and heat on medium for approximately 10 to 15 minutes. Test the oil with a small amount of the fryer batter placed gently into the pan, so as to not splash.

Bermuda Fish Chowder

Serves 10

This dish, from Chef David Garcelon in Bermuda, is a local specialty that has won several contests on the island.

¼ cup olive oil

2 sprigs fresh thyme

1 tablespoon dried oregano

1 tablespoon dried marjoram

1 tablespoon ground cinnamon

¼ cup finely diced celery

½ cup finely diced carrots

½ cup finely diced onion

4 cloves garlic, minced

½ cup chopped tomatoes

2 pounds diced whitefish
  (perch, cod, or bass)

2 quarts fish stock

¼ cup black rum

½ cup Worcestershire sauce

1 ounce Gravy Master

1 tablespoon salt

1. Heat the oil on medium in a sauté pan. Add the herbs, cinnamon, and all the vegetables except the tomatoes and sauté until soft. Add all the remaining ingredients and cook over low heat for 45 minutes to 1 hour.
2. Purée the soup lightly with a hand blender, leaving chunks.
3. Adjust seasonings to taste and serve.

Bermuda Fish Chowder

Though a Bermuda national dish, Bermuda Fish Chowder was originally a British recipe that came over with the first colonists. The soup was quickly adopted by Bermudians and today is made with a rich stock (from fresh local fish, including fish heads and tails). Other ingredients are water, bacon fat, parsley, salt and ground pepper, potatoes, onion, carrots, celery, bay leaves, peppercorns, cloves, tomatoes, and thyme.

Bermuda Onion Soup

½ cup butter

2½ pounds Bermuda onions, chopped

½ pound apples, chopped

4 cloves garlic, minced

¼ pound celery, chopped

½ pound potatoes, peeled and chopped

½ tablespoon ground coriander

1 bay leaf

1 tablespoon salt

½ teaspoon pepper

1 quart water

1 cup heavy cream

Serves 10

Another signature soup by Chef David Garcelon of the Fairmont Southampton in Bermuda. This soup is based on the Bermuda onion, which was one of Bermuda's best-known exports in the nineteenth century.

1. Melt the butter in sauté pan over medium-low heat. Sauté the onions, apples, garlic, and celery until soft. Add all the remaining ingredients except the cream, and cook over low heat for 45 minutes to 1 hour.

2. Remove and discard the bay leaf. Purée soup in a blender or food processor until smooth. Strain the soup through a fine-mesh sieve. Add the cream and adjust seasonings to taste.

Bermuda: From Agriculture to Tourism

Though today Bermuda relies on business and tourism as its main sources of revenue, in the not-too-distant past it was agriculture that fed its wealth. Once steamers began traveling to and from New York, Bermudians were able to export their goods: tomatoes, celery, potatoes, arrowroot, Easter lillies, and, most importantly, Bermuda onions. The Bermuda onion became so popular that the colony became known as "the Onion Patch," and true Bermudians still refer to themselves as "Onions."

Jerk Marinade

Yields 1 cup

Chef Walter Staib, culinary consultant for Sandals Resorts International, created this wonderful jerk marinade.

¾ pound Scotch bonnets, stems removed, deseeded, and roughly chopped

1 large onion

4 bunches green onions (white and green parts), chopped

½ pound thyme, leaves removed and stems discarded

½ cup minced fresh ginger

6 cloves garlic, minced

4 tablespoons freshly ground allspice

Salt and freshly ground black pepper, to taste

1 cup soy sauce

½ cup vegetable oil

1. Combine all the ingredients except the soy sauce and oil in food processor or blender, and purée. Transfer the mixture to a mixing bowl and add the soy sauce and oil. Store in a glass jar or clay pot.
2. To use with chicken, beef, or pork, place the meat in the marinade and let sit overnight. Remove the meat from the marinade and grill at a high temperature until cooked through. For fish, lobster, or shrimp, place the fish or seafood in the marinade for 1 hour only. (Do not overmarinate or it will break down the fibers in the fish and seafood, resulting in a mushy consistency when cooked.) Remove from the marinade and grill at a high temperature until cooked through.

What a Jerk

It all began with the Indians. The Arawak tribe had a traditional method of using Jamaican pimento (today's allspice) to season and smoke meat, mostly wild pigs. That spice, combined with hot chilies (from South America and the Caribbean), pirates who brought a medley of new spices, and escaped slaves who were experts at slow-roasting in pits, resulted in what we now call jerk. The escaped slaves, known as Maroons, are believed to have perfected this way of preserving and cooking meat during their years living in the Blue Mountains, fighting the British troops.

Avocado, Crab, and Sour Cream Timbale

½ onion, chopped
1 clove garlic, minced
2 scallions, chopped
1 tablespoon butter
8 ounces lump crabmeat
Salt and freshly ground black
  pepper, to taste
1 avocado, peeled and chopped
2 teaspoons fresh-squeezed
  lime juice
4 tablespoons sour cream
1 tablespoon chopped fresh
  parsley

1 tablespoon chopped fresh
  cilantro
1 tablespoon chopped fresh
  basil

Dressing:

2 teaspoons fresh-squeezed
  lime juice
2 teaspoons balsamic vinegar
½ cup olive oil
Pinch salt, pepper, and
  granulated sugar

> **Serves 4**
>
> This is a favorite dish of Sandals Grande St. Lucian Beach Resort and Spa. In this recipe, Chef Walter Staib uses avocados— a major staple throughout the Caribbean.

1. Sauté the onions, garlic, and scallion in the butter until soft. Add the crabmeat and cook for 2 minutes. Season to taste with salt and pepper. Chill in the refrigerator.
2. Season the avocado with the lime juice and salt and pepper.
3. Mix together the sour cream and all the herbs.
4. Assemble the timbales: Lightly oil 4 timbale molds (2½ inches in diameter and 3 inches high). Divide the avocado among the molds and press down. Next add the crabmeat and press down. Add the tomato and press down. Finally, top off with the sour cream, filling the molds and smoothing off the top. Chill in the refrigerator for 1 hour.
5. Blend together all the dressing ingredients. Slide the timbales onto serving plates and drizzle the dressing around them.

Risotto with Lobster and Parmesan

Serves 6

This recipe, by Executive Chef Ciaran Hickey of the Four Seasons Resort Great Exuma, uses spiny lobster found in the reefs of the turquoise Bahamian waters. Plain lobster also works fine.

2 shallots, diced
Vegetable oil, as needed
1 pound risotto rice
2 tablespoons dry white wine
2 pints shellfish stock
½ pound spiny lobster meat, diced
1 zucchini, diced

½ cup (1 stick) butter
½ cup Parmesan cheese, grated, plus extra for garnish
Salt and freshly ground black pepper, to taste
A few springs parsley, for garnish

1. In a large pan, cook the shallots in a little oil to release the flavor, then add the risotto.
2. Cook the risotto for about 4 minutes, and add the wine. Cook for a few minutes, then add a bit of the shellfish stock. Stir and cook until the stock is absorbed. Continue adding the stock a bit at a time and stirring until the liquid is absorbed.
3. In a small pan, sauté the diced lobster with the zucchini in a little oil, then add to the risotto.
4. Add the butter and Parmesan to the pan, and season with salt and pepper. Serve in a pasta bowl. Garnish with fresh parsley and extra Parmesan cheese.

The Making of Rum

Rum is made from fermented and distilled sugar-cane juice or, more commonly, molasses. First water is added, then yeast is introduced until the desired alcohol level is reached. Next it is distilled either in copper pot stills or columnar stills. Modern rum production only became a commercial enterprise in the 1600s, after the English and French had established their colonies. Alas, the thriving rum production relied largely on the labor of African slaves, who toiled in the sugar-cane plantations.

Appendices

Appendix A

U.S. to Metric Units Conversion

Appendix B

Gourmet Cooking Glossary

Appendix A: U.S. to Metric Units Conversion

Volume

1 teaspoon	5 milliliters
1 tablespoon	15 milliliters
¼ cup	60 milliliters
⅓ cup	80 milliliters
½ cup	120 milliliters
1 cup	240 milliliters
1 pint (2 cups)	480 milliliters
1 quart (4 cups)	.95 liter
1 gallon (16 cups)	3.8 liters

Weight

1 ounce	28 grams
1 pound (16 ounces)	454 grams

Length

1 inch	2.54 centimeters
1 foot (12 inches)	30.48 centimeters

Temperature

32°F (freezing point of water)	0°C
300°F	150°C
350°F	175°C
400°F	200°C
450°F	230°C

Appendix B: Gourmet Cooking Glossary

al dente: "To the tooth," in Italian. Pasta is cooked just to a firm texture.

allemande: In French cooking it means "in the German style." Sauce Allemande is made from veal stock, cream, egg yolks, and lemon juice.

aromatics: Seasonings to enhance the flavor and aroma—usually herbs and spices.

au jus: The natural pan drippings or juice that comes from a roasting pan after deglazing.

bain-marie: A "water bath." Food is placed in a container that is placed in a shallow dish filled with hot water, then heated in an oven or on the stovetop.

baste: To brush or spoon liquid fat or juices over meat, fish, poultry, or vegetables during cooking to help keep moisture on the surface area.

beat: Briskly whipping or stirring with a spoon, fork, wire whisk, beater, or mixer.

bias: To slice a food crosswise at a 45-degree angle.

bind: To thicken a sauce or hot liquid by stirring in ingredients such as roux, flour, butter, cornstarch, egg yolks, vegetable purée, or cream.

blanch: To partially cook vegetables by parboiling them, then cooling quickly in ice water.

blend: Mixing together two or more ingredients to obtain a distributed mixture.

bouquet garni: A bundle of seasonings, such as bay leaf, thyme, and parsley. It's used to season braised foods and stocks.

braise: To cook slowly in liquid in a covered pot.

brown: A quick sautéing/searing done either at the beginning or end of meal preparation.

brush: To coat food with melted butter, glaze, or other liquid using a pastry brush.

butterfly: To cut food down the center without cutting all the way through to open and then spread it apart.

caramelize: The process of cooking sugar until it begins to color. Also, while slowly cooking some vegetables (e.g., onions, root vegetables), the natural sugars are released and the vegetables will caramelize in their own sugars.

chiffonade: Cutting lettuces and other leafy vegetables or herbs into julienne strips.

chinoise: A very fine, conical wire-mesh strainer. Using a chinoise removes small impurities from the liquid that is strained.

chop: To cut into irregular pieces with no set size.

coat: Cover evenly.

confit: Pieces of meat slowly cooked in their own gently rendered fat until very soft and tender.

cure: Marinating to preserve an ingredient with salt and/or sugar and spices.

cut in: Working butter into dry ingredients for equal distribution. This is done with the help of a pastry blender and is an important step in making flaky pie crusts.

dash: A measure approximately equal to $\frac{1}{16}$ teaspoon, a pinch or less.

deglaze: Adding liquid to a pan in which foods have been sautéed, fried, or roasted to dissolve the baked-on bits stuck to the bottom of the pan.

dice: To cut food into cubes.

dredge: Completely coating in flour and shaking off the excess.

drippings: The liquids and bits of food left in the bottom of a roasting or frying pan after meat is cooked.

drizzle: Pouring a liquid, such as melted butter, olive oil, or other liquid, in a slow trickle over food.

dust: Sprinkling flour to lightly and evenly coat.

egg wash: A mixture of beaten eggs, yolks, whites, or both with milk or water used to coat baked goods to give them a shine when baked. Also may be used as a sealant for pieces of dough.

fillet: A boneless and skinless piece of meat cut away from the bone, usually fish.

fillet: To remove the bones from fish or meat for cooking.

flambé: To ignite liquid that contains an alcoholic substance so that it flames.

fleure de sel: A very high-quality French sea salt.

foie gras: A fattened duck or goose liver.

fold: To gently combine two or more ingredients using a bottom-to-top or side-to-side motion with a spoon or spatula.

fritter: A deep-fried sweet or savory food coated or mixed in a batter.

ganache: A chocolate filling or coating made with chocolate, egg yolks, and heavy cream. Most often used as a filling for truffles and as a coating for cakes such as Boston Cream Pie.

garnish: A decorative piece of an edible ingredient placed as a finishing touch to dishes or drinks.

glaze: A liquid that gives an item a shiny surface.

grate: To shred food into fine pieces by rubbing it against a coarse surface, usually a grater.

herbes de Provence: A French blend of herbs consisting of chervil, tarragon, chives, rosemary, and lavender.

infusion: Extracting flavors by soaking them in liquid heated in a covered pan.

jointed: Something, such as chicken, cut at the joint.

julienne: To cut into thin strips about 2 inches long.

jus: The natural juices released by roasting meats that have collected on the bottom of the roasting pan.

knead: To work dough with the heels of your hands in a pressing and folding motion until it becomes smooth and elastic.

marinate: Submerging a food in a seasoned liquid in order to tenderize and flavor the food.

medallion: Small round or oval pieces of meat (sometimes lightly pounded), such as chicken, tenderloin, pork, and veal.

mince: To chop or dice food into tiny irregular pieces.

mirepoix: A mixture of vegetables: 2 parts onions, 1 part celery, 1 part carrots. It may also contain leeks and mushrooms (in which case the amount of onions would be less).

pan-broil: Cooking food in a heavy-bottomed pan without added fat, then removing any fat as it accumulates so it doesn't burn.

parchment: A nonstick, silicone-coated, heat-resistant paper used in cooking.

pare: To peel or trim food of its outer layer of skin, usually vegetables.

pinch: A small inexact measurement, about 1/16 of a teaspoon.

poach: To simmer in liquid that is just below the boiling point.

ramekin: A small ovenproof dish used for individual servings.

reduce: To slowly or rapidly cook liquids down so that some or most of the water evaporates.

reduction: Simmering a sauce so that moisture is released, causing the remaining ingredients to concentrate, thickening and strengthening the flavors.

render: Cooking something greasy, such as bacon, to release the fat

roast: A method of cooking in an oven where the item isn't covered, allowing the dry heat to surround the item.

roux: A cooked mixture of equal parts flour and oil, fat, or butter used to thicken liquids.

sauté: To cook food quickly in a small amount of fat in a pan over regulated direct heat.

score: To tenderize meat, fish, or shellfish by making a number of shallow, often diagonal cuts across its surface.

sear: Frying meat quickly over high heat to seal in the juices.

season: To enhance the flavor of foods by adding ingredients such as salt, pepper, and a variety of other herbs and spices.

simmer: Cooking food in a liquid at just below the boiling point so that small bubbles rise to the surface.

steep: To soak dry ingredients in liquid until the flavor is infused into it.

stir-fry: Quickly frying small pieces of meats and vegetables over very high heat with continuous stirring in a small amount of oil.

stock: The liquid that results from simmering bones, vegetables, and seasonings in water or another liquid.

sweat: Cooking vegetables over low heat to release their natural juices.

zest: The thin outer part of the rind of citrus.

Index

A

Achara, 456
Acorn squash, in Sweet Simmered Squash, 480
Afghani Lamb with Spinach, 492
African dishes, 499–510
Ahi Tuna Tartar, 535
Akhni Stock, 421
All-American Barbecued Chicken, 182
Almonds
    Almond Cookies, 104
    Almond Paste, 509
    Baked Red Snapper Almandine, 257
    Baklava, 346
    Crunchy Nut Treats, 66
    Pan-Fried Flounder with Toasted Almonds, 362
    Veal Medallions in Almond Stew, 545
    Wild Rice with Apples and Almonds, 204
Aloo Tikki (Indian Potato Cakes), 413
Amaretto Cake, 86
Ancho Chili Fudge Pie, 551
Anise Oval Cookies, 40
Appetizers and dips
    Artichoke Bottoms with Herbed Cheese, 59
    Broccoli Dip, 58
    Creamy Garlic and Red Pepper Dip, 58
    Eggplant Caviar, 62
    Feta and Mint Dip, 341
    Fried Green Tomato Bruschetta, 63
    Guacamole, 126
    Herbed Clam Dip, 60
    Horseradish Vodka Dip, 530
    Hot Artichoke Dip, 64
    Louisiana Hot Wings, 60
    Parmesan Crisps, 59
    Pears Wrapped in Prosciutto on a Bed of Mixed Greens, 61
    Pepita Balls, 129
    Spinach and Ricotta Dip, 64
    Stuffed Mushrooms, 56
    Tzatziki, 341
    Vegetable Gado-Gado, 57
Apples and apple juice
    Apple and Onion Purée, 400
    Apple Blossom, 23
    Apple-Buttered Rum Pudding with Apple Topping, 87
    Apple-Cinnamon Farfel Kugel, 115
    Apple Crisp, 208
    Apple Haroset, 114
    Bermuda Onion Soup, 561
    Buttermilk Soup with Apples, 312
    Cheesy Golden Apple Omelet, 141
    Classic Apple Pie, 187
    Classic Waldorf Salad, 141
    Danish Apple Soup, 386
    Danish Christmas Goose with Apples and Prunes, 390
    Duck Confit in Phyllo with Caramelized Apples, 531
    Elderberry Soup with "Dumplings" and Apples, 328
    Flemish-Style Red Cabbage, 309
    Fruited Pork Loin Casserole, 200
    Fruit-Stuffed Pork Chops, 325
    German Baked Apple French Toast, 320
    Gorgonzola and Apple Salad, 231
    Holstein Duck, 329
    Lemony Apple Drink, 105
    Mexican Christmas Eve Salad, 35
    Old-Fashioned Baked Apples, 218
    Pickled Okanagan Apples, 532
    Roast Turkey with Fruit Stuffing, 11
    Spinach Salad with Apple-Avocado Dressing, 166
    Swedish Apple Cake, 393
    Warm Sweet Potato and Apple Salad, 14
    Westphalian Cabbage, 324
    Wild Rice with Apples and Almonds, 204
Apple wine, 320
Apricots and apricot nectar
    Apricot Sparkler, 106
    Apricot-Stuffed Pork Tenderloin, 96
    Bread and Butter Pudding, 402
    Fruited Pork Loin Casserole, 200
    Swedish Apricot and Prune Pork Loin, 392
Armenian Nutmeg Cake, 496
Artichokes
    about: how to eat, 72
    Artichoke Bottoms with Herbed Cheese, 59
    Artichokes and lamb with "Terbiye," 483
    Artichokes in Court Bouillon with Lemon Butter, 72
    Hot Artichoke Dip, 64
    Pasta with Artichokes, 76
    White Bean and Artichoke Salad, 113
Arugula
    about: 250, 431
    Portobellos Stuffed with Basil and Salmon on Arugula Leaves, 250
Asian Salad, 558
Asparagus
    about: freshness, 15; white asparagus, 324
    Asparagus with Pork, 459
    Lobster and Asparagus Salad, 248
    Oven-Roasted Asparagus, 15
    Stir-Fried Asparagus, Oyster Mushrooms, and Shrimp in Garlic Sauce, 434
    Wok-Seared Beef Medallions with Asparagus Tips, 463
Avocados
    about: pitting of, 126
    Avocado, Crab, and Sour Cream Timbale, 563
    Avocado and Peach Salad, 165
    California Garden Salad with Avocado and Sprouts, 170
    California Rolls, 476–77
    Ceviche de Pescado, 547
    Cold Avocado Soup, Atlixco Style, 542
    Guacamole, 126
    Orange-Avocado Slaw, 176
    Poached Shrimp and Avocado Appetizer, 366
    Spinach Salad with Apple-Avocado Dressing, 166
    Texas Caviar, 152
    Totopos, 121

B

Baby Back Ribs with Sauerkraut, 194
Bacano Español, 376
Bacon Dressing, 516
Bahian-Style Shrimp Stew, 409
Baja Lobster Tails, 123
Baked Alaska, Peppermint, 49
Baked Orange Roughy with Orange-Rice Dressing, 92
Baked Pear Crisp, 99
Baked Plantains with Calvados, 367
Baked Red Snapper Almandine, 257
Baklava, 346
Balsamic dressing, 557
Balsamic-Marinated Beef Tenderloin, 195

Bananas
  about: freezing, 242
  Bananas Foster, 242
  Bananas in Coconut Milk, 437
  Brazilian Bananas with Rum, 408
  Guava Fritters with Banana Syrup, 559
  Lamb Curry with Banana Raita, 415
  Polynesian Banana Salad, 167
Bangkok-Style Roasted Pork Tenderloin, 440
Bar Harbor Fish Chowder, 143
Basic Cheese Soufflé, 405
Basil, 354
Bay leaves, 246
Beans
  about: cooking, 214; fermented black beans, 458
  Barbecued Pork and Beans, 183
  Egyptian Fava Beans, 506
  Enchiladas, 129
  Green Beans in Lemon Honey, 153
  Lobster Cantonese, 458
  Risotto with Fresh Summer Vegetables, 167
  Sambal Bunchies, 443
  Scallops and Shrimp with White Bean Sauce, 73
  Snail in Black Bean and Orange Peel Sauce, 453
  Steamed Tilapia with Mushrooms and Black Bean Sauce, 451
  Summer Vegetable Slaw, 171
  Three-Bean Salad, 178
  Totopos, 121
  Vegetable Gado-Gado, 57
  White Bean and Artichoke Salad, 113
Beef
  about: grades of, 159
  Balsamic-Marinated Beef Tenderloin, 195
  Beef and Horseradish Salad, 142
  Braised Beef in Barolo, 375
  Burgers with Lemon Pepper, 158
  California Tri-tip, 159
  Carne Asada, 120
  Danish Stuffed Cabbage, 387
  Dry Ginger Beef, 468
  Easy Chili, 214
  Filet Southwestern, 140
  Finnish Sauerkraut Soup, 391
  Grilled Beef and Onion Kebabs, 193
  Grilled Rib-Eye Steaks with Onions, 160

Herbed Beef Rib-Eye Roast with Potatoes, 30
London Broil with Mushrooms, 155
Madhouse Spaghetti, 215
Moambé Stew, 503
Moussaka, 342–43
Pizza Meatballs, 213
Savory Pastitsio, 260–61
Sloppy Joes, 212
Tagine-Style Beef Stew with Lemons, 505
Thai Beef with Rice Noodles, 447
Tommy Toy's Four Seasons Fried Rice, 464
Tournento Rossini, 360
Vodka-Marinated Sirloin, 384
Watermelon with Beef and Tangerine Herb, 450
Wok-Seared Beef Medallions with Asparagus Tips, 463
Beer
  about: Belgian, 318
  Beer-Basted Sausage with Caramelized Onions and German Mustard, 321
  Beer-Braised Chicken with Endives, 305
  Beer Soup, 137
  Bread Pudding with Belgian Beer, 318
Beets
  Honey-Orange Beets, 32
  Italian Beets, 190
  Mexican Christmas Eve Salad, 35
Belgian dishes, 303–18
Belgian endives. See also Endives
  about, 308
  Belgian Endive Salad with Maple Vinaigrette, 533
  Belgian Endives in Mornay Sauce, 306
  Cream of Belgian Endive Soup, 308
  Cucumber Salad with Mint, 304
  Mussels in Wine, 313
Belgian Waffles, 317
Bellini, 90
Bergen Fish Soup, 383
Bermudan dishes, 553–64
Berry Puff Pancakes, 241
Beurre Blanc, Pesto, 299
Beverages
  about: alcohol substitutes, 132
  Apple Blossom, 23
  Apricot Sparkler, 106
  Bellini, 90

Bishop, 88
Brandy Cocoa, 25
Bubbly Berry Blast, 185
Cape Cod Punch, 173
Caribbean Sunset, 198
Champagne Charisma, 68
Champagne Cocktail, 68
Champagne Fizz, 69
Champagne Mint, 69
Cider Punch, 210
Classic Margarita, 131
Cranberry Cream Cocktail, 23
Cranberry Gin Sour, 24
Creamy Peach Drink, 105
Fish House Punch, 173
Fruity Margarita, 132
Holiday Punch, 51
Hot Cinnamon Stocking, 52
Irish Coffee, 51
Irish Cream, 66
Lemon-Spiked Pineapple Smoothie, 162
Lemony Apple Drink, 105
Mayflower Cocktail, 24
Mexican Coffee, 130
Midori Mimosa, 89
Mimosa, 149
Minted Middle Eastern Buttermilk Shake, 276
Mint Julep, 162
Nonalcoholic Champagne Punch, 70
Nonalcoholic Mulled Cider Punch, 210
Nonalcoholic Wassail, 52
Peach Bunny, 106
Perfect Eggnog, 53
Planter's Punch, 198
Rose-Flavored Yogurt Lassi, 420
Sangria, 89
Scotch Milk Punch, 67
Sparkling Citrus Punch, 219
Sparkling Fruit Drink, 131
Spiced Cranberry Glogg, 22
Tom and Jerry, 53
Turkey Shooter, 25
Valentine, 88
White Wine Cooler, 149
Bishop, 88
Blackberries, in Wild Blackberry Pie, 172
Black Forest Cherry Cake, 330
Blintzes, 485
Bliss's Fresh Plum Tomato and Basil Sauce, 360
Bliss's Gnocchi, 359

BLT: Buster Crab, Lettuce, and Tomato Sandwich, 512
Blueberries
Blueberry Soufflé, 381
Bubbly Berry Blast, 185
Champagne-Marinated Summer Berries, 197
Crispy Crepes with Fresh Fruits, 448
Lemon Blueberry Ice "Cream," 265
Simple Fruit Compote, 311
Boar, Wild, with Orzo Salad, 537
Bouillabaisse, 294
Bouquet garni, 289
Bourbon Molasses Glacé, 517
Braised Beef in Barolo, 375
Braised Conway Mussels, 401
Braised Lamb in Pomegranate Sauce, 224–25
Braised Lamb with a Sour Orange Marinade, 109
Braised Octopus with Onions, 340
Braised Squab with Caramelized Onions, 310
Braised Veal Shanks with Porcini Mushrooms, 353
Brandy Cocoa, 25
Brazilian Bananas with Rum, 408
Brazilian Hot Cocoa, 408
Brazilian Paella, 271
Bread and Butter Pudding, 402
Bread Pudding
Bread Pudding with Belgian Beer, 318
Classic Bread Pudding, 38
Breads and scones
Cranberry Nut Bread, 19
Cranberry Scones, 18
Low-Fat Garlic Toast, 76
Brie
Belgian Endive Salad with Maple Vinaigrette, 533
Truffle Oil and Brie Soufflé, 292
Warm Dungeness Crab and Brie Melt, 532
Brine-Marinated Salmon, 530
Broccoli
Broccoli and Carrot Casserole, 240
Broccoli Dip, 58
Broccoli Florets with Lemon Butter Sauce, 135
Vegetable Gado-Gado, 57
Broiled Oysters on the Half Shell, 374
Broiled Sea Bass Fillet over Tomatillo Rice, 541
Brome Lake Duck Suprême, 288

Brotzeit, 321
Brownies. See Desserts
Bruschetta, Fried Green Tomato, 63
Brussels sprouts
Brussels Sprouts a L'Orange, 160
Brussels Sprouts with Mustard Cream, 34
Cream of Brussels Sprout Soup, 307
Oven-Roasted Winter Vegetables, 37
Bubbly Berry Blast, 185
Bulgur wheat, 94
Burgers with Lemon Pepper, 158
Butter, clarified, 272
Buttered Fillet of Sole, 327
Butterfly Shrimp Tempura, 475
Buttermilk
Buttermilk Soup with Apples, 312
Minted Middle Eastern Buttermilk Shake, 276
Butternut squash
Roasted Butternut Squash Pasta, 201
Roasted Butternut Squash Soup, 520
Sweet Potato-Ginger Soup, 16
Turkey and Cranberry on Butternut Squash, 12
Buttery Mashed Potatoes, 517

C
Cabbage
Danish Stuffed Cabbage, 387
Flemish-Style Red Cabbage, 309
Hungarian Cabbage and Noodles, 226
Red Laver Sea Lettuce "Kimchi," 534
Westphalian Cabbage, 324
Cabrales cheese
Marinated Salmon with Roasted Red Peppers, 372
Radicchio Salad, 364
California Garden Salad with Avocado and Sprouts, 170
California Rolls, 476–77
California Tri-tip, 159
Calvados brandy, baked plantains with, 367
Canadian dishes, 527–37
Candy. See Desserts
Cantaloupe, in Shrimp and Melon Salad, 299
Cape Cod Punch, 173
Caramelized Pearl Onions, 29
Caramel Rum Fondue, 82
Caraway-Rubbed Chicken, 222
Carbohydrates, in wine, 232. See also Low-carb celebrations
Caribbean dishes, 553–64

Caribbean Sunset, 198
Carne Asada, 120
Carrots
Broccoli and Carrot Casserole, 240
Carrot Cake, 208
Carrot Timbales, 203
Glazed Carrots with Balsamic Vinegar, 95
Oven-Roasted Winter Vegetables, 37
Vegetable Gado-Gado, 57
Cauliflower
Cauliflower Vichyssoise, 97
Roasted Garlic Mashed Potatoes, 10
Caviar. See Roe
Celery
about: as roasting rack, 28
Elegant Cream of Celery Soup, 524
Central and South American dishes, 407–12
Ceviche de Pescado, 547
Champagne Charisma, 68
Champagne Cocktail, 68
Champagne Fizz, 69
Champagne-Marinated Summer Berries, 197
Champagne Mint, 69
Cheery Cherry Crispy, 197
Cheese. See also specific cheeses
about: cheese boards, 209; freezing, 61; moldy, 258
Artichoke Bottoms with Herbed Cheese, 59
Basic Cheese Soufflé, 405
Cheese Coins, 262
Cheese Fondue, 74
Cheesy Golden Apple Omelet, 141
Quiche in a Loaf, 229
Stilton and Cheddar Cheese Soup, 246
Zesty Feta and Olive Sandwich, 164
Cherries
Black Forest Cherry Cake, 330
Bread Pudding with Belgian Beer, 318
Cheery Cherry Crispy, 197
Cherries Jubilee, 148
Simple Fruit Compote, 311
Chicken
about: boneless, 154; cooking temperatures, 252; handling, 222; roasting, 369; roasting variety, 180
All-American Barbecued Chicken, 182
Beer-Braised Chicken with Endives, 305
Caraway-Rubbed Chicken, 222
Chicken and Soba Noodle Salad, 556
Chicken in Coconut Milk, 432
Chicken in Pomegranate Sauce, 489

Chicken in Wine, 355
Chicken Skewers with Spicy Island
    Marinade, 154
Chicken Thighs Cacciatore, 237
Chicken with Mushrooms, 491
Chicken with Nectarine Salsa, 252
Easy Chicken Cordon Blue, 144
Fire Noodles, 445
Foie Gras–Stuffed Cornish Hens, 300
Fried Chicken, 180
Fusilli with Chicken and Coriander
    Pesto, 259
Lemon Chicken, 454
Lemongrass Chicken Skewers, 442
Louisiana Hot Wings, 60
Mango Chicken, 466
Marinated Ginger Chicken, 158
Mexican Chicken Roll-Ups, 122
Mole Poblano with Chicken, 548–49
Moroccan Stuffed Chicken, 509
Pecan-Crusted Chicken, 518–19
Purim Ravioli, 227
Roasted Butternut Squash Soup, 520
Sesame Chicken, 457
Strawberry Chicken Salad, 156
Tom Ka Kai, 438
Tommy Toy's Four Seasons Fried Rice,
    464
Walnut Chicken with Plum Sauce, 236
Zucchini-Stuffed Chicken, 108
Chicory and Orange Salad, 400
Chili Prawns with Tomato Sauce, 430
Chilled Cucumber Soup, 417
Chinese dishes, 449–69
Chocolate. See also Cocoa
    about: in Belgium, 316; curling, 44;
        melting, 146; in Spain, 374
    Ancho Chili Fudge Pie, 551
    Black Forest Cherry Cake, 330
    Brazilian Hot Cocoa, 408
    Chocolate Chip Cookies, 207
    Chocolate Fondue, 146
    Chocolate Mousse, 147
    Chocolate Mousse with Goat Cheese
        Cream, 295
    Chocolate Raspberry Torte, 117
    Chocolate Soufflé, 85
    Left Bank's Chocolate Fondant, 301
    Minty Hot Chocolate, 220
    Mole Poblano with Chicken, 548–49
    Ooey, Gooey S'Mores, 218
Chopsticks, 457
Chorizo in Wine, 370

Chowders. See Soups
Christmas meals, 27–38
    Brussels Sprouts with Mustard Cream,
        34
    Caramelized Pearl Onions, 29
    Christmas Piglet, 269
    Classic Bread Pudding, 38
    Gingered Mashed Sweet Potatoes, 34
    Herbed Beef Rib-Eye Roast with
        Potatoes, 30
    Holiday Goose with Cranberries, 29
    Honey-Orange Beets, 32
    Mexican Christmas Eve Salad, 35
    Oven-Roasted Winter Vegetables, 37
    Oysters Rockefeller Soup, 36
    Pecan-Crusted Roast Pork Loin, 28
    Poached Salmon with Bearnaise
        Sauce, 32
    Sauerkraut-Stuffed Roast Duck, 31
    Twice-Baked Potatoes with Chives, 33
    Yorkshire Pudding, 38
Christmas treats, 39–53
    Anise Oval Cookies, 40
    Christmas Teacakes, 48
    Christmas Theme Sugar Cookies, 42
    Coconut Wreath Cookies, 43
    Crème Brûlée, 44
    Gingerbread Men, 45
    Gingerbread with Lemon Topping, 50
    Holiday Punch, 51
    Hot Cinnamon Stocking, 52
    Irish Coffee, 51
    Mincemeat Pie, 48
    Nonalcoholic Wassail, 52
    Peppermint Baked Alaska, 49
    Peppermint-Flavored Candy Cane
        Cookies, 47
    Perfect Eggnog, 53
    Pfeffernusse, 41
    Plum Pudding Pie, 46
    Tom and Jerry, 53
Churros, 127
Chutneys
    about, 425
    Fresh Mango Chutney, 414
    Gooseberry Chutney, 426
Cider Punch, 210
Cinco De Mayo, 119–32
    Baja Lobster Tails, 123
    Carne Asada, 120
    Churros, 127
    Classic Margarita, 131
    Enchiladas, 129

Fruity Margarita, 132
Gazpacho, 125
Guacamole, 126
Margarita Pie, 128
Mexicali Shrimp on the Grill, 124
Mexican Chicken Roll-Ups, 122
Mexican Coffee, 130
Molasses Candy, 130
Orange Liqueur Mousse, 128
Pepita Balls, 129
Sparkling Fruit Drink, 131
Totopos, 121
Cinnamon, about, 21
Citrus and Shallot Dressing, 403
Clams
    Corn Clam Chowder with Mulard Duck
        Pan Seared Foie Gras, 291
    Vietnamese Crab and Pineapple Soup,
        270
Clarified butter, 272
Classic American Potato Salad, 177
Classic Apple Pie, 187
Classic Bread Pudding, 38
Classic Margarita, 131
Classic Risotto, 357
Classic Waldorf Salad, 141
Cloudberries
    Cloudberry Cream Dessert, 385
    Cloudberry Parfait, 381
Cocktails. See Beverages
Cocoa. See also Chocolate
    Brandy Cocoa, 25
    Hot Cinnamon Stocking, 52
Coconut
    Coconut Turkey Curry, 269
    Coconut Wreath Cookies, 43
    Cold Coconut Soup, 544
Coconut milk
    about, 409
    Bananas in Coconut Milk, 437
    Chicken in Coconut Milk, 432
    Shrimp in Coconut Milk, 423
    Sweet and Savory Grilled Coconut-
        Rice Hotcakes, 441
Cod
    Bergen Fish Soup, 383
    Bermuda Fish Chowder, 560
    Bouillabaisse, 294
    Fish in Red Sauce, 110
    Gefilte Fish, 112
    Scandinavian Baked Cod with Spicy
        Plum Sauce, 268
Coffee

Irish, 51
Mexican, 130
Cold Avocado Soup, Atlixco Style, 542
Cold Coconut Soup, 544
Cold Wine Soup, 322
Cold Yogurt and Cucumber Soup, 490
Conch Chowder, 553
Cookies. *See also* Desserts
    about: cooking tip, 47
    Anise Oval Cookies, 40
    Chocolate Chip Cookies, 207
    Christmas Theme Sugar Cookies, 42
    Coconut Wreath Cookies, 43
    Cranberry-Pecan Bars, 20
    Easter Cookies, 102
    Mint Meringue Cookies, 104
    Peppermint-Flavored Candy Cane
      Cookies, 47
    Pfeffernusse, 41
Cooking equipment
    blenders and food processors, 187
    casseroles, 200
    chilled glasses, 70
    double boiler, 147
    food processor, 97
    nonstick pans, 161
    ovens, 262
    pans, 17
    skillet, testing hot, 111
    slow cookers, 31, 212, 220
Cooking techniques
    frying, 127
    parboiling, 73
    preventing curdling, 81
    sautéing, 11, 79, 234
Cooking terminology
    cooking terms and methods, 6–8
    gourmet cooking glossary, 567–69
    mixing terms, 5–6
    slicing terms, 4–5
Coquilles St. Jacques Provençal, 79
Corn
    Corn Clam Chowder with Mulard Duck
      Pan Seared Foie Gras, 291
    Corn-Pickled Okra Relish, 522
    Roasted Vegetable Salad, 546
    Sweet Corn and Cipollini Onion Soup,
      514
    Sweet Corn Pudding, 190
Corned beef, in New England Boiled
    Dinner, 206
Couscous, 488

Crab
    Avocado, Crab, and Sour Cream
      Timbale, 563
    BLT: Buster Crab, Lettuce, and Tomato
      Sandwich, 512
    Crab Cakes with Sesame Crust, 238
    Crabmeat on Red Pepper Strips, 244
    Crab Spring Rolls, 435
    Hot Dungeness Crab Appetizer, 65
    Jumbo Lump Crab Cakes, 521
    Pork and Crab Lumpia, 455
    Seafood Roll-Ups, 249
    Snapper with Jumbo Lump Crabmeat,
      516
    Vietnamese Crab and Pineapple Soup,
      270
    Warm Dungeness Crab and Brie Melt,
      532
Cranberries
    about: cooking fresh, 12
    Cranberry Cream Cocktail, 23
    Cranberry Gin Sour, 24
    Cranberry Nut Bread, 19
    Cranberry-Pecan Bars, 20
    Cranberry Salad, 525
    Cranberry Scones, 18
    Cranberry Sherbet, 17
    Fruity Citrus Spice Tea, 209
    Holiday Goose with Cranberries, 29
    Turkey and Cranberry on Butternut
      Squash, 12
    Venison Medallions with Cranberry
      Dijon Chutney, 138
    Venison with Dried Cranberry Vinegar
      Sauce, 205
Crayfish Quiche, 395
Cream of Belgian Endive Soup, 308
Cream of Brussels Sprout Soup, 307
Creamy Garlic and Red Pepper Dip, 58
Creamy Peach Drink, 105
Crème Brûlée, 44
Crème fraîche, 395
Crepes
    Crepes with Curaçao Strawberries and
      Oranges, 297
    Crispy Crepes with Fresh Fruits, 448
    Green Tea Crepes, 478
Crispy Salad of Vendace Roe, 379
Crunchy Nut Treats, 66
Cucumbers
    about: seedless, 169
    Cold Yogurt and Cucumber Soup, 490
    Cucumber Salad with Fresh Mint, 508
    Cucumber Salad with Mint, 304

    Cucumber Slices with Smoked Salmon
      Cream, 236
    Daikon Salad with Cucumber, 474
    German Cucumber Salad, 333
    Tzatziki, 341
    Yogurt and Cucumber Soup with Mint
      and Dill, 98
Cured meats, 384
Currants
    Chicory and Orange Salad, 400
    Fruit-Stuffed Pork Chops, 325
Curried Lamb Kebabs, 422
Curry, 439

D

Daikon Salad with Cucumber, 474
Danish Apple Soup, 386
Danish Christmas Goose with Apples and
    Prunes, 390
Danish Rum Raisin Muffins, 389
Danish Stuffed Cabbage, 387
Dark Bread Soup, 323
Dashi Soup Stock, 480
Desserts. *See also* Christmas treats; Cookies
    Almond Cookies, 104
    Amaretto Cake, 86
    Ancho Chili Fudge Pie, 551
    Apple-Buttered Rum Pudding with Apple
      Topping, 87
    Apple-Cinnamon Farfel Kugel, 115
    Apple Crisp, 208
    Apple Haroset, 114
    Armenian Nutmeg Cake, 496
    Bananas Foster, 242
    Black Forest Cherry Cake, 330
    Blintzes, 485
    Blueberry Soufflé, 381
    Bread and Butter Pudding, 402
    Bread Pudding with Belgian Beer, 318
    Caramel Rum Fondue, 82
    Carrot Cake, 208
    Cherries Jubilee, 148
    Chocolate Fondue, 146
    Chocolate Mousse, 147
    Chocolate Mousse with Goat Cheese
      Cream, 295
    Chocolate Raspberry Torte, 117
    Chocolate Soufflé, 85
    Churros, 127
    Classic Apple Pie, 187
    Classic Bread Pudding, 38
    Cloudberry Cream Dessert, 385
    Cloudberry Parfait, 381

Cranberry-Pecan Bars, 20
Cranberry Sherbet, 17
Crunchy Nut Treats, 66
Easter Cookies, 102
Galaktoboureko, 343
German Coffee Cake, 275
Hamantaschen, 232
Hazelnut Torte, 331
Honey Cake Lekach, 233
Jewish Honey Cake, 486
Key Lime Pie, 188
Lebanese Rice Pudding, 493
Left Bank's Chocolate Fondant, 301
Light Lemon Pudding, 101
Lingonberry Sherbet for Adults, 394
Mango Cheesecake, 427
Margarita Pie, 128
Mint Meringue Cookies, 104
Molasses Candy, 130
Moscardini, 230
Native American Pudding, 274
New Orleans Pralines, 100
Old-Fashioned Baked Apples, 218
Ooey, Gooey S'Mores, 218
Orange Liqueur Mousse, 128
Palace-Style Rose Milk Pudding, 497
Panna Cotta, 358
Passover Brownies, 115
Peanut Popcorn Fudge, 65
Peanutty Oatmeal Candy, 67
Pecan Pie, 22
Pineapple-Pear Mold, 103
Plantains with Whipped Cream, 549
Prune Tart, 315
Pumpkin Pie, 21
Purim Poppyseed Candy, 234
Red Devil Chocolate Cake, 217
Red Velvet Cake, 515
Refrigerator Pumpkin Pie with
    Macadamia Nut Crust, 253
Simple Fruit Compote, 311
Strawberry Pie, 186
Strawberry Sorbet, 161
Swedish Apple Cake, 393
Tiramisu, 357
Wild Blackberry Pie, 172
Yorkshire Pudding, 38
Deviled Eggs, 179
Diabetic diets, 235–42
    Bananas Foster, 242
    Berry Puff Pancakes, 241
    Broccoli and Carrot Casserole, 240
    Chicken Thighs Cacciatore, 237

Crab Cakes with Sesame Crust, 238
Cucumber Slices with Smoked Salmon
    Cream, 236
Fillets of Fish with Lime and Cumin,
    239
Mock Stuffed Grape Leaves, 239
Walnut Chicken with Plum Sauce, 236
Dips. See Appetizers and dips
Dry Ginger Beef, 468
Duck
    Brome Lake Duck Suprême, 288
    Duck Confit in Phyllo with
        Caramelized Apples, 531
    Holstein Duck, 329
    Roast Duckling with Orange Glaze, 148
    Sauerkraut-Stuffed Roast Duck, 31
Dumplings, Split Lentil, 425

E
Easter, 91–106
    Almond Cookies, 104
    Apricot Sparkler, 106
    Apricot-Stuffed Pork Tenderloin, 96
    Baked Orange Roughy with Orange-
        Rice Dressing, 92
    Baked Pear Crisp, 99
    Cauliflower Vichyssoise, 97
    Creamy Peach Drink, 105
    Easter Cookies, 102
    Glazed Baked Ham with Rosemary, 95
    Glazed Carrots with Balsamic Vinegar,
        95
    Lemony Apple Drink, 105
    Light Lemon Pudding, 101
    Mint Meringue Cookies, 104
    New Orleans Pralines, 100
    Peach Bunny, 106
    Pineapple-Pear Mold, 103
    Scented Escarole with Fennel, 94
    White Wine and Lemon Pork Roast, 93
    Yogurt and Cucumber Soup with Mint
        and Dill, 98
Easy Chicken Cordon Blue, 144
Easy Chili, 214
Edamame Soup à la Chef Nobu, 472
Eggnog, 402
Eggnog, Perfect, 53
Eggplant
    about: varieties, 62
    Eggplant Caviar, 62
    Eggplant Miso Soup, 473
    Moussaka, 342–43

North African Eggplant, 273
Sweet-and-Sour Eggplant Stew, 356
Eggs. See also Soufflés
    about: breaking, 229; cholesterol in,
        19; raw, 179
    Cheesy Golden Apple Omelet, 141
    Deviled Eggs, 179
    Galaktoboureko, 343
    Lemon and Egg Soup, 339
    Mined Pork, 410
    Paulista Shrimp Cake, 411
    Quiche in a Loaf, 229
    Spanish Frittata, 365
    Spinach Frittata, 116
Egyptian Fava Beans (Fool Medames),
    506
Elderberry Soup with "Dumplings" and
    Apples, 328
Elegant Cream of Celery Soup, 524
Enchiladas, 129
Endives. See also Belgian endives
    Beer-Braised Chicken with Endives,
        305
    Radicchio Salad, 364
English dishes, 397–405
Escargots in Chablis, 289
Escarole, Scented, with Fennel, 94
Ethnic favorites, 267–76
    Brazilian Paella, 271
    Christmas Piglet, 269
    Coconut Turkey Curry, 269
    French Country Mussels, 272
    German Coffee Cake, 275
    Minted Middle Eastern Buttermilk
        Shake, 276
    Native American Pudding, 274
    North African Eggplant, 273
    Scandinavian Baked Cod with Spicy
        Plum Sauce, 268
    Vietnamese Crab and Pineapple Soup,
        270

F
Fall favorites, 199–210
    Apple Crisp, 208
    Carrot Cake, 208
    Carrot Timbales, 203
    Chocolate Chip Cookies, 207
    Cider Punch, 210
    Fruited Pork Loin Casserole, 200
    Fruity Citrus Spice Tea, 209
    New England Boiled Dinner, 206

Nonalcoholic Mulled Cider Punch, 210
Roasted Butternut Squash Pasta, 201
Venison with Dried Cranberry Vinegar
    Sauce, 205
Warm Potato Salad with Balsamic
    Vinegar and Onions, 202
Wild Rice with Apples and Almonds, 204
Father's Day. *See* Mother's Day and Father's
    Day
Fats, about, 186. *See also* Low-fat
    celebrations; Oils
Fennel
    about, 192
    Fennel-and-Garlic-Crusted Pork Roast,
        192
    Norwegian Salmon Salad, 382
    Red Laver Sea Lettuce "Kimchi," 534
    Salmon Fillets in Sweet Wine with
        Orange and Fennel, 288
    Scented Escarole with Fennel, 94
    Sweet Fennel with Lemon and Shaved
        Parmigiano, 75
Fenugreek, in Split Lentil Dumplings, 425
Feta and Mint Dip, 341
Feta cheese, in Zesty Feta and Olive
    Sandwich, 164
Figs with Brie and Port Wine Reduction, 137
Filet Southwestern, 140
Fillets of Fish with Lime and Cumin, 239
Finnish Sauerkraut Soup, 391
Fire Noodles, 445
Fish and seafood. *See also* Roe; *specific fish*
    about: choosing, 140, 143, 398; fresh or
        frozen, 244; grilling, 110; handling,
        238; ink from squid, 368; lobsters,
        398; monkfish, 247; oysters, 399;
        shrimp size, 251; smoked, 256;
        substitutions, 248
    Ahi Tuna Tartar, 535
    Avocado, Crab, and Sour Cream
        Timbale, 563
    Bahian-Style Shrimp Stew, 409
    Baja Lobster Tails, 123
    Baked Orange Roughy with Orange-Rice
        Dressing, 92
    Baked Red Snapper Almandine, 257
    Bar Harbor Fish Chowder, 143
    Bergen Fish Soup, 383
    Bermuda Fish Chowder, 560
    BLT: Buster Crab, Lettuce, and Tomato
        Sandwich, 512
    Bouillabaisse, 294
    Braised Octopus with Onions, 340
    Brine-Marinated Salmon, 530

Broiled Oysters on the Half Shell, 374
Broiled Sea Bass Fillet over Tomatillo
    Rice, 541
Buttered Fillet of Sole, 327
Butterfly Shrimp Tempura, 475
Ceviche de Pescado, 547
Chili Prawns with Tomato Sauce, 430
Conch Chowder, 555
Coquilles St. Jacques Provençal, 79
Corn Clam Chowder with Mulard Duck
    Pan Seared Foie Gras, 291
Crab Cakes with Sesame Crust, 238
Crabmeat on Red Pepper Strips, 244
Crab Spring Rolls, 435
Crayfish Quiche, 395
Cucumber Slices with Smoked Salmon
    Cream, 236
Fillets of Fish with Lime and Cumin, 239
Fish and chips, 404
Fish in Red Sauce, 110
Fish Tacos, 543
French Country Mussels, 272
Gefilte Fish, 112
Glazed Champagne and Oyster Sauce,
    399
Gourmet Tuna Sandwich Spread, 364
Gravlax, 378
Green Mango and Shrimp Salad, 433
Grilled Lobster with Lemon and
    Tarragon, 80
Grilled Whitefish, 378
Herbed Clam Dip, 60
Herb Linguini with Salmon, Cream, and
    Pistachios, 83
Honey Dijon Tuna Salad, 166
Honey Walnut Shrimp, 465
Hot and Sour Prawn Soup, 436
Hot Dill Pasta with Scallops, 136
Hot Dungeness Crab Appetizer, 65
Jumbo Lump Crab Cakes, 521
Lemony Baked Parsnips with Salmon
    Roe, 385
Lobster Cantonese, 458
Lobster Korma, 419
Marinated Salmon with Roasted Red
    Peppers, 372
Marinated Teriyaki Salmon, 477
Mexicali Shrimp on the Grill, 124
Mustard-Glazed Monkfish Wrapped in
    Bacon, 247
Nasturtium-Wrapped Halibut with
    Lobster Ragout, 536
Norwegian Salmon Salad, 382
Oysters Rockefeller Soup, 36

Pad Thai, 444
Pan-Fried Fish with Rosemary, 338
Pan-Fried Flounder with Toasted
    Almonds, 362
Pan-Roasted Swordfish with Plum
    Tomatoes, 352
Pasta and Smoked Trout with Lemon
    Pesto, 256
Paulista Shrimp Cake, 411
Penne with Scallops, Bacon, and Chili
    Pepper, 349
Poached Salmon with Bearnaise Sauce,
    32
Poached Shrimp and Avocado
    Appetizer, 366
Pork and Crab Lumpia, 455
Portobellos Stuffed with Basil and
    Salmon on Arugula Leaves, 250
Red Laver Sea Lettuce "Kimchi," 534
Risotto with Lobster and Parmesan, 564
Sage-and-Pancetta-Wrapped Shrimp, 251
Salmon Fillets in Sweet Wine with
    Orange and Fennel, 288
Salmon Hash, 228
Salmon in Saffron-Flavored Curry, 424
Salmon in White Wine with Dried
    Peaches, 82
Salmon Tortellini Salad, 258
Savory Shanghai Noodles, 469
Scallops and Shrimp with White Bean
    Sauce, 73
Scallops Broiled in Sake, 472
Scandinavian Baked Cod with Spicy
    Plum Sauce, 268
Seafood Roll-Ups, 249
Seared Asian-Style Glazed Tuna, 557
Seared Scallops with Saffron Mash, 403
Shrimp and Melon Salad, 299
Shrimp in Coconut Milk, 423
Shrimp Scampi, 139
Smoked Mussels in Cream Sauce with
    Pasta, 134
Smoked Salmon Pancakes, 404
Snapper with Jumbo Lump Crabmeat,
    516
Spicy Chilled Shrimp, 191
Spicy Scallops, 446
Squid Ink Risotto, 368
Squid in Sherry, 373
Squid in Wine, 337
Steamed Prawns with Crushed Garlic,
    451
Stir-Fried Asparagus, Oyster Mushrooms,
    and Shrimp in Garlic Sauce, 434

Straits Sea Bass, 460
Tuna Ceviche, 540
Twice-Baked Lobster Soufflé, 398
Vietnamese Crab and Pineapple Soup, 270
Warm Dungeness Crab and Brie Melt, 532
Fish House Punch, 173
Five-Minute Recado, 543
Flan, Spinach-Wrapped Zucchini, 77
Flemish-Style Red Cabbage, 309
Flemish Yeast Dough, 316
Flounder, Pan-Fried, with Toasted Almonds, 362
Fois gras
Corn Clam Chowder with Mulard Duck Pan Seared Foie Gras, 291
Foie Gras–Stuffed Cornish Hens, 300
Fondue
Caramel Rum Fondue, 82
Cheese Fondue, 74
Chocolate Fondue, 146
Fourth of July, 175–88
All-American Barbecued Chicken, 182
Barbecued Pork and Beans, 183
Bubbly Berry Blast, 185
Classic American Potato Salad, 177
Classic Apple Pie, 187
Deviled Eggs, 179
Fried Chicken, 180
Fried Green Tomatoes, 178
Grilled Cinnamon Pork Tenderloins, 176
Grilled Zucchini with Balsamic Vinegar, 181
Ham Barbecue, 183
Jumbo Beer-Battered Onion Rings, 177
Key Lime Pie, 188
Orange-Avocado Slaw, 176
Strawberry Pie, 186
Summertime Strawberry Soup, 184
Three-Bean Salad, 178
French Country Mussels, 272
French dishes, 287–301
French Onion Soup, 78
"French Toast," German Baked Apple, 320
Fresh Mango Chutney, 414
Fried Chicken, 180
Fried Green Tomato Bruschetta, 63
Fried Green Tomatoes, 178
Frites, 312
Frittata, spinach, 116
Fritters, leek and meat, 111

Fromage blanc, 381
Frosting, easy, 45
Fruits. See also specific fruits
about: canned, 99; compote, 35; ripening, 264
Berry Puff Pancakes, 241
Bubbly Berry Blast, 185
Champagne-Marinated Summer Berries, 197
Chocolate Fondue, 146
Crispy Crepes with Fresh Fruits, 448
Fruited Pork Loin Casserole, 200
Fruit-Stewed Turkey, 13
Fruit-Stuffed Pork Chops, 325
Fruity Citrus Spice Tea, 209
Fruity Margarita, 132
Mexican Christmas Eve Salad, 35
Roast Turkey with Fruit Stuffing, 11
Simple Fruit Compote, 311
Sparkling Citrus Punch, 219
Sparkling Fruit Drink, 131
Wild Blackberry Pie, 172
Fusilli with Chicken and Coriander Pesto, 259

G, H

Galaktoboureko (Greek-Style Pie), 343
Galangal, 432
Game hens
about: choosing, 145
Game Hens in Red Wine, 81
Quail Baked in White Wine, 145
Garlic
about, 460; buying tips, 98; jarred, 152; "popping" of, 259
Creamy Garlic and Red Pepper Dip, 58
Fennel-and-Garlic-Crusted Pork Roast, 192
Garlic Purée, 419
Ginger-garlic Paste, 424
Low-Fat Garlic Toast, 76
Roasted Garlic Mashed Potatoes, 10
Young Garlic Soup with Crème Fraîche and Spring Pea Shoots, 513
Gazpacho, 125
Gefilte Fish, 112
German Coffee Cake, 275
German dishes, 319–33
German Syrup, 317
Ginger, 460
Gingerbread Men, 45
Gingerbread with Lemon Topping, 50

Gingered Mashed Sweet Potatoes, 34
Ginger-garlic paste, 424
Glazed Baked Ham with Rosemary, 95
Glazed Carrots with Balsamic Vinegar, 95
Glazed Champagne and Oyster Sauce, 399
Glazed Turnips with Cinnamon, 311
Glogg, 393
Glossary, gourmet cooking, 567–69
Goat cheese
Chocolate Mousse with Goat Cheese Cream, 295
Goat Cheese Cream, 296
Roasted Tomato, Zucchini, and Goat Cheese Tarts, 523
Vine Leaf Envelopes with Raisins, 484
Goose
Danish Christmas Goose with Apples and Prunes, 390
Holiday Goose with Cranberries, 29
Gooseberry Chutney, 426
Gorgonzola and Apple Salad, 231
Gourmet foods, 277–86
cooking glossary, 567–69
equipment for, 283–86
organization for cooking, 281–83
Gourmet Tuna Sandwich Spread, 364
Grapefruit, broiled, 103
Grape Leaves, Middle Eastern Stuffed, 495
Gravlax, 378
Great Britain. See English dishes
Greek dishes, 335–46
Green Beans in Lemon Honey, 153
Green Mango and Shrimp Salad, 433
Greens with Peanuts, 504
Green Tea Crepes, 478
Gremolata seasoning, 353
Grilled Beef and Onion Kebabs, 193
Grilled Cinnamon Pork Tenderloins, 176
Grilled Lobster with Lemon and Tarragon, 80
Grilled Portobello Mushroom Caps, 556
Grilled Rib-Eye Steaks with Onions, 160
Grilled Whitefish, 378
Grilled Zucchini with Balsamic Vinegar, 181
Guacamole, 126
Guavas
Guava Fritters with Banana Syrup, 559
Guava Mousse, 554
Haddock, in Bar Harbor Fish Chowder, 143
Halibut

Bergen Fish Soup, 383
Nasturtium-Wrapped Halibut with
    Lobster Ragout, 536
Ham
    Easy Chicken Cordon Blue, 144
    Glazed Baked Ham with Rosemary, 95
    Ham Barbecue, 183
    Ham with Asian Pear, 467
    Holstein Duck, 329
Hamantaschen, 232
Hazelnut Torte, 331
Herbed Beef Rib-Eye Roast with Potatoes, 30
Herbed Clam Dip, 60
Herbed Potato Salad, 326
Herb Linguini with Salmon, Cream, and
    Pistachios, 83
Herbs. See also specific herbs
    chopping fresh, 181
    crushing, 101
    fresh and dry, 113
Herring, 396
Holiday Goose with Cranberries, 29
Holiday Punch, 51
Holstein Duck, 329
Honey Cake Lekach, 233
Honeydew melon, in shrimp salad, 299
Honey Dijon Tuna Salad, 166
Honey-Orange Beets, 32
Honey Walnut Shrimp, 465
Horn of Plenty Mushroom Soup, 380
Horseradish Vodka Dip, 530
Hot and Sour Prawn Soup, 436
Hot Artichoke Dip, 64
Hot Cinnamon Stocking, 52
Hot Dill Pasta with Scallops, 136
Hot Dungeness Crab Appetizer, 65
Huckleberries, in vinaigrette, 529
Hungarian Cabbage and Noodles, 226

I, J, K

Independence Day. See Fourth of July
Indian dishes, 413–27
Irish Coffee, 51
Irish Cream, 66
Italian Beets, 190
Italian dishes, 347–60
Japanese dishes, 471–80
Jarlsberg cheese
    Basic Cheese Soufflé, 405
    Crayfish Quiche, 395
Jerk Marinade, 562
Jewish holidays, 221–34

Braised Lamb in Pomegranate Sauce,
    224–25
Caraway-Rubbed Chicken, 222
Gorgonzola and Apple Salad, 231
Hamantaschen, 232
Honey Cake Lekach, 233
Hungarian Cabbage and Noodles, 226
Mock Chopped Liver, 230
Moscardini, 230
Purim Poppyseed Candy, 234
Purim Ravioli, 227
Quiche in a Loaf, 229
Salmon Hash, 228
Yam Latkes with Mustard Seeds and
    Curry, 223
Jewish Honey Cake, 486
Jicama with Lime, 547
Jumbo Beer-Battered Onion Rings, 177
Jumbo Lump Crab Cakes, 521
Jungle Curry Paste, 431
Juniper berries, in rabbit stew, 345
Kabocha squash, in Pumpkin Curry Soup, 439
Kebabs
    Curried Lamb Kebabs, 422
    Lamb Kebabs, 507
Key Lime Pie, 188
Kids' celebrations, 211–20
    Easy Chili, 214
    Madhouse Spaghetti, 215
    Minty Hot Chocolate, 220
    Old-Fashioned Baked Apples, 218
    Ooey, Gooey S'Mores, 218
    Party Snack Mix, 216
    Pizza Meatballs, 213
    Red Devil Chocolate Cake, 217
    Sloppy Joes, 212
    Sparkling Citrus Punch, 219
    Strawberries in Butterscotch Sauce, 219
Kugel, Apple-Cinnamon Farfel, 115

L

Labor Day, 189–98
    Baby Back Ribs with Sauerkraut, 194
    Balsamic-Marinated Beef Tenderloin, 195
    Caribbean Sunset, 198
    Champagne-Marinated Summer Berries,
        197
    Cheery Cherry Crispy, 197
    Fennel-and-Garlic-Crusted Pork Roast, 192
    Grilled Beef and Onion Kebabs, 193
    Italian Beets, 190
    Orange Cups with Lemon Cream, 196
    Planter's Punch, 198

Spicy Chilled Shrimp, 191
Spicy Cold Pears, 196
Sweet Corn Pudding, 190
Lamb
    about: slow-cooking, 109
    Afghani Lamb with Spinach, 492
    Braised Lamb in Pomegranate Sauce,
        224–25
    Braised Lamb with a Sour Orange
        Marinade, 109
    Curried Lamb Kebabs, 422
    Lamb and Artichoke with "Terbiye," 483
    Lamb Curry with Banana Raita, 415
    Lamb Kebabs, 507
    Leek and Meat Fritters, 111
    Rhubarb Khoresh, 488
    Roasted Leg of Lamb with Lemon-Garlic
        Potatoes, 344
    Turkish Lamb Casserole Cooked in
        Paper, 494
La Pasta d'Angelica, 350
Lebanese Rice Pudding, 493
Leeks
    about, 291
    Leek and Meat Fritters, 111
    Stoemp with Caramelized Shallots, 314
Left Bank's Chocolate Fondant, 301
Lemons and lemon juice
    about: juicing, 90; keeping handy, 257;
        preserved, 500; for tartness, 153
    Lemon and Egg Soup, 339
    Lemon Blueberry Ice "Cream," 265
    Lemon Chicken, 454
    Lemongrass Chicken Skewers, 442
    Lemon-Spiked Pineapple Smoothie, 162
    Lemony Apple Drink, 105
    Lemony Baked Parsnips with Salmon
        Roe, 385
    Light Lemon Pudding, 101
    Orange Cups with Lemon Cream, 196
    Tagine-Style Beef Stew with Lemons, 505
Lentils
    Aloo Tikki, 414
    Split Lentil Dumplings, 425
Light Lemon Pudding, 101
Limes
    Fillets of Fish with Lime and Cumin, 239
    Key Lime Pie, 188
Lingonberry Sherbet for Adults, 394
Liver, Mocked Chopped, 230
Lobster
    about: choosing female, 398; serving, 80
    Baja Lobster Tails, 123

Grilled Lobster with Lemon and Tarragon, 80
Lobster and Asparagus Salad, 248
Lobster Cantonese, 458
Lobster Korma, 419
Nasturtium-Wrapped Halibut with Lobster Ragout, 536
Risotto with Lobster and Parmesan, 564
Twice-Baked Lobster Soufflé, 398
Lollipop Veal Chop, 519
London Broil with Mushrooms, 155
Louisiana Hot Wings, 60
Low-carb celebrations, 243–53
Chicken with Nectarine Salsa, 252
Crabmeat on Red Pepper Strips, 244
Lobster and Asparagus Salad, 248
Mustard-Glazed Monkfish Wrapped in Bacon, 247
Pork and Veal Pâté, 245
Portobellos Stuffed with Basil and Salmon on Arugula Leaves, 250
Red Snapper with Cayenne Tomato Sauce, 249
Refrigerator Pumpkin Pie with Macadamia Nut Crust, 253
Sage-and-Pancetta-Wrapped Shrimp, 251
Seafood Roll-Ups, 249
Stilton and Cheddar Cheese Soup, 246
Low-fat celebrations, 256–65
Baked Red Snapper Almandine, 257
Cheese Coins, 262
Fusilli with Chicken and Coriander Pesto, 259
Lemon Blueberry Ice "Cream," 265
Orecchiette with Summer Tomato Sauce and Olives, 263
Pasta and Smoked Trout with Lemon Pesto, 256
Pears in Orange Sauce, 264
Salmon Tortellini Salad, 258
Savory Pastitsio, 260–61

M

Macaroni, 338
Madhouse Spaghetti, 215
Mangos
Asian Salad, 558
Fresh Mango Chutney, 414
Green Mango and Shrimp Salad, 433
Mango Cheesecake, 427
Mango Chicken, 466
Mare's milk, 497

Margarita Pie, 128
Marinated Ginger Chicken, 158
Marinated Olives, 351
Marinated Salmon with Roasted Red Peppers, 372
Marinated Teriyaki Salmon, 477
Mascarpone, in Tiramisu, 357
Matzo Brei, 114
Maultaschen, 332–33
Mayflower Cocktail, 24
Mayonnaise, 363
Meal planning
terms and definitions, 4–8
tips, 1–2
Meats. See also specific meats
defatting, 10
safety, 30
slicing, 205
substituting mushrooms for, 13
Memorial Day, 151–62
Brussels Sprouts a L'Orange, 160
Burgers with Lemon Pepper, 158
California Tri-tip, 159
Chicken Skewers with Spicy Island Marinade, 154
Green Beans in Lemon Honey, 153
Grilled Rib-Eye Steaks with Onions, 160
Lemon-Spiked Pineapple Smoothie, 162
London Broil with Mushrooms, 155
Marinated Ginger Chicken, 158
Mint Julep, 162
Smoked Salmon Salad with Cilantro Dressing, 157
Strawberry Chicken Salad, 156
Strawberry Sorbet, 161
Texas Caviar, 152
Merrit Venison Carpaccio, 528
Metric equivalents, 566
Mexicali Shrimp on the Grill, 124
Mexican Chicken Roll-Ups, 122
Mexican Christmas Eve Salad, 35
Mexican Coffee, 130
Mexican dishes, 539–51
Middle Eastern dishes, 481–97
Midori Mimosa, 89
Milk. See also Buttermilk; Coconut milk
about: making condensed, 86; mare's milk, 497; using skim, 42
Palace-Style Rose Milk Pudding, 497
Scotch Milk Punch, 67
Milk-Fed Veal Cutlet with Parmesan and Truffle Crust, 348
Mimosas

Midori Mimosa, 89
Mimosa, 149
Mincemeat Pie, 48
Mined Pork, 410
Mint
about: growing, 276
Minted Middle Eastern Buttermilk Shake, 276
Mint Julep, 162
Mint Meringue Cookies, 104
Minty Hot Chocolate, 220
Moambé Stew, 503
Mock Chopped Liver, 230
Mock Stuffed Grape Leaves, 239
Molasses Candy, 130
Mole Poblano with Chicken, 548–49
Monkfish, in Mustard-Glazed Monkfish Wrapped in Bacon, 247
Moroccan Stuffed Chicken, 509
Moscardini, 230
Mother's Day and Father's Day, 133–49
Bar Harbor Fish Chowder, 143
Beef and Horseradish Salad, 142
Beer Soup, 137
Broccoli Florets with Lemon Butter Sauce, 135
Cheesy Golden Apple Omelet, 141
Cherries Jubilee, 148
Chocolate Fondue, 146
Chocolate Mousse, 147
Classic Waldorf Salad, 141
Easy Chicken Cordon Blue, 144
Figs with Brie and Port Wine Reduction, 137
Filet Southwestern, 140
Hot Dill Pasta with Scallops, 136
Mimosa, 149
Quail Baked in White Wine, 145
Roast Duckling with Orange Glaze, 148
Shrimp Scampi, 139
Smoked Mussels in Cream Sauce with Pasta, 134
Venison Medallions with Cranberry Dijon Chutney, 138
White Wine Cooler, 149
Moules Mariniere (Mussels in White Wine), 296
Mountain Huckleberry Vinaigrette, 529
Moussaka, 342–43
Muffins, Danish Rum Raisin, 389
Mung bean sprouts, in Pad Thai, 444
Mushrooms

about: cooking without fat, 237; dried, 56; "horn of plenty," 380; substituting for meat, 13
Asparagus with Pork, 459
Braised Veal Shanks with Porcini Mushrooms, 353
Chicken with Mushrooms, 491
Grilled Portobello Mushroom Caps, 556
Horn of Plenty Mushroom Soup, 380
Hot and Sour Prawn Soup, 436
London Broil with Mushrooms, 155
Oyster Mushroom and Jasmine Tea Rice, 479
Portobellos Stuffed with Basil and Salmon on Arugula Leaves, 250
Shiitake Mushroom Soup, 525
Steamed Tilapia with Mushrooms and Black Bean Sauce, 451
Stir-Fried Asparagus, Oyster Mushrooms, and Shrimp in Garlic Sauce, 434
Straits Sea Bass, 460
Stuffed Mushrooms, 56
Tommy Toy's Minced Squab Imperial, 462
Mussels
about, 313, 401
Bouillabaisse, 294
Braised Conway Mussels, 401
French Country Mussels, 272
Moules Mariniere, 296
Mussels in Wine, 313
Mustard-Glazed Monkfish Wrapped in Bacon, 247

N

Nabemono, 473
Nasturtium-Wrapped Halibut with Lobster Ragout, 536
Native American Pudding, 274
Nectarine Salsa, Chicken with, 252
New England Boiled Dinner, 206
New Orleans Pralines, 100
New Year's, 55–70
Artichoke Bottoms with Herbed Cheese, 59
Broccoli Dip, 58
Champagne Charisma, 68
Champagne Cocktail, 68
Champagne Fizz, 69
Champagne Mint, 69
Creamy Garlic and Red Pepper Dip, 58
Crunchy Nut Treats, 66
Eggplant Caviar, 62
Fried Green Tomato Bruschetta, 63
Herbed Clam Dip, 60

Hot Artichoke Dip, 64
Hot Dungeness Crab Appetizer, 65
Irish Cream, 66
Louisiana Hot Wings, 60
Nonalcoholic Champagne Punch, 70
Parmesan Crisps, 59
Peanut Popcorn Fudge, 65
Peanutty Oatmeal Candy, 67
Pears Wrapped in Prosciutto on a Bed of Mixed Greens, 61
Scotch Milk Punch, 67
Spinach and Ricotta Dip, 64
Stuffed Mushrooms, 56
Vegetable Gado-Gado, 57
Nonalcoholic Champagne Punch, 70
Nonalcoholic Mulled Cider Punch, 210
Nonalcoholic Wassail, 52
North African Eggplant, 273
Norwegian Salmon Salad, 382
Nuts. See also Almonds; Pecans; Pine nuts; Walnuts
about: freezing, 172; grinding, 331
Hazelnut Torte, 331
Herb Linguini with Salmon, Cream, and Pistachios, 83
Refrigerator Pumpkin Pie with Macadamia Nut Crust, 253

O

Octopus, Braised, with Onions, 340
Oils
for browning, 273
coconut and palm, 186
fat and, 100
flavored, 191
olive oil, 195, 371
Okra Relish, Corn-Pickled, 522
Old-Fashioned Baked Apples, 218
Olives
about, 351; olive oil, 195, 371; pitted, 157, 163
Gourmet Tuna Sandwich Spread, 364
Marinated Olives, 351
Marinated Salmon with Roasted Red Peppers, 372
Orecchiette with Summer Tomato Sauce and Olives, 263
Pasta alla Puttanesca, 354
Poached Shrimp and Avocado Appetizer, 366
Zesty Feta and Olive Sandwich, 164
Onions

about: cipollini, 524; pearl, 193; peeling without tears, 78; puréed, 419; varieties, 108
Apple and Onion Purée, 400
Beer-Basted Sausage with Caramelized Onions and German Mustard, 321
Bermuda Onion Soup, 561
Braised Octopus with Onions, 340
Braised Squab with Caramelized Onions, 310
Caramelized Pearl Onions, 29
French Onion Soup with Port, 293
Grilled Beef and Onion Kebabs, 193
Jumbo Beer-Battered Onion Rings, 177
Spanish Frittata, 365
Sweet Corn and Cipollini Onion Soup, 514
Veal and Vegetable Stew, 412
Warm Potato Salad with Balsamic Vinegar and Onions, 202
Ooey, Gooey S'Mores, 218
Orange Liqueur Mousse, 128
Orange Roughy, Baked, with Orange-Rice Dressing, 128
Oranges and orange juice
Brome Lake Duck Suprême, 288
Chicory and Orange Salad, 400
Crepes with Curaçao Strawberries and Oranges, 297
Fruity Citrus Spice Tea, 209
Greek-Style Rabbit Stew, 345
Mexican Christmas Eve Salad, 35
Norwegian Salmon Salad, 382
Orange-Avocado Slaw, 176
Orange Cups with Lemon Cream, 196
Orange Salad with Orange Flower Water, 502
Salmon Fillets in Sweet Wine with Orange and Fennel, 288
Orecchiette with Summer Tomato Sauce and Olives, 263
Ostriches, 502
Oven-Roasted Asparagus, 15
Oven-Roasted Winter Vegetables, 37
Oyster Mushroom and Jasmine Tea Rice, 479
Oysters
about, 399
Broiled Oysters on the Half Shell, 374
Glazed Champagne and Oyster Sauce, 399
Oysters Rockefeller Soup, 36

P

Pad Thai, 444
Paella, Brazilian, 271

Palace-Style Rose Milk Pudding, 497
Palm hearts, in shrimp cake, 411
Pancakes
    Berry Puff Pancakes, 241
    Potato Pancakes, 487
    Smokes Salmon Pancakes, 404
    Sweet and Savory Grilled Coconut-
        Rice Hotcakes, 441
Pancetta, in Sage-and-Pancetta-Wrapped
    Shrimp, 251
Paneer, in Mango Cheesecake, 518–19
Pan-Fried Fish with Rosemary, 338
Pan-Fried Flounder with Toasted
    Almonds, 362
Panna Cotta, 358
Pan-Roasted Swordfish with Plum
    Tomatoes, 352
Papaya
    Achara, 456
    Curried Lamb Kebabs, 422
Parmesan Crisps, 59
Parsley, 261
Parsnips
    New England Boiled Dinner, 206
    Oven-Roasted Winter Vegetables, 37
Party Snack Mix, 216
Passover foods, 107–17
    Apple-Cinnamon Farfel Kugel, 115
    Apple Haroset, 114
    Braised Lamb with a Sour Orange
        Marinade, 109
    Chocoláte Raspberry Torte, 117
    Fish in Red Sauce, 110
    Gefilte Fish, 112
    Leek and Meat Fritters, 111
    Matzo Brei, 114
    Passover Brownies, 115
    Spinach Frittata, 116
    White Bean and Artichoke Salad, 113
    Zucchini-Stuffed Chicken, 108
Pasta
    about: buying, 215; cooking, 201;
        in Greece, 338; homemade, 74;
        importance of fresh, 83
    Chicken Thighs Cacciatore, 237
    Fusilli with Chicken and Coriander
        Pesto, 259
    Herb Linguini with Salmon, Cream,
        and Pistachios, 83
    Hot Dill Pasta with Scallops, 136
    La Pasta d'Angelica, 350
    Madhouse Spaghetti, 215

Orecchiette with Summer Tomato
    Sauce and Olives, 263
Pasta alla Puttanesca, 354
Pasta and Smoked Trout with Lemon
    Pesto, 256
Pasta with Artichokes, 76
Pasta with Chilies, 550
Penne with Scallops, Bacon, and Chili
    Pepper, 349
Purim Ravioli, 227
Roasted Butternut Squash Pasta, 201
Salmon Tortellini Salad, 258
Savory Pastitsio, 260–61
Smoked Mussels in Cream Sauce with
    Pasta, 134
Paulista Shrimp Cake, 411
Peach Bunny, 106
Peaches
    Avocado and Peach Salad, 165
    Creamy Peach Drink, 105
    Salmon in White Wine with Dried
        Peaches, 82
Peanuts and peanut butter
    Greens with Peanuts, 504
    Peanut Popcorn Fudge, 65
    Peanutty Oatmeal Candy, 67
Pears
    Baked Pear Crisp, 99
    Ham with Asian Pear, 467
    Pears in Orange Sauce, 264
    Pears Poached in White Wine with
        Strawberry Sauce, 84
    Pears Wrapped in Prosciutto on a Bed
        of Mixed Greens, 61
    Pineapple-Pear Mold, 103
    Spicy Cold Pears, 196
Pecans
    Cranberry Nut Bread, 19
    Cranberry-Pecan Bars, 20
    New Orleans Pralines, 100
    Pecan-Crusted Chicken, 518–19
    Pecan-Crusted Roast Pork Loin, 28
    Pecan Pie, 22
    Purim Poppyseed Candy, 234
Penne with Scallops, Bacon, and Chili
    Pepper, 349
Pepita Balls, 129
Pepper, black, 164
Peppermint Baked Alaska, 49
Peppermint-Flavored Candy Cane
    Cookies, 47
Peppers

about: Anaheim, 122; bell, 125;
    chipotles, 182; Poblano, 124
Stuffed Red Peppers, 456
Summer Vegetable Slaw, 171
Tricolor Pepper Salad, 169
Perfect Eggnog, 53
Pesto Beurre Blanc, 299
Pestos
    Fusilli with Chicken and Coriander
        Pesto, 259
    Pasta and Smoked Trout with Lemon
        Pesto, 256
Pfeffernusse, 41
Phyllo dough
    about, 339
    Baklava, 346
    Duck Confit in Phyllo with
        Caramelized Apples, 531
Pickled Okanagan Apples, 532
Picnics. See Summer picnics
Pies. See Desserts
Pike, in Bouillabaisse, 294
Pineapple
    Fruit-Stewed Turkey, 13
    Mexican Christmas Eve Salad, 35
    Pineapple-Pear Mold, 103
    Warm Sweet Potato and Apple Salad, 14
Pine nuts
    about, 492
    Afghani Lamb with Spinach, 492
    Cucumber Salad with Fresh Mint, 508
    Spinach with Raisins and Pine Nuts,
        371
Pizza, origins of, 359
Pizza Meatballs, 213
Plantains
    Baked Plantains with Calvados, 367
    Plantains with Whipped Cream, 549
Planter's Punch, 198
Plum Pudding Pie, 46
Poached Salmon with Bearnaise Sauce, 32
Poached Shrimp and Avocado Appetizer,
    366
Polynesian Banana Salad, 167
Pomegranate Sauce, Chicken in, 494
Pork. See also Ham; Sausage
    about: fat in, 96
    Apricot-Stuffed Pork Tenderloin, 96
    Asparagus with Pork, 459
    Baby Back Ribs with Sauerkraut, 194
    Bacon Dressing, 516
    Bangkok-Style Roasted Pork
        Tenderloin, 440

Barbecued Pork and Beans, 183
Brazilian Paella, 271
Christmas Piglet, 269
Fennel-and-Garlic-Crusted Pork Roast, 192
Fruited Pork Loin Casserole, 200
Fruit-Stuffed Pork Chops, 325
Grilled Cinnamon Pork Tenderloins, 176
Lobster Cantonese, 458
Mustard-Glazed Monkfish Wrapped in Bacon, 247
Pecan-Crusted Roast Pork Loin, 28
Penne with Scallops, Bacon, and Chili Pepper, 349
Pork and Crab Lumpia, 455
Pork and Ginger Pot Stickers, 461
Pork and Veal Pâté, 245
Pork Chops with Prunes, 363
Raclette, 298
Sauerkraut-Stuffed Roast Duck, 31
Stuffed Red Peppers, 456
Swabian Stuffed Pockets, 332–33
Swedish Apricot and Prune Pork Loin, 392
Tommy Toy's Four Seasons Fried Rice, 464
White Wine and Lemon Pork Roast, 93
Portobellos. See Mushrooms
Potatoes. See also Sweet potatoes
about: testing for doneness, 202; using skins, 33
Aloo Tikki, 414
Bacano Español, 376
Bliss's Gnocchi, 359
Buttery Mashed Potatoes, 517
Classic American Potato Salad, 177
Fruited Pork Loin Casserole, 200
Herbed Beef Rib-Eye Roast with Potatoes, 30
Herbed Potato Salad, 326
Potato Pancakes, 487
Raclette, 298
Roasted Garlic Mashed Potatoes, 10
Roasted Leg of Lamb with Lemon-Garlic Potatoes, 344
Roasted Potatoes with Garlic, Lemon and Oregano, 336
Smoked Salmon Pancakes, 404
Spanish Frittata, 365
Stoemp with Caramelized Shallots, 314
Swedish Potato Dumplings, 396
Sweet Potato-Ginger Soup, 16
Twice-Baked Potatoes with Chives, 33

Warm Potato Salad with Balsamic Vinegar and Onions, 202
Young Garlic Soup with Crème Fraîche and Spring Pea Shoots, 513
Pot stickers, 461
Poultry. See Chicken; Duck; Game hens; Goose; Turkey
Pralines, New Orleans, 100
Prawns. See also Shrimp
Chili Prawns with Tomato Sauce, 430
Hot and Sour Prawn Soup, 436
Steamed Prawns with Crushed Garlic, 451
Preserved Lemons, 500
Prosciutto
Pears Wrapped in Prosciutto on a Bed of Mixed Greens, 61
Raclette, 298
Swabian Stuffed Pockets, 332–33
Prunes
Danish Christmas Goose with Apples and Prunes, 390
Fruit-Stewed Turkey, 13
Fruit-Stuffed Pork Chops, 325
Pork Chops with Prunes, 363
Prune Tart, 315
Roast Turkey with Fruit Stuffing, 11
Swedish Apricot and Prune Pork Loin, 392
Pudding. See Desserts; specific pudding names
Pumpkin
Pumpkin Curry Soup, 439
Pumpkin Pie, 21
Refrigerator Pumpkin Pie with Macadamia Nut Crust, 253
Purées, 419
Purim Poppyseed Candy, 234
Purim Ravioli, 227

Q, R

Quail Baked in White Wine, 145
Quail with Curry, 418
Quiche, Crayfish, 395
Quiche in a Loaf, 229
Rabbit
Greek-Style Rabbit Stew, 345
Rabbit in Wine, 369
Rabbit with Wild Thyme, 290
Raclette, 298
Radicchio Salad, 364
Raisins
about: soaking dry, 167

Danish Rum Raisin Muffins, 389
Vine Leaf Envelopes with Raisins, 484
Raspberries
Chocolate Mousse with Goat Cheese Cream, 295
Chocolate Raspberry Torte, 117
Crispy Crepes with Fresh Fruits, 448
Lollipop Veal Chop, 519
Recado paste, 543
Red Devil Chocolate Cake, 217
Red Laver Sea Lettuce "Kimchi," 534
Red snapper. See Snapper
Red Velvet Cake, 515
Refrigerator Pumpkin Pie with Macadamia Nut Crust, 253
Remoulade, 522
Rhubarb Khoresh, 488
Rice
about: freezing cooked, 271
Baked Orange Roughy with Orange-Rice Dressing, 92
Brazilian Paella, 271
Broiled Sea Bass Fillet over Tomatillo Rice, 541
California Rolls, 476–77
Classic Risotto, 357
Cranberry Salad, 525
Lebanese Rice Pudding, 493
Oyster Mushroom and Jasmine Tea Rice, 479
Risotto with Fresh Summer Vegetables, 167
Risotto with Lobster and Parmesan, 564
Squid Ink Risotto, 368
Tommy Toy's Four Seasons Fried Rice, 464
Wild Rice with Apples and Almonds, 204
Rich Cream Sauce, 388
Risotto. See Rice
Roast Duckling with Orange Glaze, 148
Roasted Butternut Squash Pasta, 201
Roasted Butternut Squash Soup, 520
Roasted Garlic Mashed Potatoes, 10
Roasted Leg of Lamb with Lemon-Garlic Potatoes, 344
Roasted Potatoes with Garlic, Lemon and Oregano, 336
Roasted Tomato, Zucchini, and Goat Cheese Tarts, 523
Roasted Tomato Vinaigrette, 474
Roasted Vegetable Salad, 546
Roast Turkey with Fruit Stuffing, 11
Roe
Crispy Salad of Vendace Roe, 379

Lemony Baked Parsnips with Salmon Roe, 385
Rose-Flavored Yogurt Lassi, 420
Rose water, 420
Roux, 306
Rutabaga, in Oven-Roasted Winter Vegetables, 37

S

Saffron
  about, 376
  Lobster Korma, 419
  Moroccan Stuffed Chicken, 509
  Salmon in Saffron-Flavored Curry, 424
  Seared Scallops with Saffron Mash, 403
Sage-and-Pancetta-Wrapped Shrimp, 251
Salads
  Asian Salad, 558
  Avocado and Peach Salad, 165
  Beef and Horseradish Salad, 142
  Belgian Endive Salad with Maple Vinaigrette, 533
  California Garden Salad with Avocado and Sprouts, 170
  Chicken and Soba Noodle Salad, 556
  Chicory and Orange Salad, 400
  Classic American Potato Salad, 177
  Cranberry Salad, 525
  Crispy Salad of Vendace Roe, 379
  Cucumber Salad with Fresh Mint, 508
  Cucumber Salad with Mint, 304
  Daikon Salad with Cucumber, 474
  German Cucumber Salad, 333
  Gorgonzola and Apple Salad, 231
  Herbed Potato Salad, 326
  Honey Dijon Tuna Salad, 166
  Lobster and Asparagus Salad, 248
  Mexican Christmas Eve Salad, 35
  Norwegian Salmon Salad, 382
  Orange-Avocado Slaw, 176
  Orange Salad with Orange Flower Water, 502
  Polynesian Banana Salad, 167
  Radicchio Salad, 364
  Roasted Vegetable Salad, 546
  Salmon Tortellini Salad, 258
  Shrimp and Melon Salad, 299
  Smoked Salmon Salad with Cilantro Dressing, 157
  Spinach Salad with Apple-Avocado Dressing, 166

Strawberry Chicken Salad, 156
Summer Vegetable Slaw, 171
Sunshine Bean Salad with Golden Gate Dressing, 168
Three-Bean Salad, 178
Tricolor Pepper Salad, 169
Warm Sweet Potato and Apple Salad, 14
White Bean and Artichoke Salad, 113
Wild Boar and Orzo Salad, 537
Zesty Feta and Olive Sandwich, 164
Salmon
  Brine-Marinated Salmon, 530
  Cucumber Slices with Smoked Salmon Cream, 236
  Gefilte Fish, 112
  Gravlax, 378
  Herb Linguini with Salmon, Cream, and Pistachios, 83
  Lemony Baked Parsnips with Salmon Roe, 385
  Marinated Salmon with Roasted Red Peppers, 372
  Marinated Teriyaki Salmon, 477
  Norwegian Salmon Salad, 382
  Poached Salmon with Bearnaise Sauce, 32
  Salmon Fillets in Sweet Wine with Orange and Fennel, 288
  Salmon Hash, 228
  Salmon in Saffron-Flavored Curry, 424
  Salmon in White Wine with Dried Peaches, 82
  Salmon Tortellini Salad, 258
  Smoked Salmon Pancakes, 404
  Smoked Salmon Salad with Cilantro Dressing, 157
Salt
  adding evenly to dish, 75
  reducing salty taste, 135
  using less, 114
Sambal Bunchies (Green Beans), 443
Sangria, 89
Sauces
  about, 416; deglazing, 290; roux, 306
  Bearnaise Sauce, 32
  Butterscotch Sauce, 219
  Chicken in Pomegranate Sauce, 489
  Glazed Champagne and Oyster Sauce, 399
  Lemon Butter Sauce, 135
  Mayonnaise, 363
  Mornay Sauce, 306

Orange Sauce, 264
Red Sauce, 110
Rich Cream Sauce, 388
Strawberry Sauce, 84
Sweet Vanilla Sauce, 20
Tamarind Sauce, 430
Vanilla Sour Cream Sauce, 394
White Bean Sauce, 73
Yogurt Sauce, 416
Sauerkraut
  about, 194
  Baby Back Ribs with Sauerkraut, 194
  Finnish Sauerkraut Soup, 391
  Sauerkraut-Stuffed Roast Duck, 31
Sausage
  about: types of, 370
  Beer-Basted Sausage with Caramelized Onions and German Mustard, 321
  Chorizo in Wine, 370
  Mined Pork, 410
  Pasta with Chilies, 550
  Swabian Stuffed Pockets, 332–33
Savory Crispy Wheat Cake, 482
Savory Pastitsio, 260–61
Savory Shanghai Noodles, 469
Scallion Scones, 534
Scallops
  Bouillabaisse, 294
  Coquilles St. Jacques Provençal, 79
  Hot Dill Pasta with Scallops, 136
  Penne with Scallops, Bacon, and Chili Pepper, 349
  Scallops and Shrimp with White Bean Sauce, 73
  Scallops Broiled in Sake, 472
  Seared Scallops with Saffron Mash, 403
  Spicy Scallops, 446
Scandinavian Baked Cod with Spicy Plum Sauce, 268
Scandinavian dishes, 377–96
Scented Escarole with Fennel, 94
Scones. See Breads and scones
Scotch Milk Punch, 67
Sea bass
  Broiled Sea Bass Fillet over Tomatillo Rice, 541
  Straits Sea Bass, 460
Seafood. See Fish and seafood; Roe; specific fish
Seared Asian-Style Glazed Tuna, 557
Seared Scallops with Saffron Mash, 403
Seeds, toasting, 223

Sesame Chicken, 457
Shallots
  about, 291
  Citrus and Shallot Dressing, 403
  Cream of Brussels Sprout Soup, 307
  Herbed Potato Salad, 326
  Stoemp with Caramelized Shallots, 314
Shiitake Mushroom Soup, 525
Shrimp. *See also* Prawns
  about: preparing fresh, 139
  Bahian-Style Shrimp Stew, 409
  Bouillabaisse, 294
  Butterfly Shrimp Tempura, 475
  Green Mango and Shrimp Salad, 433
  Honey Walnut Shrimp, 465
  Mexicali Shrimp on the Grill, 124
  Pad Thai, 444
  Paulista Shrimp Cake, 411
  Poached Shrimp and Avocado
    Appetizer, 366
  Sage-and-Pancetta-Wrapped Shrimp, 251
  Savory Shanghai Noodles, 469
  Scallops and Shrimp with White Bean
    Sauce, 73
  Seafood Roll-Ups, 249
  Shrimp and Melon Salad, 299
  Shrimp in Coconut Milk, 423
  Shrimp Scampi, 139
  Spicy Chilled Shrimp, 191
  Stir-Fried Asparagus, Oyster Mushrooms,
    and Shrimp in Garlic Sauce, 434
  Vietnamese Crab and Pineapple Soup, 270
Simple Fruit Compote, 311
Slaws. *See* Salads
Sloppy Joes, 212
Slow-Roasted Balsamic Tomato Soup, 500
Smoked Mussels in Cream Sauce with
    Pasta, 134
Smoked Salmon Pancakes, 404
Smoked Salmon Salad with Cilantro
    Dressing, 157
Smorgasbord, 386
Snack Mix, Party, 216
Snails
  Escargots in Chablis, 289
  Snail in Black Bean and Orange Peel
    Sauce, 453
Snapper
  Baked Red Snapper Almandine, 257
  Ceviche de Pescado, 547
  Gefilte Fish, 112
  Pan-Fried Fish with Rosemary, 338
  Red Snapper with Cayenne Tomato
    Sauce, 249

Snapper with Jumbo Lump Crabmeat, 516
Sole, Buttered Fillet of, 327
Soufflés
  Basic Cheese Soufflé, 405
  Blueberry Soufflé, 381
  Chocolate Soufflé, 85
  Truffle Oil and Brie Soufflé, 292
  Twice-Baked Lobster Soufflé, 398
Soups. *See also* Stews
  about: freezing, 184
  Bar Harbor Fish Chowder, 143
  Beer Soup, 137
  Bergen Fish Soup, 383
  Bermuda Fish Chowder, 560
  Bermuda Onion Soup, 561
  Bouillabaisse, 294
  Buttermilk Soup with Apples, 312
  Cauliflower Vichyssoise, 97
  Chilled Cucumber Soup, 417
  Cold Avocado Soup, Atlixco Style, 542
  Cold Coconut Soup, 544
  Cold Wine Soup, 322
  Cold Yogurt and Cucumber Soup, 490
  Conch Chowder, 555
  Corn Clam Chowder with Mulard Duck
    Pan Seared Foie Gras, 291
  Cream of Belgian Endive Soup, 308
  Cream of Brussels Sprout Soup, 307
  Danish Apple Soup, 386
  Dark Bread Soup, 323
  Dashi Soup Stock, 480
  Elderberry Soup with "Dumplings" and
    Apples, 328
  Elegant Cream of Celery Soup, 524
  Finnish Sauerkraut Soup, 391
  French Onion Soup, 78
  French Onion Soup with Port, 293
  Gazpacho, 125
  Horn of Plenty Mushroom Soup, 380
  Hot and Sour Prawn Soup, 436
  Lemon and Egg Soup, 339
  Oysters Rockefeller Soup, 36
  Pumpkin Curry Soup, 439
  Slow-Roasted Balsamic Tomato Soup,
    500
  Stilton and Cheddar Cheese Soup, 246
  Summertime Strawberry Soup, 184
  Sweet Corn and Cipollini Onion Soup, 514
  Sweet Potato-Ginger Soup, 16
  Tomato Egg-Flower Soup, 452
  Yogurt and Cucumber Soup with Mint
    and Dill, 98
  Young Garlic Soup with Crème Fraîche
    and Spring Pea Shoots, 513

South American dishes, 407–12
Soy sauce, 464
Spanish dishes, 361–76
Sparkling Citrus Punch, 219
Sparkling Fruit Drink, 131
Spiced Cranberry Glogg, 22
Spicy Chilled Shrimp, 191
Spicy Cold Pears, 196
Spicy Remoulade, 522
Spicy Scallops, 446
Spinach
  about: wilted salad, 171
  Afghani Lamb with Spinach, 492
  Greens with Peanuts, 504
  Oysters Rockefeller Soup, 36
  Pecan-Crusted Chicken, 518–19
  Purim Ravioli, 227
  Savory Shanghai Noodles, 469
  Spinach and Ricotta Dip, 64
  Spinach Frittata, 116
  Spinach Salad with Apple-Avocado
    Dressing, 166
  Spinach with Raisins and Pine Nuts, 371
  Spinach-Wrapped Zucchini Flan, 77
  Swabian Stuffed Pockets, 332–33
  Thai Beef with Rice Noodles, 447
Split Lentil Dumplings, 425
Squab
  Braised Squab with Caramelized
    Onions, 310
  Tommy Toy's Minced Squab Imperial, 462
Squash. *See also* Butternut squash; Zucchini
  about: as soup bowl, 16
  African Squash and Yams, 501
  Sweet Simmered Squash, 480
Squid
  about: ink from, 368
  Squid Ink Risotto, 368
  Squid in Sherry, 373
  Squid in Wine, 337
Steamed Prawns with Crushed Garlic, 451
Steamed Tilapia with Mushrooms and Black
    Bean Sauce, 451
Stews
  Bahian-Style Shrimp Stew, 409
  Greek-Style Rabbit Stew, 345
  Moambé Stew, 503
  Sweet-and-Sour Eggplant Stew, 356
  Tagine-Style Beef Stew with Lemons, 505
  Veal and Vegetable Stew, 412
  Veal Medallions in Almond Stew, 545
Stilton and Cheddar Cheese Soup, 246
Stir-Fried Asparagus, Oyster Mushrooms,
    and Shrimp in Garlic Sauce, 434

Stock, Akhni, 421
Stoemp with Caramelized Shallots, 314
Straits Sea Bass, 460
Strawberries
    about: as garnish, 156
    Bubbly Berry Blast, 185
    Champagne-Marinated Summer
        Berries, 197
    Crepes with Curaçao Strawberries and
        Oranges, 297
    Simple Fruit Compote, 311
    Sparkling Citrus Punch, 219
    Strawberries in Butterscotch Sauce, 219
    Strawberry Chicken Salad, 156
    Strawberry Pie, 186
    Strawberry Sorbet, 161
    Summertime Strawberry Soup, 184
Stuffed Mushrooms, 56
Stuffed Red Peppers, 456
Summer picnics, 163–73
    Avocado and Peach Salad, 165
    California Garden Salad with Avocado
        and Sprouts, 170
    Cape Cod Punch, 173
    Fish House Punch, 173
    Honey Dijon Tuna Salad, 166
    Polynesian Banana Salad, 167
    Risotto with Fresh Summer
        Vegetables, 167
    Spinach Salad with Apple-Avocado
        Dressing, 166
    Summer Vegetable Slaw, 171
    Sunshine Bean Salad with Golden
        Gate Dressing, 168
    Tricolor Pepper Salad, 169
    Wild Blackberry Pie, 172
    Zesty Feta and Olive Sandwich, 164
Summertime Strawberry Soup, 184
Sushi, 477
Swabian Stuffed Pockets (Maultaschen),
    332–33
Swedish Apple Cake, 393
Swedish Apricot and Prune Pork Loin, 392
Swedish Potato Dumplings, 396
Sweet and Savory Grilled Coconut-Rice
    Hotcakes, 441
Sweet-and-Sour Eggplant Stew, 356
Sweet Corn and Cipollini Onion Soup, 514
Sweet Corn Pudding, 190
Sweet Fennel with Lemon and Shaved
    Parmigiano, 75
Sweet potatoes
    African Squash and Yams, 501

Bacano Español, 376
Gingered Mashed Sweet Potatoes, 34
Herbed Beef Rib-Eye Roast with
    Potatoes, 30
Sweet Potato-Ginger Soup, 16
Veal and Vegetable Stew, 412
Warm Sweet Potato and Apple Salad, 14
Yam Latkes with Mustard Seeds and
    Curry, 223
Sweet Simmered Squash, 480
Sweet Vanilla Sauce, 20
Swiss chard, in Mock Stuffed Grape
    Leaves, 239
Swordfish, Pan-Roasted, with Plum
    Tomatoes, 352
Syrup, German, 317
Syrup substitutes, 241

T

Tacos, fish, 543
Tagine-Style Beef Stew with Lemons, 505
Tamarind Sauce, 430
Tapas, 366
Tea
    Fruity Citrus Spice, 209
    Green Tea Crepes, 478
    Oyster Mushroom and Jasmine Tea
        Rice, 479
"Terbiye," 483
Texas Caviar, 152
Thai dishes, 429–48
Thanksgiving, 9–25
    Apple Blossom, 23
    Brandy Cocoa, 25
    Cranberry Cream Cocktail, 23
    Cranberry Gin Sour, 24
    Cranberry Nut Bread, 19
    Cranberry-Pecan Bars, 20
    Cranberry Scones, 18
    Cranberry Sherbet, 17
    Fruit-Stewed Turkey, 13
    Mayflower Cocktail, 24
    Oven-Roasted Asparagus, 15
    Pecan Pie, 22
    Pumpkin Pie, 21
    Roasted Garlic Mashed Potatoes, 10
    Roast Turkey with Fruit Stuffing, 11
    Spiced Cranberry Glogg, 22
    Sweet Potato-Ginger Soup, 16
    Turkey and Cranberry on Butternut
        Squash, 12
    Turkey Shooter, 25

Warm Sweet Potato and Apple Salad, 14
Three-Bean Salad, 178
Thyme, Wild, Rabbit with, 290
Tilapia, Steamed, with Mushrooms and
    Black Bean Sauce, 451
Tiramisu, 357
Tofu
    Eggplant Miso Soup, 473
    Green Tea Crepes, 478
    Pad Thai, 444
Tom and Jerry, 53
Tomatillos, 120
Tomatoes
    about: canned for fresh, 213; varieties,
        63
    Bliss's Fresh Plum Tomato and Basil
        Sauce, 360
    Broiled Sea Bass Fillet over Tomatillo
        Rice, 541
    Fried Green Tomato Bruschetta, 63
    Fried Green Tomatoes, 178
    Roasted Tomato, Zucchini, and Goat
        Cheese Tarts, 523
    Roasted Tomato Vinaigrette, 474
    Slow-Roasted Balsamic Tomato Soup,
        500
    Tomato Egg-Flower Soup, 452
    Tomato Marmalade, 514
    Tuna Ceviche, 540
    Veal Medallions in Almond Stew, 545
Tom Ka Kai, 438
Tommy Toy's Four Seasons Fried Rice, 464
Tommy Toy's Minced Squab Imperial, 462
Totopos, 121
Tournento Rossini, 360
Tricolor Pepper Salad, 169
Trout, in Pasta and Smoked Trout with
    Lemon Pesto, 256
Truffle Oil and Brie Soufflé, 292
Truffles
    about, 292
    Milk-Fed Veal Cutlet with Parmesan
        and Truffle Crust, 348
Tuna
    Ahi Tuna Tartar, 535
    Gourmet Tuna Sandwich Spread, 364
    Honey Dijon Tuna Salad, 166
    Seared Asian-Style Glazed Tuna, 557
    Tuna Ceviche, 540
Turkey
    Coconut Turkey Curry, 269
    Roast Turkey with Fruit Stuffing, 11

Turkey and Cranberry on Butternut Squash, 12
Turkey Shooter, 25
Turkish Delight, 490
Turkish Lamb Casserole Cooked in Paper, 494
Turnips, Glazed, with Cinnamon, 311
Twice-Baked Lobster Soufflé, 398
Twice-Baked Potatoes with Chives, 33
Tzatziki (Cucumber, Garlic, and Yogurt Dip), 341

U, V, W, Y

United States dishes, 511–25
Valentine's Day, 71–90
    Amaretto Cake, 86
    Apple-Buttered Rum Pudding with Apple Topping, 87
    Artichokes in Court Bouillon with Lemon Butter, 72
    Bellini, 90
    Bishop, 88
    Caramel Rum Fondue, 82
    Cheese Fondue, 74
    Chocolate Soufflé, 85
    Coquilles St. Jacques Provençal, 79
    French Onion Soup, 78
    Game Hens in Red Wine, 81
    Grilled Lobster with Lemon and Tarragon, 80
    Herb Linguini with Salmon, Cream, and Pistachios, 83
    Midori Mimosa, 89
    Pasta with Artichokes, 76
    Pears Poached in White Wine with Strawberry Sauce, 84
    Salmon in White Wine with Dried Peaches, 82
    Sangria, 89
    Scallops and Shrimp with White Bean Sauce, 73
    Spinach-Wrapped Zucchini Flan, 77
    Sweet Fennel with Lemon and Shaved Parmigiano, 75
    Valentine, 88
Vanilla Sour Cream Sauce, 394
Veal
    Braised Veal Shanks with Porcini Mushrooms, 353
    Lollipop Veal Chop, 519
    Milk-Fed Veal Cutlet with Parmesan and Truffle Crust, 348
    Pork and Veal Pâté, 245
    Veal and Vegetable Stew, 412

Veal Medallions in Almond Stew, 545
Vegetable Gado-Gado, 57
Vegetables. *See also specific vegetables*
    blanching, 231
    cleaning root vegetables, 37
    seasoning, 240
    separating frozen, 116
Vegetarian dishes, adding smoky flavor to, 182
Vegetarianism, in India, 417
Vendace Roe, Crispy Salad of, 379
Venison, 528
    about: definition, 138
    Venison Medallions with Cranberry Dijon Chutney, 138
    Venison with Dried Cranberry Vinegar Sauce, 205
Vichyssoise, Cauliflower, 97
Vietnamese Crab and Pineapple Soup, 270
Vine Leaf Envelopes with Raisins, 484
Vodka-Marinated Sirloin, 384
Waffles, Belgian, 317
Walnuts
    Baklava, 346
    Classic Waldorf Salad, 141
    Crunchy Nut Treats, 66
    Honey Walnut Shrimp, 465
    Vine Leaf Envelopes with Raisins, 484
    Walnut Chicken with Plum Sauce, 236
Warm Dungeness Crab and Brie Melt, 532
Warm Potato Salad with Balsamic Vinegar and Onions, 202
Warm Sweet Potato and Apple Salad, 14
Wassail, Nonalcoholic, 52
Watermelon with Beef and Tangerine Herb, 450
Westphalian Cabbage, 324
White asparagus, 324
White Bean and Artichoke Salad, 113
Whitefish, Grilled, 378
White Wine and Lemon Pork Roast, 93
White Wine Cooler, 149
Wild Blackberry Pie, 172
Wild Boar and Orzo Salad, 537
Wild Rice with Apples and Almonds, 204
Wine
    about: carbs in, 232; labels, 327
    Braised Beef in Barolo, 375
    Chorizo in Wine, 370
    Cold Wine Soup, 322
    Figs with Brie and Port Wine Reduction, 137
    Game Hens in Red Wine, 81
    Glogg, 393

Pears Poached in White Wine with Strawberry Sauce, 84
Quail Baked in White Wine, 145
Rabbit in Wine, 369
Salmon in White Wine with Dried Peaches, 82
Squid in Sherry, 373
Squid in Wine, 337
White Wine and Lemon Pork Roast, 93
White Wine Cooler, 149
Wings, Louisiana Hot, 60
Wok-Seared Beef Medallions with Asparagus Tips, 463
Yams. *See* Sweet potatoes
Yeast Dough, Flemish, 316
Yin and yang, 467
Yogurt
    Chilled Cucumber Soup, 417
    Cold Yogurt and Cucumber Soup, 490
    Feta and Mint Dip, 341
    Lamb Curry with Banana Raita, 415
    Rose-Flavored Yogurt Lassi, 420
    Tzatziki, 341
    Yogurt and Cucumber Soup with Mint and Dill, 98
    Yogurt Sauce, 416
Yorkshire Pudding, 38
Young Garlic Soup with Crème Fraîche and Spring Pea Shoots, 513

Z

Zesty Feta and Olive Sandwich, 164
Zucchini
    Grilled Zucchini with Balsamic Vinegar, 181
    Pan-Fried Flounder with Toasted Almonds, 362
    Risotto with Fresh Summer Vegetables, 167
    Risotto with Lobster and Parmesan, 564
    Roasted Tomato, Zucchini, and Goat Cheese Tarts, 523
    Snapper with Jumbo Lump Crabmeat, 516
    Spinach-Wrapped Zucchini Flan, 77
    Vegetable Gado-Gado, 57
    Zucchini-Stuffed Chicken, 108